NOT SPARING THE CHILD

NOT SPARING THE CHILD

Human Sacrifice
in the Ancient World and Beyond

Studies in Honor of Professor Paul G. Mosca

Edited by

V. Daphna Arbel, Paul C. Burns, J. R. C. Cousland,
Richard Menkis, and Dietmar Neufeld

Bloomsbury T&T Clark
An imprint of Bloomsbury Publishing Plc

B L O O M S B U R Y
LONDON · OXFORD · NEW YORK · NEW DELHI · SYDNEY

Bloomsbury T&T Clark
An imprint of Bloomsbury Publishing Plc

Imprint previously known as T&T Clark

50 Bedford Square	1385 Broadway
London	New York
WC1B 3DP	NY 10018
UK	USA

www.bloomsbury.com

**BLOOMSBURY, T&T CLARK and the Diana logo are trademarks
of Bloomsbury Publishing Plc**

First published 2015
Paperback edition first published 2016

British Library Cataloguing-in-Publication Data
A catalogue record for this book is available from the British Library.

ISBN: HB: 978-0-56765-485-4
PB: 978-0-56766-958-2
ePDF: 978-0-56735-263-7

Library of Congress Cataloging-in-Publication Data
Not sparing the child : human sacrifice in the ancient world and beyond : studies in
honor of professor Paul G. Mosca / edited by V. Daphna Arbel, Paul C. Burns,
J.R.C. Cousland, Richard Menkis, and Dietmar Neufeld.
pages cm
Includes bibliographical references and index.
ISBN 978-0-567-65485-4 (hardback)
1. Human sacrifice. 2. Child sacrifice. I. Arbel, Vita Daphna, editor. II. Burns, Paul C.,
editor. III. Cousland, J. R. C., editor. IV. Menkis, Richard, editor. V. Neufeld,
Dietmar, editor. VI. Mosca, Paul G., honouree.

BL570.N68 2015
230'.420937–dc23
2014031532

Typeset by Forthcoming Publications (www.forthpub.com)

Paul G. Mosca
(and friend)

CONTENTS

ABBREVIATIONS

AB	Anchor Bible
ABDAIAK	Archäologische Veröffentlichungen / Deutsches Archäologisches Institut, Abteilung Kairo
AcA	Antike christliche Apokryphen
ANF	Ante-Nicene Fathers
AOAT	Alter Orient und Altes Testament
AOTC	Abingdon Old Testament Commentaries
ATD	Das Alte Testament Deutsch
BASOR	*Bulletin of the American Schools of Oriental Research*
BDB	Brown, F., S. R. Driver, and C. A. Briggs. *A Hebrew and English Lexicon of the Old Testament.* Oxford, 1907
BETL	Bibliotheca ephemeridum theologicarum lovaniensium
BibInt	*Biblical Interpretation*
BibOr	Biblica et orientalia
BJS	Brown Judaic Studies
BN	*Biblische Notizen*
BZAW	Beihefte zur Zeitschrift für die alttestamentliche Wissenschaft
BZNW	Beihefte zur Zeitschrift für die neutestamentliche Wissenschaft
CAD	*The Assyrian Dictionary of the Oriental Institute of the University of Chicago.* Chicago, 1956–
CBQ	*Catholic Biblical Quarterly*
CBQMS	Catholic Biblical Quarterly Monograph Series
CCSA	Corpus Christianorum. Series Apocryphorum
CIS	*Corpus inscriptionum semiticarum*
CJ	*Classical Journal*
CLUC	Halayqa, I. K. H. *Comparative Lexicon of Ugaritic and Canaanite.* Münster, 2008
CSEL	Corpus scriptorum ecclesiasticorum latinorum
DID	Didascaliae
DNWSI	*Dictionary of the North-West Semitic Inscriptions.* J. Hoftijzer and K. Jongeling. 2 vols. Leiden, 1995
DUL	Del Olmo Lete, G., and J. Sanmartín. *A Dictionary of the Ugaritic Language in the Alphabetic Tradition.* Leiden, 2004
FAT	Forschungen zum Alten Testament
FC	Fathers of the Church. Washington, D.C., 1947–
FOTL	Forms of the Old Testament Literature

FRLANT	Forschungen zur Religion und Literatur des Alten und Neuen Testaments
HALOT	Koehler, L., W. Baumgartner, and J. J. Stamm. *The Hebrew and Aramaic Lexicon of the Old Testament*. Translated and edited under the supervision of M. E. J. Richardson. 4 vols. Leiden, 1994–99
HB	Hebrew Bible
HDR	Harvard Dissertations in Religion
HSM	Harvard Semitic Monographs
HTKAT	Herders theologischer Kommentar zum Neuen Testament
IEJ	*Israel Exploration Journal*
JAOS	*Journal of the American Oriental Society*
JBL	*Journal of Biblical Literature*
JHS	*Journal of Hebrew Scriptures*
JQR	*Jewish Quarterly Review*
JSJSup	Journal for the Study of Judaism in the Persian, Hellenistic, and Roman Periods: Supplement Series
JSOT	*Journal for the Study of the Old Testament*
JSOTSup	Journal for the Study of the Old Testament: Supplement Series
JSS	*Journal of Semitic Studies*
KAI	*Kanaanäische und aramäische Inschriften*. H. Donner and W. Röllig. 2d ed. Wiesbaden, 1966–69
KTU	*Die keilalphabetischen Texte aus Ugarit*. Edited by M. Dietrich, O. Loretz, and J. Sanmartín. AOAT 24/1. Neukirchen–Vluyn, 1976. 2d enlarged ed. of *KTU: The Cuneiform Alphabetic Texts from Ugarit, Ras Ibn Hani, and Other Places*. Edited by M. Dietrich, O. Loretz, and J. Sanmartín. Münster, 1995 (= *CTU*)
KUSATU	*Kleine Untersuchungen zur Sprache des Alten Testaments und seiner Umwelte*
LCL	Loeb Classical Library
LIMC	*Lexicon iconographicum mythologiae classicae*. Edited by H. C. Ackerman and J.-R. Gisler. 8 vols. Zurich, 1981–97
LSJ	Liddell, H. G., R. Scott, H. S. Jones, *A Greek–English Lexicon*. 9th ed. with revised supplement. Oxford, 1996
LXX	Septuagint
MDAIAK	*Mitteilungen des Deutschen Archäologischen Instituts Kairo*
MT	Masoretic text
NIBC	New International Biblical Commentary
NIV	New Internationa Version
NovT	*Novum Testamentum*
NRSV	New Revised Standard Version
NTTS	New Testament Tools and Studies
OBO	Orbis biblicus et orientalis
OCD	*Oxford Classical Dictionary*. Edited by S. Hornblower and A. Spawforth. 3d ed. Oxford, 1996
OLA	Orientalia lovaniensia analecta
OTL	Old Testament Library

OTP	*Old Testament Pseudepigrapha*. Edited by J. H. Charlesworth. 2 vols. New York, 1983
PPG³	Friedrich, J., and W. Röllig. *Phönizisch-punische Grammatik*. 3d ed. Edited by M. G. Amadasi Guzzo and W. R. Mayer. Analecta Orientalia 55. Rome, 1999
RSV	Revised Standard Version
SBLDS	Society of Biblical Literature Dissertation Series
SBLRBS	Society of Biblical Literature Resources for Biblical Study
SBLSP	Society of Biblical Literature Seminar Papers
SBLSymS	Society of Biblical Literature Symposium Series
SBLWAW	Society of Biblical Literature Writings from the Ancient World
SEL	*Studi Epigrafici e Linguistici sul Vicino Oriente Antico*
SHR	Studies in the History of Religions (supplement to *Numen*)
STAC	Studien und Text zu Antike und Christentum
SubBib	Subsidia biblica
TrGF	*Tragicorum Graecorum Fragmenta*
UF	*Ugarit-Forschungen*
VT	*Vetus Testamentum*
WBC	Word Biblical Commentary
WUNT	Wissenschaftliche Untersuchungen zum Neuen Testament
ZAW	*Zeitschrift für die alttestamentliche Wissenschaft*

CONTRIBUTORS

Paul C. Burns is Emeritus Associate Professor in the Department of Classical, Near Eastern and Religious Studies at the University of British Columbia.

J. R. C. Cousland is Associate Professor of Early Christianity and Greek Religion and Mythology in the Department of Classical, Near Eastern and Religious Studies at the University of British Columbia.

Peggy L. Day is a Professor of Hebrew Bible in the Department of Religion and Culture at the University of Winnipeg.

Michel Desjardins is Professor of Religion and Culture, and Associate Dean: Research and Curriculum, in Wilfrid Laurier University's Faculty of Arts.

Thomas Hikade was tenured Assistant Professor of Egyptian Archaeology and History at the University of British Columbia, Vancouver, until 2012, and is currently working in Australian politics.

Lee Johnson is Professor Emeritus of English, the University of British Columbia.

C. W. Marshall is Professor of Greek at the University of British Columbia in Vancouver, Canada.

Aldea Mulhern is a Ph.D. candidate in the Department for the Study of Religion at the University of Toronto.

Dietmar Neufeld is Associate Professor in the Department of Classical, Near Eastern and Religious Studies at the University of British Columbia, Canada.

Jane Roy taught Near Eastern and Egyptian archaeology and world prehistory at the University of British Columbia and Simon Fraser University between 2005 and 2011, and is currently working as a publisher in Australia.

Philip C. Schmitz is a Professor in the History and Philosophy Department at the Eastern Michigan University.

Thomas Schneider is Professor of Egyptology and Near Eastern Studies at the University of British Columbia, Vancouver.

Mark S. Smith is Skirball Professor of Bible and Ancient Near Eastern Studies, New York University.

INTRODUCTION

We find that the German word *Festschrift* is a very apt designation for this volume dedicated to Paul Mosca. As the word *Fest* suggests, it is at once festive and celebratory—festive in that it acknowledges his 66th year and happy retirement, celebratory in that it allows his colleagues, students, and other friends and admirers to commemorate his achievements as a scholar, educator, colleague, and friend.

Since Paul is among other things a noted authority on child-sacrifice in Phoenicia and Carthage, and his research in this area has been and continues to be extremely influential, it seemed only fitting for us to celebrate his achievements as scholar, colleague, and educator with a volume devoted to his research topic. *Not Sparing the Child: Notions of Human Sacrifice in Ancient Worlds and Beyond* addresses infant sacrifice in its ancient Mediterranean contexts, and also considers the various ramifications of this concept as it expanded across social, geographical, and temporal boundaries. Our book sets out to illumine aspects of infant sacrifice through nuanced examinations of ancient ritual and detailed exploration of the meanings that infant sacrifice held for antiquity. These analyses are followed by studies of the concept of infant sacrifice as it came to be refracted through various cultures up to the time of the modern world. We not only present fresh insights into the social and religious meanings of this practice in its varied biblical landscapes and contexts, but also demonstrate how human sacrifice vividly captured the imagination of later writers who used its diverse cultural and religious implications to construct their own views and ideologies. All told, therefore, *Not Sparing the Child* sets out to provide valuable insights into key cultural, theological, and ideological dimensions of infant sacrifice, as well as its related associations with scapegoating, self-sacrifice, and martyrdom through biblical, post-biblical, and modern times.

It is a long way from Brooklyn to Carthage, and Paul's educational journey between the two places did not follow a direct route. Two factors helped to set Paul on his path as a scholar and educator. One was the enthusiastic support of his parents for a broadly based humanistic education; the other was his attendance at the Jesuit-run Brooklyn Preparatory

School, which he describes as the best four years of education that he had in his life. Although the teachers there were close to being uniformly excellent—introducing the students to off-Broadway theater and French cinema, museums and concerts, poetry and madrigals, even to a very young Joan Baez—it was Fr. Jack Alexander, S.J., his Latin instructor, who ultimately proved to be most influential. He immediately recognized Paul's natural aptitude for languages and his distaste for 9 a.m. classes, and by a clever exchange soon had him working his way through the first six books of the *Aeneid* in their entirety, while the rest of the class did only four. Although Paul had been contemplating doing mathematics, the regularity of Latin grammar, especially when juxtaposed with its glaringly perverse irregularities, won him over and he chose to study Classics (Latin and Greek) at Fordham.

Once at Fordham, his academic career took a further turn when he was invited to register for a summer class in Hebrew. His father urged him to take advantage of the opportunity, and here again he came under the tutelage of a gifted linguist, Fr. George Glanzmann, S.J. It was Glanzmann who sparked Paul's passion for Semitic languages and Ancient Near Eastern Studies, a passion that eventually resulted in Paul's acceptance at Harvard to pursue Near Eastern Languages and Civilizations.

At Harvard, he was to profit a third time from the instruction of a brilliant linguist, in this case, Thomas Lambdin. It was not simply that Lambdin's grammars were of an exceptional quality and thoroughness, but that he also knew how to structure a language class logically and sequentially—a skill that Paul was not slow to make his own. Paul then went on to study Northwest Semitic Epigraphy with Frank Moore Cross, developing a life-long fascination with Carthage and the Punic language. As a Pfeiffer Travelling Fellow in Biblical Archaeology (1969–70), Paul had the opportunity to spend six months in Jerusalem, three months in Beirut, and finally three months in Tunis (near Carthage). This was later followed by a productive year in Rome as a Fulbright Scholar.

Paul's friend and contemporary (and contributor to this volume), Larry Stager, provides a vivid evocation of these times:

> Back in the late 70s, Paul and I would head to the dig in Carthage, where Frank Moore Cross and later Philip King were Principal Investigators. I was Field Director, and Paul was Epigrapher. Whenever possible, Paul and I would try to 'sandwich' the excavations between stopovers in Rome for a few days. We would often go around Rome with our friend the Rev. Mitchell Dahood, an American Jesuit who taught Bible and Semitic Studies at the Pontifical Biblical Institute, was an authority on food, church architecture, the Boston Red Sox, and opera. He gave Paul and me tickets to the opera in Spoleto. There we had a memorable evening

attending a great performance of La Traviata. From Rome we flew to Tunis and then traveled on to its suburb Carthage, where we excavated in the infamous Tophet from 1975–79, a huge burial ground of cremated human and animal remains, traditionally interpreted as sacrificial offerings. This was the topic of Paul's classic thesis, entitled *Child Sacrifice in Canaanite and Israelite Religion*, written at Harvard under the direction of the renowned professor of Biblical and Near Eastern studies, Frank Cross.

In many ways, Cross was an ideal supervisor for Paul. Not only was he a brilliant and insightful scholar; he was also, in Paul's words, 'the kindest scholar I have ever met'. As one of William Albright's students, Cross had inherited much of Albright's breadth of expertise, but had also developed an overriding fascination for the intricacies of North East Semitic Epigraphy. This fascination he passed on to Paul. The result was Paul's 1975 dissertation, which substantiated Eissfeldt's insight that there was no god Moloch as such in the Hebrew Bible. Rather, the term *mlk* denoted human sacrifice by kings of their own children to their divine royal overlord(s). This practice was characteristic of the Phoenicians and came to be pervasive throughout the Phoenician settlements of the central Mediterranean, especially Carthage. As various contributions in this volume attest, Paul's dissertation has had enduring impact, and helped to frame and contextualize the ongoing debates associated with infant sacrifice.

Nor has the matter proved uncontroversial. Professor Stager relates that,

> At various international Phoenician conferences Paul and I had been challenged more than once by a well-known Semiticist from France, whose self-regard was inestimable, but whose estimation of American philologists, especially of Professor Cross and his students, was negligible. At one of the sessions at a Phoenician conference in Sicily, where this scholar was presiding and denigrating one presentation after another, Paul was about to give his paper. The Semiticist began his introduction of Mosca with a long gratuitous diatribe against our mentor Frank Cross, who wasn't even present at the colloquium. Meanwhile Paul was altering his introductory remarks: as he went to the podium he opened his lecture by dedicating it to Frank Moore Cross and in an eloquent statement praised his scholarship, his openness to students' ideas, and his fairness in all of these matters. Many stood and applauded Paul's eloquent tribute, while the Semiticist sat stone-faced.

Perhaps, however, the most eloquent tribute that Paul has made to his mentor is the extent to which he has himself embodied Cross's very same characteristics—the openness, the fairness and unparalleled kindness, and the deep respect and enduring passion for true scholarship.

For Paul, true scholarship has much to do with philology, and it comes as no surprise that for a number of years Paul had a citation of Julius Wellhausen posted on his door that read, 'Philology takes revenge on those who treat it with disdain'. This passage says a great deal about Paul both as a scholar and an educator. His scholarly interests were always marked by an enviable breadth and catholicity, with numerous articles appearing in journals as wide-ranging and diverse as *AASOR, JBL, CBQ, Biblica, Maarav, Ugarit-Forschungen,* and *Epigraphica Anatolica*— the majority display a pronounced philological component. The ones focusing on Phoenician-Punic inscriptions, for instance, are especially concerned to explicate anomalous features of the texts, and increase what is known about the language and the store of its remaining inscriptions.

The provenance of these inscriptions could be surprising. On one notable occasion he only had to walk across the courtyard between Religious Studies and Classics. A colleague from Paul's (and our) now joint department, Jim Russell, was in possession of an inscription with an unfamiliar script that he'd found in his surface explorations of southern Turkey, and he wanted help deciphering it. This inscription turned out to be Phoenician, and it resulted in a jointly written article. Other occasions, however, saw Paul having to travel a bit further afield, as when he visited Sardinia to investigate inscriptions from Nora and Tharros. Once one of the local Sardinian newspapers had found out what he was there for, he was instantly lionized in a major article—a fate not normally experienced by roving philologists. Nor, for that matter, are Semitic philologists usually called upon to write documents in Aramaic for mainstream television shows—but Paul was. In the heyday of the X-Files, one of its epigones needed a 'genuine' Aramaic document, which Paul gladly wrote for them (though rather puckishly he made it a message from Mulder to Scully!).

It goes without saying that Paul's scholarly service extended well beyond such bagatelles. He became Acting Head and then Head of UBC's Department of Religious Studies at a critical juncture in its history, and had contributed to the success of the department for decades. These responsibilities extended to graduate studies and curriculum, and he proved instrumental in Religious Studies' highly successful merger in 1995 with the Department of Classics. Along with Paul Burns and Lee Johnson (both contributors to this volume) he was also pivotal both in the formation and the oversight of the innovative program at UBC entitled Religion, Literature, and the Arts. In addition to extensive committee work, including President's Committee on Lectures, he also served on the UBC Senate, as well as the Senate Admissions Committee. His contributions in all these capacities can hardly be overestimated. Whenever the political and administrative vicissitudes of a large university threatened to harm his colleagues or department, he could always be counted upon to act as an unshifting bulwark, especially for those who were treated unjustly or otherwise overlooked. Above all, he was a calm voice of reason and commonsense when these qualities seemed to be otherwise lacking.

Paul's commitment to philology was also manifest in his teaching career, particularly in his enduring commitment to the instruction of Hebrew. He was determined that his students get the firmest foundation possible, as painlessly as possible, and to this end he was constantly revising and polishing his teaching techniques. He was equally determined that advanced students get as much language as they possibly could, and over the course of his career he would regularly offer classes in advanced Hebrew and Aramaic over and above his regular teaching load. It is not surprising, then, that his efforts have borne considerable fruit, and not a few biblical scholars owe their own grounding in Semitic languages to him.

One of them, Timothy Lim, now a world authority on the Dead Sea Scrolls, relates that,

> I was in several of Paul's classes as an undergraduate, and it was in one of his classes that I first learned about the Dead Sea Scrolls. Later, I also read portions of the Great Isaiah Scroll with him in an intermediate Hebrew course. Paul's teaching was marked by thoroughness and learning. As with his unpublished, but widely read, dissertation, his teaching reflected the urbane outlook of a man of letters. I congratulate Paul on reaching a significant milestone.

Not a few contributors to this volume could also attest to the impact his teaching has had on their own careers.

Nor was his teaching confined to philological matters; his courses on Job, Death and the Afterlife, and Archaeology and the Bible were hugely popular with students, not least because of the complexity of the issues that Paul addressed in them. Students would regularly comment in the same breath about how challenging the classes were and yet how very much they were enjoying them and profiting from Paul's insights. Testimony to his mastery of teaching came in various forms. Canada's weekly newsmagazine, *Macleans*, in its 1996 annual guide to Canada's universities singled him out as a 'notable professor' at UBC. This recognition was followed by a UBC Killam Teaching prize in 1998–99, where Professor Barry McBride, UBC's Provost and Vice President Academic, declared him a 'simply outstanding' teacher. The *UBC Report* of May 1999 added that, 'Paul Mosca is known to turn his students into disciples by the sheer force of example with his charismatic teaching'.

Yet Paul's exceptional pedagogy wasn't limited to his students—it also extended to his colleagues, especially his junior colleagues. Whether it involved attending their fledgling conference papers, reading drafts of their articles, or acting as a discerning sounding-board for their ideas, he was unstinting in his time and encouragement. Most of all, he was an exemplar of good scholarship. He had no patience for 'bulk publications' or the recycling of tired ideas. To be worth publishing, an article needed to make a significant contribution to the discipline and embody long-standing traditions associated with academic excellence. It is no surprise, therefore, that Paul was invited to serve as an Associate Editor for the *Catholic Biblical Quarterly* from 1990 to 1995.

Yet once all of Paul's teaching and scholarship have been accounted for, a large part of his person remains unaccounted for, and this can only be described as his *megalopsychia*—his greatness and generosity of spirit. Like the penumbra of pipe smoke that typically surrounds him, his great-heartedness suffuses all that he does and all his interactions with people. As Markus Bockmuehl, a friend of many years, aptly puts it, using good Semitic idiom, 'Paul has always struck me as a wonderfully genuine *mensch* with a heart of gold'. As his colleagues, students, friends and admirers over many years, we have had the privilege and great good fortune of being able to 'travel much in these realms of gold', and we present this volume to Paul with thanks for the rich legacy he has bequeathed to us all.

Daphna Arbel
Paul C. Burns
J. R. C. Cousland
Richard Menkis
Dietmar Neufeld

Part I

HISTORY, RITUAL, ARCHEOLOGY

CHILD SACRIFICE AS THE EXTREME CASE
AND CALCULATION

Mark S. Smith

1. *Introduction*

In the second half of the twentieth century, no one achieved more than Paul G. Mosca in advancing the discussion of child sacrifice in the textual sources.[1] Following Otto Eissfeldt's 1935 interpretation of BH **molk* as a sacrificial term,[2] Mosca's 1975 dissertation added fresh Punic evidence to the discussion as well as further analysis and evaluation of the biblical and classical sources. At the same time, the archaeological evidence was being engaged in a new way, thanks to excavations in Punic Carthage. For example, the evidence from this site was been thought to confirm the widespread practice of child sacrifice,[3] although

---

1. Paul G. Mosca, 'Child Sacrifice in Canaanite and Israelite Religion: A Study in *Mulk* and מלך' (Ph.D. diss., Harvard University, 1975).

2. Otto Eissfeldt, *Molk als Opferbegriff im Punischen und Hebräischen und das Ende des Gottes Moloch* (Beiträge zur Religionsgeschichte des Alterums 3; Halle: Max Niemeyer, 1935). Eissfeldt's work also received broad acceptance within Spanish scholarship. His book appeared in Spanish as *El Molk concepto Sacrificio Punico y Hebreo y final del Dios Moloch* (ed. Carlos C. Wagner and Luis Ruiz Cabreo; Madrid: Centre de Estudios Fenicios y Punicos, 2002), together with articles on the subject by Enrico Acquario, Maria Giulia Amadasi, Antonia Ciasca, and Edward Lipiński. The Phoenician evidence for the *mlk*-sacrifice has been treated by Luis Alberto Ruiz Caebreo, 'El Sacrificio Molk entre los feninicio-punicis: Cuestiones demografias y ecologicas' (Tesis, Departamento de Historia Antigua, Universidad Complutense de Madrid, 2007); reference courtesy of the author.

3. See Lawrence E. Stager, 'The Rite of Child Sacrifice at Carthage', in J.G. Pedley (ed.), *New Light on Ancient Carthage* (Ann Arbor, MI: University of Michigan Press, 1980), pp. 1-11; idem, 'Carthage: A View from the Tophet', in Hans Georg Niemeyer (ed.), *Phönizer im Westen* (Mainz am Rhein: Philipp von Zabern, 1982), pp. 155-66; and Lawrence E. Stager and Samuel Wolff, 'Child Sacrifice at Carthage: Religious Rite or Population Control? Archaeological Evidence Provides Basis for a New Analysis', *Biblical Archaeological Review* 10.1 (1984), pp. 30-51.

there was dissent.[4] More recent archaeological discussions have gone back and forth over the issue, with one side reaffirming the picture of child sacrifice at Punic Carthage and another questioning it.[5]

Mosca's work remains a cornerstone of research on the textual sources. His overall perspective on child sacrifice in Israelite religion, that it was no less a practice as elsewhere in the eastern Mediterranean, has gained widespread acceptance; it may be said to represent the general view today in critical biblical scholarship.[6] Mosca's textual work is a model of close reading, informed by a judicious use of comparative evidence and advanced by penetrating insights. Indeed, his scholarship, not to mention his warmth and humor, has inspired me. I am honored to offer a contribution to this volume in his recognition, by way of some reflections on child sacrifice as the extreme case in the historiography of 2 Kings and as an extreme calculation in the narratives of Genesis 22 and Judges 11. Before turning to these texts, two discoveries appearing in print since Mosca's early work deserve mention.

2. *Evidence at the Western and Eastern Ends of the Mediterranean*

Since Mosca's important 1975 study, information from either end of the Mediterranean thought to pertain to child sacrifice has been published. A relief carved on stones, discovered at Pozo Moro in Spain in 1971, was published in 1983.[7] This relief includes the depiction of a figure, which has been described in these terms:

4.   For example, H. Benichou-Safar, 'A propos des ossements humains du tophet de Carthage', *Rivista di Studi Fenici* 5 (1981), pp. 5-9.

5.   This view has been questioned by J. H. Schwartz, F. Houghton, R. Macchiarelli, and L. Bondioli, 'Skeletal Remains from Punic Carthage Do Not Support Systematic Sacrifice of Infants', *PLoS ONE* 5.2, e9177. doi:10.1371/journal.pone.0009177 (published February 17, 2010). See the robust refutation by P. Smith, G. Avishai, J. A. Greene, and L. E. Stager, 'Aging Cremated Infants: The Problem of Sacrifice at the Tophet of Carthage', *Antiquity* 85 (2011), pp. 859-75. Cf. the fairly meager response by J. H. Schwartz, E. D. Houghton, L. Bondioli, and L. Macchiarelli, 'Bones, Teeth, and Estimating Age of Perinates: Carthaginian Infant Sacrifice Revisited', *Antiquity* 86 (2012), pp. 738-45.

6.   See Jon D. Levenson, *The Death and Resurrection of the Beloved Son: The Transformation of Child Sacrifice in Judaism and Christianity* (New Haven: Yale University Press, 1993), esp. pp. 3-17.

7.   Martin Almagro-Gorbea, 'Pozo Moro: El monumento orientalizante, su contexto socio-culturaly sus paralelos en la arquitectura funeraria ibérica', *Madrider Mitteilungen* 24 (1983), pp. 197-201. The most detailed study is Fernando López

The monster has a human body and two heads, one above the other. The heads have open mouths with lolling tongues. In its left hand it holds the rear leg of a supine pig lying on a banquet table in front of it. In its right hand, it holds a bowl. Just over the rim of the bowl can be seen the head and feet of a small person. In the background, a figure in a long garment raises a bowl in a gesture of offering. Opposite the monster is the mutilated image of a third figure. It is standing and raising in its right hand a sword with a curved blade. Its head is in the shape of a bull or horse. Its left hand is touching the head of a second small person in a bowl on a second table or a tripod near the banquet table.[8]

The double-maw of the monstrous figure recalls the monstrous figure of Death (*mt*), who likewise has '[a lip to ea]rth, a lip to heaven, [...a to]ngue to the stars' (*KTU* 1.5 II 2-3).[9] The two enthroned Goodly Gods (*KTU* 1.23) likewise 'set a lip to earth, a lip to heaven' (*KTU* 1.23.61-62).[10] While neither is explicitly named in association with child sacrifice, these descriptions comport with the ravenous figure depicted in the Pozo Moro relief, perhaps the divine recipient of a child offering. It is apparent from other sources, as noted below, that any number of gods could be the recipient of such an offering. Without further context, it is difficult to provide specific interpretation.[11] Still, the association with the West Semitic practice of child sacrifice has been reaffirmed.[12]

An eighth-century Assyrian–Luwian–Phoenician trilingual inscription discovered at Injirli in Turkey in 1993 includes lines in Phoenician that

Pardo, *La torre de las almas: Un recorrido por los mitos y creencias del mundo fenicio y orientalizante a través del monumento de Pozo Moro* (Anejo 10; Madrid: Universidad Complutense de Madrid, 2006), pp. 145-82.

8. John S. Rundin, 'Pozo Moro, Child Sacrifice, and the Greek Literary Tradition', *JBL* 123 (2004), pp. 425-47, here 426. A good picture appears in López Pardo, *La torre de las almas*, p. 147; and Mark S. Smith, *The Sacrificial Rituals and Myths of the Goodly Gods, KTU/CAT 1.23: Royal Constructions of Opposition, Intersection, Integration and Domination* (SBLRBS 51; Atlanta, GA: Society of Biblical Literature; Leiden: Brill, 2006), p. 112.

9. Smith, *The Sacrificial Rituals*, pp. 110-13.

10. See Charles Kennedy, 'The Mythological Reliefs from Pozo Moro, Spain', in *SBL Seminar Papers 1981* (SBLSP 20; Chico, CA: Scholars Press, 1981), pp. 209-16; and Smith, *The Sacrificial Rituals*, pp. 110-13. For a different reading, see López Pardo, *La torre de las almas*, pp. 154-77.

11. For further discussion of this scene, see in addition to the references above the contribution of Peggy L. Day to the present volume. For the broader impact of Phoenicians in Spain, see Michael Dietler and Carolina López-Ruiz (eds.), *Colonial Encounters in Ancient Iberia: Phoenician, Greek, and Indigenous Relations* (Chicago: University of Chicago Press, 2009).

12. Rundin, 'Pozo Moro, Child Sacrifice', pp. 428-32, and esp. 440-41.

may also bear on child sacrifice.[13] A tentative reconstruction and translation of lines 11-15 have been offered by Stephen Kaufman (with italics representing reconstructions or unsure readings[14]):

> *There was a rebellion through the Hi[ttite] country,* and the King of Arpad *sacrificed for the benefit of Hadad-Melek* (or: *for the purpose of a molk-offering for Hadad*), and redeemed [the human sacrifice] with butchered animals parts, because Arpad *feared (a living molkomor)/(the King of Assyria. He [the wise man] arose)* and a wise man gave advice as follows: '*According* to the law of the *King of Ar*pad and Aleppo, do not sacrifice a human-[being]...*do not fe*ar, rather *offer a substitute that your province* he not destr[oy...]'[15]

In this rendering, three matters are pertinent: possibly the *mlk*-offering; the redemption of said offering by means of animal offerings; and the citation of local law that forbids human sacrifice in favor of a prescription of a substitute offering. Most of this material involves some reconstruction, if not an entire reconstruction. The only material within this complex that mostly does not entail so much reconstruction is the command: 'do not sacrifice a human-[being]' (*'l gzr/l 'd[m]*).[16]

While these discoveries have generated interpretational controversies, they suggest that at either end of the Mediterranean, child sacrifice may have been a deeply rooted practice, perhaps more so than many modern scholars have envisioned. The same may be said for the biblical

---

13. See Stephen A. Kaufman, 'The Phoenician Inscription of the Injirli Trilingual: A Tentative Reconstruction and Translation', *Maarav* 14.2 (2007), pp. 7-26. For its context, see Lynn Schwartz Dodd, 'Squeezing Blood from a Stone: The Archaeological Context of the Injirli Inscription', in Marilyn J. Lundberg, Steven Fine, and Wayne T. Pitard (eds.), *Puzzling Out the Past: Studies in the Northwest Semitic Languages and Literatures in Honor of Bruce Zuckerman* (Leiden: Brill, 2012), pp. 213-30.

14. For a precise understanding of Kaufman's system of marking these letters, see Kaufman, 'The Phoenician Inscription of the Injirli Trilingual', p. 12.

15. Kaufman, 'The Phoenician Inscription of the Injirli Trilingual', pp. 12, 15. I have added some square brackets for the translation where Kaufman's drawing of the inscription has square brackets.

16. Again, Kaufman's translation. For **gzr* for the cutting of an animal in a treaty context, see Sefire I A lines 7, 40 (3 times); and I B line 43 (and reconstructed in line 41). Sefire I A, line 40 provides the background for the usage of the word elsewhere in the inscription. Cf. the root in a covenantal context in Gen 15.17. For discussion, see Joseph A. Fitzmyer, *The Aramaic Inscriptions of Sefire* (BibOr 19; Rome: Pontifical Biblical Institute, 1967), pp. 32-33. Cf. **gzr* used in literary contexts, such as *KTU* 1.23.63 and Isa 9.19. See Smith, *The Sacrificial Rituals*, pp. 114-15.

evidence. In his discussion of Ezek 20.25-26, Moshe Greenberg charac-
terizes child sacrifice as a 'murderous pagan practice and an abomination
worthy of severest condemnation'.[17] Although these verses do not
reference the practice as non-Israelite (unlike 2 Kgs 16.3, discussed
below), Greenberg's characterization gives the impression that it was
less at home in Israel than elsewhere in the eastern Mediterranean world.
This is not clear from the available West Semitic evidence, including the
Hebrew Bible.[18] The Injirli inscription, if correctly understood, may
suggest otherwise. It stands rather close to the practice of ritual substitution, as found across the biblical legal corpora.

It would appear that the situation in ancient Israel, as perhaps elsewhere in the eastern Mediterranean, was complex. On the one hand, the
idea of child sacrifice exerted considerable symbolic power across the
biblical legal corpus, prophecy and narrative.[19] In addition to the symbolic freight involved in the sheer act of child sacrifice, the depth of its
symbolism is to be attributed in part to the central role that the first-born
plays in matters of family lineage, inheritance and land.[20] On the other

17. Moshe Greenberg, *Ezekiel 1–20* (AB 22; Garden City, NY: Doubleday,
1983), p. 369. For a more nuanced view somewhat along these lines, see Morton
Cogan, *Imperialism and Religion: Assyria, Judah and Israel in the Eighth and
Seventh Centuries B.C.E.* (SBLDS 19; Missoula, MT: Society of Biblical Literature
and Scholars Press, 1974), pp. 72, and 77-83.

18. See the critique of Greenberg on this score in Levenson, *The Death and
Resurrection*, pp. 8, 12, and 15.

19. This is abundantly clear from the treatment of Levenson, *The Death and
Resurrection*. For treatments of the relevant biblical passages, see also John van
Seters, 'From Child Sacrifice to Paschal Lamb: A Remarkable Transformation in
Israelite Religion', *Old Testament Essays* 16.2 (2003), pp. 453-63.

20. See Deut 21.15-17. As Jeffrey H. Tigay notes, inheritance by the first-born
was not rigidly fixed; see Tigay, *The JPS Commentary: Deuteronomy* (Philadelphia:
The Jewish Publication Society, 1996), p. 193. This is evident in texts from Ugarit,
specifically *KTU* 1.15 III 16 ('the youngest of them I will make the first-born
[*bkr*]'), as well as some Akkadian inheritance tablets from Ugarit, see D. Pardee,
'RS 94.2168 and the Right of the Firstborn at Ugarit', in W. H. van Soldt (ed.),
Society and Administration in Ancient Ugarit (Publications de l'Institut historique-
archéologique néerlandais de Stamboul 114; Leiden: Nederlands Instituut voor het
Nabije Oosten, 2010), pp. 94-106. Note the blessing associated with the first-born in
KTU 1.13.28, as well as the praise of Lady Huraya as 'the fair one, your first-born
child' (*KTU* 1.14 III 39, VI 25). Legal tradition of inheritance might underlie
Phoenician *bkr* ('in the field of the first-born', the latter possibly as a divine title),
but its import is not clear; see Paul G. Mosca and James Russell, 'A Phoenician
Inscription from Cebel Ires Daği in Rough Cilicia', *Epigraphica Anatolica* 9 (1987),
pp. 1-28 plus Tafel 1-4, here pp. 5-6, 9. Note *becor* in Plautus' *Poenulus* line 942,

hand, the practice itself seems to have been rare in Israel, as elsewhere in the eastern Mediterranean, employed in relatively extreme circumstances. For example, according to literary sources it was undertaken in situations of siege warfare (2 Kgs 3.27)[21] and plague (Philo of Byblos).[22] In both concept and practice, child sacrifice was not a matter of deviation and it is to be seen as a norm.[23] It is perhaps better characterized as the extreme measure long sanctioned by tradition.

It is with this notion of child sacrifice as the extreme measure that a number of narrative sources in the Hebrew Bible mentioning this practice are examined. Before proceeding to these narrative sources, child sacrifice as the extreme case in divine rulings may be briefly noted. In a number of passages, child sacrifice is stated to be a practice that God did not command (Jer 7.31; 19.5; 32.35; Ezek 20.25-26), suggesting that it

according to C. Krahmalkov, *Phoenician–Punic Dictionary* (OLA 90; Leuven: Peeters/Departement Oosterse Studies, 2000), p. 101; the word is read *dechor* in Maurice Sznycer, *Les passages puniques en transcription Latine dans le 'Poenulus' de Plaute* (Études et commentaires 65; Paris: Librairie C. Klincksieck, 1967), p. 114. See more broadly I. Mendelsohn, 'On the Preferential Status of the Eldest Son', *BASOR* 156 (1959), pp. 38-40; preference for the first-born son is attested (e.g., Middle Assyrian Laws, Mal B, #1 and Mal O, #3 in M. T. Roth, *Law Collections from Mesopotamia and Asia Minor* [ed. P. Michalowski; SBLWAW 6; Atlanta, GA: Scholars Press, 1995], pp. 176 and 191). There are also examples of latitude in Mesopotamian legal tradition (e.g., the Laws of Hammurabi #150, in Roth, *Law Collections*, pp. 108-109).

21. See Greenberg, *Ezekiel 1–20*, pp. 368-70. *KTU* 1.119.26-36 shows the practice of sacrificing in the situation of siege warfare, but it is unclear that it reflects human sacrifice. What has been thought to be the critical term in line 31 is read as *dkr*, 'male' (animal), by *KTU* and reconstructed as *[b]kr* by Dennis Pardee, *Ritual and Cult at Ugarit* (ed. T. J. Lewis; SBLWAW 10; Atlanta: Society of Biblical Literature, 2002), p. 150. For these two possibilities, see Pardee, *Les texts rituels* (2 vols.; RSO XII; Paris: Éditions Recherche sur les Civilisations, 2000), vol. 1, pp. 662, 664-65. Pardee notes that even if the word were read or reconstructed as *[b]kr*, the firstborn in this text may be an animal; see Dennis Pardee, 'Ugaritic Prayer for a City under Siege (1.88)', in William H. Hallo and K. Lawson Younger, Jr. (eds.), *The Context of Scripture*. Vol. 1, *Canonical Compositions from the Biblical World* (Leiden: Brill, 1997), p. 285 n. 23.

22. In Eusebius' *Praeparatio Evangelica* 1.10.33: 'At the occurrence of a fatal plague, Kronos immolated his only son to his father Ouranos'. For this translation along with the text, see Harold W. Attridge and Robert A. Oden, Jr., *Philo of Byblos: The Phoenician History: Introduction, Critical Text, Translation, Notes* (CBQMS 9; Washington, DC: The Catholic Biblical Association of America, 1981), pp. 56-57.

23. Deviation versus norm are the alternatives posed in Levenson, *The Death and Resurrection*, pp. 3-17. Levenson (p. 8), answers in favor of seeing child sacrifice as 'an older normative tradition'.

served as an extreme test case for interpretation (cf. prophecy posed in parallel terms in Deut 18.20; Jer 14.14; 23.32; and 29.23). Such reflections may represent early, inner-biblical instances of using such an extreme case to explore a problem in legal interpretation.[24]

3. *Child Sacrifice as the Extreme Example of Idolatry in 2 Kings*

The references to child sacrifice in 2 Kgs 16.3 and 21.6 likewise represent extremity, in these cases the outer limits of idolatry.[25] Both verses are intriguing for their brevity and perspective. 2 Kings 16.3 attributes to Ahaz the sacrifice of his son, in a clause opening with *wĕgam*, 'and also'. Elsewhere in narrative sections of 2 Kings this construction marks material layered into accounts, either to express condemnation (see also 2 Kgs 13.6; 21.16; cf. *gam* in 2 Kgs 17.19) or to note action taken against

24.   For these passages, see Corrine Carvalho, ' "I Myself Gave Them Laws That Were Not Good": Ezekiel 20 and the Exodus Traditions', *JSOT* 69 (1996), pp. 73-90; Scott Walker Hahn and John Seitze Bergsma, 'What Laws Were "Not Good"? A Canonical Approach to the Theological Problem of Ezekiel 20.25-26', *JBL* 123 (2004), pp. 201-18; Baruch Halpern, 'The False Torah of Jeremiah 8 in the Context of Seventh Century BCE Pseudepigraphy: The First Documented Rejection of Tradition', in Sidnie White Crawford et al. (eds.), *'Up to the Gates of Ekron': Essays on the Archaeology and History of the Eastern Mediterranean in Honor of Seymour Gitin* (Jerusalem: The W. F. Albright Institute of Archaeological Research/The Israel Exploration Society, 2007), pp. 337-43, esp. 339-40; Armin Lange, 'They Burn their Sons and Daughters—That Was No Command of Mine (Jer 7.31): Child Sacrifice in the Hebrew Bible and in the Deuteronomistic Jeremiah-Redaction', in K. Finsterbusch, A. Lange, K. F. Römheld, and L. Lazar (eds.), *Human Sacrifice in Jewish and Christian Tradition* (SHR 112; Leiden: Brill, 2007), pp. 109-32; Mark S. Smith, 'Textual Interpretation in 7th–6th Century Israel: Between Competition, Textualisation and Tradition', in Andrés Piquer Otero and Pablo A. Torijano Morales (eds.), *Textual Criticism and Dead Sea Scrolls Studies in Honour of Julio Trebolle Barrera: Florilegium Complutense* (JSJSup 158; Leiden: Brill, 2012), pp. 317-23. Note also Tigay, *Deuteronomy*, pp. 162-63.

25.   Based on the similarity of idiom with the *C*-stem of * '*br* in legal passages (especially those involving **mlk* in Lev 18.21; 20.1-5), it has been questioned whether 2 Kgs 16.3 and 21.6 refer to child sacrifice rather than a separate fire cult of Molech not involving child sacrifice. For this view, see M. Weinfeld, 'The Worship of Molech and the Queen of Heaven and its Background', *UF* 4 (1972), pp. 133-54; Cogan, *Imperialism and Religion*, pp. 77-83; and M. Cogan and H. Tadmor, *II Kings: A New Translation with Introduction and Commentary* (AB 11; New York: Doubleday, 1988), pp. 186, 266-67. While there are some differences of language, the conclusion drawn has been disputed by Morton Smith, 'A Note on Burning Babies', *JAOS* 95 (1975), pp. 477-79, and by Mosca, 'Child Sacrifice', pp. 135-59. Note also the review of Tigay, *Deuteronomy*, pp. 127-28 and pp. 464-65.

condemnable practices (2 Kgs 23.15, 19, 24; cf. 24.4). The distribution
of the particle for opening prose clauses suggests late or secondary
additions in at least some instances. In addition, the formulation of the
practice in 2 Kgs 16.3 fronts the direct object, 'his son', in contrast to the
verb standing first in the parallel formulation in 2 Kgs 21.6. It is thought
that this fronting of the direct object bears an additional force of some
sort ('He even consigned his son to the fire', NJPS), although this is
unclear since a son would be the expected offering in this formulation.

The report in 2 Kgs 16.3 then offers a comparison: 'like the abomination of the nations'. Here the practice is marked as the outer limits of
immoral behavior, being associated with other nations by the implied
narrator. In this way, this traditional practice is represented as the extreme
measure of Ahaz's idolatrous behavior. The context for the practice is
not supplied, although 2 Kgs 16.5 refers to the siege of Jerusalem: 'They
besieged Ahaz, but they were unable in battling'. It would be tempting to
connect the report of child sacrifice with this siege, but this oversteps the
evidence.[26] More to the point, the report of the practice charges King
Ahaz with the worst behaviors associated by this narrator with foreign
nations. This is historiography as sermon.

The similar formulation for child sacrifice in 2 Kgs 21.6 belongs to a
long catalogue of Manasseh's sins. Where in 2 Kgs 16.3 child sacrifice
heads the characterization of Ahaz's sin, in Manasseh's case in 2 Kgs
21.6 it is one item in a longer 'laundry list' of idolatrous acts. As Mosca
observed, it plays a significant role in this context. It links Manasseh to
the worst of Ahaz's acts and the northern kingdom more broadly (see
2 Kgs 17.17). The grammar of the operative phrase also calls for comment, since the verb used is not the *waw*-consecutive, as one might
expect in the context of *waw*-consecutive verbs preceding and following. The construction instead consists of a simple *waw* plus the suffix
indicative verbal form. It could suggest iterative or continuous action in
the past, and thus multiple acts of child sacrifice; or, the form is denoting
the simple past thought to be suggestive of a secondary addition.[27] Such
approaches have been debated, but they remain possibilities.

---

26. On this score, see the criticism of Cogan and Tadmor, *II Kings*, p. 186.
27. Cf. 2 Chr 33.6, with *wĕhû'* before the verbal form. Takamitsu Muraoka
(*Emphatic Words and Structures in Biblical Hebrew* [Jerusalem: Magnes; Leiden:
Brill, 1985], p. 51 n. 20) comments, 'It is remarkable that the parallel passage in
2 Kg 21.6 lacks the pronoun'. For another grammatical difference with these parallel
verses (but not of consequence for the topic at hand), see Paul Joüon and Takamitsu
Muraoka, *A Grammar of Biblical Hebrew* (2d ed.; SubBib 27; Rome: Pontificio
Istituto Biblica, 2008), paragraph 158h.

In view of the possible secondary character of the *wĕgam* clause of 2 Kgs 16.3, it may be tempting to see a comparable addition here. In any case, the practice here, as in 2 Kgs 16.3, is identified as one of the abominable acts of the other nations as in 2 Kgs 21.3. These passages may draw on strictures about the practice in Deut 18.10 (and/or perhaps 12.31; cf. 2 Kgs 17.17 and 23.10 with their closer formulations),[28] which mentions the rite of passing children through fire as well as the divinatory practices of other nations. There has been some effort to understand the passage from a historical perspective, namely that Ahaz introduced the practice into Israel.[29] At the same time, the possibility that the relevant verses are secondary additions suggests a literary effort at heaping up the sins of the kings in question; this is particularly evident with what I have called 'the laundry list' of Manasseh's sins in 2 Kgs 21.3-6. This assessment would comport with the further observation that the textual accounts of these two instances of child sacrifice with Ahaz and Manasseh do not tie them to a historical incident (so also 2 Kgs 17.17).

Compared with 2 Kgs 16.3 and 21.6, 2 Kgs 3.27 moves in a very different direction. First, this verse attributes the practice to the king of Moab and not to an Israelite king. Second, it is presented explicitly in the context of a battle siege. Third, the practice is represented without condemnation. On the contrary, it is reported as successful: the practice achieves the intended goal of turning back the Israelites. Finally, it does not partake of the formulary found in 2 Kgs 16.3 and 21.6. On the whole, the passage is remarkable for the credence given to the non-Israelite sacrificial offering of a royal son[30] (which has led to rather convoluted efforts to read the passage differently).[31] Contrary to some commentators, the passage does not seem particularly deuteronomistic, but seems to partake of a different sensibility (not to mention the difference in formulation) of what is seen in 2 Kgs 16.3 and 21.6. 2 Kings 3.27 may be

---

28. See Cogan and Tadmor, *II Kings*, p. 205.

29. See Cogan, *Imperialism and Religion*, p. 72.

30. See Levenson, *The Death and Resurrection*, pp. 14-15.

31. Anson F. Rainey and R. Steven Notley, *The Sacred Bridge: Carta's Atlas of the Biblical World* (Jerusalem: Carta, 2006), p. 205: 'the very idea that ancient Israel (at least the Deuteronomist's view) would have felt remorse at the human sacrifice of an enemy is so outlandish that it must be rejected out of hand'. To explain the verse otherwise, Rainey and Notley posit a back-story unattested in the text. To my mind, while the text is not without difficulties, this approach constitutes a sort of pseudo-historical midrash in order to avoid the passage's plain reading. For the problems, see Cogan and Tadmor, *II Kings*, pp. 50-52.

located instead in the context of a different religious worldview of trans-latability between the national gods of Israel and its neighbors.[32] In this context, the national gods of other nations would be recognized as doing for them what Yahweh the national god of Israel and Judah do for them.

In 2 Kgs 16.3 and 21.6, child sacrifice is represented as a foreign practice wholly unbefitting of Israel's kings. These passages represent the practice as the extreme case of immoral non-Israelite behavior.

4. *Human Sacrifice as the Extreme Calculation in Genesis 22 and Judges 11*

The symbolic freight of child sacrifice is put on display in two biblical narratives that present it as an extreme measure (Gen 22; Judg 11).[33] Where God goes to this extreme length to test Abraham (Gen 22.1-2), Jephthah takes this extreme measure in order to secure divine favor in battle (Judg 11.30-31, 39). Further parallels between the two passages are also notable. Both characterize the child as *yḥd* (Gen 22.2, 12, 16; Judg 11.34), a term known elsewhere, both in the Hebrew Bible (Jer 6.26; Amos 8.10; Zech 12.10),[34] and elsewhere in the West Semitic milieu.[35] For the offering of the child, both stories use the noun *'ōlâ* with

---

32. Mark S. Smith, *God in Translation: Deities in Cross-Cultural Discourse in the Biblical World* (FAT 1/57; Tübingen: Mohr Siebeck, 2008; Grand Rapids: Eerdmans, 2010), pp. 91-130, esp. 116-18.

33. See Michaela Bauks, *Jephtas Tochter: Traditions- religions- und rezeptions-geschichte Studien zu Richter 11,29-40* (FAT 71; Tübingen: Mohr Siebeck, 2010), pp. 115-21.

34. See Levenson, *The Death and Resurrection*, pp. 27-30.

35. The term appears in Philo of Byblos where the practice of offering an 'only son', said to be named Ieoud, takes place on the occasion of war (*Preparatio evangelica* 1.10.44 = 4.16.11): 'Now Kronos, whom the Phoenicians call El, who was in their land and who was later divinized after his death as the star of Kronos, had an only son by a local bride named Anobret, and therefore they called him Ieoud. Even now among the Phoenicians the only son is given this name. When war's gravest dangers gripped the land, Kronos dressed his son in royal attire, prepared an altar and sacrificed him'. See Attridge and Oden, *Philo of Byblos*, pp. 62-63, 94 n. 150. See also Albert Baumgarten, *The Phoenician History of Philo of Byblos: A Commentary* (Leiden: Brill, 1981), pp. 245-52. Baumgarten also notes the Greek equivalent, *monogene* (*huion*), reflecting *yaḥid*, in a parallel story of Kronos' immolation of his only son to his father to avert a plague (*Preparatio evangelica* 1.10.33, in Attridge and Oden, *Philo of Byblos*, pp. 56-57, 91 n. 130, noted above). The putative name, Ieoud, seems to derive ultimately from West Semitic *yaḥid*. The Neo-Punic word has been thought to be reflected in Plautus' *Poenulus*, lines 932-33: 'I would get my brother's only son (*iaed*)' (so Krahmalkov, *Phoenician–Punic*

the verbal form of * *'lh* (Gen 22.2 and 13, see *'ôlâ* also in vv. 3, 6, 7-8; Judg 11.31). They also use **hlk* (Gen 22.2, 3, 5, 6, 8, 13, 19; Judg 11.37, 38) and **šûb* (Gen 22.5, 19; Judg 11.31; cf. the verbal use, 'to take back, retract', in v. 35), although to rather different ends (see below). To express the poignancy of their respective situations, both involve a dialogue between father and child (Gen 22.7-8; Judg 11.35-38), with both children addressing their father as 'my father' (Gen 22.7; Judg 11.36). As we will see, in both texts God chooses the human offering to take. These two stories also represent child sacrifice as belonging to eras long past (relative to the time of their composition). The practice of child sacrifice in these narratives is not couched in etiological fashion; they are not rendered as accounts of why child sacrifice was practiced or out-lawed. Rather, both passages present child sacrifice as a real possibility in the past.

The two passages also offer a literary counterpoint.[36] In Genesis 22, Yahweh is said to be testing Abraham. By contrast, Jephthah initiates the offering. Abraham goes on a considerable three-day journey to the moun-tain of Yahweh (see v. 14), on what may be called an 'anti-pilgrimage'.[37] While pilgrimage to the sacred site was a communal activity involving offerings of first fruits of crops and animals, Abraham's in Genesis 22 is a journey to a sacred site undertaken by a father and son involving the offering of the first-fruit being the human son. By contrast to Abraham's offering, the setting for Jephthah's is at home; it is his daughter with her companions who journey before her demise is to take place (Judg 11.37-39).[38] Also most strikingly, in Abraham's case it is his son who is

---

Dictionary, p. 206); for a similar reading, see Sznycer, *Les passages puniques en transcription Latine dans le 'Poenulus' de Plaute*, pp. 65-66. The Latin translation in line 952 is *filium*. Note also Akkadian *wēdum*-names, such as E-du-sal-lim, 'Keep-the-Only-Child-Safe', in *CAD E*:37a, #2'.

36. See Levenson, *The Death and Resurrection*, pp. 13-14; and Bauks, *Jephtas Tochter*, pp. 115-21.

37. Mark S. Smith, with contributions by Elizabeth M. Bloch-Smith, *The Pilgrimage Pattern in Exodus* (JSOTSup 239; Sheffield: Sheffield Academic Press, 1997), pp. 138-40.

38. For recent discussions, see Michaela Bauks, 'La fille sans nom, la fille de Jephthé', *Études Théologiques et Religieuses* 81 (2006), pp. 81-93, and idem, *Jephtas Tochter: Traditions- religions- und rezeptionsgeschichte Studien zu Richter 11,29-40* (FAT 71; Tübingen: Mohr Siebeck, 2010); Renate Egger-Wenzel, 'Jiftachs Tochter (Ri 11,29-40)—Die Töchter von Schilo (Ri 21,19-25). Ursprung und Ausführung einer kultischen Feier durch Frauen?', *BN* 129 (2006), pp. 5-16; David Janzen, 'Why the Deuteronomist Told about the Sacrifice of Jephthah's Daughter', *JSOT* 29 (2005), pp. 339-57. Among older studies, see Peggy L. Day, 'From the

involved, as expected for child sacrifice from what we have noted above. This stands in contrast to Jephthah's daughter.[39] Finally, Abraham's act generates blessing (Gen 22.17-18), while Jephthah's issues in a lamentable result (see Judg 11.35). God commends Abraham while Jephthah directs blame at his daughter.[40]

Within this broader context, I would like to focus attention on the formulation of Jephthah's vow in Judg 11.30-31 and specifically on one clause within the apodosis. The apodosis of Jephthah's vow does not name a specific offering, only 'the one that comes, who comes out to meet him'. The expression seems open-ended (not to mention convoluted). One clue is perhaps the masculine singular form of the verbs (as well as the object suffix on the verb in v. 31b). On a first reading, it might be supposed that Jephthah is represented as having a male animal in mind that he thinks he will see 'coming out of the doors of my house to meet me' and that he will offer in fulfillment of his vow. His offer of an *'ōlâ* offering in v. 31b would accord with the *'ōlâ* offering of Lev 1.2 involving a male (*zākār*) from the cattle, and with Lev 1.10's reference to the male (*zākār*) from the sheep or goats. It also accords with the common sacrificial usage of the cognate accusative expression with the *C*-stem verb of **'lh* (Deut 27.26; Josh 22.23; 1 Sam 10.8; 13.10; Ezek 43.18; Ezra 3.2, 6; 1 Chr 16.40; 2 Chr 23.18; 29.27, etc.). At first glance, Jepththah's vow might seem little different from the vow made by Demarous 'to offer a sacrifice in return for his escape' from battle.[41]

Child Is Born the Woman: The Story of Jephthah's Daughter', in Peggy L. Day (ed.), *Gender and Difference in Ancient Israel* (Minneapolis: Fortress, 1989), pp. 58-74. This part of the text lies beyond the scope of the discussion here.

39. Compare the notable use of **bkr* with respect to only females in the story of Kirta, specifically in *KTU* 1.15 III 16 ('the youngest of them I will make the firstborn'), and in the praise of Lady Huraya in *KTU* 1.14 III 39, VI 25 ('the fair one, your first-born child').

40. While the similarities as well as the contrasts might suggest that Gen 22 could have served as a model for Judg 11 on these matters, the features shared are fairly general. I do not see sufficient basis for proposing that one of these texts alludes to or echoes the other according to the criteria discussed by Benjamin B. Sommer, *A Prophet Reads Scripture: Allusion in Isaiah 40–66* (Stanford, CA: Stanford University, 1998), pp. 6-31. In connection with this issue, it is to be noted that Judg 11 shares with other texts some central features that are missing from Gen 22. See Levenson, *The Death and Resurrection*, p. 24. An intertextual approach to Gen 22 and Judg 11 would seem to be more promising.

41. For text and translation of *Preparatio evangelica* 1.10.29, in Attridge and Oden, *Philo of Byblos*, pp. 52-55.

This interpretation seems unlikely, as what would normally 'come out of the doors of a house' would be a person (cf. Judg 19.26-27) and not an animal (cf. Judg 14.5), as critics have noted. Thus the vow appears to raise the specter of the *'ôlâ* offering consisting of a human sacrifice, as seen with the human son of the king of Moab in 2 Kgs 3.27.[42] This ominous offering also takes place in the context of battle, although the timing imagined for Jephthah's offering seems unusual and seems more in keeping with votive offerings post-battle.[43] By contrast, the son offered in 2 Kgs 3.27 involves not a post-battle situation, but one in the heat of battle. In any case, given the masculine form of the participle 'the one who comes out, who comes out from the doors of my house to meet me' in the post-battle context of victory might evoke a male member from his household.

As an alternative, the masculine forms could cover female gender. Indeed, this grammatical sensibility is required by the later appearance of Jephthah's daughter (in vv. 34-40). Jephthah might be also presented as understanding that a female could come out to meet him upon his return, as it was a female role to greet the hero on his return from battle. So Lauren A. S. Monroe concludes: 'There is no escaping that Jephthah had in mind a human, female sacrifice—and the sacrifice of his only heir at that'.[44] Monroe rightly compares 1 Sam 18.6, in which women from all the towns likewise 'go out' singing and dancing 'to meet' the victorious Saul with timbrels. In 2 Sam 6.20, Michal also 'goes out to meet' David (without music or dance) upon his return following his celebration of his military victory.[45] The same expression in these two passages indicates that a celebrating female might be expected. Given the narrative outcome in vv. 34-40, it would appear that the form of the vow as given seems

---

42. According to Ziony Zevit, the vow that Jephthah makes is what he calls 'a private *ḥerem*'. See Zevit, 'Mesha's *Ryt* in the Context of Moabite and Israelite Bloodletting', in Lundberg, Fine, and Pitard (eds.), *Puzzling Out the Past*, p. 237; cf. A. Logan, 'Rehabilitating Jephthah', *JBL* 128 (2009), p. 682.

43. An unnecessary, rash vow made without prompting by the deity before battle is known also in the story of Kirta (*KTU* 1.14 IV 31-43). This vow later gets Kirta in trouble because he apparently forgets to fulfill the vow (*KTU* 1.15 III 22-30). By contrast, Jephthah appears prepared to fulfill his vow.

44. Lauren S. Monroe, 'Disembodied Women: Sacrificial Language and the Deaths of Bat-Jephthah, Cozbi, and the Bethlehemite Concubine', *CBQ* 75 (2003), p. 36. In view of the sacrificial language, the passage would seem to point to a child and not Jephthah's wife, as also entertained by Tony Cartledge, *Vows in the Hebrew Bible and in the Ancient Near East* (Sheffield: Sheffield Academic Press, 1992), p. 179.

45. Cf. Judg 4.18 where Jael goes out to meet Sisera.

designed to anticipate his daughter who comes out to meet the victorious hero, in this case, Jephthah's unnamed daughter. Yet, if he had had his daughter specifically in mind as Monroe suggests, then Jephthah's speech could have used feminine verbal forms. Or, why not name 'my daughter' as his intended offering? It also is unclear why he would blame her in v. 35 unless he knowingly or self-deceptively 'blames the victim'.

The specific nature of Jephthah's vow is, however, left unnamed unlike other vows. He may be represented as thinking that he would offer any person in order to secure divine help in battle. As a result, commentators such as David Marcus believe that he may be rash in pronouncing the vow as he has.[46] Alice Logan argues instead that in this military context the offering of a child would be expected of Jephthah and that here he is not thoughtless or rash, but cagey, leaving it to the deity to decide which person to select for the vow's payment.[47] For Logan, Jephthah knows full well that his daughter is a real possibility because of the traditional practice of women meeting the returning hero, yet he feels compelled to offer his only child per the warfare practice of child sacrifice, and he hopes against hope that someone else will greet him instead. If this is what the audience is to suppose, the question remains: from within the world of the story, who could it be that Jephthah might have hoped to come out from the house upon his return home?

While the general expectation might have been that females greet warriors upon their return from battle, it is not only women who do so. In Num 31.13, it is the non-military leaders of the community who meet the returning army. The larger literary context in Judges 11 generates a strong contrast between the masculine forms here in v. 31 in the vow and the female who will fulfill these conditions in vv. 34-40. In the immediate context of Jephthah's vow as he voices it, the masculine grammatical forms may evoke a male. In theory, Jephthah could have in mind the sacrifice of a male member of his household. Since, as the audience learns later, Jephthah has no male children, Jephthah would not have a

---

46. David Marcus, *Jephthah and His Vow* (Lubbock, TX: Texas Tech Press, 1986). This interpretation is an old one, as noted by Marcus. According to *b. Taan.* 4a, Samuel ben Nahmani said in the name of Jonathan that Jephthah was one of three men who 'asked not in a proper manner' (i.e., haphazardly). The other two, Eliezer (Gen 24.14) and Saul (1 Sam 17.25), the passage continues, 'were fortunate in the reply they received, and one was not' (namely Jephthah). For this passage, see also David B. Weisberg, *Leaders and Legacies in Assyriology and Bible: The Collected Essays of David B. Weisberg* (Winona Lake, IN: Eisenbrauns, 2012), p. 242.

47. Logan, 'Rehabilitating Jephthah', p. 678. So also Cartledge, *Vows in the Hebrew Bible*, p. 179.

son in mind. While one might entertain an unnamed servant of the household as a possible candidate,[48] this alternative stands outside of the story. The only male figures of the household named in the story are his half-brothers who had expelled him in vv. 1-3. Perhaps one of them—or more—was the object of his wishful thinking. Or, more in line with the traditional expectation that females of the household would greet and celebrate the returning hero, perhaps Jephthah hoped that he would see any one of the possibly many females related to his half-brothers,[49] but not his only child, his daughter. Perhaps the emphasis on his daughter as his only child is to hint at the many females that might have belonged to the households of his half-brothers. In this reading, the vow would be offered in the hope that it would accomplish two goals, victory in battle and revenge on his half-brothers.[50] In this case, Jephthah would be negotiating with Yahweh in a way that perhaps parallels his cagey negotiation with the elders in vv. 4-11, as Logan observes.

The comparison between Genesis 22 and Judges 11 serves to shine a harsh light on Judges 11 and perhaps on Genesis 22 as well. In both texts, God chooses the human offering at stake. In Genesis 22, God calculates in testing Abraham by means of the extreme measure of sacrificing his son. It may be that for Abraham it lies beyond his hope that God will intervene. In Judges 11 Jephthah calculates in making God choose the human offering. Here Jephthah is perhaps hoping that God will not choose his only child. Indeed, it marked an extreme calculation in both stories.

48. A slave is suggested by Pamela Tamarkin Reis, 'Spoiled Child: A Fresh Look at Jephthah's Daughter', *Prooftexts* 17 (1997), p. 281. She also reads the vow of offering to be metaphorical and not literal, though without any particular evidence. She also assumes that the whole household knows of the vow as it was made in the same place, in Mizpah. On this score, this is unclear given the two different spellings of the geographical name in vv. 29 and 34.

49. I owe this suggestion to Corrine Carvalho, personal communication.

50. This view does not require an original literary unity of the material under discussion. On the contrary, vv. 1-11, 12-13 + 28-32, and vv. 34-40 may be viewed as parts of what Luis Alonso Schökel calls a 'secondary unity' (the latter two parts sutured together by vv. 30-31, as noted by Aviva Richman): 'A later writer could take already completed pieces and bring them together skillfully to form a new and complex unity'. Alonso Schökel, *A Manual of Hebrew Poetics* (Subsidia biblica 11; Rome: Pontificio Istituto Biblico, 1988), p. 189. For the literary-redactional issues of Judg 11, see Walter Gross, *Richter* (HTKAT 5A; Freiburg: Herder, 2009), pp. 555-65. Verses 14-25 (+ 26-27?) may be an older speech about Moabites dating from Omride-period conflicts inserted into an updated story concerning conflict with the Ammonites.

HUMAN SACRIFICE IN PRE- AND EARLY DYNASTIC EGYPT: WHAT DO YOU WANT TO FIND?*

Thomas Hikade and Jane Roy

Is it true, the saying that you know how to reattach a head which has been cut off?
Dedi said: Yes, I do know, Sovereign. Life, prosper, and health, my Lord.
His Majesty [King Cheops] said: Let there be brought to me a prisoner who is in confinement, that his punishment may be inflicted.
And Dedi said: But not indeed to a man, the august cattle.

(Papyrus Westcar ca. 4000 years old)

Introduction

This year sees the commemoration of the 100th anniversary of the outbreak of the First World War. The landing at the Gallipoli Peninsula of the Australian and New Zealand Army Corps (ANZAC) on 25 April 1915 marks a particular and crucial point in the history of Australia. The Australian governments of the day fully supported Great Britain, but there was a new sense and mood in the young country: this was where a new nation could be forged and an opportunity to show the independence and importance of this federation on the international stage.

The Gallipoli Campaign (25 April 1915 to 19 December 1915) under the command of the British and French was designed to open the Dardanelles but ended in utter failure. On 25 April 1916, the first anniversary of the landing at Gallipoli, ceremonies and services were held throughout Australia to honour the sacrifices made by so many men overseas. This day is known as ANZAC Day. During our time at UBC we marked this day by hosting a barbeque for friends and faculty from CNRS.

Paul Mosca was a regular guest at our ANZAC events. In the following our intention is to connect Paul's interest in the practice of human

* We would like to thank Jana Jones, D'arne O'Neill and Kate Hickey for reading earlier drafts and providing helpful comments.

sacrifice with the evidence from Pre- and Early Dynastic Egypt and a surprise find from the Predynastic site at Maadi, which brings us finally back to ANZAC.

Ancient Egypt was 'discovered' by a Georgian England and revolutionary France, at a time when Europe was either rejecting or riding on the wave of the Age of Enlightenment. Scholars were pushing into lands of which they had only ever read or dreamed. What did they expect? What did they hope to find? And what expectations and preconceptions did they bring with them?

Exploration of Egypt (ancient and modern) began with the Napoleonic Expeditions in 1798. But it was from the nineteenth century on that excavations uncovered the first evidence for dismemberment and manipulation of the deceased, finds which often led to sensational interpretations, including headhunting,[1] cannibalism[2] and human sacrifice.[3] Petrie even went so far as to conclude that some individuals were partially conscious when they were buried at the same time as their masters—this based solely on the awkward positions, such as dropped jaws, of the skeletons.[4]

The idea of human sacrifice in First Dynasty Egypt is still very much alive in Egyptology.[5] The subsidiary chambers from this time have been interpreted as the 'ghostly internment of an entire royal court'[6] and the whole funerary landscape as 'spaces of sacrifice'.[7]

---

1. B. G. Trigger, 'The Rise of Egyptian Civilization', in B. G. Trigger, B. J. Kemp, D. O'Connor and A. B. Lloyd, *Ancient Egypt: A Social History* (Cambridge: Cambridge University Press, 1983), pp. 1-70.

2. W. M. F. Petrie and J. E. Quibell, *Naqada and Ballas* (London: Quaritch, 1896).

3. É. Crubézy, S. Duchesne and B. Midant-Reynes, 'Les sacrifices humains à l'époque prédynastique: l'apport de la nécropole d'Adaïma', *Archéo-Nil* 10 (2000), pp. 21-40. T. Wilkinson, *Early Dynastic Egypt* (London: Routledge, 1999); M. Hoffman, *Egypt before the Pharaohs* (London: Routledge & Kegan Paul, 1980).

4. W. M. F. Petrie, *The Tombs of the Courtiers and Oxyrhynkhos* (London: Quaritch, 1925), p. 8.

5. As recently E. F. Morris, '(Un)dying Loyalty: Meditations on Retainer Sacrifice in Ancient Egypt and Elsewhere', in R. Campbell (ed.), *Violence and Civilization: Studies of Social Violence in History and Prehistory* (Oxford: Oxbow Books, 2014), pp. 61-93.

6. R. Stadelmann, 'A New Look at the Tombs of the First and Second Dynasties at Abydos and Sakkara and the Evolution of the Pyramid Complex', in K. Douad, S. Bedier, and S. Abd el-Fatah (eds.), *Studies in Honor of Ali Radwan* (Cairo: Conseil Suprême des Antiquités de l'Égypte, 2005), pp. 361-75 (362).

7. D. Wengrow, *The Archaeology of Early Egypt: Social Transformation in North-East Africa, 10,000 to 2650 BC* (Cambridge: Cambridge University Press, 2006), pp. 245-48.

It seems that the idea of human sacrifice is almost the desired concept from our 'modern' perspective, but what evidence can we expect to indicate the practice of human sacrifice in ancient Egypt? Is it to be found in the pathology of buried individuals such as consistent and widespread physical trauma? Is it to be found in the architectural situation where we can clearly see that the main burial and its subsidiary burials were sealed, for example by a layer of mud plaster, at the same time? Is it the iconographical record that shows people being killed, which of course could be interpreted as human sacrifice or executions if we don't know the exact context? Or is it oral and written tradition that speaks of it? And for the evidence most often cited for the Pre- and Early Dynastic periods, are other interpretations equally, if not more valid?

We would like to revisit the sites of Adaima, Hierakonpolis, Saqqara and especially Abydos to cast a critical eye over the possible evidence for human sacrifices there, before briefly visiting the site of Maadi and giving some thoughts on the nature of sacrifice itself.

Scalping, Beheading, and Mutilation at Predynastic Adaima and Hierakonpolis

The Evidence from Adaima

The site of Adaima lies about 550km south of Cairo and was initially excavated, in part, at the beginning of the twentieth century, but the major phase of excavation took place between 1989 and 2005.[8] The site comprises a Predynastic settlement and two cemeteries labelled the Western Cemetery and the Eastern Cemetery. In all, 881 graves, yielding 800 morphologically well-preserved skeletons, were excavated and were studied by osteoarchaeologists and anthropobiologists.

---

8. N. Buchez, 'Adaïma (Upper Egypt): The Stages of State Development from the Point of View of a "Village Community"', in R. F. Friedman, and P. N. Fiske (eds.), *Egypt at its Origins 3: Proceedings of the Third International Conference 'Origin of the State: Predynastic and Early Dynastic Egypt', London, 27th July–1st August 2008* (OLA 205; Leuven: Peeters, 2011), pp. 31-40; É. Crubézy, S. Duchesne and B. Midant-Reynes, 'The Predynastic Cemetery at Adaima (Upper Egypt), General Presentation and Implications for the Population of Predynastic Egypt', in B. Midant-Reynes and Y. Tristant (eds.), *Egypt at its Origins 2: Proceedings of the International Conference 'Origin of the State: Predynastic and Early Dynastic Egypt', Toulouse (France), 5–8 September 2005* (OLA 172; Leuven: Peeters, 2008), p. 289-310; B. Midant-Reynes, É. Crubézy and T. Janin, *Adaïma*. Vol. 2, *La nécropole prédynastique* (Fouilles de l'Institut français d'archéologie orientale 47; Cairo: Institut français d'archeologie orientale, 2002). B. Midant-Reynes and N. Buchez, *Adaïma*. Vol. 1, *Économie et habitat* (Fouilles de l'Institut français d'archéologie orientale 45; Cairo: Institut français d'archeologie orientale, 2002).

Apart from the burials in the cemeteries, the people of Adaima also sometimes laid very young children to rest inside the settlement, some equipped with provisions for the afterlife and adornments such as bracelets.[9]

The Western Cemetery was already badly damaged during the Predynastic period, with some graves obviously obliterated, and had once contained many more tombs than the 301 that could still be studied. Primarily adults were buried in this cemetery. The earliest internment of six individuals (one adult, one adolescent, and four children) was prepared around 3700/3600 BCE, about the time when people first settled at Adaima. The tomb (S55) was set on top of a small mound and no archaeological remains were discovered in its vicinity. All individuals of S55 died and were buried at the same so that the tomb has been considered the 'original first tomb', possibly even triggering the settlement of people at Adaima.[10] The Western Cemetery was then used for the next 600 to 700 years as a final resting place, and in fact multiple burials remained nothing unusual for the next 100 years.

In one case, extraordinary care was taken over the placement of the bodies creating an image of love expressed by the funerary party as much as a gesture of tenderness between a woman and a child. In burial S11 the body of the child was placed in such a way that the child's neck was resting on the woman's arm while her fingertips were touching the child's forehead.[11]

Interestingly for this study, in several other tombs in the area, those buried showed clear cut marks on the upper vertebrae. It seems clear that the skulls were removed after decomposition of the corpses.[12]

Around 3400 BCE Egypt saw a dramatic change in society. Elites emerged, monumental architecture appeared, such as can be seen at Hierakonpolis,[13] and a growing wealth is reflected by an increase of grave goods in Upper Egypt.

9. Crubézy, Duchesne and Midant-Reynes, 'The Predynastic Cemetery at Adaima', p. 295, fig.5.

10. Crubézy, Duchesne and Midant-Reynes, 'The Predynastic Cemetery at Adaima', p. 296, fig. 6.

11. Crubézy, Duchesne and Midant-Reynes, 'The Predynastic Cemetery at Adaima', p. 297, fig. 7, p. 302.

12. Crubézy, Duchesne and Midant-Reynes, 'The Predynastic Cemetery at Adaima', p. 306.

13. R. F. Friedman, 'Hierakonpolis', in E. Teeter (ed.), *Before the Pyramids: The Origins of Egyptian Civilization* (Chicago: Oriental Institute of the University of Chicago, 2011), pp. 33-44. T. Hikade, 'Origins of Monumental Architecture: Recent Excavations at Hierakonpolis HK29B and HK 25', in Friedman and Fiske (eds.), *Egypt at its Origins 3*, pp. 81-107.

At Adaima larger and deeper tombs were cut and the number and quality of grave goods increased. The tombs of this phase of about 200 years in the Western Cemetery are those of people of high rank within the community, and the spatial closeness to the original tomb S55 on top of the mound is evidence for strong collective memory and veneration of the ancestors. It is interesting to note that the tombs of the following 50 to 100 years at the Western Cemetery do not match the general trend for elite tombs, which usually had underground chambers lined with mud-bricks and even mudbrick superstructures. These later burials, without any ceramic vessels, sometimes considered 'poor', were often placed in leather bags and wrapped with a mat.

At Adaima it seems that members of the elite were now buried else-where. Overall the Western Cemetery does not display a chronological sequence of a village population; it changed its character over time—at times a resting place for the elite, later for those of lower status.

The Eastern Cemetery is divided into a northern and southern section by a gap formed by an old wadi of around 15m width. The southern section contained only graves of children, many placed in vessels, and dates mainly to around 3400/3300–3200 BCE with some younger tombs dated to around 3150–3050 BCE.[14] The northern section was later used for children and adults from around 3000 BCE until the Third Dynasty (ca. 2700/2600 BCE). It would appear that the Eastern Cemetery was used by a community of only 10 to 30, perhaps just one or two extended families.[15] In a similar case to the careful display of a woman and a child in S11 on the Western Cemetery, the Eastern Cemetery allows further insight into rituals performed during the funeral, albeit difficult for us today to understand. In one case, burial S166, a young individual was laid to rest in a clay chest without any offerings. However, the corpse's right arm had been detached when the body was still fresh, with the severed arm subsequently replaced at the correct spot, although anatomically incorrectly.[16]

For about 200 years, starting around 3400 BCE, we see the Western Cemetery containing the elite tombs while the Eastern Cemetery con-tained the non-elite tombs, thus complementing one another.[17]

14. Crubézy, Duchesne and Midant-Reynes, 'The Predynastic Cemetery at Adaima', p. 293.

15. Crubézy, Duchesne and Midant-Reynes, 'The Predynastic Cemetery at Adaima', p. 301.

16. Crubézy, Duchesne and Midant-Reynes, 'The Predynastic Cemetery at Adaima', pp. 302-4, fig. 12.

17. Crubézy, Duchesne and Midant-Reynes, 'The Predynastic Cemetery at Adaima', p. 302.

It is also clear that the tombs fall into two different categories of care. On the one hand, burials which seems to have been done in a haphazard way, such as children buried in vessels without offerings or adults simply placed in a leather bag. On the other hand are the 'choreographed' funerals, sometimes including manipulation of the bodies, with a meaning that is sometimes understood by us, and sometimes not. However, there are no clear signs of human sacrifice at the site.

The 'Working-class' Cemetery HK43 at Hierakonpolis

Predynastic Hierakonpolis, about 20km south of Adaima, has been under excavation for almost 120 years and has yielded some of the most intriguing finds from the fourth millennium BCE.[18] Hierakonpolis, or ancient Nehkhen, was the legendary capital of Upper Egypt in the fourth millennium BCE and the major cult centre for the falcon god Horus, whose earthly human incarnation was the divine reigning king of Egypt.

For the purposes of the present study we would like to focus on Cemetery HK43 (ca. 3600–3400/3300 BCE), and the elite cemetery HK6. HK43, excavated between 1996 and 2004, is described as being non-elite or 'working-class'; the excavated area contains 453 burials.[19] The cemetery is located south of the Predynastic settlement, where the lower desert meets the alluvial plain.

At HK43 the bodies were placed on their left side, head to the south, face to the west in simple pit tombs. Often the bodies at HK43 were wrapped in linen shrouds with a mat placed over and under them. Only half the burials at HK43 were equipped with grave goods, generally one or two ceramic vessels. Around 40% of the internments at HK43 were women and men who had died between the ages of 20 and 35 years. At the opposite end young children (0 to 5 years) account for around 10%, while almost 6% were adults aged 50 years and older.[20] A study into the approximate age at death gave an average age at death of 38.5 years.[21]

18. Friedman, 'Hierakonpolis', 'About Hierakonpolis', http://www. hierakonpolis-online.org/index.php/about-the-site.

19. S. P. Dougherty and R. F. Friedman, 'Sacred or Mundane: Scalping and Decapitation at Predynastic Hierakonpolis', in Midant-Reynes and Tristant (eds.), *Egypt at its Origins 2*, p. 312, fig 1, p. 330.

20. E. K. Batey, 'Palaeodemography in Predynastic Upper Egypt: Investigations of the working-class cemetery at Hierakonpolis', in Midant-Reynes and Tristant (eds.), *Egypt at its Origins 2*, p. 258, fig. 2.

21. A. Huard, 'Reassessing age at death through tooth wear using the population at HK43', in Midant-Reynes and Tristant (eds.), *Egypt at its Origins 2*, p. 346.

Of all the tombs, 14 contained 15 individuals with lacerated vertebrae indicative of decapitation, and the skeletal remains of a 20- to 35-year-old male also exhibiting cut marks on the skull[22] similar to those at Adaima. It is thus possible that we are facing a similar ritual at Hierakonpolis at the very same time. In respect to grave goods this group fared the same as the overall population of the cemetery. The young woman (15 to 18 years) of Burial 85 received special treatment, with her hands and neck wrapped and packed with fine linen.[23] Where it was possible to assign age and sex, most individuals in this group were young men. The lacerations were conducted by several blows with a light implement generally aimed at the second and third cervical vertebrae.[24] It is unclear if complete decapitation was the intent but when that appears to have happened the head was subsequently placed in the correct anatomical position as is the case in the Burial 438 of a man aged 30 to 35 years.[25] The skeletal remains of the man (aged 20 to 35) of Burial 350 featured, apart from cuts to the vertebrae, more than 60 cut marks on the skull. This links his skull to a further four skulls from a disturbed area at HK43 where in one case almost 200 cuts were counted.[26] The pattern of the cuts is such that they are more severe and frequent at the middle of the front of the skull, becoming less in number and intensity towards the top and back of the skullcap, indicating a sophisticated method of gradually removing the flesh from the bone. However, as there are no other cut marks on the skulls, the purpose of the cuts at HK43 was merely scalping and not de-fleshing the whole skull.[27]

While there are manipulations of the body in some tombs at HK43, there is no evidence that these were done *perimortem*, so the sacrifice of a living human cannot be attested. However, the case seems slightly different at the elite cemetery HK6 located in a wadi over 2km from the alluvial plain and the Predynastic settlement.[28] The status of HK6 can

22. Dougherty and Friedman, 'Sacred or Mundane', p. 314, table 1.
23. Dougherty and Friedman, 'Sacred or Mundane', p. 317, fig. 4. A. J. Jones, 'Bound for Eternity: Examination of the Textiles from HK43', *Nekhen News* 13 (2001), pp. 13-14.
24. Dougherty and Friedman, 'Sacred or Mundane', p. 321.
25. Dougherty and Friedman, 'Sacred or Mundane', p. 322, fig. 9A.
26. Dougherty and Friedman, 'Sacred or Mundane', p. 324, fig 11.
27. Dougherty and Friedman, 'Sacred or Mundane', p. 328.
28. B. Adams, *Excavations in the Locality 6 Cemetery at Hierakonpolis 1979–1985* (BAR International Series 903; London: Egyptian Studies Association, 2000). B. Adams, 'Excavations in the Elite Predynastic Cemetery at Hierakonpolis Locality HK6: 1999–2000', *Annales du Service des Antiquités de l'Égypte* 78 (2004), pp. 35-52.

easily be described as exceptional and unique. Among the extraordinary finds are several unique pottery masks from Tomb 16.[29] Tomb 16 is a brick-lined subterranean tomb (4.3 × 2.6 × 1.45m) dated to around 3200 BCE which had been placed inside a larger tomb roughly 300 years older and to which the pottery masks probably belonged.[30] Tomb 16, like so many other tombs at HK6, was heavily plundered and yet it still contained around 120 ceramic vessels.

Tomb 16 is part of a larger funerary complex, possibly 60 × 40m, that also contained subsidiary graves surrounded by individual fenced enclosures.[31] In the immediate vicinity at least 12 tombs for humans and a minimum of ten tombs for 28 animals were arranged. In the case of subsidiary Tomb 32 it was itself flanked by two interments of animals: two adult dogs (Feature D) and one young hippopotamus (Feature H).[32] The latter was kept in captivity before its final end at HK6. Among the animal burials Tomb 33 and tomb 24 stand out. Both contained the remains of elephants; the former contained the lower half of a 10-year-old male elephant placed on a mat on its left side and covered with textiles and additional mats. They had been kept in captivity for some time with the stomach contents of the elephant in tomb 24 showing it had been fed on rushes during its last days.[33] A nearby burial of aurochs from Tomb 19 was probably part of the same burial rituals as the elephant. Further wild animals were buried at HK6, such as a baboon in Feature B, but domesticated animals like goats and cattle were also present, with at least twenty dogs found.[34]

29. B. Adams, 'Seeking the Roots of Ancient Egypt: A Unique Cemetery Reveals Monuments and Rituals from before the Pharaohs', *Archéo-Nil* 12 (2002), pp. 11-28 (pp. 17-19, fig. 4a-f).

30. Friedman, 'Hierakonpolis', p. 1188.

31. R. F. Friedman, W. Van Neer, and V. Linseele, 'The Elite Predynastic Cemetery at Hierakonpolis: 2009–2010 Update', in Friedman and Fiske (eds.), *Egypt at its Origins 3*, p. 161, fig. 3.

32. Friedman, Van Neer, and Linseele, 'The Elite Predynastic Cemetery at Hierakonpolis: 2009–2010 Update', p. 166.

33. Friedman, Van Neer, and Linseele, 'The Elite Predynastic Cemetery', pp. 175-77, fig. 11. Friedman, 'Hierakonpolis'; W. Van Neer, V. Linseele, and R. F. Friedman, 'Animal Burials and Food Offerings at the Elite Cemetery HK 6 at Hierakonpolis', in S. Hendrickx, R. F. Friedman, K. M. Ciałowicz, and M. Chłodnicki (eds.), *Egypt at its Origins: Studies in Memory of Barbara Adams: Proceedings of the International Conference 'Origin of the State: Predynastic and Early Dynastic Egypt', Krakow, 28 August–1 September 2002* (OLA 138; Leuven: Peeters, 2004), pp. 67-130.

34. Friedman, Van Neer, and Linseele, 'The Elite Predynastic Cemetery at Hierakonpolis: 2009–2010 Update', pp. 180-83.

A large number of marked ceramic vessels, beads, a drop pendant of carnelian, and some resin and malachite could be indicators of the high social esteem that the women and children possessed during their lives.[35] So far thirty-six individuals could be identified: 13 of them female, 8 male, 11 juvenile, and 4 unknown.[36] Their age range is from 8 to 35 years. Males seem to be slightly older at the time of death than women. The juveniles are mostly teenagers aged between 10 and 15 years.

While there is evidence to indicate that tomb 16 and its surrounding animal and human burials were fenced, in at the same time this does not mean that all burials happened at the same time. If they *were* buried at the same time does it follow that the peripheral tombs were sacrificial? Certainly the arrangement of the complex around tomb 16 was not random. The appearance of a large and wealthy central burial and its surrounding graves seems to be similar to the situation at Adaima, where over the course of time a central tomb became the focus and preferred burial place of succeeding generations of high-status people. Yet the social stratification around tomb 16 allows for the interpretation that retainers followed their master into the afterlife. Despite the evidence, when this journey to the afterlife began for the retainers remains open.

Early Dynastic Subsidiary Graves at Abydos

The Early Dynastic period is the time when the foundation stone of Egyptian civilization was laid.[37] By the end of the fourth millennium BCE we can detect from the archaeological record certain centres or polities in Upper Egypt, such as Hierakonpolis, Naqada, and Abydos. These entities are sometimes called 'proto-states'. They fought for supremacy in the south of Egypt before a 'proto-kingdom' of Upper Egypt was established, which finally won control of all of Egypt.[38] The political and societal processes that led to a united Egypt still remain under debate but perhaps can be seen simply as 'big fish eat little fish'.[39] Whatever the process, at its end stood a unified Egypt and the beginning of the Dynastic Period.

35. Friedman, Van Neer, and Linseele, 'The Elite Predynastic Cemetery at Hierakonpolis: 2009–2010 Update', pp. 171-72.

36. Friedman, Van Neer, and Linseele, 'The Elite Predynastic Cemetery at Hierakonpolis: 2009–2010 Update', p. 174, table 1.

37. Wengrow, *The Archaeology of Early Egypt*; Wilkinson, *Early Dynastic Egypt*.

38. B. J. Kemp, *Ancient Egypt: Anatomy of a Civilization* (London: Routledge, 2006), pp. 73-78.

39. D. O'Connor, *Abydos: Egypt's First Pharaohs and the Cult of Osiris* (London: Thames & Hudson, 2009), pp. 137-39.

The Pre- and Early Dynastic Period at Umm el-Qa'ab

Throughout the fourth millennium BCE Cemetery U at Abydos was the burial ground for a local population. This cemetery became an increasingly isolated final resting place for the uppermost stratum of society, and around 3200 BCE Tomb U-j was constructed at Abydos, the largest Predynastic mudbrick tomb ever to be found.[40] This 12-chamber tomb contained some of the earliest forms of Egyptian writing, hundreds of imported vessels full of wine attesting to the wealth of its owner and the international trade of the time, but most significantly, a crook sceptre, part of the royal regalia of the later Pharaohs of Egypt. So it comes as no surprise that it is at Abydos where the early rulers of a unified Egypt ultimately found their final resting place. Abydos was the royal cemetery for all the rulers of the First Dynasty (from ca. 3050 BCE onwards), including Queen Meretneith, the mother of King Den for whom she had reigned when he was still in his minority, and the last two kings of the Second Dynasty (ending ca. 2700 BCE, see fig. 1). All the tombs were disturbed at various times prior to the modern excavation. During a civil war in the First Intermediate Period most tombs at the site were set on fire. In the Twelfth Dynasty the tombs were reopened as the Egyptians believed this was the burial ground of the god Osiris. Some repairs were made to the mudbrick walls and the tomb of King Djer was designated as that of Osiris. From this time on for almost 2500 years Egyptians made pilgrimages to Abydos, where they left offerings in pottery vessels and worshipped Osiris.[41] The extensive pottery debris left on the desert surface gave rise to its current name, Umm el-Qa'ab (Arabic for 'Mother of Pots'). Some damage was done by the Copts in an attempt to stop the cult, and during the Medieval Period the site may even have featured in a book for treasure hunting.[42]

---

40. G. Dreyer et al., 'Umm el-Qaab. Nachuntersuchungen im frühzeitlichen Königsfriedhof 9./10. Vorbericht', *MDAIK* 54 (1998), pp. 77-167; U. Hartung, *Umm el-Qaab II. Importkeramik aus dem Friedhof U in Abydos (Umm el-Qaab) und die Beziehungen Ägyptens zu Vorderasien im 4. Jahrtausend v.Chr.* (Mainz am Rhein: P. von Zabern, 2001).

41. U. Effland, J. Budka, and A. Effland, 'Studien zum Osiriskult in Umm el-Qaab/Abydos. Ein Vorbericht', *MDAIK* 66 (2010), pp. 19-91.

42. U. Effland, '"Grabe im Zentrum des erstbesten Grabes..."—Mitteralterliche Schatzsuche in Abydos', in E. M. Engel, V. Müller, and U. Hartung (eds.), *Zeichen aus dem Sand. Streiflichter aus Ägyptens Geschichte zu Ehren von Günter Dreyer*: (Wiesbaden: Harrassowitz, 2008), pp. 71-81 (77-78).

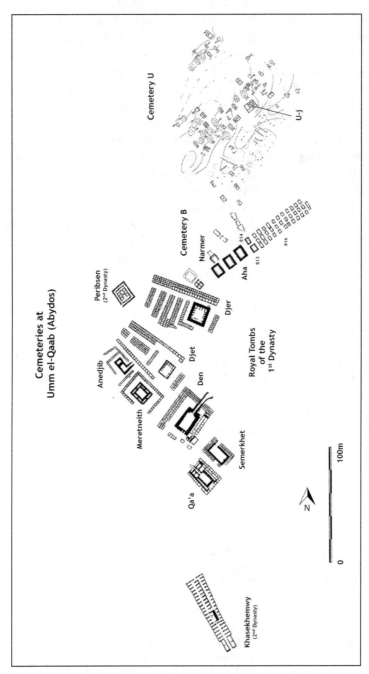

Figure 1. *Cemetery U and the Royal Cemetery at Abydos after Petrie 1901 and Dreyer et al. 2003*

First diggings at the site were conducted by Amélineau in 1895–98,[43] followed in 1899/1900 by Flinders Petrie,[44] and later in 1911–12 by Naville[45] and Peet.[46] In 1977 modern research was resumed by the German Archaeological Institute (DAI)[47] and continues to this day. Petrie conducted further investigations around the large funerary enclosures in the area known as Abydos North[48] and today this area is again under excavation by the Yale-Pennsylvania expedition.[49]

For the royal tombs a large pit of various sizes was dug into the solid sand and mudbrick walls were built inside the pit. Over time the tombs increased considerably and the central royal burial chamber was surrounded by dozens if not hundreds of subterranean subsidiary chambers for graves and storage.

The first tomb, which belongs to King Narmer, consists of two rectangular chambers, labelled B17 and B18. It was cut into the desert floor and lined with mudbricks. No smaller chambers accompany Narmer's tomb; it was his successor, King Aha, who added this feature. In the case of King Aha, three chambers (B19, B15, B10) were made for the king's internment and for the grave offerings. Northeast of them are a further 36 subterranean chambers.

After Aha the royal tombs of the First Dynasty increased dramatically in size, with only one main chamber for the rulers. Aha's successor King Djer had rows of 326 chambers at a distance of a few meters laid out around the royal burial chamber. Queen Meretneith's tomb was surrounded by 41 chambers, while her son Den increased his provision to 121. Several dozens of Den's subsidiary burials were re-examined. Six

43. E. Amélineau, *Les nouvelles fouilles d'Abydos (1897–1898)* (4 vols.; Paris: E. Leroux, 1898–1905).

44. W. M. F. Petrie, *The Royal Tombs of the First Dynasty, Part 1* (London: Egypt Exploration Fund, 1900); Petrie, *The Royal Tombs of the Earliest Dynasties, Part 2* (London: Egypt Exploration Fund, 1901).

45. É. Naville, *Cemeteries of Abydos. Pt. 1. 1909–1910. The Mixed Cemetery and Umm el-Ga'ab* (London: Egypt Exploration Fund, 1914).

46. T. E. Peet, *Cemeteries of Abydos. Pt. 2. 1911–1912* (London: Egypt Exploration Fund, 1914).

47. W. Kaiser and P. Grossmann, 'Nachuntersuchungen im frühzeitlichen Königsfriedhof 1. Vorbericht', *MDAIK* 35 (1979), pp. 155-63.

48. Petrie, *The Tombs of the Courtiers and Oxyrhynkhos.*

49. M. D. Adams, 'Abydos North', in K. A. Bard (ed.), *Encyclopedia of the Archaeology of Ancient Egypt* (London: Routledge, 1999), pp. 106-9; M. D. Adams and D. O'Connor, 'The Royal Mortuary Enclosures of Abydos and Hierakonpolis', in Z. Hawass (ed.), *Treasures of the Pyramids* (New York: Barnes & Noble, 2003), pp. 78-85; D. O'Connor, 'Abydos, Early Dynastic Funerary Enclosure', in Bard (ed.), *Encyclopedia*, pp. 102-4; O'Connor, *Abydos*, pp. 9-14.

of them were positioned next to the so-called Southwest Annex, a room that most likely housed a statue of the king and from here pointing south one would reach the opening of a large wadi once believed to be the entrance to the Netherworld. The location of this group and the fact that two of them are by far larger than any other subsidiary burials attests to the high status of the occupants.[50] This hierarchy is already visible around the tombs of Djer and Djet. In Djer's case the subsidiary chambers to the north (closest to the principal burial) and the L-shaped row of chambers to the west and south also display larger chambers. Two chambers also once contained a pair of coffins. It also became clear that the subsidiary chambers for Den were built in several phases, sometimes even leaving a gap between various groups of chambers.[51] After Den there is a steady decline of the numbers of subsidiary graves and by the end of the First Dynasty under King Qa'a there were only 26 such chambers. Some were mere storage rooms for grave offerings but others clearly once contained the burials of retainers. Human skeletal remains, coffins and the roughly 200 known stelae with non-royal names and sometimes with titles of the deceased are clear evidence for this. Among the subsidiary graves of King Djet, Petrie also discovered names of retainers painted in red on the wall.[52]

Other major changes in funerary architecture at Abydos were the introduction of a stairway leading down to the central chamber under King Den, which meant that it was possible for the tomb to be reopened after the funeral. The last two kings of the First Dynasty, Semerkhet and Qa'a, had the subsidiary chambers abutting the walls of the central chamber.

Although no superstructures were found, we assume that some of the royal burial chambers were once covered by a small tumulus and all of them covered by a larger superstructure. A pair of large stone stelae with the royal name placed outside the tomb served to identify the tomb owner.

The Enclosures

A second complementary part of the funerary complex of the first kings of Egypt were the so-called funerary cult enclosures (or Talbezirke, valley precincts) that were located around 1.5km to the north of Umm

---

50. G. Dreyer et al., 'Umm el-Qaab. Nachuntersuchungen im frühzeitlichen Königsfriedhof 3./4. Vorbericht', *MDAIK* 46 (1990), pp. 53-90 (78-79).

51. G. Dreyer et al., 'Umm el-Qaab. Nachuntersuchungen im frühzeitlichen Königsfriedhof 5./6. Vorbericht', *MDAIK* 49 (1993), pp. 23-62 (57-60, pl. 10-1).

52. Petrie, *The Royal Tombs of the First Dynasty*, p. 8, pl. LXIII.

el-Qa'ab close to the alluvial plain. These were giant rectangular mud-brick buildings and part of the royal funerary complex. The largest of them, mainly intact after 5000 years, is that of the last king of the Second Dynasty, Khasekemwy. It is ca. 134m long, 80m wide and stands up to a height of 11m!

The enclosures also possessed subsidiary graves. They show a similar development in numbers increasing from six under Aha to a peak of 269 under King Djer, then dropping to 154 under King Djet and 79 under Queen Meretneith.[53]

For the purposes of the present study we would like to focus on recent research of the subsidiary burials around the tomb and enclosures associated with King Aha, the second ruler of the First Dynasty and the subsidiary chambers adjacent to the tomb of King Qa'a, the last ruler of the First Dynasty.

The Tomb and Enclosures of King Aha
As mentioned, the tomb of King Aha has three individual subterranean chambers lined with mudbrick with another thirty-six subsidiary chambers adjacent. The three main chambers were built into pits of 11.5–12m × 9–9.5m and possessed massive walls of 1.5–2m thickness.[54] Wooden posts supported a wooden shrine that was set into the chambers. The chambers were once covered by a grid of beams, matting, layers of mudbrick and plaster. A large tumulus then covered all three chambers. It seems that the chambers were not constructed in one building phase. Initially the western-most was built and the desire or need for more room for offerings and luxury goods led to the addition of two more chambers.[55] Of the subsidiary chambers, 33 were lined up in three rows while one elongated chamber with a partition wall marks the northeastern end of the complex and two clearly larger chambers are located west of the three rows. The latter are, at ca. 18sqm and 22.5sqm, more than twice the size of the smaller chambers. The subsidiary chambers clearly decrease in size the further away they are from the king's chambers. This could be an indication of the lower status of the people buried further away from the main chambers. The brick-lined pits were once covered with wooden beams, reed matting, mudbrick and a layer of mud plaster on top.[56] Like

53. Petrie, *The Tombs of the Courtiers and Oxyrhynkhos*, pl. XX-XXI.
54. W. Kaiser and G. Dreyer, 'Nachuntersuchungen im frühzeitlichen Königsfriedhof 2. Vorbericht', *MDAIAK* 38 (1982), pp. 214-15.
55. Kaiser and Dreyer, 'Nachuntersuchungen', p. 219.
56. Dreyer et al., 'Umm el-Qaab. Nachuntersuchungen im frühzeitlichen Königsfriedhof 3./4', pp. 63-64.

the chambers for the king, it appears that the subsidiary chambers were built in two phases. First the large chambers next to the king's were constructed along with the majority of smaller chambers. In a second phase the remaining chambers were added to the west. It is also noteworthy that any finds from the subsidiary burials made in recent excavations by the DAI appeared only in the first five strips of the chambers.[57] In one of the two larger subsidiary graves (B14) three objects with the name *Bnr-jb* ('Sweet of Heart') were found. This was interpreted to be a queen or a daughter of the king.[58]

Although all tombs were heavily disturbed and the bones scattered on the desert surface, an attempt was made to assign the human bones to the various subsidiary chambers.[59] Remains of 29 individuals (about 50%) could be classified as male, roughly 17% as probably male, and around 24% as adult. In twelve cases it was possible to give an age. Eight individuals died between the age of 18 and 30 and four died between 17 and 20 years of age. None of the buried was older than 30 years of age. It is obvious that most buried retainers of King Aha were young men. Considering the initial interpretation of the owner of chamber B14 as a queen or daughter of the king, it is interesting that the skeletal remains assigned to chamber B14 probably belonged to an adult male. Pathologies could only be detected for one individual, who apparently suffered from chronic anaemia. The apparently young age of these mostly male individuals has sometimes been seen as further evidence for the case of sacrificial burials.

The examination of the animal bones delivered some fascinating results.[60] In addition to the expected cattle bones, skeletal remains of the colourful Nile goose, and the remains of at least seven lions were found in the area of the elongated chamber. The youngest of the lions was just six months at the time of its death. The lions had bent bones and they suffered from rickets. Whether they were all born in captivity is impossible to say but, based on the deformed bones, they were certainly raised at the court of King Aha.

57. Dreyer et al., 'Umm el-Qaab. Nachuntersuchungen im frühzeitlichen Königsfriedhof 3./4', p. 66.

58. Petrie, *The Royal Tombs of the Earliest Dynasties*, p. 5.

59. S. Klug, 'Die menschlichen Skelettreste', in Dreyer et al., 'Umm el-Qaab. Nachuntersuchungen im frühzeitlichen Königsfriedhof 3./4', pp. 81-86

60. J. Boessneck and A. von den Driesch, 'Die Tierknochenfunde', in Dreyer et al., 'Umm el-Qaab. Nachuntersuchungen im frühzeitlichen Königsfriedhof 3./4, pp. 86-89.

In 2001 an enclosure of King Aha was discovered around 150m north of the large enclosure of King Khasekhemwy.[61] It came as a big surprise when a few years later two more, yet much smaller, enclosures were discovered just north of the first.[62] As inscriptions on pottery and seal impressions only have the name of King Aha it is evident that all enclosures date to the same reign. The largest enclosure, called Aha I, measured ca. 33m × 22m. There are two gateways in the northeastern wall and a cult chapel in the southeastern part of the enclosure. Inside one of the rooms a bench and offering pottery was excavated, essentially making the enclosure the mortuary temple for the king.[63] The two smaller enclosures, labelled Aha II and Aha III, have only one entrance on the south of the northeastern wall. Aha I was surrounded by six individual chambers while Aha II and Aha III each possessed three subsidiary burials. The subsidiary tomb northeast of Aha III featured an undisturbed corpse with offering jars; yet its southern wall was cut by a later tomb.[64] Only three ovoid jars were found placed at the feet of the body.[65] The person buried in this grave was a 25- to 34-year-old woman of about 165cm.[66] She was of good health, apart from a chronic respiratory problem, and no signs for her cause of death could be detected. All the bodies found around the smaller enclosures were in fact those of women.

The question is: For whom were the three enclosures constructed? That the largest belonged to the king himself should be beyond doubt. The smaller enclosures are possibly linked to the owners of the two larger subsidiary graves right next to the king's chamber at Umm el-Qa'ab.[67]

61. Adams and O'Connor, 'The Royal Mortuary Enclosures of Abydos and Hierakonpolis'.

62. L. Bestock, 'The Evolution of Royal Ideology: New Discoveries from the Reign of Aha', in Midant-Reynes and Tristant (eds.), *Egypt at its Origins 2*, pp. 1091-1106; L. Bestock, 'An Undisturbed Subsidiary Burial from the Reign of Aha', in Engel, Müller, and Hartung (eds.), *Zeichen aus dem Sand*, pp. 41-57; L. Bestock, *The Development of Royal Funerary Cult at Abydos: Two Funerary Enclosures from the Reign of Aha* (Wiesbaden: Otto Harrassowitz, 2009).

63. Bestock, 'The Evolution of Royal Ideology', p. 1093.

64. Bestock, 'An Undisturbed Subsidiary Burial', p. 43, fig. 2.

65. Bestock, 'An Undisturbed Subsidiary Burial', p. 52, fig. 10.

66. Bestock, 'An Undisturbed Subsidiary Burial', p. 53.

67. Bestock, 'The Evolution of Royal Ideology', pp. 100-104.

The Tomb of King Qa'a

The tomb of King Qa'a is situated on the southwestern ridge of the plateau at Umm el-Qa'ab and it was originally excavated by Amélineau and then Petrie. In the 1990s the German Archaeological Institute excavated the tomb again.[68] One of the major results was certainly the detailed insight into the construction phases which, given Petrie's neat plans,[69] had not been obvious for the tomb of King Qa'a nor his predecessor King Semerkhet, under whom, for the first time in the First Dynasty, the subsidiary chambers were built immediately next to the central royal burial chamber.[70]

The tomb of King Qa'a was built into a deep pit measuring roughly 30 × 20m in the desert surface. The walls were made of sundried mud-bricks. It became clear that the tomb was built in eight phases.[71] Phase I comprised the central chamber, a row of fourteen small chambers on the east, west, and south side and two storage rooms to the north. A staircase leads from the north to the central chamber and is flanked by the two mentioned storage rooms. Later, another ring of twenty-one chambers was added on the east, west, and south. A further extension of the steps to the north saw the addition of two more storage chambers for organic materials, vessels, and objects that required labels.[72] In phase V one chamber was added to the outer eastern chambers to the north, and two on the west. A final extension to the north (phase VII) mirrored the prior phase so that at the end six storage rooms flanked the stairway, several corridors were located immediately next to the central burial chamber, and a ring of 26 outer chambers for the burial of retainers and storage formed the outside of the construction. Petrie discovered twelve seemingly undisturbed burials, among them a dwarf.[73] *Leichenschatten* could be traced in a few more of the outer chambers.

---

68. E.-M. Engel, 'Grabkomplex des Qa'a', in G. Dreyer et al., 'Umm el-Qaab. Nachuntersuchungen im frühzeitlichen Königsfriedhof 7./8. Vorbericht', *MDAIAK* 52 (1996), pp. 57-71, idem, 'Das Grab des Qa'a in Umm el-Qaab. Architektur und Inventar' (Ph.D. diss., University of Göttingen, 1997, microfiche 1998).

69. Petrie, *The Royal Tombs of the First Dynasty*, pl. LX.

70. E.-M. Engel, 'Grab des Semerchet', in G. Dreyer et al., 'Umm el-Qaab. Nachuntersuchungen im frühzeitlichen Königsfriedhof 11./12. Vorbericht', *MDAIAK* 56 (2000), pp. 119-22; idem, 'Grab des Semerchet', in Dreyer et al., 'Umm el-Qaab. Nachuntersuchungen im frühzeitlichen Königsfriedhof 7./8. Vorbericht', pp. 93-98.

71. Engel, 'Grabkomplex des Qa'a', pp. 58-61; idem, *Das Grab des Qa'a in Umm el-Qaab. Architektur und Inventar*, pp. 76-95.

72. Engel, 'Grabkomplex des Qa'a', p. 63.

73. Petrie, *The Royal Tombs of the First Dynasty*, pl. LX.

During the First Dynasty the central royal chamber was once covered by a roof of wooden beams, reed matting and layers of mudbrick and a tumulus surrounded by a retaining wall of mudbricks. All these were parts of the subterranean structure and all of them remained below the level of the desert surface. Later, a larger tumulus of sand and gravel with a retaining wall and a top layer of mudbricks and plaster marked the funerary monument. The inner tumulus possibly had a religious significance and resembled the primordial mound.[74] It is, however, also conceivable that the initial smaller tumulus was merely for protection and to give the tomb a more or less complete form before the construction of the larger superstructure that defined the grave site.[75] Several options for the final appearance of the Royal Tombs at Abydos have been proposed. Just to name two, Hoffman suggested a tumulus just for the central chamber for Qa'a excluding the storage rooms and the subsidiary graves.[76] Others have proposed a large mastaba (Arabic for 'bench') that would have covered the subsidiary graves, or for some tombs at Umm el-Qa'ab, even a stepped mastaba similar to the later Step Pyramid of King Djoser at Saqqara.[77]

At the tomb of King Qa'a it was possible to trace the direction of the tunnels made by tomb robbers. Some of these tunnels actually started on a higher level than the subterranean mudbrick walls and thus it seems unlikely that the whole area was covered by one large mound. Hence the recent excavator proposes a large tumulus of around 2.5m in height, with the storage rooms merely covered with sand and a flat surface remaining on top of them, while the ring of subsidiary tombs was covered by individual tumuli of around 1m in height.[78]

The whole burial complex of King Qa'a would have required dozens of workers who would first start digging the pit, manufacturing tens of thousands of mudbricks, and constructing all the walls and finally piling the tumuli, re-using some of the material that was initially excavated.

74. G. Dreyer, 'Zur Rekonstruktion der Oberbauten der Königsgräber der 1. Dynastie in Abydos, Festschrift Werner Kaiser', *MDAIAK* 47 (1991), pp. 93-104.

75. W. Kaiser, 'Zu den überbauten Strukturen in den grossen Nischengräbern der 1. Dynastie in Sakkara', in Engel, Müller, and Hartung (eds.), *Zeichen aus dem Sand*, (2008), pp. 364-65.

76. Hoffman, *Egypt before the Pharaohs*, p. 271, fig. 66.

77. G. A. Reisner, *The Development of the Egyptian Tomb Down to the Accession of Cheops* (Cambridge, Mass.: Harvard University Press, 1936), p. 326, fig. 173, pp. 330-31.

78. Engel, *Das Grab des Qa'a in Umm el-Qaab. Architektur und Inventar*, p. 113, fig. 71.

If work continued throughout the whole year an estimate for the construction time lies around two years at a minimum.[79] No additional
funerary enclosure at Abydos has been identified as belonging to King
Qa'a.

King Qa'a apparently enjoyed a long reign—he celebrated two jubilee
festivals, the first of which, in later periods, was generally performed
after 30 years on the throne. Several tags and labels made from bone give
us some insight into the administration and life of King Qa'a.[80] We hear
of several inspections and visits of the carpenters in Lower Egypt by the
supervisor of the carpenters of Upper Egypt, Henuka and Nefer. Timber
was shipped from the north to the south. On other labels the festival of
the Apis Bull is mentioned as is a reference to tax collection.

As we have seen, there is no conclusive archaeological evidence that
would allow the firm interpretation that when the king was buried, the
subsidiary tombs were filled with retainers. It is very obvious that the
burials were of major importance and were organized on a large scale.
There is certainly a closeness and yet deliberate separation in space
between the burial chamber of the regent and the subsidiaries. Yet the
long construction phase and the interpretation of the inner tumulus as a
temporary measure to await the ultimate completion of the burial
complex[81] would allow a period of many months or even years for the
final finish of the royal burial complexes at Umm el-Qa'ab.

A Brief Look at the First Dynasty Elite Cemetery at North Saqqara

As the First Dynasty elite burials at North Saqqara bear some similarities
to those at Abydos, a brief examination is worthwhile. These mastaba
tombs were excavated by Emery between 1935 and 1946.[82] They have a
niched mudbrick substructure and a large mudbrick superstructure with a
niched façade (see fig. 2). Both structures contain several chambers with
the main burial chamber in the centre of the substructure.

---

79. E.-M. Engel, 'The Royal Tombs at Umm el-Qa'ab', *Archéo-Nil* 18 (2008),
pp. 30-41 (33).

80. Engel, *Das Grab des Qa'a in Umm el-Qaab. Architektur und Inventar*,
pp. 433-81.

81. Kaiser, 'Zu den überbauten Strukturen in den grossen Nischengräbern der 1.
Dynastie in Sakkara.'

82. W. B. Emery, *The Tomb of Hemaka* (Cairo: Government Press, 1938);
Emery, *Hor-Aha* (Cairo: Government Press, 1939); idem, *The Great Tombs of the
First Dynasty* (3 vols.; Cairo: Government Press, 1949–58).

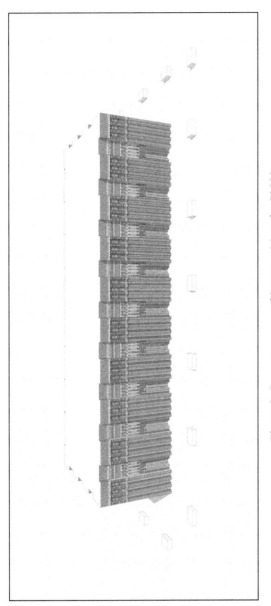

Figure 2. *Reconstruction of Saqqara Mastaba S3503*
(courtesy of Franck Monnier)

Several of the large mastaba tombs can be assigned to a specific reign of the First Dynasty:[83] S3357 (Aha), S2185, S3471 (all Djer), S3504 (Djet), S3503 (Meretneith), S3035, S3036, S3057, S3506, S3507 (all Den), S3038, S3111 (Adjib), S3500, S3505 (Qa'a). It has to be pointed out that not all of these mastabas actually had subsidiary chambers raising the interesting question of the selection criteria.

In the oldest mastaba S3357 (ca. 42 × 16m) the scattered remains of four women were found in the subterranean chambers while the body of the owner had been removed by plunderers.[84] The tomb stands out for its 19m boat grave.[85]

Mastaba S3504 (ca. 49.5 × 20m) belonged to the Seal Bearer of the King of Lower Egypt, Sewedj-ka, and contained 62 subsidiary burials.[86] The tombs were laid out in rows on the south, east and west sides of the enclosure wall that surrounded the mastaba. Only nine tombs could be categorized as unplundered or undisturbed. Out of the 58 individuals five were women, three children, and one was a dwarf. However, the majority were male (37), amongst them 16 young and three older individuals. Two adult women stand out with their undisturbed equipment; one containing more than a dozen ceramic vessels and both with a set of flint blades and so-called bi-truncated regular blade tools, the latter one of the most widely distributed flint tools of its time.[87] It is interesting to note that the tomb was remodelled and repaired several decades later under King Qa'a.

Mastaba S3503 (ca. 42 × 16m), whose major occupant could have been a Meretneith or an individual named Seshemka, is surrounded by twenty individuals in subsidiary chambers. A few fragile bones were found in the main burial chamber.[88] The rows of subsidiary burials are located ca. 5m from the superstructure of the mastaba and outside its enclosure wall. Fourteen of the individuals were men, second women, and in four cases the gender could not be determined. They were lying in a contracted position on their left sides with the hands in front of their

83. E. F. Morris, 'On the Ownership of the Saqqara Mastabas and the Allotment of Political and Ideological Power at the Dawn of the State', in Z. Hawass, and J. Richards (eds.), *The Archaeology and Art of Ancient Egypt: Essays in Honor of David B. O'Connor* (Cairo: Conseil Supreme des Antiquites de l'Egypte, 2007), pp. 171-90 (179-86).

84. Emery, *Hor-Aha*, p. 77.

85. Emery, *Hor-Aha*, pls. 3 and 5.

86. Emery, *The Great Tombs of the First Dynasty II*, pp. 5-6, 13, 24-37.

87. Emery, *The Great Tombs of the First Dynasty II*, pp. 28-32, figs. 9 and 12.

88. Emery, *The Great Tombs of the First Dynasty II*, pp. 133-58, pl. XLVIII-LI.

faces. Given the finds that accompanied the dead it seems that the people belonged to the household of the unknown owner of S3503.[89] For example, Burial A contained a copper implement and the special wooden box of a craftsman. The high number of pots accompanying the man in Burial B could make him a potter, while the cow horn in Burial D might identify the man as a herder. In Burial E 14 small shallow vessels with green, red, black and yellow paint hint at the owner being a painter. Burial H was possibly the tomb of the personal oarsman given the clay models of boats.

The number of subsidiary chambers drops to half in the time of King Den with Mastaba S3506 (ca. 48 × 20m) of the official Setka.[90] Each subsidiary tomb was built separately, on average around 4m apart from each other. The pits had a modest size of ca. 2.15 × 1.60 × 1.25m. Four burials remained undisturbed. For the total of ten subsidiary burials age and gender are as follows: five adult male, one female, one young female, one child, one young adult, and one adult. It is, to date, the only case in which we have a child. The equipment of a child in Burial 5 and of a young female in Burial 3 is comparable to the richer tombs in S3504.[91] Oddly enough, the woman in Burial 3 was found on her back with legs apart and flexed, which casts doubts on the claim that the burial was undisturbed.

In Mastaba S3111 (ca. 29 × 12m), belonging probably to the official Sabu, one intact subsidiary burial of an adult male was discovered on the western façade of the mastaba.[92] The man was positioned on his left side, head to the north. Four stone and seven ceramic vessels were placed into the pit outside the wooden coffin.

Mastaba S3500 (ca. 37 × 24m), whose owner is unknown, contained the four subsidiary graves that were built against the inside of the south wall of the enclosure.[93] Their architecture is quite unusual as the brick tombs were not subterranean chambers but built on the floor of the corridor. They also had vaulted brick roofs. One of the tombs was plundered, one was for a middle-aged male, one for an old man, and the fourth for an old woman. The bodies were wrapped in coarse linen and a reed mat was placed on top of the coffin. The middle-aged man and the old woman had 'dummy' cylinder seals of wood and foreign pottery with

89. Emery, *The Great Tombs of the First Dynasty II*, pp. 144-48.
90. Emery, *The Great Tombs of the First Dynasty III*, p. 37-72, pls. 40, 45-49.
91. Emery, *The Great Tombs of the First Dynasty II*, p. 47, pl. 72A, B and C.
92. Emery, *The Great Tombs of the First Dynasty I*, p. 99, pl. 42B.
93. Emery, *The Great Tombs of the First Dynasty III*, pp. 103-104, pls. 121-22.

them. Given the small number and the age of the individuals these burials do not seem to comprise a household but might have been 'wise consultants' and 'confidants' of the owner of S3500.

The large Mastaba S3505 (65 × 40m) from the reign of King Qa'a seems to be a rather debatable case.[94] Based on a stela found near a completely ransacked tomb on the east corridor with the name of Merka and dug below the façade, S3505 was originally seen as a subsidiary burial for King Qa'a by the excavator, as he saw the large mastabas at Saqqara as the real burial places of the Early Dynastic kings of Egypt. Later, S3505 was assigned to Merka himself.[95] Merka bore several important titles, among them 'district administrator of the desert regions', 'controller of the royal bark', 'controller of the palace', and 'controller of the audience hall'. Recently, however, the original location of the stela, the connection and ownership of Mastaba S3505 by Merka has been questioned once again.[96]

If we assume that some of the retainer burials represent the household of the high official, then Mastabas S3504 and S3503 could be examples that confirm this in both size of the household and variety of professions. However, it would be difficult to explain the four subsidiary burials of mastaba S3500 in terms of a household as the skeletal remains are those of elderly individuals. The biggest obstacle in regard to the idea would be to explain why a few mastabas have retainer burials while others do not. Clearly, it was neither mandatory nor necessary for the elite to be accompanied in the afterlife by their household and servants.

Human Sacrifice—An Alternative Approach

Human sacrifices are rare in history, yet are known from several cultures from around the world. One of the most striking examples for the region of the Near East is the Royal Cemetery at Ur, the most famous being the grave of Queen Puabi and the Great Death Pit.[97]

94. Emery, *The Great Tombs of the First Dynasty II*, pp. 5-36.

95. B. J. Kemp, 'The Egyptian 1st Dynasty Royal Cemetery', *Antiquity* 41 (1967), pp. 22-32; E. C. Köhler, 'Early Dynastic Society at Memphis', in Engel, Müller, and Hartung (eds.), *Zeichen aus dem Sand*, pp. 385-88; D. O'Connor, 'The Ownership of Elite Tombs at Saqqara in the First Dynasty', in K. Douad, S. Bedier and S. Abd el-Fatah (eds.), *Studies in Honor of Ali Radwan*, pp. 223-31.

96. G. T. Martin, 'The Stela and Grave of Merka in Saqqara North', in Engel, Müller, and Hartung (eds.), *Zeichen aus dem Sand*, pp. 461-66.

97. P. Collins, 'The Tomb of Puabi', in J. Aruz (ed.), *Art of the First Cities: The Third Millennium B.C. from the Mediterranean to the Indus* (New Haven: Yale University Press, 2003), pp. 108-19; J. Reade, 'The Royal Tombs of Ur' and 'The

The situation at Ur seems clear-cut. In several cases the principal burial is accompanied, in the same tomb, by dozens of well-equipped and adorned retainers, primarily women, all appearing to have died and been laid out at the same time, probably as part of the funerary ritual. However, even here the notion of large-scale human sacrifice can be called into question. Some of the individuals appear to have been reburied, which may indicate that they died earlier and were initially buried elsewhere. While the majority of skeletal remains were not kept by Woolley after excavations, the skulls of two individuals (a male soldier and a female) were recently re-examined in Pennsylvania, and clearly displayed blunt force trauma to the head, which was probably the cause of death.[98] While the sacrifice of these individuals at Ur is clear, the archaeological evidence from Pre- and Early Dynastic Egypt is far more ambiguous and often lacking entirely. While the archaeological evidence from Hierakonpolis and Adaima clearly show the severing and manipulation of body parts, there is no evidence that this was done *perimortem*. At the Royal Cemetery of Abydos we have hundreds of subsidiary graves of mostly lower-ranking people buried in wooden coffins. But there is no evidence that the tombs were filled and used at the time of the king's burial.

How Many Subsidiary Burials?
The number of subsidiary graves around the Royal Tombs of the First Dynasty at Umm el-Qa'ab, and the contemporary enclosures, amounts to a minimum of about 1,400 burials, assuming that each chamber contained at least one retainer. On average this represents only seven deceased individuals per year for the entire First Dynasty.

If we take the assumed lengths of reigns[99] into consideration the following estimates can be given:

Great Death Pit at Ur', in Aruz (ed.), *Art of the First Cities*, pp. 93-107 and 120-32, respectively; L. Woolley, *The Royal Cemetery: A Report on the Predynastic and Sargonid Graves Excavated between 1926 and 1931* (2 vols.; London: British Museum, 1934).

98. This information was accessed from the site, 'Iraq's Ancient Past: Rediscovering Ur's Royal Cemetery' at the University of Pennsylvania Museum of Archaeology and Anthropology (http://www.penn.museum/sites/iraq/?page_id= 233#) accessed 4 May 2013.

99. J. von Beckerath, *Handbuch der ägyptischen Königsnamen* (Mainz am Rhein: von Zabern, 1999), p. 283. Wilkinson, *Early Dynastic Egypt*, pp. 67-82.

King	Estimated regnal years	Subsidiary chamber at tomb	Subsidiary chambers at enclosure	Average dead persons per year
Narmer	?	n/a	n/a	n/a
Aha	ca. 32	36	6	minimum of 1
Djer	ca. 47	306	269	ca. 13
Djet	ca. 13	174	154	ca. 25
Meretneith	ca. 5-10	41	79	12-24
Den	ca. 47	121	unknown	minimum of 3
Anedjib	ca. 6 (Beckerath) Sed-festival (Wilkinson)	63	unknown	minimum of 11
Semerkhet[100]	ca. 8	64	unknown	minimum of 8
Qaà	ca. 25	26	unknown	minimum of 1
Total	minimum of 183	851	509	n/a

Table 1. *Estimated Average Subsidiary Burials at Umm el-Qa'ab during the First Dynasty*

Names, Ranks and Titles

One indication of the social position of a person is certainly the effort that was put into his tomb. As essentially all tombs at Umm el-Qa'ab are disturbed and plundered it is impossible to recreate the tomb assemblages to estimate the wealth and social standing of the tomb owner. Since size mattered, a look at the area and size of the subsidiary tombs around the royal tombs and the enclosures might give an impression of social hierarchy.[101] A small grave is defined by the size of up to 3sqm and a large tomb occupies the space of 3 to 9m². There are two complexes that stand out, the one of King Aha and the one of King Qa'a. In both instances the overwhelming majority of subsidiary chambers are large, with almost 100% for Aha and around 70% for Qa'a. For the tombs of all the other kings the small chambers make up between 66 and 100%. Hence it is safe to say that there is a hierarchical differentiation based on tomb size and most of the tombs belonged to people of lower status.

Today almost 400 private stelae are known from Umm el-Qa'ab, with almost 50% excavated by Petrie, 20% found by Amélineau, and almost 25% that have come to light during the recent excavations by the German

---

100.   Martin 2011, p. 15 figure 2.
101.   Reisner, *The Development of the Egyptian Tomb*, pp. 76-117.

Archaeological Institute.[102] The stelae were made of local limestone with a rounded top and approximately 30–45cm in height. Although Petrie assigned many of the stelae he found to various subsidiary chambers, one should not forget the disturbances and plundering of the past and that the contents of the tombs were 'ransacked and scattered hither and yon'.[103] Around 270 different names are carved on the stelae and most of them occur only once.[104]

Based on the female determinatives, it seems that most (141) of the stelae were carved for women of the royal court, while 41 of the stelae bear a male determinative. Three of the women were called *Iwt* and one of them was a priestess of the goddess Seshat.[105] Three of the males were in fact dwarves named *Dd*, *Hd*, and *St*.[106] It is interesting to note that the recent excavations at the tomb of King Semerkhet revealed the skeletal remains of a dwarf,[107] while the closest find spot of the dwarf stelae is from the tomb of Den/Djet.

Around eighty various titles are known.[108] Many are compositions that refer to the god Horus, i.e. the king, and show the definite affiliation of those retainers with the royal household. A group of seven stelae of women is associated with King Den as they all bear the title 'she who ornaments the Horus Khasety' (one of the names of Den).[109] Others, like *Htp-skhm* and *Htp-nb*, were butchers and a certain *Pt* worked in the granary.[110] However, the most common title is that of a *sekhen-ȝkh*, which is attested 34 times and associated with both men and women. The rather enigmatic title can be translated as 'spirit seeker'. It is tempting to see this as a hint that these individuals are indeed associated with a special funerary ritual, even sacrifice, but in fact its role remains unclear.[111] Some of the stelae show determinatives of a hound and were possibly meant for pets.[112]

---

102. G. T. Martin, *Umm el-Qaab VII: Private Stelae of the Early Dynastic Period from the Royal Cemetery at Abydos* (Wiesbaden: Harrassowitz, 2011).

103. Martin, *Umm el-Qaab VII*, p. 2.

104. Martin, *Umm el-Qaab VII*, pp. 216-18.

105. Martin, *Umm el-Qaab VII*, cat. nos. 16, 25, 146.

106. Martin, *Umm el-Qaab VII*, cat. nos. 58, 186, 201.

107. Engel, 'Grab des Semerchet', pp. 121-22. A. Zink, 'Von Riesen und Zwergen—besondere anthropologische Befunde aus dem prä- und frühdynastischen Grabanlagen in Abydos', in Engel, Müller, and Hartung (eds.), *Zeichen aus dem Sand*, pp. 700-703.

108. Martin, *Umm el-Qaab VII*, pp. 215-16.

109. Martin, *Umm el-Qaab VII*, cat. nos. 21, 120-25.

110. Martin, *Umm el-Qaab VII*, cat. nos. 24, 260, 103

111. Martin, *Umm el-Qaab VII*, pp. 2, 215.

112. Martin, *Umm el-Qaab VII*, cat. nos. 173 and 178.

Finally, it has to be emphasized that the stela of Sabef found in the tomb complex of Qa'a remains the absolute exception for a person with a higher position in the royal administration.[113] Almost 85cm in height, this monument is also at least double the size of the other stelae. Sabef carried the title of 'administrator of the hall in the funerary estate [Sa]-ha-neb', 'administrator of the Per-akh of the temple of Horus of Pe, the Harpooner', 'courtier of the King's palace', 'one privy to the secrets of (judicial) decisions', '*smr* of the Hall of Anubis beside Pe', and 'master of the *sdd*'.

It is safe to say that, with the exception of Sabef, none of the titles seem to be high enough to have given the owners direct contact with the king. The concept that the selection of the retainers was based on a close bond between retainer and king[114] seems rather unlikely given the low ranks and lack of personal proximity to the king in life of those buried in the subsidiary chambers. Indeed, it is worth noting that in the case of King Qa'a the subsidiary chambers closest to the king were not reserved for retainers but for the storage of luxury goods for the afterlife.

Now, as we know roughly how many people were buried around the royal tombs and enclosures at Abydos and some of the First Dynasty mastabas at Saqqara, and their social status, we would like to propose an alternative to human sacrifice—the taking of human life as the ultimate and extreme form of conspicuous consumption—involving the factors 'time' and 'mortality rate' and the very Egyptian concept of *Ma'at*.

The Alternative
Unsurprisingly, studies on skeletal material from Umm el-Qa'ab have revealed that small children and women of child-bearing years were at greater mortality risk.[115] What was striking in the findings at Abydos was that a normal population of at least 133 individuals studied at the Predynastic Cemetery U shows the mortality rate for infants (ca. 20%), compared to almost 70% in nineteenth-century CE Egypt, was unexpectedly low. However, a peak of the mortality rate was for adults aged

113.   Martin, *Umm el-Qaab VII*, cat. no. 48. Petrie, *The Royal Tombs of the First Dynasty*, pl. XXX, XXXVI.

114.   B. Midant-Reynes, 'Sacrifices humains et mort d'accompagnement: le casse-tête Égyptien', in J. Guilaine (ed.), *Sépultures et sociétiés. Du néolithique à l'histoire* (Paris: Errance, 2009); É. Vaudou, 'Les sépultures subsidiaries des grandes tombes de la 1re dynastie égyptienne', *Archéo-Nil* 18 (2008), pp. 148-65.

115.   A. G. Nerlich and A. Zink, 'Anthropologische und palaopathologische Untersuchungen des Skelettmaterials', in G. Dreyer et al. 'Umm el-Qaab. Nachuntersuchungen im frühzeitlichen Königsfriedhof 13./14./15. Vorbericht', *MDAIK* 59 (2003), pp. 24-136.

21 to 30 years.[116] Almost one in five of the 133 individuals studied also showed signs of diseases, such as chronic anaemia or vitamin D deficiency. Around 16% showed chronic wear of the joints and degenerated bones.

Skeletons of more than 1,000 individuals from the cemetery at the Old Kingdom cemetery on Elephantine Island near Aswan and the Qubbet el-Hawa opposite give an interesting insight into life-expectancy and domestic life in the third millennium BCE.[117] Apart from general information that men were on average 168cm tall and women 155cm, there were some severe wounds observed. Several individuals show healed skull fractures, most likely caused by a club. Broken noses and parry fractures of the lower arm on women, for example, are clear indications for domestic violence. Overall there is, as at Cemetery U, a peak in the mortality rate among adults aged 20 to 29 years.[118]

Another study of almost 600 individuals from newborns to senile dating from the Middle and New Kingdom from Western Thebes shows a very similar distribution, with the majority being between 20 and 40 years of age at death.[119] Even at the capital of Pharaoh Akhenaten at Tell el-Amarna, life was characterized by hardship for the majority of the population of the 20,000–30,000 people.[120] Skeletal remains from more than 200 graves from the South Cemetery of individuals aged between 3 and 25 years show signs of scurvy and rickets. Most of the adults had arthritis and healed fractures.

It seems obvious that malnutrition, certain diseases such as tuberculosis, and domestic violence are major factors for the short life-expectancy in ancient Egypt, and reaching 30 years of age was an uphill battle for most of the population. Thus the age distribution of burials at the tomb of King Aha is very much according to the standard, and not an exceptional concentration of 'young' men which, as mentioned earlier, was seen as evidence they had been sacrificed.

---

116. Nerlich and Zink, 'Anthropologische', p. 127, figs. 22 and 23.

117. F. W. Rösing, *Qubbet el Hawa und Elephantine. Zur Bevölkerungsgeschichte von Ägypten* (Stuttgart: G. Fischer, 1990).

118. Rösing, *Qubbet el Hawa*, p. 110, fig. 110.

119. A. G. Nerlich and A. Zink, 'Anthropological and Palaeopathological Analysis of Human Remains in the Theban Necropolis: A Comparative Study on Three "Tombs of the Nobles"', in N. C. Strudwick and J. H. Taylor (eds.), *The Theban Necropolis; Past, Present and Future* (London: British Museum, 2003), pp. 218-28.

120. B. Kemp, A. Stevens, G. R. Dabbs, M. Zabecki, and J. Rose, 'Life, Death and Beyond in Akhenaten's Egypt: Excavating the South Tombs Cemetery at Amarna', *Antiquity* 87, no. 335, (2013), pp. 64-78.

At the same time we know little about the schedule for the actual funerals of Early Dynastic kings. At which point of the reign, if at all, did the tomb building start? Was there even a tomb designed before the king died? The changes in the construction of the tomb of King Qa'a clearly show that alterations were possible.

As we saw, the estimate for the construction of the tomb of King Qa'a may have taken up to two years. Some of the larger funerary complexes at Umm el-Qa'ab certainly took longer, not to mention the enclosures. But no matter when the construction started there was always ample time for servants of the royal household to 'simply die'—be it during the reign of their regents and living gods or during the construction of the tomb, should it have been started after the royal death. We must also keep in mind that there was no standard number of servants that were needed, and at the same time we saw that tombs were enlarged at Umm el-Qa'ab and chambers added.

Reburying people was not unknown in ancient Egypt. One only has to recall the actions by the Theban necropolis administration reburying some royal mummies by the end of the New Kingdom. Later, in the tenth century BCE, priests relocated more than fifty mummies of kings, queens, lesser royalty and nobility to cache DB320 at Deir el-Bahri.[121]

We propose a rather straightforward solution to explain the hundreds and hundreds of retainer burials during the First Dynasty in Egypt: members of the royal households and some of the nobility received the privilege of serving their masters in the afterlife.

They died during the reign of the kings, were buried, and later re-interred at Abydos or Saqqara. This could, for instance, explain the exception of Sabef at the tomb of King Qa'a and at the same time serve to explain why the number of subsidiary burials peaked under King Djer, with almost half of all known subsidiary burials at Abydos: it was simply the long reign of this ruler that allowed a large entourage to be collected and buried at Abydos after his death!

The alteration of human bodies from Pre- and Early Dynastic Egypt have long been linked with later texts, such as the Pyramid Texts, that speak of the mutilation of bodies and reassembling body parts.[122] Yet it

---

121. N. Reeves and R. H. Wilkinson, *The Complete Valley of the Kings: Tombs and Treasures of Egypt's Greatest Pharaohs* (London: Thames & Hudson, 1996), pp. 190-207.

122. G. A. Wainright, 'The ritual of dismemberment', in W. M. F. Petrie, G. A. Wainright, and E. Mackey, *The Labyrinth, Gerzeh and Mazguneh* (London: School of Archaeology in Egypt, University College, 1912), pp. 11-15; G. R. H. Wright, 'The Egyptian Sparagmos', *MDAIAK* 35 (1979), pp. 345-58.

seems difficult to transform the content of these Pyramid Texts over almost 1,000 years and to trace the line of Predynastic body mutilation of seemingly ordinary people to the royal ideological sphere. If one would do this one would equally be allowed to introduce the concept of *Ma'at*, known from the Pyramid Age onward, to argue against human sacrifice. *Ma'at* is considered to be the essential harmony of the universe. On a human level *Ma'at* encompasses connective justice and vertical solidarity.[123] This also means the responsibility of the king for his subjects. The king was the good shepherd for his people. Killing them was a punishment and not a reward. Assuming the concept of *Ma'at* developed long before the Pyramid Age when Egyptian royal ideology was formed in the late fourth and beginning third millennium BCE, this would clearly stand in the way of human sacrifice.

To sum up: as long as we have no clear evidence of a violent and/or common death from the skeletal remains, the final proof for human sacrifice for the First Dynasty in Egypt is missing. Even a mudfloor applied to seal subsidiary tombs all at the same time seems insufficient, given the mortality rate that we have to consider in Egypt 5,000 years ago. People may have been buried in one place at the same time but it does not necessarily follow that they died (or were deliberately killed) at the same time.

Predynastic Maadi and a Surprise Modern Find

Archaeology at Maadi
Just south of Cairo lies the modern city of Maadi, which is also the name for a Prehistoric site of the fourth millennium BCE. Early excavations were undertaken by the Egyptian University in Cairo just after WWI from 1920 to 1932[124] and the Department of Geography at the University of Cairo from 1930 to 1953.[125] Further excavations were conducted at the site in the late 1970s and again in the early 1980s.[126] Work resumed in

123. J. Assmann, *Ma'at. Gerechtigkeit und Unsterblichkeit im Alten Ägypten* (Munich: Beck, 1990).

124. O. Menghin, and M. Amer, *The Excavations of the Egyptian University in the Neolithic Site at Maadi: First Preliminary Report, Season 1930–31* (Cairo: Misr-Sokkar Press, 1932); O. Menghin and M. Amer, *The Excavations of the Egyptian University in the Neolithic Site at Maadi: Second Preliminary Report, Season 1932* (Cairo: Government Press, 1936).

125. I. Rizkana and J. Seeher, *Maadi* (4 vols.; AVDAIAK 64, 65, 80, 81; Mainz am Rhein: Verlag Philipp von Zabern, 1987–90).

126. I. Caneva, et al., 'Predynastic Egypt: New data from Maadi', *African Archaeological Review* 5 (1987), pp. 105-14; I. Caneva et al., 'Recent Excavations

the mid-1980s,[127] before, finally, a rescue project conducted by the German Archaeological Institute in Cairo took place between 1999 and 2002.[128]

The site is located on a strip that is around 1.5km long but only 150 to 200m wide. When we arrived with the German Archaeological Institute in 1999, most of the settlement had been destroyed or built over and only a small part (400 × 200m) on the western side remained. Here the foundations of a radio station had caused further destruction.

The cultural layers are about 40 to 60cm thick and pottery and stone tools of the first half of the fourth millennium could be found right on the sandy surface of the site. The architecture of the settlement consisted of simple huts with fences and fireplaces. Storage facilities were constructed in the form of pits into which large vessels were placed. The sustenance of the village relied on agriculture, husbandry, and fishing. The people of Maadi raised sheep and goats, as well as cattle and pigs. Imports of artefacts and raw materials from Upper Egypt and Palestine strongly suggest regional trade. Foreign-style subterranean buildings also show that for some time immigrants from the Levant arrived at Maadi and lived alongside the indigenous Egyptian population.

Life-expectancy was between 25 and 30 years.[129] In the cemetery at Maadi the skeletal remains tend to show degeneration of the intervertebral disks and exostosis, resulting from hard work in the field and carrying heavy objects. Tooth abscesses were also common, while a few skeletons showed healed fractures.[130]

at Maadi (Egypt)', in L. Krzyzanik and M. Kobusiewicz (eds.), *Late Prehistory of the Nile Basin and the Sahara* (Poznan: Poznan Archaeological Museum, 1989), pp. 287-93.

127.   F. A. Badawi, 'Kurzbericht über die neuen ägyptischen Ausgrabungen in Ma'adi (Prädynastisch)', *Mitteilungsblatt der Archaeologica Venatoria e.V.* 12 (1987), pp. 58-60; Badawi, 'Kurzer Bericht aus dem spät-prädynastischen Fundort Maadi', in Z. Hawass and A. Milward Jones (eds.), *Eighth International Congress of Egyptologists, Cairo 28 March–3 April 2000, Abstracts of Papers* (Cairo: The American University in Cairo Press, 2000), p. 25; Badawi, 'Preliminary Report on the 1984–1986 Excavations at Maadi-West', *MDAIAK* 59 (2003), pp. 1-10.

128.   U. Hartung, 'Rescue Excavations in the Predynastic Settlement of Maadi', in Hendrickx, Friedman, Ciałowicz, and Chłodnicki (eds.), *Egypt at its Origins*, pp. 337-56; U. Hartung et al. 'Vorbericht über neue Untersuchungen in der prädynastischen Siedlung von Maadi', *MDAIAK* 59 (2003), pp. 149-98.

129.   K.-G. Beck and S. Klug, 'The Anthropology of the Predynastic Sites of Maadi and Wadi Digla', in Rizkana and Seeher, *Maadi*, vol. 4, p. 136.

130.   Beck and Klug, 'The Anthropology of the Predynastic Sites', p. 124, tables 4.10 and 4.11.

Overall the cemetery at Maadi gives no insight into any violence that might have caused the death of any individual. There is, however, one occurrence to be mentioned where the body had apparently been treated before internment: the body of a young man between 17 and 21 years of age was apparently cut in half before being placed in Tomb MA 61.[131]

The Diggers at Maadi

By the outbreak of WWI modern Maadi was a small community of just 61 houses and mainly British.[132] The so-called Anglo-Egyptians were members of the military or police, administrators, bank comptrollers, or working in branches of the Egyptian Government run by the British at the time. While Egypt as a whole was faced with the threat of being invaded by the Ottoman Empire, Maadi was in fact 'overrun by the men from the bush',[133] as it became the training ground and launching-pad for troops from Australia, New Zealand, South Africa and other British colonies.

On the Australian side initially the 1st Light Horse Brigade (LHB) and later the 2nd LHB set up their camp in an empty site just south of Road 84 in Maadi, west of the Khashab Canal extending all the way to the Digla freight line in the east. As part of the 1st LHB, the 1st Light Horse Regiment (LHR) was drawn in New South Wales (NSW) from existing Militia Regiments, i.e. trained soldiers. The 2nd Light Horse Brigade was made up of the 5th, 6th, and 7th Regiments, of which the latter two were exclusively recruited from New South Wales.[134]

A lot has changed at Maadi since 1918, so we were quite surprised when we discovered several sheets of old newspaper just after surface cleaning, side-by-side with finds from the fourth millennium BCE (see images 1 and 2). Even more surprising was that the newspaper could be identified as the *Cootamundra Liberal*, Cootamundra being a rural town in New South Wales approximately 350km southwest of Sydney.

---

131. Beck and Klug, 'The Anthropology of the Predynastic Sites', pp. 150-51. Rizkana and Seeher, *Maadi*, vol. 4, p. 21, pl. V.

132. S. W. Raafat, *Maadi 1904–1962: Society and History in a Cairo Suburb* (Cairo: Palm Press, 1994), p. 44.

133. Raafat, *Maadi 1904–1962*, p. 48.

134. L. G. Berrie, *Under Furred Hats: 6th A.L.H. Regt* (Sydney: W.C. Penfold, 1919); J. D. Richardson, *The History of the 7th Light Horse Regiment A.I.F.* (Sydney: Eric N. Birks, 1923, repr. 2009).

Images 1 and 2. *Fragments from the Cootamundra Liberal found at Predynastic Maadi (authors' photos)*

The newspaper is dated to Wednesday 9 December 1914. Among the advertisements for farm equipment, community meetings and general news items one can read the vision of Sir Max Waechter of a 'federation of Europe' and his prophecy that the United States would declare their adherence to this European Union. This was a vision to ensure long-term peace even while war raged. And the war was also found in the pages of the *Cootamundra Liberal*. For instance, we also learn what awaited the Slouch Hats on the battle field:

> ...he [Stanley Anderson from NZ] says that the men who were in the South African war declare that the war was a picnic compared with this. 'We have been having a fairly busy time of it', he writes, 'and I think we have given the Germans a busy time, too. They don't like standing up to the British soldier. We had a hot time of it at Mons and Le Cateau, but we

gave them more than we got. The Germans came up to us in thousands and went back in hundreds This is not the old style of fighting with a battle once a month. We have been at it continuously, or nearly so, for the last five weeks, and sleeping besides the guns in the trenches where we now are. The Germans have a big siege gun, which we have christened "Little Willie", and it is throwing shells around us that make a hole in the ground you could bury a horse in.'

Australia had a population of around 4 million at the time of WWI. Around 416,000 men between the age of 18 and 44 enlisted, which was almost 40% of this age group. Australia suffered a casualty rate of 65% relative to the number of total embarkations—the highest rate of all countries in WWI!

The Gallipoli Campaign alone resulted in more than 8,000 Australian casualties. Still, the highest losses were suffered by the Turkish forces, which lost around 80,000 men (some estimates are even higher). Today at Anzac Cove, the landing place of the Australian and New Zealand troops, and on the Kemal Ataturk Memorial in Canberra, visitors can read the words of the Turkish President Kemal Ataturk, commander of the Turkish 19th Infantry Division at Gallipoli, honouring the fallen soldiers of both sides:

> Those heroes that shed their blood, and lost their lives…
>
> You are now lying in the soil of a friendly country.
> Therefore, rest in peace.
> There is no difference between the Johnnies
> And the Mehmets to us where they lie side by side,
> Here in this country of ours.
> You, the mothers, who sent their sons from far away countries…
> Wipe away your tears.
> Your sons are now lying in our bosom and are in peace.
> After having lost their lives on this land, they have
> Become our sons as well.

The Diggers who left Australia towards the end of 1914 for Egypt could not foresee their fate on the battlefields of Europe and the Near East. Yet reading the newspapers they were pretty aware of the grim and fierce fighting that was ahead of them—as did the young soldier who brought a copy of the *Cootamundra Liberal*, even in these very early stages of the war.

While human sacrifice in the ancient past seems to be a rare thing executed by only a few cultures around the globe, making sacrifices in order to protect your family, people, and country is experienced in the modern world on a vaster scale—and this time it does include the taking of human life.

GOD'S INFANTICIDE IN THE NIGHT OF PASSOVER: EXODUS 12 IN THE LIGHT OF ANCIENT EGYPTIAN RITUALS

Thomas Schneider

1. *Introduction*

In his Exodus commentary, Thomas Dozeman paints the vision of the night of Passover as the cataclysmic final battle of Yahweh and Egypt:

> The absence of light indicates a cosmological battle. Yahweh, the Storm God, is attacking the land of Egypt. Death is on the Horizon. It has enveloped the land. The only oases from the consuming darkness are the individual Israelite houses. Each is lit up in the sea of darkness. They now become the setting for the drama of Passover.[1]

The 'drama of Passover' in Exodus 12, the killing of the firstborn of Egypt by Yahweh or his 'destroyer' who is prevented by a blood rite from carrying out his slaughtering in the houses of the Israelites, is the most momentous of all infanticides described in the Hebrew Bible. It constitutes the narrative trigger for Israel's exodus to the promised land, 'a defining moment, perhaps the defining moment in ancient Israelite tradition'.[2] The drama of scholarship on this biblical chapter, on the other hand, is far from such a transformative moment. The most disparate views are held on the relationship of the different narrative cycles—in the received text of the Hebrew Bible, the institution of Passover is linked to the plague cycle imposed on Egypt[3] and the Exodus narrative— the delineation, date and motivation of the different textual layers in Exodus 12, and the significance, genuine origin and dates of association

---

1. T. B. Dozeman, *Commentary on Exodus* (Eerdmans Critical Commentary; Grand Rapids, MI: Eerdmans, 2009), p. 267.

2. E. Gruen, 'The Use and Abuse of the Exodus Story', *Jewish History* 12.1 (1998), p 93.

3. On the exegesis of the plague narrative, see L. Schmidt, 'Die vorpriesterliche Darstellung in Ex 11,1–13,16*', *ZAW* 117 (2005), pp. 171-88; B. Lemmelijn, *A Plague of Texts? A Text-critical Study of the So-called 'Plagues Narrative' in Exodus 7:14–11:10* (Leiden: Brill, 2009).

of the different motifs and regulations mentioned—of *Pesaḥ* and *Maṣṣot*, the *mašḥit*, the blood rite, the celebration at nightfall and in the spring, or the significance of the firstborn.

The purpose of this contribution that I am so honoured to offer to Paul Mosca, is to present, after a careful overview of previous scholarship (§§2.1–3), new evidence that has been entirely absent from the past debate: ancient Egyptian motifs and rituals for a drama that is indeed set in Egypt by the narrative itself, in particular the killing of the firstborn by a nocturnal demon, as well as the ritual put in effect to protect the Israelites. I hope that this new evidence will be apt to provide a new angle of view and to thus reorient the dialogue on this text in biblical scholarship.[4]

2. *Exodus 12 in Recent Scholarship*

Exodus 12.12-13, 23, 29-30 reads as follows in the NIV:

> [12] 'On that same night I will pass through Egypt and strike down every firstborn of both people and animals, and I will bring judgment on all the gods of Egypt. I am Yahweh. [13] The blood will be a sign for you on the houses where you are, and when I see the blood, I will pass over you. No destructive plague will touch you when I strike Egypt… [21] Then Moses summoned all the elders of Israel and said to them, 'Go at once and select the animals for your families and slaughter the Passover lamb. [22] Take a bunch of hyssop, dip it into the blood in the basin and put some of the blood on the top and on both sides of the doorframe. None of you shall go out of the door of your house until morning. [23] When the Lord goes through the land to strike down the Egyptians, he will see the blood on the top and sides of the doorframe and will pass over that doorway, and he will not permit the destroyer to enter your houses and strike you down… [29] At midnight the Lord struck down all the firstborn in Egypt, from the firstborn of Pharaoh, who sat on the throne, to the firstborn of the prisoner, who was in the dungeon, and the firstborn of all the live-stock as well. [30] Pharaoh and all his officials and all the Egyptians got up during the night, and there was loud wailing in Egypt, for there was not a house without someone dead.

---

4. This study, preceded by a different introduction situating it within the context of the conference for which it was written, is also published as 'Modern Scholarship Versus the Demon of Passover: An Outlook on Exodus Research and Egyptology through the Lense of Exodus 12', in Thomas E. Levy, Thomas Schneider and William H. C. Propp (eds.), *Israel's Exodus in Transdisciplinary Perspective: Text, Archaeology, Culture, and Geoscience* (Quantitative Methods in the Humanities and Social Sciences; Cham, Switzerland: Springer, 2014), pp. 537-53. I am indebted to David Frankfurter who has kindly read the text and provided comments.

I will first provide an overview of the debates on the exegesis of Exodus 12 (§2.1), on the relationship between the Passover and the Plague/ Exodus narratives (§2.2), and on the proposed origins of the protection ritual contained in the Passover narrative (§2.3), before presenting ancient Egyptian rituals that can elucidate important elements of the Passover narrative (§3).

2.1. *The Textual, Literary, and Redaction History of Exodus 12*
Scholarship on Exod 12.1-20 commonly distinguishes a P section in vv. 1-13. For the following vv. 14-20, different interpretations have been proposed. I mention three possibilities: Propp identifies as P as well vv. 14-17a, 18-20, and as a redactor's note, v. 17b.[5] Albertz views vv. 1-13 on the Passover law as the original priestly source (PB[1] = *erste priesterliche Bearbeitung* etc.) with the *Maṣṣot* prescriptions (vv. 14-17: PB[2]),[6] vv. 18-20 (PB[4]) and v. 12b (PB[5]) as later priestly additions.[7] Utzschneider and Oswald regard vv. 1-13, 18-20 as priestly and vv. 14 und 15-17 as late editorial additions at the time of the redaction of the Tora ('Tora-Komposition').[8] The following vv. 21-27 are regularly set apart by scholars as a passage of different origin. Of all texts analyzed in pentateuchal literary criticism, this section is among those with the most controversial assessments.[9] The recent demise of former certainties in the historical-critical analysis of the Pentateuch has increased the difficulties, to the extent that Fischer and Markl, in their 2009 Exodus commentary, have decided to focus on the transmitted text, regarding it as impossible to reconstruct earlier stages of text formation.[10] Similarly, Diana Edelman decided 'not to include the initial Exodus story in Exodus 12–13 in my review because the date when this aetiological legend that commemorates the Exodus was first developed and then

---

5. He considers that, alternatively, v. 14 might be R (added by a redactor), as might be 18-20. W. H. C. Propp, *Exodus 1–18: A New Translation with Introduction and Commentary* (AB 2; New Haven: Yale University Press, 1999), p. 374.

6. According to Albertz, PB[2] is close to the redactor of the Holiness Law in Lev 17–26.

7. R. Albertz, *Exodus 1–18* (Zürcher Bibelkommentare; Zürich: Theologischer Verlag, 2012), pp. 21-23, 25f., 199f.

8. H. Utzschneider and W. Oswald, *Exodus 1–15* (Internationaler Exegetischer Kommentar zum Alten Testament; Stuttgart: Kohlhammer, 2013), pp. 280-89.

9. Utzschneider and Oswald, *Exodus 1–15*, p. 281. Sh. Bar-On, 'Zur literar-kritischen Analyse von Ex 12,21-27', *ZAW* 107 (1995), p. 18.

10. G. Fischer and D. Markl, *Das Buch Exodus* (Neuer Stuttgarter Kommentar. Altes Testament 2; Stuttgart: Katholisches Bibelwerk, 2009), p. 24.

subsequently committed to its present form is unknown'.[11] Traditional exegesis identified this text as J or partially J; Gerhard von Rad, for instance, recognized J in vv. 21-23, 27b, with a dtr addition in 24-27a.[12] Propp regards the presence of 'D-like material' as undeniable.[13] He identifies the non-P section of Exodus 12 as entirely Elohistic, 'with the author quoting a D-like document or more likely using D-like language himself',[14] The crisis of Pentateuchal criticism has now removed the Yahwist and the Elohist as undisputed interpretive models.[15] Instead, scholarship has adopted the umbrella term 'Non-P' for the non-priestly stages of the Pentateuch. Dozeman notes the affinity of vv. 21-27 with Deuteronomy and the Deuteronomistic History and assigns them to the 'Non-P History', which he places in the exile or, more likely, in the post-exilic period, but before P.[16] At the same time, he assumes vv. 21-23 to include an earlier 'ancient rite'. David Carr sees vv. 25-27 as a secondary D-like instruction to the early non-P Passover law in Exod 12.21-24.[17] According to Schmidt,[18] the older, non-P layer consists of 12.21–23.27b.

11. D. Edelman 'Exodus and Pesach/Massot as Evolving Social Memory', in C. Levin and E. Ben Zvi (eds.), *Remembering (and Forgetting) in Judah's Early Second Temple Period* (FAT 85; Tübingen: Mohr Siebeck, 2012), pp. 161-93.

12. G. von Rad, *Das zweite Buch Mose: Exodus* (2d ed.; ATD 5; Göttingen: Vandenhoeck & Ruprecht, 1961), p. 72.

13. Propp, *Exodus 1–18*, p. 377.

14. Propp, *Exodus 1–18*, p. 377: 'We might impute the D-like diction to a literary *topos* rooted in didactic tradition. It need not be specific to a single source'.

15. For the history of scholarship, see D. M. Carr, 'The Formation of the Moses Story: Literary-Historical Reflections', *Hebrew Bible and Ancient Israel* 1 (2012), pp. 11-12. Cf. K. Schmid, 'The So-Called Yahwist and the Literary Gap Between Genesis and Exodus', in T. B. Dozeman and K. Schmid (eds.), *A Farewell to the Yahwist? The Composition of the Pentateuch in Recent European Interpretation* (SBLSymS 34; Atlanta: SBL, 2006), p. 30 n. 4: the observations that led Graupner to reemphasize the existence of the Elohist are true but they lead to the distinction between P and non-P texts, not between J and E.

16. Dozeman, *Commentary on Exodus*, pp. 39-40. According to U. Dahm, *Opferkult und Priestertum in Alt-Israel. Ein kultur- und religionswissenschaftlicher Beitrag* (BZAW 327; Berlin: W. de Gruyter, 2003), pp. 137-41, both Exod 12.21-27 and Exod 12.1-14 originated in the same circles ('gleicher Verfasserkreis'). She assigns 12.1-14 to an 'Aharon layer' from the second half of the fourth century BCE, and 12.21-27 to her so-called 'Zadokite Mose layer' from the end of the fifth century BCE.

17. D. M. Carr, *The Formation of the Hebrew Bible: A New Reconstruction* (Oxford: Oxford University Press, 2011), p. 267. For his literary assessment of the Exodus narrative, see Carr, 'The Formation of the Moses Story: Literary-Historical Reflections'.

18. Schmidt, 'Die vorpriesterliche Darstellung in Ex 11,1–13,16*'.

Some scholars, unlike the majority of exegetes, consider vv. 21-27 to be younger than the priestly text in vv. 1-13(-20). Bar-On[19] suggests that 21-27 is a commentary-like priestly continuation of vv. 1-20. Gertz[20] recognizes both priestly and deuteronomistic elements in vv. 21-27 and assigns them to the final redaction of the Pentateuch. Albertz[21] ascribes the verses to the late-deuteronomistic redactor D whom he places chronologically later than his priestly layers PB[1] and PB[2]. Berner[22] sees in vv. 21-27 a post-priestly supplement in which three layers of halakhic regulations (vv. 21-23, v. 25, vv. 26-27a) and a narrative addition (v. 27b) appear amalgamated.

In turn, arguments for a date of these verses prior to the priestly passage of vv. 1-13, 18-20 have again been proposed in Utzschneider and Oswald's latest[23] evaluation of the literary history of Exodus 12, which identifies 12.21-27 as a uniform piece belonging to the deuteronomistic history.[24] While Dozeman[25] concedes that 'a firm date for the Non-P History is not necessary for interpreting Exodus', this is certainly not true for a historical contextualization of the texts in their development during the first millennium BCE.[26] Given the common

---

19.   Bar-On, 'Zur literarkritischen Analyse von Ex 12,21-27'.

20.   J. C. Gertz, *Tradition und Redaktion in der Exodus-Erzählung. Untersuchungen zur Endredaktion des Pentateuch* (FRLANT 186; Göttingen: Vandenhoeck & Ruprecht, 2000), pp. 38-50.

21.   R. Albertz, *Exodus 1–18* (Zürcher Bibelkommentare; Zurich: Theologischer Verlag, 2012), pp. 212, 220-21.

22.   C. Berner, *Die Exoduserzählung, Das literarische Werden einer Ursprungslegende Israels* (FAT 73; Tübingen: Mohr Siebeck, 2010), pp. 331-39.

23.   Utzschneider and Oswald, *Exodus 1–15*.

24.   See also Utzschneider and Oswald's diagram, *Exodus 1–15*, p. 280.

25.   Dozeman, *Commentary on Exodus*, pp. 39-40.

26.   Cf. here the critical comments by W. Morrow, Review of T. B. Dozeman, *Commentary on Exodus*, *JHS* 12 (2012). Online: http://www.jhsonline.org/reviews/reviews_new/review584.ht): 'for the most part, Dozeman declines to reconstruct the literary history of the non-P and P Histories. One consequence of Dozeman's methodology, therefore, is a certain flattening in historical perspective when accounting for the origins of the book. For some readers this will stand out as a weakness in the commentary. Dozeman does an excellent job of describing the status of source critical debates on various segments of the text, but these concerns are subordinate to the author's stated aims, which are focused on mapping the dimensions of the non-P and P Histories and explaining their viewpoints and relationships. A good example of his approach is found in the discussion about the altar law in Exod 20.24–26. While he recognizes its associations with centralization ideas in Deuteronomy, ultimately he leaves the question open as to whether the law is an older expression of a theological perspective appropriated by Deuteronomy or derivative of Deuteronomic thinking. What the reader is presented with is a description of the function of

acceptance of deuteronomistic material in Exod 12.20-27, any dating depends on assumptions about the Deuteronomistic tradition where the state of the debate is similarly opaque.[27]

2.2. *The Relationship between Passover and the Plague/Exodus Narrative*

The literary and historical relationship between the celebrations commemorating the Exodus in the received text of Exodus 12 (*Pesaḥ* and *Maṣṣot*) and the exodus and plague narratives has been the subject of an intense debate. A view widely held in scholarship today sees the association of the two festivals with the exodus as secondary, the result of a gradual transfer of institutions of different origins to commemorative events of Israel's departure from Egypt.[28] By way of example, I mention here Willi-Plein,[29] Bar-On,[30] Levinson,[31] Propp,[32] Dahm,[33] Russell,[34] and

---

the altar law within the final form of the non-P History. A particular bias emerges with discussions of proposals regarding post-Priestly redaction(s) of Exodus. While he acknowledges this hypothesis, Dozeman does not appeal to it in his interpretative comments. By implication, this means that post-P insertions or authorial activity are negligible and, for all practical purposes, either non-existent or non-identifiable.'

27. T. Römer, *The So-Called Deuteronomistic History: A Sociological, Historical and Literary Introduction* (London: T&T Clark International, 2005); R. F. Person Jr. (ed.), *In Conversation with Thomas Römer: The So-Called Deuteronomistic: A Sociological, Historical and Literary Introduction* (London: T&T Clark International, 2005).

28. Propp, *Exodus 1–18*, p. 429.

29. I. Willi-Plein, *Opfer und Kult im alttestamentlichen Israel* (Stuttgart: Katholisches Bibelwerk, 1993), p. 19.

30. Bar-On, 'Zur literarkritischen Analyse von Ex 12,21-27': 'Das Passa als außerheiligtümliches Hausopfer mit seinem apotropäischen Hauskult wird zum historischen Passa der Auszugsgeschichte ("Pessach Mizraim") degradiert'.

31. B. M. Levinson, *Deuteronomy and the Hermeneutics of Legal Innovation* (Oxford: Oxford University Press 1997), p. 59. He speaks of the apotropaic origin of the Passover blood ritual 'with no inherent connection to the plagues or to the events of the exodus', and sees a sympathetic effect at work.

32. Propp, *Exodus 1–18*, p. 429, stating that *Pesaḥ* and *Maṣṣot* only gradually evolved into commemorations of the Exodus.

33. According to Dahm, *Opferkult und Priestertum in Alt-Israel*, p. 136, Pesah and Massot were unconnected originally, and practiced independently from the exodus tradition.

34. S. C. Russell, *Images of Egypt in Early Biblical Literature: Cisjordan-Israelite, Transjordan-Israelite, and Judahite Portrayals* (BZAW 403; Berlin: W. de Gruyter, 2009), p. 77: 'The biblical descriptions of the Passover festival allow for the possibility that an original pastoralist festival may have been unconnected with the exodus, as has been argued. If so, it may have been through the Passover that pastoralist imagery came to be associated with the exodus.'

Albertz.[35] Dozeman has called this process the 'historization' of the festivals ('The Passover is clearly historicized into the exodus in the P History, where it is merged with the Feast of Unleavened Bread'[36]) although it might be more appropriate to speak of the *mythologization of historical festivals*, festivals that had a historical origin and a history of practice.[37]

Proposals of how the exodus narrative and the festival prescriptions were interwoven over time are very complex. Here I present the latest three scenarios by Albertz,[38] Utzschneider and Oswald,[39] and Dozeman:[40]

(1) Albertz,[41] who assigns vv. 20-27 to the late-deuteronomistic redactor D, posits that this passage presupposes at least the first priestly version (*erste priesterliche Bearbeitung*, PB[1]), and that the regulations set forth there make good sense in post-priestly times (which he later defines as post-PB[1-2]). In his view, Passover was celebrated decentrally in Israelite families in pre-dtn times, probably reflecting a situation of decampment in a nomadic or semi-nomadic society, such as transhumance, in this case the movement of groups from winter to summer pastures. The blood rite's function would have been apotropaic, to prevent demons of illness from entering the houses.[42] At the end of the seventh century BCE, the deuteronomic legislators would have linked Passover to the Festival of Unleavened Bread, which according to Albertz had been connected with the exodus since the end of the eighth century BCE. This correlation would have tied Passover to the Exodus and to the temple cult.[43] In his view, the killing of the firstborn was genuinely part of the plague narrative and completely unrelated to Passover and *Maṣṣot*[44]—it stands in marked contrast to the Passover

35. Albertz, *Exodus 1–18*, p. 197.

36. Dozeman, *Commentary on Exodus*, p. 262.Cf. also p. 261: 'The Passover was not originally associated with the Exodus'.

37. Cf. here the statement made by R. Albertz, 'Exodus: Liberation History against Charter Myth', in J. W. van Henten and A. Houtepen (eds.), *Religious Identity and the Invention of Tradition: Papers Read at a NOSTER Conference in Soesterberg, January 4–6, 1999* (Assen: Van Gorcum, 2001), p. 135, according to which, in adopting the Exodus as a charter myth of the Northern kingdom, 'a historical event was mythologized in some way'.

38. Albertz, *Exodus 1–18*.

39. Utzschneider and Oswald, *Exodus 1–15*.

40. Dozeman, *Commentary on Exodus*.

41. Albertz, *Exodus 1–18*, pp. 200-201 and 212.

42. Albertz, *Exodus 1–18*, pp. 212-13.

43. Albertz, *Exodus 1–18*, p. 213.

44. Albertz, *Exodus 1–18*, p. 197.

ritual, which provides protection for all the Israelites.[45] Albertz dates the genesis of the plague/exodus *narrative* to the first half of the seventh century, that is, between the exodus/*Maṣṣot* correlation and the *Pesaḥ/ Maṣṣot* one, and believes it was formed in response to the Assyrian menace.[46] At the end of the sixth century BCE, the priestly authors (Albertz's 'PB¹') would have restored the domestic celebration of *Pesaḥ* and established a different relation to the Exodus via the blood rite in vv. 12-13. Only when the temple was rebuilt did PB² insist on renewing the connection between Passover and *Maṣṣot*, at the beginning of the fifth century BCE (vv. 14-17). A later addition (PB⁵) would have expanded the Passover event to a judgment on all Egyptian gods in 12.12b.[47] As this put the blood rite in danger of receding into the background, the late-deuteronomistic redactor would have re-emphasized the ritual in modified form in vv. 21-27, for the sake of Israel's cultural memory.[48]

(2) Utzschneider and Oswald's scenario[49] takes its point of departure from the pre-dtr 'older Exodus account' which reported, after the failed negotiations with the pharaoh, the killing of the firstborn and the release of Israel (12.29-33). Legal regulations would have been added in the deuteronomistic *Fortschreibungsphase* for three reasons:

1. DtrH's definition of *Pesaḥ* as a pilgrimage festival. Within the context of the narrative, Exod 12.21-23 pertain to the exodus occurrence, whereas vv. 24-27a point beyond the exodus to a recurrent practice, the temple festival. Unlike other scholars, Utzschneider and Oswald regard the prohibition to leave the house as a motif confined to the Egypt event and thus not a contradiction to the Passover regulations in Deut 16.1-8. In the dtr version, the blood rite lacks any explanation. Since vv. 21-27 do not mention the firstborn but speak exclusively about Yahweh striking Egypt, it follows that the dtr Passover was linked to the exodus but not in any way to the killing of the Egyptian offspring and the salvation of the Israelite one (as in Deut 16.1-8 in contrast with P). While the theme of the firstborn was known to DtrH from the older Exodus narrative and/or the tradition, DtrH links it with the consecration of the firstborn in Exod 13.11-16 and not with the Passover.

45. Albertz, *Exodus 1–18*, p. 208.
46. Albertz, *Exodus 1–18*, p. 216.
47. Albertz, *Exodus 1–18*, p. 206.
48. Albertz, *Exodus 1–18*, p. 206, mentioning that both forms of Passover (home, temple) are attested in post-exilic times, for example, in Elephantine.
49. Utzschneider and Oswald, *Exodus 1–15*, pp. 280-89.

2. the establishment of *Maṣṣot* as a reenactment of the Exodus by the DtrH, and

3. the correlation of the consecration of the firstborn and the *Maṣṣot* festival. DtrH provides the history of Israelite faith as the justification for the re-enactment of exodus (*geschichts-theologische Begründung*).

The priestly author discontinued this correlation by depriving the *Maṣṣot* festival of any *Vergegenwärtigungscharakter* and focussing all historical remembrance on *Pesaḥ* which was understood as a domestic celebration. In P's arrangement, it is no longer the consecration of the firstborn that re-enacts the killing of the Egyptian firstborn and the salvation of the Israelite one, but the blood rite (12.7, 13) which was left without any explanation in vv. 20-27. Different layers of P can be distinguished in additions to the text.[50] At the stage of the Torah's composition, the final redactor would have harmonized the dtr and P scenarios.

The main discrepancies regarding the earlier history of the rituals addressed in Exodus 12 are these: in Utzschneider and Oswald's view, dtr Passover was linked to the Exodus but not to the killing of the Egyptian offspring and the salvation of the Israelite one. The blood rite is part of the dtr Passover account and thus the Exodus nexus. It was only DtrH who established *Maṣṣot* as a re-enactment of the Exodus and correlated the consecration of the firstborn and the *Maṣṣot* festival. P's use of the blood rite is a reinterpretation of the blood rite transmitted by DtrH. By contrast, in Albertz's view, there was a genuine connection between Exodus and *Maṣṣot* dating back to the eighth century. Passover was genuinely a domestic rite unrelated to them but containing an apotropaic blood rite. Deuteronomic legislators would have connected Passover to *Maṣṣot* (and thus implicitly, to the exodus). The blood rite was a mechanism re-employed by P to link Passover and Exodus when they redefined Passover as a domestic celebration.

(3) Different again is a third option proposed by Dozeman. He argues (unlike both Utzschneider/Oswald and Albertz) that while Passover is not originally linked to the exodus event, it yet commemorates an occurrence that happened in Egypt: the killing of the firstborn, and Israel's escape from the plague of death. He comments on the Non-P History version of Passover in Exod 12.21-27 (which he assumes to include an earlier 'ancient rite' in vv. 21-23) that if Passover was originally

---

50. For example, regarding the year reckoning, the minimization of meat consumption, the explanation of Passover, and additions to the exodus account. No theological explanation is given of the Feast of Unleavened Bread.

independent, then v. 23 must be seen as an addition to vv. 21-22 'to accommodate the ritual to the narrative context of the exodus'.[51] In *God at War* he elaborates:

> The passover instruction in Exod 12:21-27 presents strong points of similarity to both Exod 13:1-16 and Deut 6.4-25... Some of the differences can be accounted for by the place of passover within the deuteronomistic interpretation of the exodus. Passover occurs in Egypt at Ramses and is separated from the promulgation of *massot*/firstlings at Succoth. This geographical separation indicates that passover is not a festival about the exodus. Rather it commemorates Israel's escape from the plague of death in Egypt. The absence of the exodus motif reinforces this conclusion. The exodus motif is defined narrowly in deuteronomistic tradition in relationship to Israel's march out of Egypt—so narrowly, in fact, that its introduction into the larger story of the exodus has even been separated geographically from the passover legislation... The placement of passover at Ramses in Egypt raises the suspicion that this festival is meant to function in the larger context of the plagues, of which the death of the Egyptian firstborn is the culmination. The instruction in 12:27 reinforces such a suspicion, since it states that passover commemorates Israel's protection from the plague of death. Once the close relationship between passover and the larger plague cycle is noted, then the deuteronomistic insertion of instruction at the outset of the plague of locusts (10:1b-2a) also takes on a larger function in relationship with passover (12:21-27)...[52]

This view is also shared by Gertz, who holds:

> Der überkommene nicht-priesterliche Textbestand zum Passa *[12,21b-23, as explained in the previous sentence, TS]* gehört vermutlich mitsamt seines szenischen Rahmens in 12,21a.27b—ursprünglich oder redaktionell—zu einer nichtpriesterlichen Plagenerzählung.[53]

The killing of the firstborn is part of the non-P plague narrative.[54] This is precisely the assessment given by William Propp for the narrative thread of E (= non-P according to Dozeman and Gertz) and P: from the announcement of the imminent death of the Egyptian firstborn and that

51. Dozeman, *Commentary on Exodus*, p. 273.
52. T. B. Dozeman, *God at War: Power in the Exodus Tradition* (New York: Oxford University Press, 1996), p. 57.
53. Gertz, *Tradition und Redaktion in der Exodus-Erzählung*, p. 73.
54. Gertz, *Tradition und Redaktion in der Exodus-Erzählung*, pp. 185-86. Although Albertz, in his own commentary, advocates a different literary-critical analysis of Exod 12 than Gertz and Dozeman, he also thinks that the killing of the firstborn was genuinely part of the plague narrative (and completely unrelated to Passover and *Maṣṣot*).

Israel should prepare for departure (10.24–11.8) to the instruction about how to escape Yahweh's destroyer by the *Pesaḥ* ritual in 12.20-27 and the hasty departure. Propp sees the priestly text as a commentary following this outline and supplying details absent from the older legislation, ending abruptly with the consecration of the firstborn in 13.1-2.[55]

2.3. *The Origins of the Protection Ritual of the Passover Narrative*

The blood ritual employed to avert the destroyer (משחית) has seen an intense debate and often been described as a pastoralist and/or domestic ritual.[56] Such assumptions have sometimes acquired the status of firm declarations ('Passover, in contrast, was originally an apotropaic rite from Israel's nomadic period'[57]) although research about Israel's early history has shown that nomadism might be at most the form of subsistence of one of many elements that amalgamated in Israel (and, as has been remarked, contradicts the mention of doorsteps). The term 'domestic', in turn, is suggested by the application of the blood to the doorsteps; it does not help in contextualizing the ritual in terms of its actual origin. In their recent Exodus commentary, Utzschneider and Oswald sum up the debate as follows:[58]

> Das Wort משחית ist ein substantivisches Partizip Hifil der Wurzel שחת. Es kann als unpersönliches Nomen in der Bedeutung 'Vernichtung' oder 'Verderben' gebraucht werden oder personal als 'Verderber' verstanden werden. Als Nomen wird es häufig 'mit *lᵉ* konstruiert, um zum Ausdruck zu bringen, dass das jeweilige Geschehen auf die definitive Vernichtung der Betroffenen abzielt...'. Diese Bedeutungsvariante liegt auch in Ex 12,13 vor. In Ex 12,23 hingegen ist das Wort mit Bezug auf eine personale Größe gebraucht, auf eben den 'Verderber', der an JHWHs Stelle die Erstgeburt der Ägypter tödlich schlägt, von Gott aber daran gehindert wird, dies auch den Israeliten zuzufügen. Die religionsgeschichtliche Forschung ist sich darin einig, dass diese Gestalt als Dämon zu verstehen ist. Die ältere Forschung hat dazu die Hypothese eines Päsachfestes aus der nomadischen Frühzeit der Israeliten aufgestellt, das der Abwehr

55. Propp, *Exodus 1–18*, p. 379.

56. See Willi-Plein, *Opfer und Kult*, p. 119; Propp, *Exodus 1–18*, pp. 440-42; Dahm, *Opferkult*, pp. 168-72; Bar-On, 'Zur literarkritischen Analyse'; Albertz, *Exodus 1–18*, pp. 197, 200-201, 212-13.

57. J. G. McConville, 'Deuteronomy's Unification of Passover and Massot: A Response to Bernard M. Levinson', *JBL* 119 (2000), pp. 47-58 (49). Cf. also R. S. Hess, 'Multiple-Month Ritual Calendars in the West Semitic World: Emar 446 and Leviticus 23', in J. K. Hoffmeier and A. B. Millard (eds.), *The Future of Biblical Archaeology: Reassessing Methodologies and Assumptions* (Grand Rapids, MI: Eerdmans, 2004), p. 249.

58. Utzschneider and Oswald, *Exodus 1–15*, p. 55.

gefährlicher Dämonen im Wanderleben der Hirten diente. Der nächste 'Verwandte' des personifizierten 'Verderbers' ist aber eher der 'Verderberengel' (מלאך המשחית) in 2Sam 24,16, der wegen einer als sündhaft empfundenen Volkszählung Davids das Volk mit der Pest schlagen sollte. In der Version der Plagenerzählung, die sich in Ps 78,48–51 findet, ist von 'Unheilsengeln' (V. 49 מלאכי רעים) die Rede, in deren Gefolge Tod und Pest zunächst über das Vieh und dann auch über die Erstgeborenen der Ägypter hereinbrechen. So spricht viel dafür, dass das Modell für die Handlung, die Mose den Ältesten gebietet, 'ein apotropäischer Ritus gegen den Pestdämon' gewesen ist. In Ps 78,48 (vgl. auch Dtn 32,24) erscheinen weitere Unheilsbringer, die רשפים (*rešāpîm*) genannt werden. Religionsgeschichtlich ist die Vermutung naheliegend, dass sich in diesen Gestalten die zum Dämon degradierte kanaanäische Pest- und Unheilsgottheit Rescheph spiegelt.

While many parallels have been adduced to explain the ritual and the destroyer from the modern Middle East (from the Arabic *fidya*[59] to the Moroccan *tfaska* ritual[60]) and several ancient Near Eastern cultures (e.g., Neo-Assyrian purification rituals[61]), it is surprising to notice that for a ritual linked in the plot to one of the plagues imposed on Egypt and purportedly employed there for the first time, none of the many commentators has ever signaled comparable ancient Egyptian rituals.[62] In the next section I will examine such rituals and explore to what extent they are conducive to the interpretation of Exodus 12.

3. *Egyptian Rituals as Comparanda*

The formation of the grand exodus narrative in the first millennium BCE owes many of its themes and motifs to Egyptian texts and ideas. The editors of the narrative appropriated such texts and ideas for the Israelite cause, to mention only studies by Rendsburg and Schipper.[63] While

---

59. Propp, *Exodus 1–18*, pp. 434-39. Like *fidya*, *Pesah* and *Maṣṣot* are for Propp rites of passage, pp. 435 and 443.
60. Dahm, *Opferkult und Priestertum in Alt-Israel*, pp. 156-60.
61. Dahm, *Opferkult und Priestertum in Alt-Israel*, p. 151.
62. Propp, *Exodus*, p. 442, mentions bloodsmearings in fourth-century CE Egypt in conjunction with the vernal equinox. This is one millennium after the time of late Israel and Judah and does not seem to have precursors in contemporary Late Period Egypt.
63. G. A. Rendsburg, 'The Egyptian Sun-God Ra in the Pentateuch', *Henoch* 10 (1988), pp. 3-15; Rendsburg, 'Moses as Equal to Pharaoh', in G. M. Beckman and T. J. Lewis (eds.), *Text, Artifact, and Image: Revealing Ancient Israelite Religion* (Brown Judaic Studies 346; Providence: Brown Judaic Studies, 2006), pp. 201-19. See also the following works by B. Schipper, 'Ägypten und Israel. Erkenntnisse und

Egyptian texts have often been used for comparisons with biblical motifs, such texts were mostly taken from the well-published literature of the second millennium, rather than the millennium after the Egyptian New Kingdom (1,100–100 BCE), the time of Israel's historical existence, the composition of the texts of the Hebrew Bible and their later redactions. I also contend that we need to compare Egyptian magical and ritual texts as the most likely source of inspiration because major parts of the Exodus narrative expose magical and ritual activities (the contest between Moses and pharaoh, the plagues, the Passover ritual, the parting of the sea, the Golden Calf). Establishing this level of comparison can shed significant new light on the interpretation and origin of elements of the Exodus narrative, and on the ritual of the Passover night that interests us here.[64]

3.1. *A General View: Rituals and the Aversion of Plagues and Threats*
In terms of how the ritual action is classified by the Egyptian titles of protection rituals,[65] the focus is either on the type of threat from which protection is sought ('To pacify Sakhmet'), or on the individual person

Perspektiven', *Theologische Literaturzeitung* 134 (2009), pp. 1153-64; 'Die "eherne Schlange"'. Zur Religionsgeschichte und Theologie von Num 21,4-9', *ZAW* 121 (2009), pp. 369-87; 'Egypt and Israel: The Ways of Cultural Contact in the Late Bronze- and Iron-Age', *Journal of Ancient Egyptian Interconnections* 4.3 (2012), pp. 30-47; 'Kultur und Kontext—Zum Kulturtransfer zwischen Ägypten und Israel/ Juda in der 25., und 26. Dynastie', *Studien zur altägyptischen Kultur* 29 (2001), pp. 307-19; 'Schlangenbeschwörung in Ägypten und Israel', in F. Hartenstein and M. Pietsch (eds.), *Israel zwischen den Mächten—Studien zum Alten Testament in seiner altorientalischen Umwelt* (FS S. Timm) (AOAT 364; Münster: Ugarit Verlag, 2009, pp. 265-82; *Israel und Ägypten in der Königszeit., Die kulturellen Kontakte von Salomo bis zum Fall Jerusalems* (OBO 170; Fribourg: Academic Press; Göttingen: Vandenhoeck & Ruprecht, 1999. For a comprehensive study of the significance of Egypt in Rabbinic Judaism, see R. Ulmer, *Egyptian Cultural Icons in Midrash* (Berlin: W. de Gruyter, 2009).

    64. For the debate, see Propp, *Exodus 1–18*, pp. 427-61.

    65. For general treatments of Egyptian magic and rituals, see M. Etienne, *Heka. Magie et envoûtement dans l'Egypte ancienne* (Paris: Éditions de la réunion des musées nationaux, 2000); Y. Koenig, *La magie en Egypte: à la recherche d'une définition. Actes du colloque organisé par le Musée du Louvre, les 29 et 30 septembre 2000* (Paris: Documentation française, 2002); T. Schneider, 'Die Waffe der Analogie. Altägyptische Magie als System', in K. Gloy and M. Bachmann (eds.), *Das Analogiedenken. Vorstöße in ein neues Gebiet der Rationalitätstheorie,* (Freiburg: K. Alber, 2000), pp. 31-85. For rituals in Graeco-Roman Egypt, see J. F. Quack (ed.), *Ägyptische Rituale der griechisch-römischen Zeit* (Orientalische Religionen in der Antike; Tübingen: Mohr Siebeck, 2013).

or object that needs protection ('Protection of the flesh of pharaoh'). The most menacing threats were deities (such as Sakhmet, the goddess of plague and pestilence[66]) and demons[67] inflicting illnesses and death, particularly during dangerous periods of the year (e.g., after the annual Nile inundation when the 'plague of the year' occurred; at night; during the five epagomenal days [361–365] of the Egyptian year). Such demons often acted in groups and were the executioners of the divine will of major deities, but they also acted individually and were described with their particular demonic features and skills. The most significant targets needing protection were the ordered existence of this world, and the Egyptian king as its earthly guarantor. I give here a number of representative quotes pertaining to the 'plague of the year' caused by Sakhmet, from texts ranging from the New Kingdom to the Ptolemaic period:

> The might of the Flame appears…
> When she has smashed the Two Lands with the fear of her,
> When she has burned everything to ashes,
> As life and death belong to her at her discretion.
> When she has given disaster throughout the two lands
> And assigned all slaughterers to their massacres.[68]
> *(The goddess is addressed)*
> One performs for you the sacrifices in the form of what you love.
> When you turn your face to the south, north, west and east,
> The fear of you is in them,
> Wherever you emerge on the (valley-)roads and the mountains.
> You instill the fear of you in the gods.

---

66. For a recent treatment of some aspects of Sakhmet, see A. von Lieven, 'Wein, Weib und Gesang: Rituale für die Gefährliche Göttin', in C. Metzner-Nebelsick (ed.), *Rituale in der Vorgeschichte, Antike und Gegenwart. Neue Forschungen und Perspektiven von Archäologie, Ägyptologie, Altorientalistik, Ethnologie und vergleichender Religionsgeschichte. Interdisziplinäre Tagung vom 1.–2. Februar 2002, Berlin* (Leidorf: Rahden, 2003), pp. 47-55. For spells against Seth, see N. Fiedler, 'Sprüche gegen Seth. Bemerkungen zu drei späten Tempelritualen' (Ph.D. diss., Universität Heidelberg 2011. Online: www.ub.uni-heidelberg.de/archiv/13643.

67. R. Lucarelli, 'Demonology during the Late Pharaonic and Greco-Roman Periods in Egypt', *Journal of Ancient Near Eastern Religions* 11 (2011), pp. 109-25, and 'Demons (benevolent and malevolent)', in Jacco Dieleman and Willeke Wendrich (eds.), *UCLA Encyclopedia of Egyptology* (Los Angeles, 2010). Online: http://escholarship.org/uc/item/1r72q9vv.

68. J.-C. Goyon, *Le rituel du sḥtp Sḫmt au changement de cycle annuel. D'après les architraves du temple d'Efou et textes parallèles, du Nouvel Empire à l'époque ptolémaique et romaine* (Bibliothèque d'étude 141; Cairo: L'institut Français d'archéologie orientale, 2006), p. 27. I follow Goyon's translation but have made some changes on the basis of the Ptolemaic text here and in the following passages.

Your plague is throughout the country's populace.
You devour blood,
You equip the gods who are over the fetters
On the days of your 'wanderers'.[69]
You have split the mountains with your plagues,
You have killed all the livestock through fear of you,
Lady of fear, who causes great trembling,
Who captures the gods in her radiance.[70]
(The goddess speaks)
I am the mighty one, I have power over my enemies,
I make the demons go out on their tasks
Millions tremble before me, being docile.[71]
A Spell for Purifying Anything in/from the plague
May your emissaries be burned, Sakhmet!
Let your slaughterers retreat, Bastet.
No year(-demon) passes along to rage against my face!
Your breeze will not reach me!
I am Horus, (set) over the wanderers, oh Sakhmet.
I am your Horus, Sakhmet, I am your Unique One, Uto!
I will not die on account of you—I am the Rejoiced One.
I am the Jubilated one, oh son of Bastet!
Do not fall upon me, oh Devourer!
Tousled ones, do not fall upon me, do not approach me—
I am the King inside his shrine!
[an instruction follows of how to speak this spell over an amulet]
A means to scare away the plague,
to ward off the passing of slaughterers along anything edible,
as well as along a bedroom. (from Pap. Edwin Smith)[72]

A correlation between the protection of the king and the protection of Egypt that is visible here occurs in many other texts, such as a Late Period naos from Bubastis[73] or a ritual papyrus in Vienna with the title 'Protection of the flesh of pharaoh'.[74] In the latter, Sakhmet's plague is additionally averted from cattle, birds, and the fish in the Nile:

69. Goyon, *Le rituel du shtp Shmt*, p. 28. A type of demon, see the discussion below.

70. Goyon, *Le rituel du shtp Shmt*, p. 41.

71. Goyon, *Le rituel du shtp Shmt*, p. 42.

72. J. F. Borghouts, *Ancient Egyptian Magical Texts* (Leiden: Brill, 1978), p. 17.

73. V. Rondot, 'Une monographie bubastite', *Bulletin de l'Institut Français d'Archéologie Orientale* 89 (1989), pp. 249-70.

74. N. Flessa, *'(Gott) schütze das Fleisch des Pharao'. Untersuchungen zum magischen Handbuch pWien Aeg 8426* (Corpus Papyrorum Raineri Archeducis Austriae 27; Munich: K. G. Saur, 2006).

Withdraw your Impure one, Sakhmet,
may you loosen your arrow, Bastet.
Your rage to the ground!
This fury of yours which is the plague,
Retreat!…
Her rage is in the cattle,
The plague is in the birds,
Her fury is in the fish in the Nile.'[75]

In Exodus 12, the Passover demon slays human firstborns as well as the firstlings of the *bᵉhema*, a term used for cattle, domestic livestock, and animals in general. Instead of all the firstborn and firstlings of Exodus 12, a note from the Egyptian *Calendar of Lucky and Unlucky Days* that will be quoted below (see p. 70) more specifically says that all newborn children will necessarily die from the plague. In the context of the larger plague narrative of Exod 7.14–11.10 (continued in the killing of the first-born in Exod 12), it is worth noticing that many motifs of the biblical plagues have their precise equivalents in ritual texts describing the effects of the annual plague in Egypt, or the actions taken by particular demons.[76]

3.2. A Specific View: The Ritual for the Protection of Pharaoh at Night
For the more specific context of Exod 12, I propose to discuss an Egyptian ritual for the protection of pharaoh at night, called 'Bedroom of the Palace'.[77] It is preserved in Theban Papyrus Cairo 58027 of the late Ptolemaic period and the mammisi (birth sanctuaries of divine children) of Dendera and Edfu where the ritual is transferred to the protection of the child gods of Graeco–Roman temples. When the original text was

75. Flessa, *'(Gott) schütze das Fleisch des Pharao'*, p. 54. My translation differs from Flessa's in several instances.

76. By way of example, I mention the 'seven arrows' of the goddess Bastet (a possible form of appearance of Sakhmet), a group of demons that both menaced Egyptians but could also be instrumentalized for the protection of Egypt against enemies (see Rondot, 'Une monographie bubastite'). The fifth of these demons whose names are attested since the reign of Osorkon I (924–889 BCE) was called 'The one who is in the Nile flood who makes blood' (J. Osing, *Hieratische Papyri aus Tebtunis/1* [Copenhagen: Museum Tusculanum Press, 1998], p. 253). This could be understood as a demon who creates carnage in the Nile, and thus turns the Nile into blood (Exod 7.17-20).

77. A. H. Pries, *Das nächtliche Stundenritual zum Schutz des Königs und verwandte Kompositionen. Der Papyrus Kairo 58027 und die Textvarianten in den Geburtshäusern von Dendara und Edfu* (Studien zur Archäologie und Geschichte Altägyptens 27; Heidelberg: Heidelberger Orientverlag, 2009). For a general description of the text and its structure, see pp. 1-19.

composed is unclear, although the division of the text follows the New Kingdom (and later) books of the Underworld; the language is Middle Egyptian, although with some interference of later Egyptian grammatical forms.[78] Elements of the ritual are attested in a variety of other ritual texts that are more specifically conceived to offer protection from the annual plague after the Nile inundation, and for mothers and their newborn children, and which date back to the Middle and New Kingdoms. Comparable in structure and purpose is the late apotropaic ritual 'protection of the house', which was equally carried out before nightfall, originally for the king and secondarily for the temple house of gods.[79]

The ritual of Pap. Cairo 58027 offers protection of the pharaoh during the twelve hours of the night. It contains a specific recitation for every subsequent hour of the night when a protective deity is invoked who has to ward off malevolent demons that would harm pharaoh.[80] Pharaoh himself is equated with a specific god in every hour so as to assume divine powers himself. The standard wish of protection is as follows:

> May you be vigilant in your hour, may you watch over pharaoh, may you spread terror among (or: make tremble) those who are in the deep night, may you keep the wanderers away from his bedroom.[81]

The malevolent demons are called *wš3.w* 'Those of the night' and *šm3y.w*, 'wanderers', in related texts also *h3ty.w* ('slaughterers', and other terms; see the texts cited above), and are seen as being sent by Sakhmet or Bastet, variant appearances of the goddess of plague and pestilence. The designation *wšз.w* used for the demons ('those who are in the night') uses an Egyptian term (*wšз*) denoting the hours around midnight (the deep night), when according to other texts Osiris was believed to have been killed and Re was most remote on his nocturnal

---

78. Pries, *Das nächtliche Stundenritual*, p. 2 and passim for the grammatical forms; cf. Flessa, *'(Gott) schütze das Fleisch des Pharao'*, p. 14.

79. Pries, *Das nächtliche Stundenritual zum Schutz des Königs und verwandte Kompositionen*, p. 4. For the text, D. Jankuhn, *Das Buch 'Schutz des Hauses' (sз-pr)* (Bonn: R. Habelt, 1972).

80. Other texts invoke the divine protection of the king for both the day and the night, such as in a ritual comprising four clay spheres ritually equated with four deities and deposited in the places that needed protection (preserved in Edfu and Pap. Vienna Aeg 8426): 'One from among you is in the palace of the king of Upper and Lower Egypt / Another one from among you is behind him. / Another one from among you is the protection of his throne. / Another one from among you is the protection of his bed chamber / in order to make him safe day and night, and vice versa' (Goyon, *Le rituel du shtp Shmt*, p. 125).

81. Pries, *Das nächtliche Stundenritual zum Schutz des Königs und verwandte Kompositionen*, passim.

journey. For the sixth hour leading to midnight, the Theban papyrus is not preserved. In the version from Dendara, the pharaoh is indeed identified with the underworldly (Osirian) form of Re and is protected by Isis and Min, whereas as the attacking demon the Seth animal is mentioned. In the seventh hour (the hour after midnight), the king is given the protection of the sun god in the form of a winged scarab amulet and is equated with the sun god himself in an attempt to dispel the darkness of the night: 'The appearance of pharaoh is that of a living lion whose eyes are fire, and whose face is daylight'.[82] The endangerment by demonic forces at night is also a recurrent theme in other texts: In spells for the 'Lighting of the Torch', the torch is identified with Re and said to dispel 'Seth's might which is in the darkness',[83] and Pyramid Text §1334 already invokes protective gods to 'slay Seth and protect the Osiris NN (the deceased king) from his hand until it dawns'.[84]

The text of the hourly recitations is followed by a detailed description of the ritual procedure: images of the protective deities invoked for the successive hours of the night were drawn in ochre around the king's bed, and additionally an *udjat* eye in front of the bed in whose pupil the king had to be seated at the beginning of the ritual (more likely, a figurine of the king). In addition, the recipient of the ritual was anointed with a special unguent whose ingredients are explicated in a prescription,[85] and the same ointment was to be placed on 'every window [or: opening, *wsj*] of his house'.[86] The procedure of applying such unguents to windows and doors of the house reoccurs in a supplement to the papyrus aimed at the specific protection of the king in the night of New Year[87] and in other ritual texts.[88] In the case of bedrooms that were already contaminated with the plague of the year, brushing them with specific medicinal plants would cleanse them again (Pap. Edwin Smith 19, 18-20, 8),[89] a motif

---

82. Pries, *Das nächtliche Stundenritual*, p. 44; cf. pp. 46-47 for parallels of this motif.

83. D. C. Luft, *Das Anzünden der Fackel. Untersuchungen zu Spruch 137 des Totenbuches* (Studien zum altägyptischen Totenbuch 15; Wiesbaden: Harrassowitz, 2009), p. 43.

84. Luft, *Das Anzünden der Fackel*, p. 37.

85. Pries, *Das nächtliche Stundenritual*, pp. 87-90.

86. Pries, *Das nächtliche Stundenritual*, p. 89.

87. Pries, *Das nächtliche Stundenritual*, pp. 95-98. This is interesting with regard to the proclamation of the Passover event as the beginning of a new system of time-reckoning in Exod 12.2, either reference to a different calendric system or a symbolic new era, a question extensively discussed in the literature.

88. Pries, *Das nächtliche Stundenritual*, p. 89.

89. Pries, *Das nächtliche Stundenritual*, p. 89 n. 511.

noteworthy with regard to the use of a bunch of marjoram (Syrian hyssop)[90] to distribute the blood in Exod 12.22.

The ointment contains five (or six, in the second prescription) medicinal plants, anointing oil, goose fat, honey, and another liquid.[91] In more general terms, anointing is an activity providing power and legitimacy.[92] It is interesting to notice that ointments played a significant role in the protection of Osiris at night in the *Stundenwachen* performed for him.[93] The fragrance of unguents also had a smoothing effect, maybe desirable in the appeasement of Bastet, a form of the plague goddess, who seems to have had a close genuine association with ointments.[94]

In contrast to the Egyptian ritual texts, in Exodus 12 blood from sacrificed sheep or goat is applied on the doorposts. On the significance of this rite, opinions differ widely, ranging from proposals to see it as a repellent, to the use of blood in purification rites.[95] From an Egyptological viewpoint, the blood of sacrificial animals can signify the blood of killed enemies of the world order and signal the triumph over inimical forces.[96]

90. Propp, *Exodus 1–18*, p. 407.

91. Pries, *Das nächtliche Stundenritual zum Schutz des Königs und verwandte Kompositionen*, pp. 88 and 94-95.

92. E. Martin-Pardey, 'Salbung', *Lexikon der Ägyptologie* 5 (1985), pp. 367-69.

93. H. Junker, *Die Stundenwachen in den Osirismysterien nach den Inschriften von Dendera, Edfu und Philae* (Vienna: Hölder, 1910), p. 2. For the text, see now H. Pries, *Die Stundenwachen im Osiriskult* (Wiesbaden: Harrassowitz, 2011).

94. A. K. Capel and G. E. Markoe (eds.), *Mistress of the House, Mistress of Heaven: Women in Ancient Egypt* (Cincinnati: Cincinnati Art Museum, 1996), p. 209. Her name means 'The one from the city of ointment'.

95. Dahm, *Opferkult und Priestertum in Alt-Israel*, pp. 141-68; C. Eberhart, *Studien zur Bedeutung der Opfer im Alten Testament: die Signifikanz von Blut- und Verbrennungsriten im kultischen Rahmen* (Neukirchen–Vluyn: Neukirchener Verlag, 2002), pp. 277-78; Propp, *Exodus 1–18*, pp. 435-39; H.-U. Weidemann, *Der Tod Jesu im Johannesevangelium: Die erste Abschiedsrede als Schlüsseltext für den Passions- und Osterbericht* (BZNW 122; Berlin: W. de Gruyter 2004), pp. 427-29.

Acording to C. Berner, it would be no more than a narrative invention by P to provide an etiology for Passover. C. Berner, *Die Exoduserzählung, Das literarische Werden einer Ursprungslegende Israels* (FAT 73; Tübingen: Mohr Siebeck, 2010), pp. 84-85.

96. Sacrifical animals are equated with evil forces; in a mythological episode preserved in the ritual of 'Breaking Open the Soil', Seth and his followers, who had taken the form of goats to attack Osiris, were slaughtered; their blood soaked the soil. W. A. Guglielmi, 'Erdaufhacken', *Lexikon der Ägyptologie* 1 (1975), pp. 1261-63.

3.3. *The Passover Demon in an Egyptian Perspective*

On the demonic nature of the *mašḥit* who strikes blindly and does not tell the Israelite houses from the Egyptian ones, compare the comments made by W. H. C. Propp and J. D. Levenson:

> The paschal blood rite seems out of character with biblical theology. Throughout Exodus 7–11, Yahweh easily distinguished between Hebrew and Egyptian households, without the help of blood. But now, even though the Destroyer is an aspect of God himself, Yahweh instructs Israel to treat it as an amoral being that slays blindly unless checked—i.e., a demon; compare Yahweh's quasi-demonic behavior in 4:24-26. The very name *Pesaḥ* 'protection' suggests inherent apotropaic powers. Not too far beneath the surface, then, we glimpse a primitive Israelite or pre-Israelite belief that, in some fashion, the paschal blood averts a supernatural threat.[97]

> The Destroyer is YHWH in his aspect of slayer of the first-born son. This is not an aspect of the Deity that the biblical tradition is inclined to celebrate, and for obvious reasons. It is, after all, an aspect that recalls Molech and the monster on the Pozo Moro Tower more than the gracious and delivering god of the Exodus.[98]

Rather than to ascribe this feature to a 'primitive Israelite belief' and see it as 'out of character with biblical theology', it seems a genuine example of *divine* and *demonic ambiguity*, well represented in deities and demons engineering disaster in ancient Egypt, as we will see below. In a response to an article by Rita Lucarelli,[99] David Frankfurter has recently commented on such *demonic ambiguity*:

> Lucarelli's paper demonstrates how the identification *of* the demonic and protection *from* the demonic in ancient cultures involved, first and foremost, the description of *liminality*: what lies *between* here and there, *beyond* the village or *before* sacred zones; how to evaluate the ambiguous theophany, the *wrath* of a temple god, and the vicious weaponry of a gate-protector. By describing, naming, and listing liminal zones and beings you can control their powers; you can *re-place* those beings as either minions of demon-masters, or as verbally vanquished by a protector god, or as fulfilling a *locative* function as a gate-keeper that the incomer can pacify with the right spell. As hard as it may be to understand from a modern (American) vantage, steeped as we are in

---

97. Propp, *Exodus 1–18*, p. 436.

98. J. D. Levenson, *The Death and Resurrection of the Beloved Son: The Transformation of Child Sacrifice in Judaism and Christianity* (New Haven: Yale University Press, 1993), p. 46.

99. Lucarelli, 'Demonology during the Late Pharaonic and Greco-Roman Periods in Egypt'.

apocalyptic Protestantism, demons in the ancient and late antique Mediterranean world were rarely 'evil' but rather hovered in a zone of uncertainty.[100]

As 2 Sam 24.16 and Ps 78.48-51 indicate (see Utzschneider and Oswald's comments cited above, pp. 60-61), the *mašḥit* of Exodus 12 was most likely the demon of plague. William Propp also quotes *Jub.* 49.15 from the second century BCE as articulating *Pesaḥ*'s primal significance: 'The plague will not come to kill or to smite during that year when they have observed the Passover in its (appointed) time'.[101] This evidence correlates the *mašḥit* closely with the demons sent by the Egyptian goddess of plague, Sakhmet/Bastet, both of whom display merciless and all-encompassing rage. In the Book of the Heavenly Cow, Sakhmet has to be averted from killing the humans by means of a trick: a field is flooded with beer made to appear like blood by mixing it with red ochre, and the blood-thirsty Sakhmet thus becomes drunk and placated.[102] The hemerologies of the New Kingdom (*Calendar of Lucky and Unlucky Days*) indicate for the third month of the inundation season, day 20:

> Coming forth of Bastet, the lady of Ankhtawy, in front of Re,
> so furious that the god could not withstand in her proximity.
> Whoever is born on this day dies of the plague of the year.[103]

As the most powerful divine source of destruction, the goddess was at the same time the most powerful potential defender of human life if it was possible to placate her and to obtain her mercy.[104] Sakhmet offers protection to whoever was not struck by the death inflicted by her 'wanderers';[105] Bastet protects the king from the slaughterers of Atum and their arrows; she is a bastion against any malignant fever, and against any evil wind of the year.[106] Their avatar Hathor/Ernutet is called 'the shutter of a window that cannot be opened',[107] as opposed to the

---

100. D. Frankfurter, 'Master-Demons, Local Spirits, and Demonology in the Roman Mediterranean World: An Afterword to Rita Lucarelli', *Journal of Ancient Near Eastern Religions* 11 (2011), p. 129.

101. Propp, *Exodus 1–18*, p. 437.

102. E. Hornung, *Der Mythos von der Himmelskuh. Eine Ätiologie des Unvollkommenen* (3d ed.; OBO 46; Fribourg: Academic Press; Göttingen: Vandenhoeck & Ruprecht, 1997).

103. C. Leitz, *Tagewählerei: das Buch ḥȝt nḥḥ pḥ.wy ḏt und verwandte Texte* (2 vols.; Ägyptologische Abhandlungen 55; Wiesbaden: Harrassowitz, 1994), p. 134.

104. Cf. the hymns in Goyon, *Le rituel du sḥtp Sḥmt*, pp. 34, 92.

105. Goyon, *Le rituel du sḥtp Sḥmt*, p. 76.

106. Goyon, *Le rituel du sḥtp Sḥmt*, p. 93.

107. Goyon, *Le rituel du sḥtp Sḥmt*, p. 75.

window as a dangerous access way for demons that needed to be protected (as aimed at in the ritual). A supplication to Sakhmet-Bastet-Ernutet asks for the king to be spared:

> O goddess, you have spoken with your own mouth,
> Spare your beloved son, the son of Re,
> From the wanderers who are in your retinue.
> Do not cause the destruction of the king of Upper and Lower Egypt
> In the uproar since he is a member of your crew.
> He knows your name and he knows the name of the wanderers and the slaughterer in your following.
> May you smite, in his place, one man from the million in the plague of the year.[108]

This twofold nature was a preponderant theme in Egyptian theology and the need of appeasement a major cultic concern. The ritual texts describe in detail placation offerings for these goddesses that were carried out at dawn, mainly consisting of meat and bread.[109] In the first millennium BCE, this cultic worship for the purpose of appeasement was also extended to demons who were thus turned into protective deities; an interesting case for this *demonic ambiguity* comprises twelve gods, as in the ritual 'Bedroom of the Palace' adduced above.[110]

4. *Conclusion and Historical Context*

Commentators on Exodus 12 perceive it as an amalgamation of rituals from different original contexts that were secondarily reinterpreted and combined with the plague and Exodus narrative. In his encyclopedic

---

108.   Goyon, *Le rituel du sḥtp Sḥmt*, p. 116.

109.   E.g., Goyon, *Le rituel du sḥtp Sḥmt*, pp. 63, 76: offerings of antelopes, cranes, ducks and other meat, bread and white bread, cakes, beer, and frankincense; p. 92: offerings of grilled meat, fat, and ducks; p. 104: offerings of different kinds of bread.

110.   M. J. Raven, 'Charms for Protection during the Epagomenal Days', in J. van Dijk (ed.), *Essays on Ancient Egypt in Honour of Herman te Velde* (Leiden: Brill, 1997), pp. 275-92. Pap. Leiden I 346 starts with a copy of the *Book of the Last Days of the Year*, invoking twelve gods identified as 'slaughterers who stand in waiting upon Sakhmet, who have come forth from the Eye of Re, messengers everywhere present in the districts, who bring slaughtering about, who create uproar, who hurry through the land, who shoot their arrows from their mouths, who see from afar', followed by a protection ritual 'to save a man from the plague of the year…to placate the gods in the retinue of Sakhmet and Thoth'. In the following 'Book of the Five Epagomenal Days', a vignette depicts the twelve invoked demons/gods who are drawn on linen amulets and placed 'at a man's throat' for his protection.

Exodus commentary, William Propp identifies three major questions about *Pesaḥ*: 'Why is it limited to the evening, the doorway and the springtime?'[111] He concludes that these aspects of the festival can be answered by seeing it as a specialized form of the *fidya* ritual known from the Islamic Middle East—if the latter was indeed pre-Islamic and pre-Israelite. Both *Pesaḥ* and *Maṣṣot* (the latter maybe a rite of annual purification) would later have been attached to the Moses tradition and reinterpreted as commemorative events: 'There arose the etiological legend of the first *Pesaḥ* of Egypt, when the rite redeemed Israel from two predicaments: a plague (*via* vicarious sacrifice) and servitude'.[112] A similar attachment would have occurred with the previously independent and pre-Israelite idea of God's special relationship with firstborn sons: 'Again, there was an effort to attach the institution to Moses. The story arose that, on the paschal night, Yahweh killed Egypt's firstborn, while Israel, God's firstborn, was ransomed.'[113]

As there is no scholarly consensus on the historical context of these rituals and reinterpretations, nor a less disparate situation of exegetical scholarship to allow for any clarity about the stages and the historical contexts of the narrative itself, the approach adopted here is more modest: it introduces to the scholarly dialogue Egyptian ritual texts that have been entirely absent from the debate in the past. The suggestion is that the rituals and motifs that the narrative places within an ancient Egyptian context could be indeed borrowed from the Egyptian ritual repertoire, rather than seeing in them a secondary reinterpretation of (pre-)Israelite institutions when there arose a narrative about Israel's salvation from Egypt. This repertoire provides Egyptian parallels for the figure and the ritual context of the demon of Passover sent by Yahweh in the form of the demons sent by the Egyptian goddess of plague Sakhmet during the 'plague of the year' and other perilous times such as the epagomenal days and the night. The protection ritual 'Bedroom of the Palace' protects the house of pharaoh and his life during the night; it is equally celebrated at nightfall and comprises a ritual not identical but similar to the Passover one in which the openings of the house were anointed in order to avert the attack of demons. The Egyptian rituals also presuppose a similar nexus between a more general plague and, more specifically, the death of pharaoh('s son) as it is visible in Exodus 12's continuation of the plague cycle in Exodus 7–11.

111.   Propp, *Exodus 1–18*, p. 440.
112.   Propp, *Exodus 1–18*, p. 457.
113.   Propp, *Exodus 1–18*, p. 457.

In this vein, the ritual to prevent the demon from entering the house of Israelites and instead to have the demon kill the king's son (and the other firstborn Egyptians) could be an *appropriation of Egyptian rituals aimed at that very protection.* By removing the divine protection from the Egyptians, assigning it to Israel, and dispatching his slaughtering demon to pharaoh's palace, Yahweh indeed 'brings judgment on all the gods of Egypt' (Exod 12.12)—the gods who had failed as the protective deities of the twelve hours of the night.[114] The idea of an adoption of these elements of Egyptian rituals by Israelite authors suits particularly well certain of the exegetical models presented above, such as those suggesting a genuine connection of the plague cycle, the killing of the firstborn, and the blood rite,[115] but it does in no way preclude other scenarios. It is outside the scope of the present study to suggest a precise historical scenario in which such an appropriation[116] would have taken place,[117] and probably outside of what can currently be inferred on the

114.   Admittedly, Exod 12.12 is commonly seen as a late addition to the text. As a side note, it is intriguing to notice the invocation of the protective god of the 11th hour, Horus of Dawn, which states: 'You are the perfect golden calf belonging to the breast of Hathor, the appearance of the lord of the sky and of the two lands, the lord of the land of turquoise (= the Sinai)' (Pries, *Das nächtliche Stundenritual zum Schutz des Königs und verwandte Kompositionen*, pp. 72-74). It may be interesting to explore further this tradition of Horus as the 'golden calf and lord of the Sinai' in the context of the discussion of the golden calf episode in Exod 32. For the debate on the golden calf, see H.-C. Schmitt, 'Die Erzählung vom Goldenen Kalb Ex. 32* und das Deuteronomistische Geschichtswerk', in S. L. McKenzie, T. Römer and H. H. Schmid (eds.), *Rethinking the Foundations: Historiography in the Ancient World and in the Bible* (FS J. van Seters; BZAW 294; Berlin: W. de Gruyter, 2000), pp. 235-50; repr. in H.-C. Schmitt, *Theologie in Prophetie und Pentateuch. Gesammelte Schriften* (BZAW 310; Berlin: W. de Gruyter, 2001), pp. 311-25.

115.   E.g., Dozeman's according to which the killing of the firstborn was part of the non-P plague narrative, as was the older passage on the *Pesaḥ* ritual in 12.20-23. These later verses comprise a protection ritual but lack elements (most importantly, the Passover meal) extant in the P version. It seems feasible that such elements are a secondary addition, and not part of the original ritual practice.

116.   Cf. the demonstration, on the later traditions of the 'lepers' episode, by Gruen, 'The Use and Abuse of the Exodus Story', pp. 113-14: 'Jewish inventiveness expropriated Egyptian myth in order to insert their own heroes, their religious superiority, and even their military triumphs... The Jews freely adapted the Exodus legend and infiltrated native fables in order to elevate their own part in the history of their adopted land.'

117.   A general familiarity with the Egyptian 'plague of the year' can probably be inferred from the statement Amos 4.10, 'I send a plague among you in the way of Egypt'. New consideration also deserves the hypothesis that the term *Pesaḥ* is

basis of the opaque situation of scholarship. If it occurred, it gave ancient Egyptian rituals, embedded and refracted within memories of the exodus story, a continuous reception until the present.[118]

Egyptian ('the striking'; cf. Exod 12.12, 23, 29; as a name of the occurrence, not the agent, in modification of a hypothesis first suggested by M. Görg, 'Paesah [Pascha]: Fest des "schlagenden" Gottes?', *BN* 43 [1988], pp. 7-11; repr. in M. Görg [ed.], *Aegyptiaca—Biblica* [Wiesbaden: Harrassowitz, 1991], pp. 168-72 [festival of 'the smiting god']).

118.   William Propp (*Exodus 1–18*, p. 439) has proposed that the plague demon itself lives on in a transfigured form: 'Though demons may be repelled or ignored, they are harder to kill. Our paschal demon survived, so to speak, by donning various disguises. Most obviously, he was absorbed into Yahweh's persona as the Destroyer. I also suspect that the characterization of the Pharaoh of the oppression as a would-be baby-killer (1.16, 22) owes an unconscious debt to the paschal demon. And the antique sprite is still with us, but defanged, as it were. He has become a kindly being, in fact a Jew. The Hebrews of Egypt bloodied their door frames in order to shunt the Destroyer onto their enemies. Nowadays the traditional Passover Seder ends with the opening of a door and a call for the destruction of infidels. But then a genial spirit is symbolically invited into each house to share the "blood of the grape": none other than the prophet Elijah, harbinger of the Messiah.'

A LATE PUNIC NARRATIVE ABOUT DISRUPTED SACRIFICE? HR. MEDEINE N 2

Philip C. Schmitz

Dedicating this study to Paul Mosca provides a welcome opportunity to honor one of the finest scholars of the linguistic and cultural tradition generally called 'Phoenician'. Our connection goes back to 1975, when we met in Vancouver. Some years later, Paul graciously agreed to serve on my dissertation committee. His comments prevented more than one error in my text, and in the years since then he has offered anchoring wisdom in critiques of several other projects I undertook. The argument below has not had the benefit of his review; nonetheless, I hope that it will serve as a tribute to his important contributions to the study of Punic sacrifice, Semitic epigraphy, and the larger world of the Western Phoenicians. I offer it with warm sentiments of friendship.

The Neo-Punic and Latin bilingual dedication Hr. Medeine N 2 was discovered during excavations by Alfred Merlin in Temple L at ancient Althiburos, modern Hr. Medeine.[1] The surviving Neo-Punic text is inscribed on one of three fragments of soft limestone, conserved in the Musée du Bardo, Tunis. The Neo-Punic and Latin texts were first published in 1908 by Poinssot,[2] with further treatments offered in the following decades by Clermont-Ganneau,[3] Merlin,[4] Vassel,[5] Chabot,[6] Février,[7]

1. A. Merlin, *Forum et maisons d'Althiburos* (Paris: Leroux, 1913), p. 14.

2. L. Poinssot, 'Note sur les foullies à Medeina, l'ancien Althiburos', *Bulletin archéologique du Comité des Travaux historiques et scientifiques* (1908), p. ccxxiv, and pl. xlv.

3. C. Clermont-Ganneau, *Annuaire du Collège de France* 65 (1909).

4. Merlin, *Forum et maisons*, p. 59.

5. E. Vassel, 'Sur la bilingue d'Althiburos', *Revue Tunisienne* (1916), pp. 278-85.

6. J.-B. Chabot, 'Inscriptions carthaginoises', *Bulletin archéologique du Comité des Travaux historiques et scientifiques* (1943–45), pp. 289-90.

7. J. Février, 'Une corporation de l'encens à Althiburos', *Semitica* 4 (1951–52), pp. 19-23.

and Röllig.[8] The critical edition of the Neo-Punic text appears as Hr. Medeine N 2 in Jongeling's handbook.[9] The Latin text is published also as *CIL* viii, 27774, and separately by ben Abdallah.[10]

From the published photographs[11] it is difficult to establish the right-hand margin of the original text with much precision. In the transcription of the text below, I suggest a restoration of six letters at the beginning of line 2. The length of the restoration appears to fit within the probable space of the original right margin of the text. There can nonetheless be no certainty about the correctness of this restoration. The suggested restoration at the beginning of line 4 is likewise uncertain; in line 5 restoration is only partial, and mostly speculative. The first line of the extant Neo-Punic text continues a portion of a narrative that must already have begun in a preceding column, now lost.

Neo-Punic Text

1   [']š ytn' lyt 'ktrt b 'ym š k 'rnm
2   [w k'rm ']š 'y šl nqšm yk ytb wbyt š 't
3   [lk'rm b]ṣ 'n k 'tšwmywš knš' š 't
4   [whk'rm š]ṭ' š 'ṭrnyn' bn š 'ṭr
5   [nyn' . . y]šb š 't brkb 'l bn mtn
6   [ ]š 't

Translation of Neo-Punic Text

1   [w]ho placed green garlands on the helixes (of the horns) of their rams.
2   [And rams t]hat they had not caught were ensnared. Stricken, they bleated, and ewes were coming
3   [to the rams in the] flock as ewes gathered *correspondingly*,
4   [and the rams roa]med about. Saturnine son of Satur-
5   [nine . . retu]rned the ewes of Barikbal son of Mattan
6   [ ] ewes

8. Röllig in *KAI*, inscription no. 160 (transliterated text); vol. 2, pp. 149-50 (commentary).

9. Karel Jongeling, *Handbook of Neo-Punic Inscriptions* (Tübingen: Mohr Siebeck, 2008), pp. 157-8.

10. Zeinab Benzina ben Abdallah, *Catalogue des Inscriptions Latines Paiennes du musée du Bardo* (Publications de l'École française de Rome 92; Rome: École Française de Rome, 1986), p. 148, no. 380a-b; pl. 380a-b. The photograph published in this *Catalogue* as pl. 380a is one of the best published photographs of the Neo-Punic text.

11. Poinssot, 'Note', pl. xlv; ben Abdallah, *Catalogue*, pl. 380a-b.

Latin Text[12]

(a)
Quod bonum, fau[stum, fe]/[l]ixque sit sodalibus?]
/ [- - - - - -] isigne qui u[elit - - -] / [- - - - -]
-]ISA Iouis [- - - / - - - in] templo po[nere] / [- - -
- ae]difici [- - - - - -]

(b)
- - - - - -]NI (denarios) L/[- - - - - -]animo / [- - -
- - -]IC Aescu/[lapi]i et Iovis.
[sac(erdos) publ]ic(us) ?

Before discussing the Neo-Punic portion of the inscription, I must consider the apparent relationship between the Latin and Late Punic versions.[13] The inscription appears to have been bilingual in its original condition. An architectural frieze runs along the upper margin of the stone.[14] Immediately beneath the frieze is the extant portion of the inscription in Neo-Punic script. Centered below the fifth line in Neo-Punic script is an incised horizontal palm-frond decoration that serves as a separator. Below the decoration are centered six lines of Latin characters (on the main fragment and a smaller joining piece). A third fragment[15] bears the end portions of four additional lines in Latin characters.

The opening clause of the Latin text[16] employs the formula 'bonum, fau[stum, fe]/[l]ixque', the first two adjectives of which are approximated in the Late Punic expression *n 'm wbrk*, 'pleasant and blessed'.[17] The formula *bym n 'm wbrk*, 'on a pleasant and blessed day', occurs at the beginning[18] of Late Punic votive inscriptions from Dougga, Sidi Ahmed el-Hachmi, Teboursouk, Ksar Lemsa, Constantine, and Ksiba

---

12. The editor summarizes the content thus: 'Il est probablement question d'un don de 50 deniers fait au temple d'Esculape et de Jupiter par un groupe de donateurs, membres d'une association(l. 2: *sodalibus*?)' (ben Abdallah, *Catalogue*, p. 148).

13. Neo-Punic refers to the script style of the inscription; Late Punic refers to the language of the text.

14. ben Abdallah, *Catalogue*, p. 148 and pl. 380a.

15. Ibid., pl. 380b.

16. Ibid., p. 148 and pl. 380a.

17. For examples, see *DNWSI* 451 (s.v. ywm 7), and Jongeling, *Handbook of Neo-Punic Inscriptions*, p. 4 (Hr. Ghayadha N 1), p. 176 (Teboursouk N 1); and p. 391 (s.v. ym).

18. At Hr. Ghayadha, the formula concludes the text of the inscription.

Mraou.[19] Because the formula occurs at the beginning of the Latin version of the inscription, it seems reasonable to assume that an equivalent formula began the Late Punic version of the inscription. Because the extant fragments represent different sections of their respective inscriptions, however, I do not attempt to correlate the Latin and Punic versions, but present only an interpretation of the Punic version.

Commentary on Punic Text

Line 1
[']*š ytn' lyt 'ktrt b'ym š k'rnm*
[w]ho placed green garlands on the helixes (of the horns) of their rams

> *lyt* ($\sqrt{lwy_1}$?) n.f. pl. /luyūt/[20] 'garlands'; cf. Biblical Hebrew *loyâ* 'wreath' (RSV); 'spiral' (NJPS) 1 Kgs 7.29-30; see (*HALOT* 528); cf. *liwyâ* 'wreath', Prov 1.9 (BDB 531); Ugaritic *lyt₁* 'garland' (*DUL* 507; *CLUC* 208).
>
> '*ktrt* adj. f. pl. /'aktarūt/. This adjective is probably cognate to the Middle Hebrew color term *'aktar* 'greenish'.[21] The etymon of both terms is probably Lat. *citr(us)* > Gk. κίτρον (LSJ 954).[22] The color of the citron ranges from medium to light green.[23]
>
> '*y* ($\sqrt{ġwy}$) G part. pl. /'uyyīm/[24] 'curves, helixes'; cf. Biblical Hebrew '*wh* 'be bent', D 'twist' (*HALOT* 796-97); cf. Ugaritic *ġwy* v. D 'twist' (*CLUC* 144).
>
> *k'r* (*kar* < $\sqrt{krr_2}$) n.m. 'ram' (*DNWSI* 535); cf. Biblical Hebrew *kar* 'ram' (*HALOT* 496); Ugaritic *kr* 'ram' (*DUL* 454; *CLUC* 190 s.v. *krr₂*). The letter *'ayin* {'} is a vowel sign in Neo-Punic orthography, here indicating /a/ or /ā/ (Kerr 2010: 39-42).

---

19. A. Ferjaoui, 'À propos de la formule *bym n'm wbym brk* dans les inscriptions néopuniques', in Yann Le Bohec (ed.), *L'Afrique, la Gaule, la Religion, à l'époque romaine: Mélanges à la mémoire de Marcel Leglay* (Collection Latomus 226; Brussels: Latomus, 1994), pp. 9-12; Jongeling, *Handbook of neo-Punic Inscriptions*, p. 176.

20. Possibly with assimilation *w > y*, /luwyūt/ > /luyyūt/.

21. M. Jastrow, *A Dictionary of the Targumim, the Talmud Babli and Yerushalmi, and the Midrashic Literature* (New York, 1903; repr., New York, Judaica Press, 1985), p. 66 s.v.

22. R. S. P. Beekes, *Etymological Dictionary of Greek* (Leiden: Brill, 2010), p. 705, s.v. κίτριον, classifies the stem κίτρ- as a borrowing from Latin.

23. Compare 'capital [architectural term]', *DNWSI*, p. 548, and Jongeling *Handbook of Neo-Punic Inscriptions*, pp. 157-58.

24. Possibly with assimilation *w > y*, /'uwyīm/ > /'uyyīm/.

Line 2

[wk'rm ']*š 'y šl nqšm yk ytb wbyt š't*
[And rams t]hat they had not caught were ensnared. Stricken, they
bleated. And ewes were coming

'y 'not' (*DNWSI* 43-44).
šl (√*šll₂*) v. G 3pl. /šallū/ 'they captured'; cf. Biblical Hebrew *šll₂*
　'plunder, capture, rob' (*HALOT* 1531); Ugaritic *šll* 'plunder, rob'
　(*DUL* 817; *CLUC* 323).
nqš (√*yqš*) v. N pl. /noqəšīm/ 'they were ensnared'[25]; cf. Biblical Hebrew
　yqš N 'be caught, ensnared' (*HALOT* 432); Ugaritic *yqš* 'fowler'
　(*DUL* 976; *CLUC* 365).
yk (√*nky*) v. K pass. pl. /yukkū/ 'stricken' (*DNWSI* 730); cf. Biblical
　Hebrew *nkh* Hip'īl 'strike, smite' (*HALOT* 697-98); Ugaritic *nkyt*
　'beaten' (*DUL* 632; *CLUC* 236).
ytb (√*ybb*) v. Yitpa'ēl perf. /yittabbū/ '(they) bleated/shouted' (cf. *DNWSI*
　431); Biblical Hebrew *ybb* in Judg 5.28 (*HALOT* 382); Jewish
　Aramaic *ybb* 'Etpa'ēl 'to shout' (Jastrow, *Dictionary*, p. 560).
byt (√*bw'*) G part. /bayyūt/ '(they f.) were entering' (*DNWSI* 146-47).
š't (*š'h₂*) n.f. pl. /šat/ 'ewes' (collective) (*DNWSI* 1094-95). Note Old
　Aramaic *š't* (*KAI* 222 A 21).[26]

My restoration of this line creates a complete line of text comprising 27
letters. I have adjusted all other line lengths to that length as an average.

Line 3

[l k'rm b]*ṣ'n k 'tšwmywš knš' š't*
[to the rams in the] flock as ewes gathered *correspondingly*,

ṣ'n n. 'flock (of sheep)' (*DNWSI* 954).
'tšwmywš adv. < Gk. ἀντί + ἰσόωμαι 'make equal': *ἀντισουμάιως
　'opposing on equal terms' (see LSJ 210 s.v. ἀντισόομαι 'oppose on
　equal terms', Th. 3.11).[27]
knš' (√*knš₁*) v. G 3pl. '(they) gathered' (*DNWSI* 520).

The word *'tšwmywš* transliterates an otherwise unattested adverbial
derivation from the attested Greek verb ἀντισόομαι. The final suffix -ως is
common in Greek adverbs of manner.[28] The verb is a nonce-word in

25. Note the parallel morphology of *nšt'm* 'they were feared' (*KAI* 26 A ii 4;
PPG³ 87 §141).
　26. The letter *{'}* is not etymological in Late Punic *š't*, but a vowel sign
representing /ā/ in this word (see R. M. Kerr, *Latino-Punic Epigraphy* [FAT 2/42;
Tübingen: Mohr Siebeck, 2010], pp. 39-42).
　27. On the verb ἰσόωμαι see H. von Frisk, *Griechisches etymologisches Wörter-
buch* (3 vols.; Heidelberg: Winter, 1960–72), p. 738 s.v. ἰσός.
　28. H. W. Smyth, *A Greek Grammar for Colleges* (rev. Gordon M. Messing;
Cambridge, Mass.: Harvard University Press, 1984), p. 100 §343; J. H. Moulton,

Classical Greek, appearing only in Thucydides (3.11), although it also occurs in several late-period sources, e.g., Josephus, *A.J.* 18.3.4 (ἀντισουμένων).[29]

The Late Punic spelling of the prefix *'t-* is to be vocalized /att-/ and must represent Greek ἀντ-,[30] with assimilation of the /n/ to the following /t/.[31] The Late Punic letter {w} probably represents the diphthong ου that appears in derived stems in the late period.[32] The use of {w} in the final syllable to represent the vowel of the adverbial suffix requires further consideration. Kerr observes that 'in Neo-Punic, {w} is not usually used to render /o/ (originally /ô/ < /aw/)'.[33] Neo-Punic does employ {w} for /o/ in a limited number of cases.[34] The sparsity of attested examples of this orthography in North African Neo-Punic introduces a degree of uncertainty whether the Neo-Punic spelling of the suffix *-ywš* represents Greek -ιως or the Latin *-ius*.[35]

An additional feature of the orthography of *'tšwmywš* merits comment: the intervocalic glide is represented by the consonant {y}. Phoenician representations of Greek words employ this orthography to represent an intervocalic glide as early as the eighth century BCE, as in the title *krntryš*, representing the Archaic Greek adjective *κορυνητηριος (*KAI* 26 A II 19; III 2-3, 4; C III 17, 19; IV 20).[36] Phoenician *-y-* also represents a glide in *bznty*, Greek Βυζαντια, both words that occur in a

and W. F. Howard, *A Grammar of New Testament Greek*. Vol. 2, *Accidence and Word-formation, with an Appendix on Semitisms in the New Testament* (Edinburgh: T. & T. Clark, 1929), pp. 163-64. I wish to thank Larry Hurtado for the second reference, and to express my appreciation to him and also to Markus Egetmeyer for valuable consultation concerning possible explanations of the presumed Greek form. The early version of my analysis that we discussed proved inaccurate, yet my gratitude remains undiminished.

29. Stephanus, *Thesaurus graecae linguae*, vol. 1, col. 988.

30. On the form, see P. Chantraine, *Dictionnaire étymologique de la langue grecque* (Paris: Klincksieck, 1968–80), p. 92 s.v. ἀντα (3).

31. *PPG*³ 30-31 §57. Middle Hebrew orthography represents Greek ἀντι-, as אנטי-, as in אנטיגרפין = ἀντίγραφον (S. Krauss, *Griechische und Lateinische Lehnwörter im Talmud, Midrasch und Targum* [Berlin: S. Calvary, 1898], vol. 1, p. 67; vol. 2, p. 599; M. Jastrow, *Dictionary*, p. 83 s.v).

32. Classical ἰσό-, later ἰσου- (Stephanus, *Thesaurus*, vol. 1, col. 988). Concerning {w} representing /u/ or /ū/, see Kerr, *Latino-Punic Epigraphy*, pp. 52-54.

33. Kerr, *Latino-Punic Epigraphy*, p. 54.

34. Kerr, *Latino-Punic Epigraphy*, p. 54.

35. That is, singular neuter of the comparative of the corresponding adjective, in Latin the regular comparative form of the adverb.

36. P. C. Schmitz, 'Phoenician KRNTRYŠ, Archaic Greek *ΚΟΡΥΝΗΤΗΡΙΟΣ, and the Storm God of Aleppo', *KUSATU* 11 (2009), pp. 119-60.

bilingual inscription (*KAI* 56). From the Persian period, the word *trpy* probably represents Greek τρόπαιο(ν).[37] Two impressions of a bilingual seal from the Hellenistic administrative building at Tel Kedesh (northeast quadrant, Corridor CB 3.8, Sealing A [K00 BL316], and Sealing B [K00 BL462]) read *kyndmyn* in the Phoenician legend (line 2), and in the Greek legend κοινοδημιον.[38] Glides in Greek final syllables are consistently represented with -*y*- in Phoenician orthography. The same spelling continues in Neo-Punic inscriptions. For example, the name *shlkny* (Hr. Maktar 64.16) derives from a personal name incorporating the Greek toponym Σελεύκεια.[39]

In writing the form *'tšwmywš* /attisuma[i]us/, the author of this Late Punic inscription employed a rare Greek word that had entered the language as a loanword.[40] The word's meaning involves the notion of equal and opposite action. My translation 'correspondingly' attempts an adequate expression of these elements.

Line 4
[whk'rm š]*ṭ' š'ṭrnyn' bn š'ṭr*
[and the rams roa]med about. Saturnine son of Satur-

[š]*ṭ'* ($\sqrt{šwṭ}$) v. 3 pl. /šaṭū/ 'they roamed about' (*DNWSI* 1116 s.v. *šwṭ₁*); cf. Biblical Hebrew *šwṭ₁* 'roam about' (*HALOT* 1439-40).

37. M. Yon and M. Sznycer, 'Une inscription phénicienne royale de Kition (Chypre)', *Comptes-rendus de l'Académie des inscriptions et belles-lettres* (1991), p. 807; *KAI* 288.1, 4.

38. D. T. Ariel and J. Naveh, 'Selected Inscribed Sealings from Kedesh in the Upper Galilee', *BASOR* 329 (2003), p. 66; Schmitz, 'Phoenician KRNTRYŠ', pp. 125-26.

39. Most likely as the Latin personal name *Selicanius*; see P. C. Schmitz, 'The Large Neo-Punic Inscription from Hr. Maktar: A Narrative of Military Service', *Studi Epigrafici e Linguistici* 28 (2011), p. 69 and n. 10. Concerning the final vowel, see *PPG*³ 142 §210b. On the interpretation of Latin personal names represented in Punic with final -*y* as vocatives, see Kerr, *Latino-Punic Epigraphy*, pp. 44, 68-74.

40. The assimilation of /n/ to the following /t/ in the prefix (see above and n. 31) is characteristic of Phoenician-Punic phonology, and can be interpreted as an indication that the word had become incorporated in the target language. Note the relevant summation by Noonan: 'loanwords typically evince various kinds of phonological and morphological adaptation, whereas code-switching does not', in Benjamin James Noonan, 'Foreign Loanwords and *Kulturwörter* in Northwest Semitic (1400–600 B.C.E.): Linguistic and Cultural Contact in Light of Terminology for Realia' (Ph.D. dissertation, Hebrew Union College—Jewish Institute of Religion, Cincinnati, 2012), pp.13-14. I am thankful to Dr. Noonan for providing me with a copy of his dissertation.

Line 5

[nyn' . . y]šb š't brkb 'l bn mtn

[nine . . . . retu]rned the ewes of Barikbal son of Mattan

[y]šb (√šwb) v. K 3 sing. 'he returned' (*DNWSI* 1114-15). In biblical law, the obligation to return (√šwb Hiph'il) stray sheep is established in Deut 22.1.

Line 6

[ ]š't

[ ] ewes (?)

It is difficult for a modern reader to fathom the purpose of such a dedicatory text as this. Not limiting itself to established formulas regularly employed in dedicatory contexts (and indeed evident in the Latin version of the text), the inscription includes a succinct narrative about the behavior of sheep in the course of a sacrificial offering.

The sacrificial context can be inferred because most surviving ancient dedications in Punic record some kind of sacrifice. Lexical hints of sacrifice occur in the phrase *lyt 'ktrt* 'green garlands', decorations which, according to the interpretation defended above, had been applied to the horns of the rams to be sacrificed. This procedure was common from the classical period, and can reasonably be anticipated at Hr. Medeine (Altiburus) in the Roman period.[41] The narrative character of the text is unusual when compared to most pre-Roman examples of Punic dedications,[42] but extended narratives become more frequent in Late Punic dedicatory inscriptions of the Roman period.[43]

41. Concerning this site, see Merlin, *Forum et maisons*, and Mongi Ennaïfer, *La cité d'Althiburos et l'édifice des Asclepieia* (Bibliothèque archéologique 1; Tunis: Ministère des Affaires Culturelles, 1976).

42. Although the Carthaginian Punic inscription *CIS* I 5510 (= *KAI* 302), apparently a votive dedication from 405 B.C.E., includes a significant narrative portion: C. R. Krahmalkov, 'A Carthaginian Report of the Battle of Agrigentum 406 B.C. (*CIS* I 5510.9 11)', *Rivista di Studi Fenici* 2 (1974), pp. 171-77; P. C. Schmitz, 'The Name "Agrigentum" in a Punic Inscription (*CIS* I 5510.10)', *Journal of Near Eastern Studies* 53 (1994), pp. 1-13; M. G. Amadasi Guzzo, 'Epigrafia e storia politica fenicia e punicha in Sicilia', in *Guerra e pace in Sicilia e nel Mediterraneo antico, VIII-III sec. a.C.: Arte, prassi e teoria della pace e della Guerra. Giornate internazionali di studi sull'area elima e la Sicilia occidentale 5th, 2003, Erice, Italy* (Pisa: Edizioni della Scuola Normale, 2006), pp. 693-702.

43. Note, for example, the important study by François Bron, 'Notes sur les inscriptions neo-puniques de Henchir Medeina (Althiburos)', *JSS* 54 (2009), pp. 141-47. The present writer has also recently studied Late Punic narrative dedications from Hr. Medeine-Altiburus: P. C. Schmitz, 'The Large Neo-Punic Inscription

The scene described in the Late Punic part of the inscription studied in the present context appears to involve a sacrifice of rams (LPun *k 'rnm*, 'their rams', line 1) in the course of which ewes (LPun *š 't*) from the same flock (LPun *ṣ 'n*) impulsively gathered. If my translation of *yk ytb* as 'stricken, they bleated' (line 2) is accurate,[44] and if the cry of the (presumed) rams is the motivation for the ewes' movements,[45] then the inscription may be expressing a concern about the procedure of the sacrifice. The intrusion of a Greek word in this context is all the more perplexing.

The writer may perhaps be forgiven for speculating that the circumstances of the sacrifice described in Hr. Medeine N 2 (= *KAI* 160) would not have been recorded in detail if they had been routine. As I understand the text, sacrificial procedures had been disrupted by a panic among the ewes, and some effort was required to recover frightened animals and restore them to their owners. I think it possible that such a situation could have been viewed as inauspicious.

The cause of the panic and inferred disruption appears to have been the 'striking' (√*nky*) of the rams that had been 'captured' (√*šll₂*) or 'esnared' (√*yqš*) (line 2). The brief account offers only a vague picture of events, but seems to involve the sacrifice of some portion of the rams (implied by the mention of garlands) and the less orderly capture and

---

(*KAI* 159) from Henchir Medeine (Althiburus) Translated and Interpreted', *Studi Epigrafici e Linguistici* 27 (2010), pp. 39-57; and Maktar: P. C. Schmitz, 'Late Punic Words for Textiles and Their Production', *Studi Epigrafici e Linguistici* 27 (2010), pp. 33-38; Schmitz, 'Large Neo-Punic Inscription from Hr. Maktar', *Studi Epigrafici e Linguistici* 28 (2011), pp. 67-94.

44. In the archaic Hebrew verse passage Judg 5.28, the verb *ybb* expresses the cry of anguish emitted by Sisera's mother upon learning of his death.

45. The oracle of Jer 25.34-36 employs an ironic role reversal in an implied comparison of military destruction to ritual sacrifice: הָרֹעִים הֵילִילוּ וְזַעֲקוּ, 'Wail, you shepherds, and cry' (Jer 25.34 [RSV]); הַצֹּאן אַדִּירֵי וִילְלַת הָרֹעִים צַעֲקַת קוֹל, 'the cry of the shepherds, and the wail of the lords of the flock' (Jer 25.36 [RSV]). Jer 25.34a appears to be paraphrased in Joel 11.3. In these passages, the shepherds (whatever their precise social correlate), rather than the *sheep*, emit cries of panic. This literary device of metaphoric correlation, set up explicitly in Jer 12.3 ('pull them out like sheep for the slaughter, and prepare them for the day of slaughter'), possibly discloses a latent and typically unvoiced social anxiety about the routine killing of animals in sacrifice. The metaphor itself replicates Assyro-Babylonian royal propaganda, e.g. 'I slaughtered like sheep the armies of the Hittites and Aḫlamu' (Shalmaneser I), as translated by A. Kirk Grayson, *Assyrian Royal Inscriptions*. Vol. 1, *From the Beginning to Ashur-resha-ishi* (Records of the Ancient Near East 1; Wiesbaden: O. Harrassowitz, 1972), p. 82, §531.

slaughter of others (implied by their vocalizations [√*ybb*]).[46] The variety of modes may further illustrate Sheid's conclusion that 'there were a lot of modalities of sacrifice, which altogether gave...a coherent picture of the "social" hierarchy in this world and defined implicitly the nature of divinity'.[47]

Recalling the late imperial context of the inscription, Latin sources can provide relevant analogies. Roman piety gave place on occasion to anxiety about failures or disruptions of prescribed sacrificial procedure,[48] and a similar anxiety may have supplied a motive to record the circumstances of the sacrifice at Altiburus.

An ongoing discussion among classicists concerns the degree to which ancient Greeks and Romans experienced, or sought to avert, potential or actual fear and guilt consequent to the sacrificial slaughter of animals. Recent views tend to reframe questions about this anxiety. Bremmer[49] draws attention to the scarcity of testimonies concerning sacrificial fear or guilt. Naiden,[50] addressing the 'fallacy of the willing victim', cites Bremmer as well as a number of additional scholars who minimize the significance of fear or guilt as an aspect of classical sacrifice.[51] The context of the question itself has shifted considerably: 'Forty years after

46. Graf stresses that 'the actual kill' is rare in graphic depictions of animal sacrifice 'on vases and votive reliefs' (Fritz Graf, 'One Generation after Burkert and Girard: Where Are the Great Theories?', in Christopher A. Faraone and F. S. Naiden [eds.], *Greek and Roman Animal Sacrifice: Ancient Victims, Modern Observers* [Cambridge: Cambridge University Press, 2012], p. 46).

47. John Scheid, 'Roman Animal Sacrifice and the System of Being', in Faraone and Naiden (eds.), *Greek and Roman Animal Sacrifice*, p. 95.

48. For example, the *ver sacrum* (sacred spring) ceremony of 195 B.C.E. (Livy 33.44.2) was repeated the following year because it had not been properly carried out (34.44.2). On the history of theorizing the question of anxiety in sacrificial ritual, see Jennifer Wright Knust and Zsuzsanna Várhelyi, 'Images, Acts, Meanings and Ancient Mediterranean Sacrifice', in Jennifer Wright Knust and Zsuzsanna Várhelyi (eds.), *Ancient Mediterranean Sacrifice* (Oxford: Oxford University Press, 2012), pp. 7-10.

49. Jan N. Bremmer, *Greek Religion* (Greece and Rome: New Surveys in the Classics 24; Oxford: Oxford University Press, 1994), p. 41.

50. F. S. Naiden, 'The Fallacy of the Willing Victim', *Journal of Hellenic Studies* 127 (2007), pp. 61-73.

51. For example: S. Peirce, 'Death, Revelry, and *thusia*', *Classical Antiquity* 12 (1993), pp. 219-66; Stella Georgoudi, 'L' "occultation de la violence" dans le sacrifice grec: données anciennes, discours modernes', pp. 115-47 in Stella Georgoudi, Renée Koch Piettre, and Francis Schmidt (eds.), *La cuisine et l'autel: les sacrifices en questions dans les sociétés de la méditerranée ancienne* (Bibliothèque de l'Ecole des Hautes Études; Turnhout: Brepols, 2005).

the publication of [Walter Burkert's] *Homo Necans*, "sacrifice" is a category of the thought of yesterday'.[52] Having no direct means of knowing whether Punic towns of North Africa were beset with ritual anxiety or free (or nearly so) from general angst over sacrificial violence inflicted on animals, contemporary readers may find this Late Punic text all the more interesting.

One feature of the Latin text merits comment. The text of the third fragment[53] mentions the deities *Aescu[lapi]i et Iovis*. The Roman festivals in which these two gods were associated were the *Vinalia Priora* (April 23)[54] and the *Meditrinalia* (October 11), an autumnal vintage sacrifice sacred to Asculapius.[55] One of these festivals may have been the occasion of the sacrifice recorded in the Neo-Punic text.

In a manner that remains obscure to us, this text atypically witnesses to a case of sacrifice disrupted. If this interpretation is allowed, then the brief narrative may have more to communicate to future readers about cultural transmission and performance. Additional attention to the text and its message may disclose this.

52. Christopher Faraone and F. S. Naiden, 'Introduction', in Faraone and Naiden (eds.), *Greek and Roman Animal Sacrifice*, p. 10. Similar views can be attributed to Marcel Detienne and Jean-Pierre Vernant, *The Cuisine of Sacrifice among the Greeks* (trans. Paula Wissing; Chicago: University of Chicago Press, 1989), p. 20. In noting the allusion, Hollmann remarks that Detienne did not question the validity of sacrifice as an ancient category, and cautions against a general dismissal of 'sacrifice' as an ancient category of practice as well as a category of inquiry (Alexander Hollmann, Review of Christopher A. Faraone and F. S. Naiden [eds.], *Greek and Roman Animal Sacrifice: Ancient Victims, Modern Observers*, Bryn Mawr Classical Review 2013.4.44. Online: http://bmcr.brynmawr.edu[2013-04-44.html]).

53. ben Abdallah, *Catalogue des inscriptions*, p. 148 and pl. 380b.

54. The *Vinalia Priora*, celebrating the foundation of the temple of Venus Erycina (a Phoenician cult) was sacred to Jupiter, who remained at least implicit in all vintage rites (Festus, *De Verborum Significatu* 65, 374).

55. Emma J. Edelstein and Ludwig Edelstein, *Asclepius: Collection and Interpretation of the Testimonies, with a New Introduction by Gary B. Ferngren* (2 vols.; Baltimore: The Johns Hopkins University Press 1998), vol. 2, p. 184 and n. 9. Arnobius (*Adversus Nationes* 8.32) associates Aesculapius with the vintage season (Edelstein and Edelstein, *Asclepius*, vol. 1, p. 219 §574). The corresponding Greek festival was the Πιθοίγια, whose association with Asclepius is less evident (p. 184 n. 9). Wine served as a general tonic, and was thus sacred to Asclepius.

Part II

TEXTUAL, CULTURAL AND SOCIAL ASPECTS

IS THE LANGUAGE OF CHILD SACRIFICE USED FIGURATIVELY IN EZEKIEL 16?

Peggy L. Day

Among the Hebrew Bible texts widely accepted by scholars to reference child sacrifice[1] is Ezek 16.20-21. While this basic understanding is shared by commentators who focus on Ezekiel 16 (or on ch. 16 as a

1. It is well beyond the scope of this essay to examine in detail the issues involved in determining what, precisely, the practice of child sacrifice entailed, whether it was carried out somewhat routinely or only in crisis situations, whether מלך in relevant contexts should be understood as the proper name of the deity to whom the sacrifice was offered or as a technical term (in the sense that e.g. עֹלָה is a technical term) for the offering itself, whether child sacrifice was ever an acceptable Yahwistic cult practice, whether sacrifice of the first born was a separate category, and so on. For a review of previous scholarship, an extensive bibliography and discussion of these and other issues, see most recently Heath Dewrell, 'Child Sacrifice in Ancient Israel and Its Opponents' (Ph.D. diss., The Johns Hopkins University Press, 2012). To Dewrell's bibliography, add the recent articles by Corinne Bonnet, 'On Gods and Earth: The Tophet and the Construction of a New Identity in Punic Carthage', in Erich S. Gruen (ed.), *Cultural Identity in the Ancient Mediterranean* (Los Angeles: Getty Research Institute, 2011), pp. 373-87, and, in the same volume, Josephine Crawley Quinn, 'The Cultures of the Tophet: Identification and Identity in the Phoenician Diaspora', pp. 388-413; Stephanie Budin, 'Stand Alone Complex and the Problem of Ancient History', *The Ancient World* 42 (2011), pp. 223-26, 234-42; Jason Tatlock, 'The Place of Human Sacrifice in the Israelite Cult', in Christian A. Eberhart (ed.), *Ritual and Metaphor: Sacrifice in the Bible* (Atlanta: Society of Biblical Literature, 2011), pp. 33-48; J. H. Schwartz, F. D. Houghton, L. Bondioli and R. Macchiarelli, 'Bones, Teeth, and Estimating the Age of Perinates: Carthaginian Infant Sacrifice Revisited', *Antiquity* 86 (2012), pp. 738-45. Regarding the Hebrew Bible usage of the term, I will follow Paul Mosca's understanding of child sacrifice, as argued in his dissertation, as referring to the practice in ancient Judah of immolating infants or young children by fire as *mulk* offerings in an area called the Tophet, a practice that was at some junctures and/or in certain circles considered a legitimate feature of Yahweh's cult.

part of the book of Ezekiel as a whole),[2] as well as scholars who bring
vv. 20-21 to bear on the topic of child sacrifice,[3] to my knowledge there
has been no sustained consideration of these verses by someone grounded
in both of these bodies of scholarship. It is my honour and pleasure to
address this lacuna in a volume dedicated to Paul Mosca, a truly swell,
unfailingly kind and deeply generous human being who I was most
fortunate to have as my Masters Degree supervisor at the University
of British Columbia, and who has remained a valued colleague and

2. Though scholars in this category overwhelmingly identify child sacrifice as
the topic of the aforementioned verses, there is a range of opinion as to what this
topic entails, and some scholars evidence a much greater familiarity with the
pertinent issues than others do. In general, however, Ezekiel commentators pay
relatively little attention to these verses. Rather, they focus their attention and their
indignation upon the chapter's depiction of personified Jerusalem as a licentious and
whoring wife. For further discussion and bibliography prior to 2005, see Peggy L.
Day, 'The Bitch Had It Coming to Her: Rhetoric and Interpretation in Ezekiel 16',
BibInt 8 (2000), pp. 231-54, and 'Yahweh's Broken Marriages as Metaphoric
Vehicle in the Hebrew Bible Prophets', in Martti Nissinen and Risto Uro (eds.),
*Sacred Marriages: The Divine-Human Sexual Metaphor from Sumer to Early
Christianity* (Winona Lake, IN: Eisenbrauns, 2008), pp. 219-41. More recent works
include Margaret S. Odell, *Ezekiel* (Smyth and Helwys Bible Commentary; Macon,
GA: Smyth & Helwys, 2005), pp. 179-204; Hilary B. Lipka, *Sexual Transgression in
the Hebrew Bible* (Sheffield: Sheffield Phoenix, 2006), esp. pp. 148-56; Paul M.
Joyce, *Ezekiel: A Commentary* (New York: T&T Clark International, 2007), pp. 130-
35; Sharon Moughtin-Mumby, *Sexual and Marital Metaphors in Hosea, Jeremiah,
Isaiah, and Ezekiel* (Oxford: Oxford University Press, 2008); Steven Tuell, *Ezekiel*
(NIBC; Peabody, MA: Hendrickson, 2009), pp. 87-97; Nancy R. Bowen, *Ezekiel*
(AOTC; Nashville: Abingdon, 2010), pp. 83-91, and Brian Neil Peterson, *Ezekiel in
Context: Ezekiel's Message Understood in its Historical Setting of Covenant Curses
and Ancient Near Eastern Mythological Motifs* (Princeton Theological Monograph
Series; Eugene, OR: Pickwick, 2012), pp. 173-225.
3. A few scholars disagree. Moshe Weinfeld, 'The Worship of Molech and the
Queen of Heaven and its Background', *UF* 4 (1972), pp. 133-54 (esp. 140-44), is
one among a small group of scholars who argue that the term 'child sacrifice' is a
misnomer. In Weinfeld's view, the practice involved the dedication of children, not
their immolation. He (mis)reads the sexual language of Ezek 16 to mean that, in
vv. 20-21, 'the children born of cultic prostitution associated with [the god] Molech
were presumably delivered to idolatrous priests' (p. 144). Objecting on different
grounds, the absence of the terms מלך and תפת in Ezek 16 has prompted Francesca
Stavrakopoulou, *King Manasseh and Child Sacrifice: Biblical Distortions of
Historical Realities* (BZAW 338; New York: W. de Gruyter, 2004), pp. 161-65, to
aver that there is not sufficient evidence to read vv. 20-21 as referring to child
sacrifice, though she does maintain that bona fide child sacrifice entailed immolation
by fire and not merely dedication.

friend. Both in his doctoral dissertation[4] and in a recent article[5] in *Studi Epigrafici e Linguistici sul Vicino Oriente Antico* (hereafter *SEL*), Paul[6] too has discussed Ezek 16.20-21 as a reference to child sacrifice.[7] My purpose in this essay is to draw upon certain of Paul's insights regarding references to child sacrifice in the Hebrew Bible (hereafter HB) and Phoenician/Punic texts and determine whether they should be applied to Ezek 16.1-43[8] in a way that is consistent with that passage's extensive utilization of figurative language. Concisely stated, I will be exploring whether there is a metaphorical dimension to any of the terminology that the author of Ezekiel 16 employs in vv. 20-21. I will establish the plausibility of this endeavour by taking a close look at Isa 30.27-33, a text that Paul has shown to draw metaphorically upon the language and imagery of child sacrifice to envision Yahweh's defeat of the Assyrian foe, and will demonstrate that Jer 19.1-13 provides another instance of child-sacrificial language used metaphorically. I will then turn to illuminating Ezek 16.20-21's appropriation of the vocabulary of animal sacrifice by examining other HB texts that unambiguously deploy terminology from the domain of animal sacrifice metaphorically to achieve a visceral description of killing humans. But first I will offer a brief overview of Ezek 16.1-43 as well as review of what Paul has had to say about vv. 20-21 in the context of his analysis of the vocabulary of child sacrifice.

Ezekiel 16.1-43 is a diatribe against what its author[9] perceives as a history of apostasy and political infidelities and intrigues that justifies

4. Paul Mosca, 'Child Sacrifice in Canaanite and Israelite Religion: A Study in *Mulk* and מלך' (Ph.D. diss., Harvard University, 1975), pp. 231-32.

5. Paul Mosca, 'The *tofet*: A Place of Infant Sacrifice?', *The Tophet in the Phoenician Mediterranean* (Verona 2013) (= *SEL* 29–30) (2012–13), pp. 119-36.

6. Aside from standard footnote citations of his dissertation and *SEL* article, I cannot bring myself to call him Mosca, so I will be calling him Paul.

7. In his forthcoming 'The *tofet*', Paul questions whether 'sacrifice' is indeed the appropriate descriptor of the practice, and he has suggested to me (oral communication) that 'infant offering' better captures what the practice was about. Nevertheless, I will continue to use the term 'child sacrifice' as it is the one in common scholarly parlance and there has been no opportunity for the scholarly community to discuss and assess the proposition that 'infant offering' is a more accurate term.

8. A new narrative unit begins at v. 44. See the standard commentaries for details.

9. I accept the basic premise that the original composition of what is now Ezek 16.1-43 was the work of a Jerusalemite priest who was among a group of elites deported to Babylonia in the aftermath of Nebuchadnezzar's invasion of Jerusalem in 597 BCE to re-impose vassal status on Judah. For further information, see the standard commentaries and Avi Hurvitz, *A Linguistic Study of the Relationship Between the Priestly Source and the Book of Ezekiel: A New Approach to an Old Problem* (Cahiers de la Revue Biblique 20; Paris: Gabalda, 1982).

Yahweh's impending utter destruction of Jerusalem at the hands of an alliance of foreign military forces. What complicates matters tremendously is that the author does not present his case in anything approaching a straightforward manner. Rather, he employs what Julie Galambush has analysed as an extended use of metaphor,[10] in which Jerusalem is personified as Yahweh's sexually promiscuous and murderous wife whose behaviour is so outrageous that it justifies putting her to death. The author employs the emotionally charged language of a wife's betrayal of her husband and slaughter of her children as a rhetorical strategy to win his audience over to agreeing with his conviction that Jerusalem is deserving of the severest of punishments, i.e. the conquest and destruction of the very city that is the home of Yahweh's Temple and the seat of the Davidic dynasty. The author expected that the punishment to be meted out for Jerusalem's cultic and political improprieties was to be the conquest and ruination by foreign military forces and the subsequent exile of survivors threatened as consequences of covenant disobedience (e.g. Lev 26.1-39, esp. 27-39; Deut 28.25-26, 47-57, 63-64). The verses with which we are concerned occur in a section of the narrative in which Jerusalem, personified as unmindfully hubristic and lavishing her sexual attentions on every passer-by (v. 15),[11] is accused of constructing places of illicit worship (במות, v. 16) and of taking the fine

---

10. Julie Galambush, *Jerusalem in the Book of Ezekiel: The City as Yahweh's Wife* (SBLDS 130; Atlanta: Scholars Press, 1992), pp. 78-81. This book remains by far the best analysis of the use by the author of Ezek 16 and 23 of figurative language in the context of Ezekiel as a whole. Her discussion of models of metaphors (pp. 4-10) is brief but articulate and informative. Since Galambush wrote this book, developments in the cognitive sciences and social sciences have moved beyond conceptual metaphor theory to a theory called conceptual blending, which subsumes metaphor. I have found Gilles Fauconnier and Mark Turner, *The Way We Think: Conceptual Blending and the Mind's Hidden Complexities* (New York: Basic Books, 2002), especially helpful; Joseph E. Grady, Todd Oakley and Seanna Coulson, 'Blending and Metaphor', in Raymond W. Gibbs and Gerard J. Steen (eds.), *Metaphor in Cognitive Linguistics: Selected Papers from the Fifth International Cognitive Linguistics Conference, Amsterdam, 1997* (Philadelphia: John Benjamins, 1999), pp. 101-24, is an excellent article, focussed specifically on metaphor. For application to a HB text, see, for example, Pierre J. P. Van Hecke, 'Conceptual Blending: A Recent Approach to Metaphor Illustrated with the Pastoral Metaphor in Hos 4,16', in P. Van Hecke (ed.), *Metaphor in the Hebrew Bible* (BETL 187; Leuven: Leuven University Press, 2005), pp. 215-31.

11. Qal verbal and participial forms of עבר appear at key junctures four or five times (vv. 6, 8, 15, 25 and perhaps 37) in Ezek. 16.1-43, a point to which I shall return.

food, clothing and jewelry that husband Yahweh had provided for her and using them instead for the production and care of male (cult) images (vv. 17-21):

> You took your beautiful possessions made from my gold and my silver which I gave to you and you fashioned for yourself male images and you whored with them. You took your embroidered garments and covered them, and you set (נָתַתְּ *Qere*) my oil and my incense before them. My food which I gave you, fine flour and oil and honey[12] that I provided for you to eat, you set it before them for a pleasing aroma (לריח ניחח) and it was so: oracle of Adonai Yahweh. You took your sons (בניך) and your daughters (בנותיך) who you bore to me and you sacrificed them (ותזבחים) to them for devouring (לאכול). Were your whorings not enough? You slaughtered my children (ותשחטי את־בני) and you delivered them (ותתנים) by passing (בהעביר) them over to them.

In this passage, as in Ezekiel 16 in general, the accusation of whoring (vv. 17 and 20) is clearly metaphorical. The question is whether the accusation that personified Jerusalem sacrificed her children to the male images is intended to be taken figuratively as well, as this action seems to be in addition to, and not subsumed by, the whoring (vv. 20-21; see also v. 36 and, if ושפכת דם is not a later addition, v. 38).

The technical terminology properly associated with child sacrifice in the HB was a topic that Paul treated at length in his 1975 thesis. Following a basic observation made by Moshe Weinfeld, Paul maintained that the vocabulary used of child sacrifice in 'legal-historical' HB passages should be distinguished from that used in 'prophetic-poetic' materials, as the former genres can be expected to employ technical terminology.[13] In this former category Paul placed Lev 18.21 and 20.2-4, Deut 12.31 and 18.10, and 2 Kgs 16.3, 17.17, 31, and 21.6. In the Leviticus (more specifically, the Holiness Code) passages, Paul observed that נתן, 'to give', is used with or without העביר, 'to transfer (or pass) over', and in the passages from Deuteronomy and the Deuteronomistic History (i.e. the remainder of the passages in this category), העביר is the verb used when the reference is to Israelite child sacrifice and שרף, 'to burn', is used of non-Israelites carrying out the practice.[14] Thus Paul surmised that נתן and העביר are technical terms indicative of child sacrifice, and their presence in Ezek 16.20-21 indicated to him that child sacrifice is indeed being referenced in these verses. However, Paul noted that vv. 20-21 also

---

12. דבש, 'honey', is specifically prohibited (Lev 2.11-12) from providing a ריח ניחח, 'pleasing aroma', for Yahweh.

13. Mosca, 'Child Sacrifice', p. 144.

14. Mosca, 'Child Sacrifice', pp. 139 and 146.

employ sacrificial terminology that the legal-historical sources do not. These terms are זבח and שחט, both of which, Paul argued, are properly used of the sacrifice of animals. Paul viewed Ezekiel 16's use of these terms in connection with child sacrifice as 'entirely inappropriate' and 'intended to equate child sacrifice with animal sacrifice'; he further observed that 'the tendentiousness implicit in their use' was made apparent by adding לאכול, 'to eat', which was never the purpose of child sacrifice.[15] That the author of the verses portrays child sacrifice as being made to male images rather than to Yahweh was, for Paul, additional evidence that Ezekiel 16 presents an intentionally skewed and polemical description of the practice.[16] While he no longer categorizes the practice of passing children over to a deity as sacrificial, in his recent *SEL* article Paul reasserts the importance of noting the terminological dichotomy between the legal-historical and the prophetic-poetical texts and reiterates that the author of Ezekiel 16 intentionally distorted the practice by equating the offering of children with the sacrifice of animals made to idols to provide them with food.[17] And although Paul does not characterize the reference to the sacrifice of children in Ezekiel 16 as metaphorical, in his thesis he discussed at length another prophetic text that speaks of child sacrifice, Isa 30.27-33, in which he saw metaphor at work.[18] It is to Paul's superb but, outside the circle of scholarship on child sacrifice *per se*, grossly underappreciated[19] explication of this Isaianic text that I shall now turn.

In his approach to Isa 30.27-33, and unlike previous commentators on the passage, Paul posited that this section of Isaiah constituted '*a potentially coherent poetic work*'.[20] He also postulated that there were six instances in the passage where ה rather than ו was the *mater lectionis* used to indicate final –ō, and he convincingly demonstrated the author's use of *inclusio* to structure the passage.[21] As his translation and critical

15.   Mosca, 'Child Sacrifice', p. 232.

16.   Mosca, 'Child Sacrifice', p. 232.

17.   Mosca, 'The *tofet*'.

18.   Mosca, 'Child Sacrifice', pp. 195-220 and 261-66. The reference to metaphor is on p. 217.

19.   None of the Isaiah commentaries I cite below reference Paul's work on the passage. And whereas most of the child sacrifice scholars' post-1975 works I consulted do engage his translation and discussion of v. 33, none of them treats v. 33 at any length in the context of vv. 27-33 as a whole.

20.   Mosca, 'Child Sacrifice', p. 197 (italics in the original). On pp. 195-98 Paul discusses why previous scholars found the passage so problematic.

21.   Mosca, 'Child Sacrifice', pp. 203 and 207-208.

notes for the passage have been so underutilized, and because I find them so compelling, I will diverge only twice from the translation presented in his thesis:[22]

> (27) 'Look! The Name of Yahweh comes from afar,
>   Blazing his anger, ominous his pronouncement,[23]
>   His lips full of fury, his tongue like a devouring flame,
> (28) His breath like a raging torrent, his bow drawn back,[24]
>   To yoke the nations with a yoke[25] of destruction,
>   On the jaws of the peoples a bridle leading to ruin.'
> (29) Such shall be your song, as on the night a feast is celebrated,
>   With gladness of heart, as when one marches (in procession) with the flute,
>   To enter the mountain of Yahweh, to the Rock of Israel.

22. Mosca, 'Child Sacrifice', pp. 201-207. I have, however, opted not to reproduce his strophic analysis.

23. MT וְכֹבֶד מַשָּׂאָה has proved problematic and has elicited various solutions. This is the first instance where Paul (p. 203) read the final ה as a *mater* for -ō, indicative of the third person masculine singular (hereafter 3 m.s.) suffix 'his'. He understood the phrase, in the context of the storm imagery used to describe Yahweh's theophany, to be a reference to the rumbling of thunder. The context is widely recognized to be theophanic: see, for example, Marvin A. Sweeney, *Isaiah 1–39 with an Introduction to Prophetic Literature* (FOTL 16; Grand Rapids: Eerdmans, 1996), p. 394, and Willem A. M. Beuken, 'Isaiah 30: A Prophetic Oracle Transmitted in Two Successive Paradigms', in Craig C. Broyles and Craig A. Evans (eds.), *Writing and Reading the Scroll of Isaiah: Studies of an Interpretive Tradition*, vol. 1 (Leiden: Brill, 1997), pp. 369-97. For discussion of alternative translations, see especially Hans Wildberger, *Isaiah 28–39: A Continental Commentary* (trans. Thomas H. Trapp; Minneapolis: Fortress, 2002 [1982]), pp. 186, 197.

24. As Paul noted ('Child Sacrifice', p. 204), MT עד־צואר יחצה is usually translated with reference to Isa 8.8, in which Assyrian invasionary forces are spoken of as a flood that will reach up to the neck. For examples of this line of interpretation, see Ronald E. Clements, *Isaiah 1–39* (NCB Commentary; Grand Rapids: Eerdmans, 1980), p. 253; Göran Eidevall, *Prophecy and Propaganda: Images of Enemies in the Book of Isaiah* (Winona Lake, IN: Eisenbrauns, 2009), pp. 60-61 and Otto Kaiser, *Isaiah 13–39: A Commentary* (OTL; Philadelphia: Westminster, 1974), p. 307. Paul demurred ('Child Sacrifice', p. 204) because חצה 'to divide' up to the neck makes poor sense; he posited instead a text-critically based solution that leads to a hypothetical, pre-Exilic עד צוארה חצה, 'his arrow (חץ) to (the back of) his neck', in which ה is twice the *mater* for a 3 m.s. suffix. Paul explained ('Child Sacrifice', p. 207) that 'the image here is that of Yahweh, the Man of War, with His bow drawn back, ready to release the arrow of lightning'.

25. Paul ('Child Sacrifice', p. 205) followed H. L. Ginsberg ('An Obscure Hebrew Word', *JQR* 22 [1931–32], pp. 143-45) in attributing the meaning 'yoke' rather than 'sieve' to both the nominal and verbal forms of נוף in this strophe.

(30) 'Yahweh has made heard the crash[26] of His voice,
      The down-sweep of his arm he has displayed,
      With hot wrath and flame of consuming fire,
      Cloudburst and flood and hailstone(s)'.
(31) Yes! At the voice of Yahweh Asshur will cower—
      With staff He will beat (him).
(32) Every passage of the rod of His punishment[27]
      Which Yahweh will lay upon him
      Will be to the sound of timbrels and lyres;
      With uplifted weapons[28] He will fight against him.[29]
(33) For his Tophet[30] has already[31] been prepared,

26. Paul ('Child Sacrifice', p. 205) read MT הוד as הֵד, 'crash (of thunder)', but allowed that MT's 'majesty' might also be correct.

27. Paul ('Child Sacrifice', p. 205) followed a number of Hebrew manuscripts and the Syriac in reading ר rather than MT's ד, as do many other commentators, for example Joseph Blenkinsopp, *Isaiah 1–39* (AB 19; New York: Doubleday, 1964), p. 423; William H. Irwin, *Isaiah 28–33: Translation with Philological Notes* (Biblica et Orientalia 30; Rome: Biblical Institute, 1977), p. 99, and, implicitly, Brevard S. Childs, *Isaiah* (OTL; Louisville, KY: Westminster John Knox, 2001), p. 223. This is also another instance where Paul read final ה as a *mater* for a 3 m.s. suffix, yielding the translation 'His punishment'.

28. I am following here the translation of Jacob Milgrom, 'The Alleged Wave-Offering in Israel and in the Ancient Near East', *IEJ* 22 (1972), pp. 33-38 (34 n. 8); cf. Willem A. M. Beuken, *Isaiah. Part II. Vol. 2, Isaiah Chapters 28–39* (trans. Brian Doyle; Leuven: Peeters, 2000), pp. 134 and 137-38. Paul ('Child Sacrifice', pp. 207 and 211) cited Milgrom's article but left תנופה untranslated because of the word's resonance in both the military and the cultic spheres. I find the lack of a translation confusing. For a negative assessment of Milgrom's proposed translation, see Gary A. Anderson, *Sacrifices and Offerings in Ancient Israel: Studies in their Social and Political Importance* (HSM 41; Atlanta: Scholars Press, 1987), pp. 133-35.

29. Paul ('Child Sacrifice', p. 202) read MT בה as 'against him [i.e. personified Assyria]', another example of ה as *mater* for a 3 m.s. suffix.

30. Paul ('Child Sacrifice', pp. 202, 206) once again read the final ה in תפתה as a *mater* for a 3 m.s. suffix, referring here to Assyria. The Tophet was the precinct designated for *mulk* offerings. According to Jeremiah (7.31-32 and 19.6; cf. 32.35), it was located outside Jerusalem, in the Valley of Ben Hinnom. This location of the *mulk* precinct outside city walls is consistent with the Phoenician and Punic evidence: see, for example, Michel Gras, Pierre Rouillard and Javier Teixidor, 'The Phoenicians and Death', *Berytus* 39 (1991), pp. 127-76 (150).

31. Paul ('Child Sacrifice', p. 202) translated MT מאתמול as 'has long been' prepared. My translation reflects Dewrell's observation ('Child Sacrifice in Ancient Israel', pp. 175-76) that אתמול does not refer to the distant past. I understand the time reference 'already' to refer not to how long the Tophet had been in existence but to the Tophet firepit already having been arranged (ערוך) in preparation for personified Assyria. Note that in Leviticus (e.g. 1.7), albeit in the context of animal sacrifice, ערך can refer to arranging the wood on the altar fire in preparation for the sacrificial victim.

He [*Ketib*, i.e. Assyria] himself is installed as a *mōlek*(-victim).[32]
(Yahweh) has made its fire-pit deep and wide,
With fire and wood in abundance.
The breath of Yahweh, like a torrent of sulphur, sets it ablaze!

As is widely recognized, Isa 30.27-28a depicts a theophany of Yahweh. What commentators do not emphasize enough is that the storm imagery employed in this theophany marks Yahweh's appearance as being specifically in the role of a divine warrior whose weaponry is the thunder, lightning and raging torrents of water that are the phenomena that accompany a powerful storm.[33] Fully appreciating that Yahweh is manifest as a warrior here makes v. 28b more readily intelligible. The images of the yoke and the bridle are employed to depict warrior Yahweh's treatment of his conquered foes.[34] After an interlude (v. 29) that Paul integrated into the composition as a whole by understanding it as the author's contextualizing of the singing of the theophanic battle

32. MT reads לַמֶּלֶךְ, 'to the king'. Some Isaiah commentators, including Childs (*Isaiah*, p. 223) and John H. Hayes and Stuart A. Irvine (*Isaiah the Eighth-century Prophet: His Times and his Preaching* [Nashville: Abingdon, 1987], p. 345), see this as a reference to the king of Assyria; some re-vocalize (e.g., Sweeney, *Isaiah 1–39*, pp. 395-36, and Blenkinsopp, *Isaiah 1–39*, pp. 422-23) to arrive at the reading Molech/Molek (i.e. the alleged name of a deity to whom child sacrifices were made). I follow Paul and understand the reference to be a technical term for both the type of sacrifice and the sacrificial victim.

33. Compare, for example, 2 Sam 22.7-16 // Ps 18.7-15. The classic study of Yahweh as divine warrior is Patrick D. Miller Jr., *The Divine Warrior in Early Israel* (Cambridge, MA: Harvard University Press, 1973); see also and importantly Frank Moore Cross, *Canaanite Myth and Hebrew Epic* (Cambridge, MA: Harvard University Press, 1973), pp. 77-194. For overflowing rivers and raging wadis in the HB as figurative language for human invasionary troops, see, for example, Isa 8.7-8, Jer 47.1-4 and Ps 124.1-5. For the raging storm and floodwaters as figurative language for divine wrath, battle weapon and aggressive enemy in Akkadian sources, see Joan Goodnick Westenholz, 'Symbolic Language in Akkadian Narrative Poetry: The Metaphorical Relationship Between Poetical Images and the Real World', in M. E. Vogelzang and H. L. J. Vanstiphout (eds.), *Mesopotamian Poetic Language: Sumerian and Akkadian* (Cuneiform Monographs 6; Groningen: Styx, 1996), pp. 183-206.

34. Wildberger, *Isaiah 28–39*, pp. 198-99, perceives this meaning regarding the bridle. He remarks that 'prisoners of war had a ring through their noses or a hook was shoved in their jaws'. Eidevall, *Prophecy and Propaganda*, p. 61 offers a somewhat different interpretation when he says 'the metaphor in v. 28bβ pictures these [Assyrian] soldiers and officers, responsible for the deportations of vast populations, as cattle about to be led away', but he certainly does apprehend that the image of the bridle is connected with conquest in battle. For figurative uses of the noun עֹל, a more common word for 'yoke', that signals human servitude, see BDB, p. 760.

hymn of vv. 27-28 in the *Sitz im Leben* of the festival procession that
accompanied a *mulk* sacrifice,[35] the author resumes drawing upon the
battle hymn's lyrics (v. 30). Here again, Yahweh as divine warrior is
manifest in the storm. Then, beginning in v. 31, the author particularizes
the thus far generic enemies of the hymn. The object of warrior
Yahweh's wrath becomes an historical enemy, the Assyrians, personified
(albeit minimally) as a single individual. The actual historical foe thus
identified, v. 32 proceeds to merge the language and imagery characteristic of Yahweh's theophanic battles with that of sacrificial rite in preparation for the fusion of the 'theophanic-military' and 'liturgical-sacrificial'
in the grand climax of v. 33.[36] Introduced by ערוך, a word that once again
reverberates in both the military and cultic domains,[37] v. 33 expresses the
author's conviction that Assyria's defeat is a foregone conclusion.
Figuratively speaking, Assyria's firepit has already been arranged in
readiness for his installation[38] as a *mulk* sacrifice, and Yahweh's 'theophanic lightning [כאש אכלת v. 27 and אש אוכלה v. 30] will set the
sacrificial pit ablaze'.[39] For my purposes, what I would like to stress is
that the author of Isa 30.27-33 vividly employs the language and imagery

35. Mosca, 'Child Sacrifice', p. 215.

36. Mosca, 'Child Sacrifice', pp. 210-11. As Paul noted, v. 32's תנופה evidences
both military and cultic connotations; see Milgrom, 'Wave Offering', for further
discussion and examples. Paul ('Child Sacrifice', p. 211) analyzed the phrase
מעבר מטה as partaking of both spheres because the latter term 'clearly refers to the
weapon wielded by the Divine Warrior' while the former 'suggests the technical
sacrificial phrase העביר באש, "make pass into the fire,"' which prepares the reader
for v. 33's references to תפת, 'Tophet', and מלך, '*mulk* sacrifice'. The juxtaposition
of timbrels and lyres (as instruments of festival celebration) with uplifted weapons
also serves to merge the cultic and military arenas.

None of the Isaiah scholars I have cited discusses v. 32 in terms of the merging of
military and cultic terminology. The most prevalent interpretation of v. 32 involves
seeing the people of Israel joyfully celebrating while the Assyrians are being
physically assaulted; see, for example, Clements, *Isaiah 1–39*, p. 253; Blenkinsopp,
Isaiah 1–39, p. 423, and Eidevall, *Prophecy and Propaganda*, p. 62.

37. Mosca, 'Child Sacrifice', p. 211, cited Lev 6.5 and Gen 14.8 as representative
examples. See BDB, p. 789 for additional citations.

38. The Hebrew here is הוכן, a Hophal of כון, a verb that is frequently used in the
Niphal (e.g. 2 Sam 5.12; 7.16; 1 Kgs 2.45; Pss 89.38; 93.2) of kingship being
established. Paul aptly pointed out, the irony of using a verb associated with both
divine and human kingship in conjunction with being established not as a מֶלֶךְ,
'king', but as a מֹלֶךְ, '*mulk* sacrifice' ('Child Sacrifice', p. 216). Recognizing this
word play can also be adduced as evidence that גם־הוא למלך should not be deleted as
a later addition, as *BHS* suggests doing.

39. Ibid., p. 208.

of child sacrifice metaphorically in v. 33 to envisage warrior Yahweh's victory over a dangerous enemy.[40] In this metaphoric usage, an adult human is depicted as a victim of child sacrifice.

Whereas Isaiah 30 draws upon the language and imagery of death by *mulk* sacrifice to belittle mighty Assyria, Jer 7.30-34 and 19.1-13 use references to the Tophet for purposes inimical to Judah and Jerusalem. In both passages, Jeremiah is portrayed delivering an oracle of Yahweh that threatens, 'days are coming…when it will no longer be called the Tophet or the valley of Ben Hinnom, but rather the valley of Slaughter (Jer 7.32)'.[41] As the contexts of both passages make clear, it is the people of Judah and Jerusalem (7.30, 34; 19.7) who are threatened with impending slaughter (הרגה), though 19.7 and 9 are more explicit than 7.34 that the slaughter will be in the context of warfare, at the hands of invasionary

40. So also, implicitly, Jon D. Levenson, *The Death and Resurrection of the Beloved Son: The Transformation of Child Sacrifice in Judaism and Christianity* (New Haven: Yale University Press, 1993), p. 10. Levenson does not translate and discuss Isa 30.27-33 in its entirety, but he does consider vv. 30-33. He states that 30.30-33 'really does not speak about child sacrifice at all. It talks only of the gruesome death of a hated foe'. To my knowledge, the only other child sacrifice scholar who discusses v. 33 with even a modicum of attention to its textual context is George C. Heider, *The Cult of Molek: A Reassessment* (JSOTSup 43; Sheffield: JSOT, 1985), pp. 319-26. Like Levenson, though more explicitly, Heider (p. 325; see also p. 326) describes Isaiah's 'usage of Molek [*sic*] cult imagery' as 'meta-phorical'. Of the Isaiah scholars, Hayes and Irvine (*Isaiah*, p. 345) describe Isaiah's choice of language in v. 33 as 'highly metaphorical and dramatic, drawing on the cultic imagery of the decimation by Yahweh of any enemies attacking Zion'. Eidevall (*Prophecy and Propaganda*, p. 61) is uncertain whether v. 33 refers 'meta-phorically to some kind of holocaust sacrifice (an offering of the "Molech" type, at the Tophet site in the Hinnom Valley), or literally to the burning of corpses left on the battlefield'. Wildberger (*Isaiah 28–39*, pp. 191, 193) is adamant that v. 33 'speaks not of preparations for an offering but simply about burning the bodies of the fallen foes;' so also his statement that 'the text actually talks about a fire pit where the fallen Assyrians are to be burned'. Beuken (*Isaiah Part II*, pp. 149-50) similarly states that 'Assyria comes to its end on a bonfire similar to the Tophet' and, more enigmatically, that the king of Assyria 'is himself put to death in the oven which once symbolized his invincible power in its technical construction and richly available fuel'. For Kaiser (*Isaiah 13–39*, p. 309), it is a literal storm that Yahweh brings upon the enemy in front of the gates of Jerusalem, and those who have been thusly 'struck by Yahweh's lightnings will be burnt up there in an immense pit'.

41. Jer 19.6 reads ולא יקרא למקום הזה rather than ולא יאמר. See the standard commentaries for discussion of the redactional layers of Jeremiah as well as the relationship between 7.31-33 and 19.5-6. Jeremiah 7.1–8.3 and 19.2b-9, 11b-13 are prose compositions commonly ascribed to a redactional layer with close affinities to Deuteronomy and the Deuteronomistic History.

forces. Both passages also describe the extent of the slaughter by envisioning the Tophet precinct itself turned into a general burying ground
(7.32; 19.11),[42] and both passages also picture unburied human corpses
as food (מאכל, 7.33; 19.7) for the birds of the heavens and the beasts of
the earth (cf. Deut 28.26), while 19.9 depicts Yahweh forcing the Jerusalemites, under siege, to eat (Hiphil of אכל) the flesh of their own sons
and daughters (cf. Deut 28.33) as well as that of their neighbours. Though
hyperbolic and projected into a hypothetical future, it is nonetheless
possible to imagine that the threats made up to this point in chs. 7 and 19
were intended to be understood literally. However, in 19.12-13, Yahweh
is said to declare his intention to make Jerusalem like [the] Tophet and
the houses of Jerusalem and its kings defiled like the Tophet precinct.
The initial simile is not transparent about the point(s) of comparison but
may well be likening Jerusalem to the Tophet in that the besieged city
is threatened with a fiery end,[43] whereas the second simile seems to be
alluding to the human corpses that will defile the conquered city (cf.
2 Kgs 23.10 and 14).[44] Thus in Jeremiah as well as in Isaiah, the language of child sacrifice is applied figuratively to the prospective losers of
a military encounter; in this instance, however, it is not warriors personified as a single adult male who is envisaged as a *mulk* victim, but rather
the men, women and children in Jerusalem alike. While these passages
do not prove that Ezek 16.20-21 employs the language of child sacrifice
similarly, they at least make a case for considering the possibility.

As we have seen above, in addition to using technical terminology that
Paul associated with child sacrifice, Ezek 16.20-21 draws upon language
that is normally applied to animal, rather than human, sacrifice. Specifically, personified Jerusalem is accused of sacrificing (זבח) the sons and

---

42. MT's ובתפת יקברו מאין מקום לקבור in 19.11 is absent from the Old Greek and
so is arguably an addition in that context. On this point see, for example, Geoffrey
H. Parke-Taylor, *The Formation of the Book of Jeremiah: Doublets and Recurring
Phrases* (SBLMS 51; Atlanta: Society of Biblical Literature, 2000), pp. 192-95, and
Leslie C. Allen, *Jeremiah: A Commentary* (OTL; Louisville, KY: Westminster John
Knox, 2008), pp. 221, 223.

43. Note that Deut 13.13-17 (Eng. vv. 12-16) prescribes that any city whose
inhabitants have been beguiled into serving other gods shall be invaded, its inhabitants killed, and all the booty gathered up inside the city and 'the city and all its booty
shall be set on fire as a whole burnt offering (כליל) to Yahweh your God' (v. 17).
Thus, similarly, Deut 13 envisages a fiery end for an apostate city by comparing its
destruction to a sacrifice that entails fire.

44. So also Robert P. Carroll, *Jeremiah: A Commentary* (Philadelphia: Westminster, 1986), p. 389. Cf. Terence E. Fretheim, *Jeremiah* (Smyth and Helwys Bible
Commentary; Macon, GA: Smyth & Helwys, 2002), pp. 284-85.

daughters she bore to Yahweh for devouring (לְאָכוֹל), and of slaughtering (שׁחט) Yahweh's sons/children. I will now turn to examining three passages that use זבח metaphorically with reference to human beings in a military context. In addition, each of these three passages speaks of gorging on human flesh and being satiated with human blood.

Usually considered proto-apocalyptic and assigned to an author other than First Isaiah, Isaiah 34 opens (vv. 1-4) with Yahweh's castigation of all nations and peoples in general and features imagery that may allude to the collapse of the heavens back to pre-creation chaos.[45] Appended to this introduction is an oracle directed specifically at Edom,[46] and it is the first three verses of this section that are my main concern. These verses (vv. 5-7) read:

> For my [=Yahweh's] sword has appeared[47] in the heavens
> And is about to descend upon Edom,
> Upon a people I have dedicated to destruction[48] in judgment.
> Yahweh has a sword, it is full of blood, it is gorged with fat,
> With the blood of male lambs and goats,
> With the fat of the kidneys of rams.
> For Yahweh has a sacrifice (זֶבַח) in Bozrah,
> And a mass slaying (טבח גדול) in the land of Edom.
> Wild oxen shall go down with them
> And young steers along with bulls,
> And their land will be glutted with blood,
> And their soil will be made rich with fat.

Though superficially depicting the sacrifice of animals, it has long been recognized in biblical scholarship that certain male animal names are commonly used metaphorically in the HB to designate rulers, chiefs,

---

45. For discussion see, for example, the pages referenced for Isa 34 in the biblical citations index of Cross, *Canaanite Myth and Hebrew Epic*, p. 359.

46. This juxtaposition of the cosmic with the specific usually has been explained as Edom functioning as either 'a concrete illustration of the fate of the nations, or as a symbol of them', in the words of Claire R. Mathews, *Defending Zion: Edom's Desolation and Jacob's Restoration (Isaiah 34–35), in Context* (New York: W. de Gruyter, 1995), p. 30. For a different assessment, see Elie Assis, 'Why Edom? On the Hostility Towards Jacob's Brother in Prophetic Sources', *VT* 56 (2006), pp. 1-20.

47. Reading with 1QIsaᵃ. See, for example, Beuken, *Isaiah Part II*, p. 281.

48. The Hebrew term here is חרם. As this term is not present in Ezek 16 or in the other two passages to which I am drawing attention, I will not be giving it close consideration here. For a general discussion see, for example, Philip D. Stern, *The Biblical Ḥerem: A Window on Israel's Religious Experience* (BJS 211; Atlanta, GA: Scholars Press, 1991), and Susan Niditch, *War in the Hebrew Bible: A Study in the Ethics of Violence* (New York: Oxford University Press, 1993). Stern discusses the Isa 34 references on pp. 189-92 and Niditch on pp. 39-40, 46, 50-51 and 54-55.

nobles and warriors.[49] Regarding the animals listed in Isa 34.5-7, all but
כרים, 'male lambs', are evidenced as epithets applied to male warriors
and elites.[50] By depicting warrior Yahweh's sword descending from the
heavens for the purpose of dedicating the Edomites to destruction (חרם),
v. 5 sets up the culturally informed reader's expectation that what
follows will describe a martial encounter. Verse 6aα is consistent with
that expectation, but 6aβ's הדשנה מחלב introduces vocabulary that has
strong sacrificial associations (e.g. for דשן, Exod 27.3; Lev 1.16; Num
4.13; for חלב, Exod 29.13; Lev 3.16-17; 17.6; Num. 18.17).[51] Verse 6b
reinforces the sacrificial associations by naming animals fit for sacrifice
and by pairing blood, a substance of special import to Yahweh's cult
(e.g. Gen 9.4; Lev 1.5, 11; 3.8; 4.5-7), with the fat found around both
kidneys, a part of the sacrificial animal specifically reserved as a food
gift (אשה)[52] that will produce a pleasing aroma (ריח ניחח) for Yahweh
(e.g. Lev 3.3-5, 10-11, 15-16) or will otherwise be immolated by fire
(e.g. Lev 4.9-10; 9.10, 19-20). However, the common figurative use of
the animals' names to denote male elites and warriors would continue to
reverberate in the martial milieu for the informed reader, especially given
that a sword is an appropriate weapon for killing enemies on a battlefield
but not for slaughtering sacrificial victims. Verse 6c continues to build a
metaphorical relationship between the sacrificial and martial domains by
envisioning Yahweh's conquest of Edom and Bosrah, its capital city, in
terms of the deity hosting a זֶבַח, 'animal sacrifice', a term which, more
specifically, indicates an animal sacrifice, the cooked flesh of which is
eaten by the offerer and his guests.[53] In v. 7a, however, the double meaning of the animals' names in both the sacrificial and martial domains is

49. See, for example, the relevant listings in BDB and Patrick D. Miller, 'Animal
Names as Designations in Ugaritic and Hebrew', *UF* 2 (1970), pp. 177-86.

50. Miller ('Animal Names', pp. 180-84) discusses and provides citations for
אביר, 'bull', איל, 'ram', עתודים, 'he-goats', and פר, 'bull'; see also the standard Isaiah
commentaries. כרים, 'male lambs', is used in Jer 51.40 in a simile that depicts weak
enemies as being like lambs for slaughtering. Cf. the description of troops defecting
to Esarhaddon as tumbling about like lambs in Barbara Nevling Porter, *Images,
Power, and Politics: Figurative Aspects of Esarhaddon's Babylonian Policy* (Philadelphia: American Philosophical Society, 1993), p. 25.

51. See BDB for numerous additional examples.

52. For discussion of this term and translation of it as food gift, see Jacob
Milgrom, *Leviticus 1–16: A New Translation with Introduction and Commentary*
(AB 3; New York: Doubleday, 1991), pp. 161-62.

53. Milgrom (*Leviticus 1–16*, pp. 204, 217-18 and 713-15) discusses this specific
meaning in the Priestly source. It may also be noteworthy that v. 6c uses the
sacrificial term זבח of Yahweh's actions in Bosrah, as this city was located on a
raised plateau with steep inclines, thus perhaps suggesting a sacrificial platform.

compromised by reference to wild oxen and mighty bulls, which are figurative epithets for powerful men but are not appropriate sacrificial animals.[54] In v. 7b the (battle)ground is glutted[55] with blood and gorged with fat, a pairing that resonates with the sword full of blood and gorged with fat in v. 6a and v. 6b.

That Isa 34.5-7 draws upon the language and imagery of sacrifice and sacrificial feast to envision Yahweh's routing the Edomite foe is widely recognized among scholars who have studied the passage.[56] Drawing upon conventional metaphorical language in which warriors are spoken of as powerful animals, the author here cleverly confounds conventional expectations by transforming the brawny beasts *qua* mighty warriors into sacrificial victims. In other words, humans become the victims of animal sacrifice through the agency of metaphor. And although the personification is minimal, Yahweh's sword (and, by extension, Yahweh himself) is spoken of as drinking blood and eating fat, components of the sacrificial animal strictly reserved for the deity, to satiation.[57] In v. 6b, it is in particular the fat around the kidneys that smells so enticingly delicious when being cooked on the altar that the sword is gorged on. Yahweh's mass slaying (טבח גדול, v. 6c) of the Edomite enemy is portrayed metaphorically as a זֶבַח,[58] a type of animal sacrifice whose roasted meat

---

54.   Johan Lust ('Isaiah 34 and the *Ḥerem*', in Jacques Vermeylen [ed.], *The Book of Isaiah. Le Livre d'Isaïe: les oracles et leurs relectures: unité et complexité de l'ouvrage* [BETL 81; Leuven: Leuven University Press, 1989], pp. 275-86 [279]), Wildberger (*Isaiah 28–39*, p. 331), and Beuken (*Isaiah Part II*, p. 296) note that ראמים, 'wild oxen', are never depicted in the HB as sacrificial animals, and I would point out that the only reference to אבירים, 'bulls', as sacrificial animals, in Ps 50.13, is complicated by being contextualized in a rhetorical question.

55.   Hebrew רותה, 'be glutted', may well be cognate to Moabite *ryt*, a term used in line 12 of the Mesha Stele, an inscription that employs the Moabite cognate of Hebrew חרם. For the text of the Mesha Stele and discussion, see Kent P. Jackson and J. Andrew Dearman, 'The Text of the Mesha' Inscription', and Kent P. Jackson, 'The Language of the Mesha' Inscription', in Andrew Dearman (ed.), *Studies in the Mesha Inscription and Moab* (Atlanta: Scholars Press, 1989), pp. 93-95, 96-130. For רותה in Isa 34.5 in particular, see also Stern (*Biblical Ḥerem*, pp. 32-33, 190) and Niditch (*War*, p. 39).

56.   Of the scholars I consulted, Lust ('Isaiah 34', p. 279) is the only possible exception; he denies that v. 7 has any 'sacrificial overtones' or 'cultic connotations' whatsoever.

57.   Niditch (*War*, p. 40) also notes that the sword is personified.

58.   Much to my delight, even Milgrom (*Leviticus 1–16*, p. 714) explicitly refers to the usage of זבח in v. 6 as metaphorical. In his 'The Role of Sacrificial Language in Prophetic Rhetoric', Eberhart (ed.), *Ritual and Metaphor*, pp. 49-61, Göran Eidevall suggests that passages such as Isa 34.5-7 draw vocabulary from the domain

is eaten. The appetite of Yahweh's sword and the metaphorical זֶבַח that victor Yahweh will host are also the prominent themes of Jer 46.10:

> Now that day for Lord Yahweh of the heavenly armies
> Is a day of vengeance, [a day] for taking vengeance on his foes.
> His[59] sword will eat (אכלה) and be sated,
> Will be satiated (רותה) with their blood.
> For Lord Yahweh of the heavenly armies is holding a sacrifice (זֶבַח)
> In a northern land, near the Euphrates river.

The broader context (vv. 1-12) makes it clear that, once again, Yahweh's sacrificial victims are envisaged as foreign warriors that lay slain on the battlefield. In this case, however, the enemy warriors are not referred to by animal names; it is clearly humans who are imagined as the sacrificial fare. And if the allusion in this passage is to the 605 BCE battle of Carchemish in particular, as v. 2 suggests,[60] then the oracle of which 46.10 is a part may have been known to the author of Ezekiel 16.

The third passage I wish to present that features זֶבַח in a military context and speaks of feasting on humans is Ezek 39.17-20.[61] There is a range of scholarly opinion regarding the authorship of this passage: should it be assigned to the primary author of Ezekiel, or does it belong to a subsequent redactional layer? To engage this issue properly is beyond the scope of the present study and so I will not privilege this passage in relation to Ezekiel 16. Verses 17-20 read:

of sacrifice to describe the defeat of enemies on the battlefield because, 'since warfare was commonly regarded as divinely decreed, military battles and religious festivals...would tend to have one thing in common: the notion of killing in the name of YHWH'. Westenholz ('Symbolic Language', p. 192) presents several instances in Akkadian literature that employ the metaphor of battle as a festival celebration. Cf. Wildberger, *Isaiah 28–35*, p. 331.

59. I am positing here a 3 m.s. suffix, lost in the MT through haplography.

60. For discussion see, for example, Carroll, *Jeremiah*, pp. 754-55 and 760-65; Parke-Taylor, *The Formation*, pp. 115-17; Duane L. Christensen, *Transformations of the War Oracle in Old Testament Prophecy* (HDR 3; Missoula, MT: Scholars Press, 1975), pp. 215-18; and William L. Holladay, *Jeremiah 2: A Commentary on the Book of the Prophet Jeremiah Chapters 26–52* (Hermeneia; Minneapolis: Fortress, 1989), pp. 313-14 and 318-22.

61. I have opted not to present Zeph 1.7-8 as a fourth example. This passage speaks of Yahweh having prepared a זֶבַח, but it is not entirely clear that the humans mentioned in v. 8 are the intended fare. Were this passage to be considered along with the other three, I would note that an upper class subset of Judah/Jerusalem are the intended victims here.

And as for you, human, thus says Lord Yahweh: Say to the birds of every kind and to all the beasts of the field, 'Gather together and come assemble yourselves from round about at my sacrifice (זִבְחִי) that I am preparing (זבח) for you, a great sacrificial feast (זֶבַח גָדוֹל) on the mountains of Israel, and you will eat flesh and drink blood. You will eat the flesh of warriors and the blood of princes of the earth you will drink, rams, male lambs and he-goats, bulls, all of them fatlings of Bashan.[62] And you shall eat fat (חלב) until you are sated and drink blood until you are intoxicated from my sacrificial feast (זִבְחִי) which I have prepared (זבחתי) for you.

Because both the sacrificial and martial domains are clearly enunciated, this passage is more transparently metaphorical to the cultural outsider than the previous two. Here, birds and beasts that can be imagined actually to feed on unburied human corpses are called upon to gather together, but what in reality would be a chaotic and savage feeding frenzy is transformed, through the metaphor of the sacrificial feast, into a divinely sanctioned celebration. The superimposition of the sacrificial feast upon the carnage of the battlefield creates in this image the dissonance characteristic of metaphor, and this dissonance is strengthened by noting further anomalies: all animals and birds and not solely carnivores participate in the eating of flesh and fat and the drinking of blood, animals are eating humans at this זֶבַח and not the other way around, they are gorging on portions of the sacrifice reserved for the deity, and so on. Again, that the three passages just studied all employ זֶבַח figuratively in a military context does not prove that Ezekiel 16 uses the verb זבח figuratively as well, but it does make such a reading plausible.

As previously noted, זבח in Ezek 16.20 is used in conjunction with the verb אכל, 'to eat', and this verb is often used figuratively in the HB. As we have already seen, a sword can be said to eat (human flesh) and be sated; indeed, a devouring sword is a common martial figure of speech (e.g. Deut 32.42; 2 Sam 2.26; 11.25; Isa 1.20).[63] Fire is also a common subject of the verb אכל used metaphorically. In sacrificial contexts it can denote, for example, fire that was believed to issue from Yahweh (Lev 9.24; cf. Isa 30.33 above) consuming the burnt offering (1 Kgs 18.38) until only ashes are left (Lev 6.3 [Eng. 6.10]), or devouring the fat pieces reserved for the deity (Lev 9.24). In the context of warfare, fire can be said to eat through the bar of city gates (Nah 3.13) or to consume a city's

---

62. Perhaps 'of Bashan' should be deleted.

63. For discussion and additional examples, see Magnus Ottosson, 'אכל', in *TDOT*, vol. 1, pp. 236-39. For the idiom 'mouth of the sword', see Daniel Bodi, *The Book of Ezekiel and the Poem of Erra* (OBO 104; Göttingen: Vandenhoeck & Ruprecht, 1991), pp. 242-43 and figures 3-6, pp. 244-45.

inhabitants (Ezek 15.6). Perhaps in a sense extended from an invading army's actual devouring of cereal crops and domesticated animals (e.g. Lev 26.16; Deut 28.5; cf. Isa 1.7), one people or nation can be said to devour others (e.g. Deut 7.16; Jer 8.16; 10.25; 51.34; cf. Num 14.9), i.e. conquer them or virtually wipe them out. In Lev 26.38, Yahweh threatens an idolatrous Israel with exile by saying 'you shall perish among the nations, and the land of your enemies will consume (וְאָכְלָה) you'. Spoken of in the guise of young lions, Ezek 19.3 and 6 each accuses a latter-day king of Judah of having devoured humans (אָדָם אָכַל), seemingly a way of saying that they oppressed and/or were responsible for the deaths of their own people. Micah 3.1-3 vividly depicts the leaders of Jacob/Israel as individuals who eat (אָכְלוּ) their people's flesh and Hos 7.7 describes those involved in political intrigue as having devoured (וְאָכְלוּ) their rulers.

The second verb drawn specifically from the domain of animal sacrifice that the author of Ezekiel 16 employs to describe personified Jerusalem's treatment of 'her sons' is שׁחט. This verb does not appear in any of the three passages investigated above that utilize זָבַח figuratively in a military context.[64] In his Leviticus commentary, Jacob Milgrom[65] presents his results of a word study of שׁחט in the context of comparing it with זבח. Among his conclusions he states that, 'in metaphoric usage, [both שׁחט and זבח designate] the mass slaughter of persons', and cites ten instances (Num 14.16; Judg 12.6; 1 Kgs 18.40; 2 Kgs 10.7 and 14; Jer 39.6 [twice]; 41.7; 52.10 [twice]) where he sees שׁחט used in this fashion.[66] Indeed, all of these passages involve the killing of many persons, but what I find potentially significant is that *none* of the persons killed in these passages is killed in the heat of battle, and *all* of the cases involve the prospective victims having been first rendered defenceless, often having been caught off guard by trickery, deceit or subterfuge.[67] A few examples must suffice.

64. שׁחט also does not appear in Zeph 1.7-8.
65. Milgrom, *Leviticus 1–16*, pp. 713-18.
66. Milgrom, *Leviticus 1–16*, p. 715. Milgrom's list does not include 2 Kgs 25.7, perhaps because the incident is recounted in Jer 39.6 and 52.10.
67. This aspect of deception, often connoted by שׁחט used metaphorically, is captured beautifully in Jer 9.7 (Eng. v. 8), another occurrence that Milgrom (*Leviticus 1–16*, p. 715) does not include in his tabulation and categorization of the passages that employ שׁחט figuratively. The author of Jer 9.7 is speaking about his compatriots. The NRSV translates: 'Their tongue is a deadly arrow (שׁוֹחֵט חֵץ); it speaks deceit through the mouth. They all speak friendly words to their neighbors, but inwardly are planning to lay an ambush.'

In Jeremiah 52, the famine that has resulted from Nebuchadrezzar's prolonged siege of Jerusalem prompts King Zedekiah and his entourage to attempt an escape. Nebuchadrezzar's troops pursue, capture Zedekiah and bring him to the Babylonian king at Riblah, where Zedekiah's sons and all the nobles of Judah are slaughtered (v. 10, וישחט...שחט) before his eyes. In Judg. 12.4, Jephthah and the Gileadites engage in a military conflict with the Ephraimites from which Jephthah's forces emerge victorious. In the aftermath of that victory the Gileadites take up a position at the fords of the Jordan in order to intercept any Ephraimite escapees (פליטי אפרים), whom they identify as Ephraimite by their pronunciation of 'shibboleth' as 'sibboleth' (vv. 5-6). Each Ephraimite thusly identified the Gileadites seize and slaughter (וישחטוהו), for an eventual tally of 42,000 dead (v. 6). In 1 Kings 18, Yahweh's prophet Elijah and the prophets of Baal are engaged in a contest of determining which of the two gods was indeed God; the required feat was for the deity to set a burnt offering on fire. Baal's prophets fail to demonstrate that Baal can set the sacrifice alight, but Elijah and Yahweh succeed (vv. 25-39). Elijah then says '"Seize the prophets of Baal; do not let even one of them escape."' So the gathered Israelites 'seized them, and Elijah brought them down to the Wadi Qishon, and slaughtered them (וישחטם) there' (v. 40). Finally, in Jeremiah 41, after assassinating Gedaliah (and murdering his entourage) because the king of Babylonia had chosen him to be governor (vv. 1-2), a certain Ishmael, a member of the royal family, devises a ruse so that a contingent of eighty men en route to Yahweh's temple does not discover what he has done (v. 5). Weeping as he walks, Ishmael goes out of Mizpah to meet them and bids them to come with him to see Gedaliah (v. 6). Once they are inside the city, he has them slaughtered (וישחטם, v. 7). In short, utilized figuratively, I think it is fair to say that זבח/זֶבַח and שחט are antithetical in that the former can be applied to the demise of humans in the context of warfare while the latter denotes the virtual execution of victims already subdued or taken by surprise.

The final point that I would like to make before returning to Ezekiel 16 is that the terms בנים, 'sons/children' and בנות, 'daughters' are also commonly used figuratively, or with extended meanings,[68] in the HB. For example, in the phrase בני ישראל, 'the sons/children of Israel', 'sons/ children' should not be taken to mean that the persons spoken of are all young human beings. Rather, the phrase can mean, for example, all the

---

68. Fauconnier and Turner (*The Way We Think*, pp. 140-43) place the notion of extended meaning and that of metaphor on a continuum, which they illustrate by considering numerous statements that employ the kinship word 'father'.

descendants of the eponymous ancestor Israel, or all those of that ancestry living at a particular time, or, in contrast to בני יהודה, 'the sons/children of Judah', בני ישראל can refer to the Israelite inhabitants of the northern kingdom of Israel. The adult female inhabitants of a city or country are included in the designation 'daughters' of a particular place such as בנות מואב, 'female Moabites' (e.g. Num 25.1), or בנות ירושלם, 'female Jerusalemites' (e.g. Cant 1.5). In Ezekiel specifically, בני plus the name of a city, country or deity can be used to denote members of a nation-state, such as בני אשור, 'Assyrians' (16.28; 23.7, 9, 12, 23), and בני בבל, 'Babylonians' (23.15, 17, 23). Thus I would suggest it behooves us to consider seriously that when the author of Ezek 16.20-21 speaks of the sons and daughters that personified Jerusalem bore to Yahweh, the references may be to the city's/Judah's inhabitants and not, or at least not solely, to Judahite infants and young children.[69]

Returning to Ezekiel 16, let us look again at the vocabulary of vv. 20-21. In v. 20 the author says to personified Jerusalem, 'You took your sons and your daughters who you bore to me and you sacrificed them to them [= male images] for devouring'.[70] If זבח is indeed an inappropriate term to apply to *mulk* offerings and *mulk* offerings were never intended to be food, as Paul has argued, then perhaps these incongruities are clues that the author, a priest steeped in sacrificial language and ritual, intended the statement to be understood figuratively. Perhaps what the author of Ezekiel 16 is alluding to is a metaphorical זֶבַח for the devouring of Judah/Jerusalem's inhabitants, which is to say the loss of numerous lives in the context of warfare, a situation for which the author holds Jerusalem, i.e. the decision-makers in the royal court,[71] responsible. If this is the case, Ezekiel may include the entire population (את־בניך ואת־בנותיך)

69. William H. Brownlee, *Ezekiel 1–19* (WBC 28; Waco, TX: Word, 1986), p. 231, is the only commentator on Ezek 16.20-21 who I noted having made the observation that, figuratively, all Jerusalem's residents would be her children, but he nevertheless opted for a literal reading here.

70. ותקחי את־בניך ואת־בנותיך אשר ילדת לי ותזבחים להם לאכול.

71. Throughout the book, Ezekiel directs his invective against various groups. If we understand Yahweh's sons and daughters here to refer generally to Judah/Jerusalem's inhabitants, it seems likely that Ezekiel is placing the blame for their demise on the city's elite. Cf. 7.20, in which the wealthy are accused of using their beautiful ornament to make abominable images; 17.1-21, which (when deciphered) pins the blame for the deportations of 597 and 587 BCE on Jehoiakim and Zedekiah respectively; 19.1-9, in which the behavior of the princes (נשיאים, v. 1) lead to their exile; 22.1-7, in which the princes (נשיאים, v. 6) are held responsible for idolatry and for shedding the blood of Jerusalem's inhabitants; and 34.1-6, in which Judah's rulers in the guise of metaphoric shepherds are accused of sacrificing (תזבחו, v. 3) their sheep.

in the debacle because he is not alluding to a battle fought on foreign soil, but rather to (a) military encounter(s) that had taken place in Judah and Jerusalem at the hands of foreign invaders (cf. Jer 19). In the context of warfare, the language of devouring humans alludes to their destruction. In addition to the passages, discussed above, that presage a deity's slaughter of foreign enemies by using the figure of feasting on the defeated humans, and as we have seen, the sword can be said to devour, fire devours, one nation or people can be said to devour another and deportation can be referred to as being devoured by a foreign land. That 16.20 reads 'and you sacrificed them to them [i.e. male cult images] for devouring/destruction' may be playing on the notion that (non-human) sacrifice in the ancient Near East was envisaged as feeding the gods; but understood figuratively, the people's destruction could be a consequence of their homage. In support of this interpretation, note the vivid description, in Ezek 6.4-5 and 13 (cf. Lev 26.30), of the corpses of Judahites slain by the sword thrown down in front of their idols and their bones strewn round about.[72]

Verse 21 continues, 'You [Jerusalem] slaughtered my [Yahweh's] children, and you delivered them by making them pass over to them'.[73] Again, as we have seen, Paul has argued that שחט, a word very much at home in the vocabulary of animal sacrifice, is an inappropriate term to be applied to a *mulk* sacrifice. That Jerusalem, personified as a woman, is said to do the slaughtering may be another clue that שחט is to be taken metaphorically, as it was exclusively males who immolated animal victims in Judahite cult practice.[74] If in light of these incongruities we once again understand 'my sons/children' in the extended sense of 'Yahweh's people', then the author may be understood as accusing the powers-that-be in Jerusalem of having been responsible for the deaths of Judahites in (a) situation(s) in which they had already been defeated or

72. The book of Ezekiel includes several additional figurations of humans being eaten and/or treated as animal meat. Particularly noteworthy are chs. 11 and 24, in which Jerusalem functions as a pot in which human rather than animal flesh is cooked and 34.13-14, in which the mountains of Israel(?) are relieved of the accusation of eating humans (אכלת אדם). In 43.7-8, Yahweh is said to devour (ואכל) the house of Israel/their kings.

73. ותשחטי את־בני ותתנים בהעביר אותם להם.

74. S. Tamar Kamionkowski, 'Gender Reversal in Ezekiel 16', in Athalya Brenner (ed.), *Feminist Companion to the Latter Prophets* (Sheffield: Sheffield Academic Press, 2001), pp. 170-85, in her discussion of שחט, makes the point that women were excluded from sacrificial slaughtering, but she incorrectly states that this verb is at home in the context of warfare (pp. 179-80).

subdued.[75] Interpreted in this manner, the author would seem to be saying that a slaughter thus endured by Yahweh's people was tantamount to the offering up of infants or young children in that both involved killing defenseless humans. And in that the making a child pass over to the deity accomplished by *mulk* sacrifice took place through Tophet immolation, 16.21 could be seen to share with Jer 19.12 the notion that the inhabitants of Jerusalem perished like Tophet victims (cf. Isa 30.33). Alternatively and even more tentatively I would suggest that, if a figurative interpretation is indeed what the author intended, then 'you delivered them by passing them over to them' might allude to deportation. As previously noted, Qal forms of עבר occur four and perhaps five times at important junctures in Ezek 16.1-43 (vv. 6, 8, 15, 25; the occurrence in v. 37 is disputed). In the first two instances Yahweh comes by personified Jerusalem from elsewhere, once to rescue infant Jerusalem and the second time to marry her. In v. 15, Jerusalem begins to betray husband Yahweh by bestowing her sexual favours על־כל־עובר, 'upon every passerby', thus inaugurating her relationship with the (implicitly foreign) male images; in v. 25 she spreads her legs לכל־עובר, 'for every passerby', thereby initiating her associations with foreign nations. What I am suggesting is that by virtue of these Qal usages, Jerusalem's delivering her inhabitants up בהעביר might figuratively imply delivering them by causing them to be transferred into a foreign territory,[76] an experience that the author of Ezekiel presumably underwent himself.

---

75. I suspect that this nuance in metaphorical usage of having been subdued prior to slaughter derives from the sacrificial animal being bound or otherwise secured prior to having its throat slit (which is the technical meaning of שחט for the Priestly source: see Milgrom, *Leviticus 1–16*, pp. 715-18), but I have been unable to find definitive textual proof of this. However, I find it hard to imagine the controlled slaughter of especially large and powerful animals in close quarters and the collection of their blood (e.g. Lev 1.5; 3.2; 4.3-8) without them being restrained. I have witnessed the slaughter of pigs for ritual occasions in the extended family compounds of Balinese friends, and the men make very sure the pig's legs are securely bound and they hold the pig down while one of them slits the pig's throat and another neatly collects the blood in a bowl. An additional strategy is to sneak up on the pig while it is sleeping and subdue it while it is still groggy.

76. Both Eidevall, 'The Role of Sacrificial Language', pp. 58-60, and Milgrom, *Leviticus 1–16*, p. 163; cf. Hurvitz, *A Linguistic Study*, p. 57, note that Ezek 20.41 uses a sacrificial metaphor when saying that Yahweh will accept Israel 'like a pleasing odor' (בריח ניחח) when they return from exile, and Eidevall, 'The Role of Sacrificial Language', pp. 55-57, also observes that Isa 66.20 applies a sacrificial metaphor to the return from exile by stating that the nations 'will bring all of [the exiles'] kindred out from all the nations (as) an offering (מנחה) to Yahweh'.

Did the author of Ezekiel intend 16.20-21 to be understood figuratively? If so, these verses are more compressed and significantly less transparent than the passages I have suggested may be appropriate for comparison, and a figurative interpretation leads to a reading of 16.20-21 that is uncomfortably and perhaps even implausibly unique. At best, the readings offered here are inconclusive. But Ezekiel is an author prone to decidedly odd and sometimes forced imagery who seemed to realize that his propensity for enigmatic speech (Ezek 21.5 [Eng. 20.49]) left him open to being perennially misunderstood.

MOCKING BOYS, BALDNESS, AND BEARS:
ELISHA'S DEADLY HONOUR (2 KINGS 2.23-24)

Dietmar Neufeld

Introduction

The honoree of this Festschrift has had a long history with his colleagues at UBC. His warmth, contagious humour, and fearless willingness to challenge the institutional regulations that impinged upon his department and colleagues negatively will be remembered. Unafraid, he took them on with aplomb and we all benefitted from his interventions. His fascination with the cult of *molek* and child sacrifice in ancient Israel was the butt of countless jokes (even though a humourless topic) and fueled many animated conversations in the hallway. Paul G. Mosca's research focused on Phoenician-Punic epigraphy in the Eastern and Central Mediterranean world that stretched from the Late Bronze Age (1550–1200 BCE) down to the Roman period. This volume honours Paul's long preoccupation with the Punic and biblical evidence for child sacrifice and their common derivation in Phoenicia. He spent considerable energy in reconstructing an original form of the word *mulk*, suggesting 'kingdom', 'royalty'. He consequently argued that the word was first applied to the rite of child sacrifice because it involved sacrifice by kings of their own children to gods bearing the title 'king'. As he states, 'it is the offering of royalty, by royalty, to royalty'.[1]

His defense of Eisfeldt's classic hypothesis of the cult of *Molek* in ancient Israel has received broad acceptance and, indeed, helped to moor its lasting significance in scholarship. It is a privilege for me to contribute to this volume in tribute to his learning and friendship. My contribution will not focus on the cult of child sacrifice per se but on the slaughter of forty-two boys by two she-bears—the result of Elisha's intemperate curse upon them for mocking him.

---

1. Paul Mosca, 'Child Sacrifice in Canaanite and Israelite Religion: A Study in *Mulk* and מלך' (Ph.D. diss., Harvard University, 1975).

Negative reaction to the story has been unequivocal in scholarship.[2] Modern sensibilities cannot easily countenance what looks to be an unjustified and deadly outburst of violence against innocent children foolishly humiliating a powerful prophet. More intolerable for modern readers is that the narrative supports the anger of Elisha and a deity who sanctions the mauling of forty-two young boys.[3] What do we make of the story? Taming the harsh reality of the story to fit our sensibilities imposes an ethnocentric reading upon the narrative not fitting for its time and telling. In the social milieu of ancient Israel, Elisha's deadly eruption of anger was acceptable and even expected. He was the target of undeserved mockery by a gang of juveniles that required a robust response from him. He was a prophet of high standing who had just inherited the mantel of Elijah. His honour was on-the-line and retaliation was required to keep it—even when the perpetrators were juveniles only. Elisha's loss of face would have been deadly to his honour had he not engaged in a riposte in kind.

Before proceeding down this path it will be instructive to examine briefly how commentators have interpreted the meaning of this passage—given that it sanctions gratuitous violence. These interpretations will be shown to fall short because they have failed to root the narrative in its ancient Israelite social context where mockery and the shame it triggered frequently erupted into what was considered justifiable violence in defence of honour.

Previous and Current Scholarship on Boys, Baldness and Bears

Explanations vary in their attempt to explain this difficult narrative. They employ a variety of methods, from ancient media studies to modern literary theory, from historical-critical tools to narrative criticism. A recent narrative-critical approach to the tale points out that the repeated taunt of the little boys, 'go up baldy, go up baldy', is mild and does not justify Elisha's deadly curse (2 Kgs 2.23). Yet because the slur is maliciously intending to make an invidious contrast between the hairless

2. Eric J. Ziolkowski, 'The Bad Boys of Bethel: Origin and Development of a Sacrilegious Type', *History of Religions* 30 (1991), pp. 331-58.

3. Alan F. Segal, *Sinning in the Hebrew Bible: How the Worst Stories Speak for its Truth* (New York: Columbia University Press, 2012). Segal notes that many of the stories in the Hebrew Bible 'are unattractive, downright terrible, and even immoral... Thus the Hebrew Bible presents us with many unexpected moral problems that are horrifying to contemplate. These difficult stories demand greater explanation' (p. 1).

Elisha and the hairy Elijah (2 Kgs 1.8), Elisha's fury is perhaps comprehensible. Whatever one is to make of the vicious outburst of anger, however, the incident permits the author to demonstrate this emerging prophet's power to call down a divine curse. The tale is designed to stimulate in the reader a strong respect for the authority of Elijah's successor.[4]

While at the level of narrative this explanation makes good sense, no attempt is made to situate Elisha's violent reaction in the ancient Israelite social context of mocking and being mocked and the extraordinary sensitivity to maintaining honour in the face of cruel mockery.

Theological approaches to the incident abound. Most of them either skirt the moral difficulties of the episode or rationalize it in a moralizing way. An extreme example of rationalizing the nasty response of Elisha to the taunting he received is found in Matthew Henry's Concise Commentary. The commentator writes,

> The little children of Bethel…mocked him as if he had been a fool. It was his character as a prophet that they designated to abuse. The honor God had crowned him with should have been sufficient to cover his bald head and protect him from their scoffs. These children said as they were taught: they had learned of their idolatrous parents to call foul names and give bad language, especially to prophets… The prophet must be justified, for he did it by divine impulse. He intended here to punish the parents to make them afraid of God's judgments.[5]

Whatever lesson this brief incident was projected to convey it certainly was not intended to rebuke parents or instill fear in them. Others have supposed that the tale's moral point was to enhance the prophet's fame, to confirm Elisha's inheritance of Elijah's miraculous powers, and to enforce the warning that Elisha is a powerful man with whom not to trifle.[6]

Marvin A. Sweeney observes that respect for elders hardly depletes the literary function of this pericope. Sweeney argues that this narrative is placed here 'to validate Elisha's role as Elijah's prophetic successor by demonstrating that Elijah's powers have passed to Elisha'.[7] While such

---

4. R. L. Cohn, D. W. Cotter, and J. T. Walsh (eds.), *2 Kings* (Berit Olam. Studies in Hebrew Narrative and Poetry; Collegeville, MN: Liturgical Press, 2000), p. 17.

5. Matthew Henry, *The Matthew Henry Study Bible: King James Version* (Peabody, MA: Hendrickson, 2010), p. 593.

6. Volkmar Fritz, *1 & 2 Kings: A Continental Commentary* (Minneapolis: Fortress, 2003), p. 239.

7. Marvin A. Sweeney, *I & II Kings: A Commentary* (Louisville: Westminster John Knox Press, 2007), p. 275.

meanings are extractable from the narrative, they have not been suffi-
ciently moored in the social milieu of mockery and its power to corrode
Elisha's honour standing in the company of prophets. By situating the
pericope in the social context of ancient Israelite culture of mockery and
avoiding shame, the story stands as an awful example of Elisha defending his honour.

A study by Ziolkowski explores how this pericope in 2 Kings became
foundational for a Western literary motif about male children. This motif
presented them as sacrilegious type—'ancient precursors to the "punks",
"skinheads", and "wilding" youths who stalk the streets of modern
metropolises'.[8] The author shows through analysis of classic literary
examples the kinship between boys, irreligiousness, and 'evil' that
undermines 'the virtual beatification of children traditionally embraced
by Christianity'.[9]

Ziolkowski's work is a fascinating analysis of the reception of the
bad-boys-of-Bethel motif in classic literature and puts to rest the notion
of the innocence of children. His analysis, however, does little to help
understand the incident from the perspectives of the social values of
Elisha's day.

Some studies have focused on baldness, suggesting that Elisha's
baldness was a symbol signifying his prophetic vocation or that it was
intended as a slur in sharp contrast to the well-haired Elijah.[10] Other
analyses have cast their attention upon the curse and the harsh punishment of the boys for what seemed to be a momentary lapse on their part
not worthy of such violence.[11] Still others do away with the need to
justify the curse by dismissing it and suggesting instead that a mauling
incident happened near Bethel that coincided with Elisha's visit. The
mauling therefore was not the direct result of Elisha's curse in the name
of God but a mere coincidence the author used to enhance Elisha's
character as powerful prophet.

That the small boys from Bethel mocked Elisha is clear, and that
Elisha responded aggressively to their ridicule is also clear. In the
ancient world, mockery unseated the powerful and the powerful, in
response, resorted to dramatic actions designed to retain their honour.
Hence, Elisha responded swiftly, incisively, and strongly. Not to do so

---

8. Ziolkowski, 'The Bad Boys of Bethel', pp. 332-33.

9. Ziolkowski, 'The Bad Boys of Bethel', p. 333.

10. Sweeney, *I & II Kings: A Commentary*, p. 275.

11. A. D. Fraser, 'The Ancient Curse: Some Analogies', *The Classical Journal* 17, no. 8 (1922), pp. 454-60; Brian Britt, *Biblical Curses and the Displacement of Tradition* (Sheffield: Sheffield Phoenix, 2011).

would have indicated his weakness and the loss of status, shame and the stigma that followed. Understanding the social elements of honour in such a context will make clear why Elisha's only recourse was to invoke his deity to destroy the little boys from Bethel making a mockery of him.

The next section will set out the social functions of mockery and why ancients avoided its damaging vector. Helpful in this regard will be to make use of the social sciences and what they have to say about the larger societal forces of mockery, honour, and shame as a reflection of the ancient Israelite cultural setting. The use of social-scientific insights to investigate the Hebrew Bible has become increasingly popular in recent years because it permits the interrogation of texts of the Hebrew Bible in new ways and thus produce meaningful insights into the society behind the texts.[12] And, these insights also allow us to understand the culture, values, behaviors, and practices of the ancient Israelites from their perspectives rather than from ours. This study will therefore set out the parameters of mockery and its profound influence on issues of honour and shame by canvassing Greek and Roman sources for discussions of these important social behaviours in the belief that our findings are also broadly applicable to the ancient Mediterranean world inhabited by the Israelites. In the assessment of the Elisha story, I will be using the Greek text of the Septuagint.

Mockery, Honour, Visibility and Shame

Mockery and laughter are complex human behaviours that have the capacity both to warm and to wound. We have all felt the sting of a pointed barb and its damaging aftermath. In a recent US Public Diplomacy White Paper, 'Ridicule: An Instrument in the War on Terrorism', J. Michael Waller discusses the transformation of American public diplomacy and strategic communication, and the use of ridicule as a weapon 'against terrorists, against weapons proliferators, despots, and international undesirables'.[13] Ridicule, he continues, 'leverages the emotions and simplifies the complicated and takes on the powerful, in politics,

---

12.   Norman K. Gottwald, *The Tribes of Yahweh: A Sociology of the Religion of Liberated Israel 1250–1050 B.C.E* (Maryknoll, NY: Orbis Books, 1979); Philip F. Esler (ed.), *Ancient Israel: The Old Testament in its Social Context* (Minneapolis: Fortress, 2005); Charles E. Carter and Carol L. Meyers (eds.), *Community, Identity, and Ideology: Social Science Approaches to the Hebrew Bible* (Winona Lake: Eisenbrauns, 1996).

13.   M. J. Waller, 'Ridicule: An Instrument in the War on Terrorism' (*USA Today*: Public Diplomacy White Paper No. 7: Washington, 2006), p. 1.

law, entertainment, literature, culture, sports, and romance'.[14] Moreover, an argument, image, or kinetic force can be countered, but few defences can be marshalled 'against the well-aimed barbs that bleed humiliation and drip contempt'.[15] The point is that ridicule is a highly charged medium of personal and social interactions, and an integral part within a repertoire of socially enacted behaviour and means of communication.

Ancients recognized that insulting words had the potential to wound deeply—especially those words that damaged honour and exposed shame. A passage from the ancient novel *Leucippe and Clitophon*, by Achilles Tatius, makes this abundantly clear.

> Speech is the father of shame, grief, and anger: like arrows aimed at a target and hitting it dead centre, words pierce the soul and wound it in many places. One verbal arrow is insult, and the wound it leaves is called anger: another is exposure of one's misfortunes, and this arrow causes grief: a third is lectures on one's faults, and this arrow is known as shame. One quality common to all these weapons is that they pierce deeply but draw no blood. The only remedy for them is counterattack with the same weapons. The wound caused by one's sharp tongue is healed by the razor's edge of another. This softens the heart's anger and assuages the soul's grief. If one is prevented by *force majeure* from uttering one's defense, the wounds silently fester. Unable to reject their foam, the waves swell up in labor, distended by the puffing breath of words within. (2.29)[16]

As much as the ancients felt the salty sting of scorn, so also we feel the sting of ridicule because it targets core attitudes and values on matters pertaining to sex, status, ethnicity, identity, politics, religion, economics, culture, food and drink, and a whole host of other social registers. Commentary or laughter of a derisive kind on any of these issues touches us to the core of our identities and causes personal wounds that frequently cannot be repaired.

Ridicule that pokes at core issues often triggers anger and physical antagonism. The passage above is clear that scornful words stimulate the emotion of anger (*iracundia/orgē*). Romans were acutely aware of the dangers that uncontrolled anger represented. Anger created heated actions and words that if not restrained frequently provoked crimes of murder and vengeance. Angry rulers unable to restrain their anger were a danger to the body politic and its citizens; angry fathers and mothers

---

14. Waller, 'Ridicule', p. 2.

15. Waller, 'Ridicule', p. 2.

16. Translated by T. Whitmarsh, *Leucippe and Clitophon* (Oxford: Oxford University Press, 2002); taken from D. F. Watson, *Honor Among Christians: The Cultural Key to the Messianic Secret* (Minniapolis: Fortress, 2010), p. 51.

were a danger to their children; angry children were a menace to ageing, vulnerable parents; angry religious authorities were a threat to the laws and customs of religious polity and to the many adherents beholden to their dictates; angry prophets were a menace to mocking children. Cicero wrote a letter to his young brother Quintus (60–59 BCE) to give him advice on anger control:

> [P]assions, curses and insults are not only inconsistent with literary culture and *humanitas*, they are inimical to the dignity of the imperial office, for if one's outbursts of anger are implacable, that is a sign of extreme harshness [*acerbitatem animi*], but if they are capable of being mollified, that is a sign of frivolity—which is, however, to be preferred to harshness. (*Quint. fratr.* i.1.37-40)[17]

In an excellent study of anger in Greek and Roman philosophical texts, Harris points not only to the ambivalence in attitudes towards anger but also to its many social functions in the creation of harmony or disharmony between siblings, emperors and their citizens, masters and their slaves, mothers and fathers and their children, and wives and husbands.[18] There were times when anger was justified, but for the most part anger was such a powerful emotion that it had to be restrained. Uncontrolled anger expressed itself in vengeance (*vindicta*) and violence. On occasion, anger acted out in vengeance was deserved, but generally it was frowned upon, especially when driven by a personal desire for reprisal. Under the influence of the Stoic philosophical tradition enjoining *humanitas*, harmony, mildness (*epieikesteran/clementiorem*) and dignity, Musonius Rufus argued that the wise man should abandon anger and instead opt for mildness of character—even abandoning going to court, despite having suffered a grievous injustice (*hybris*) that required restitution.

Of course, it was difficult to resist an outburst of anger. For example, Cicero writes that 'when *viri fortissimo*, vigorous public men, are injured they resent it, when they are angered they are carried away (*efferuntur*). When they are provoked they fight' (Cicero, *Cael.* 21). Most often were heard the ill-timed words of scorn from a friend or foe that caused the blood to boil over in anger. Excessive shame spawned deep hatred for

---

17. W. V. Harris, *Restraining Rage: The Ideology of Anger Control in Classical Antiquity* (Cambridge, MA: Harvard University Press, 2001), p. 205; *idem*, 'The Rage of Women', in S. Braund and G. W. Most (eds.), *Ancient Anger: Perspectives from Homer to Galen* (Cambridge: Cambridge University Press, 2004), pp. 212-43.

18. S. H. Braund and C. Gill (eds.), *The Passions in Roman Thought and Literature* (Cambridge: Cambridge University Press, 1997); Braund and Most (eds.), *Ancient Anger*; Harris, *Restraining Rage*, pp. 201-28.

the instigators of the shame. Suffering the embarrassment of exposure in the eyes of others provoked fury and the desire for vengeance.[19]

Elisha was rooted in a social system where mockery and laughter operated as a set of social behaviours intertwined with the fabric of daily life, with specific local circumstances and with the cosmos as a whole. And because mockery touched virtually every aspect of human life, authors utilized its potency as a weapon to control people and malevolent forces in the social and cosmic realms. It is thus that the author of 2 Kings, aware of mockery's flexible applicability to all areas of life, utilized it to promote the public ethos (persona) of a powerful prophet who had just inherited the mantel of Elijah. The slighting and Elisha's violent riposte served to ingrain this ethos in the imagination of the author's audience.

Mockery, however, did not work on its own; for effectiveness, it worked in tandem within the elaborate economy of Roman honour and shame. The mechanisms of shame were not unilateral but operated along a continuum from the fear of being exposed to public shame to the resigned acceptance of being tested in the eyes of public scrutiny. In the limelight of potentially becoming a public spectacle, mockery was potent because it had the power to inflame and inflict shame and create shame-bound anxiety.

Mockery and the Power to Inflict and Inflame Shame

We have already observed that mockery traded on the currency of shame and fear—the fear of being revealed to the view of public shame. Cicero, for example, notes:

> The best citizens are not deterred [from disgraceful behaviour] by fear of a punishment that has been sanctioned by laws, as much as by the sense of shame that has been instilled by nature and a kind of fear of just censure (*vituperationis non iniustae*). The founder of the state used public opinion to cause this sense of shame to grow and refined it through both established custom and training. As a result, shame, no less than fear, keeps the citizen from doing wrong. (*Resp.* 5.6)

Hence, mockery's focus was something to be feared, avoided and yet, ironically, also embraced in a culture of visibility. In such a culture, where wielding mockery's public power to cause damage to others was common, escaping the embarrassment of exposure was of paramount

---

19. C. A. Barton, *Roman Honor: The Fire in the Bones* (Berkeley: University of California Press, 2001), pp. 262-66.

importance.[20] On the positive side, ridicule also traded on the currency of honour—its establishment, maintenance and defence. Men, women, children, slaves and retainers, each in their respective courts of reputation, sought it, fought for it, gained and lost it, and manipulated it to gain advantage over friend and foe alike. Cicero, noting children at play, writes,

> With what earnestness they pursue their rivalries. How fierce their contests. What exaltation they feel when they win, and what shame when they are beaten. How they dislike reproach. How they yearn for praise. What labours will they not undertake to stand first among their peers. How well they remember those who have shown them kindness and how eager to repay. (*Fin.* 5.22.61)

Shame and honour were flip sides of the same coin, powerfully contributing to the formation of the character and reputation of each inhabitant in the ancient Mediterranean world. Honour was a wide-ranging force in society, created and maintained by individuals and public opinion, and thus a form of power that moved people. Aristotle, in a long discussion of the vices and virtues related to honour, makes clear how valuable a commodity it was:

> Now the most valuable of the external goods, we may assume, is the thing we offer to the gods, and which is most prized by noble/generous persons, and that is honour. It is clearly the greatest of external goods. Indeed, concerning honour and dishonour, the noble/generous person is the one who gets it right. (*Eth. Nic.* 4.3.9-12)

Pliny the Younger deemed 'that [the] man happiest of all [is he] who enjoys the anticipation of a good and abiding fame, and who, assured of posterity's judgment, lives now in possession of the glory that he will then have' (*Ep.* 9.3, '*fama...gloria*'). Seneca noted that honour was based on the favourable opinion of respectable persons publicly given (*Ep.* 102.8). A person's honour was a public verdict of his or her good standing and personal qualities. Indeed, observed Dio Chrysostom, scarcely a person could be found out of a multitude to do what was deemed noble for himself unless it were mediated through the public recognition and approval process of others (*Orations* 31.17; Cicero, *Arch.* 28-29). In his study of honour and influence in the Roman world, Lendon concluded that weighing honour was an unceasing process: generals and soldiers waged war for it; persons of influence schemed for

---

20. Stephen Halliwell, *Greek Laughter: A Study of Cultural Psychology from Homer to Early Christianity* (Cambridge: Cambridge University Press, 2008), p. 25.

it; philosophers argued philosophically for it; teachers sought for it; orators spoke for it—and, in the case of prophets divined for it.[21]

A pecking order maintained and defined by honour was normal for the inhabitants of the ancient Mediterranean world. Establishing notable credentials, along with ranking each other on a social scale, was done through the currency of honour. One's claim of an honour standing before one's peers was exchanged by them into the material worth of honour.[22] Hence, honour was never an assured element because it could be gained or lost at a moment's notice, as courts of reputation distributed judgments at whim. For esteem to exist, it had to find affirmation before those in the position to grant it.

Honour was either ascribed or achieved. Ascribed honour included high birth, illustrious home town, wealth (preferably not gained by insatiable lust), grand house, legal status, expensive clothes, proper education, accent, words, posture and bearing. Aristotle, for example, notes that 'a characteristic of noble birth is that he who possesses it is more ambitious; for all men, when they start with any good, are accustomed to heap it up, and noble birth is a heritage of honour from one's ancestors' (*Rhet.* 2.15.2). Those of ascribed honour never needed to ask about genealogies to realize their place on the honour map. All it took was a glance. For those who managed to achieve honourable standing, it took more than a glance. For them, great lengths were necessary to defend their achieved positions.

Achieved honour included prowess in athletic or military undertakings, and anything else in which one excelled that was noticed and for which one received credit. Honour arose from the recognition of various qualities deemed praiseworthy. Elisha's reputation as a prophet increased exponentially as rumours of his achievements spread—he gained grandeur because upon observing his deeds from a distance a company of prophets willingly granted honour to him (2 Kgs 2.15). Moreover, this acquired glory eventually became part of Elisha's general prestige as his reputation spread. The author of Kings records many an incident that graphically illustrated the increasing status of the prophet (2 Kgs 3.13-20; 4.1-7, 17, 32-37; 6.1-23)

---

21. J. E. Lendon, *Empire of Honour: The Art of Government in the Roman World* (Oxford: Oxford University Press, 1997), p. 35. See Mark Harding, *Early Christian Life and Thought in Context: A Reader* (London: T&T Clark International, 2003), pp. 235-38.

22. Lendon, *Empire of Honour*, p. 37.

Honour, Power and Influence

Lendon makes the important point that honour was a character trait one possessed—especially among the elite with inherited honour.[23] Even when conferred by one's opinion community, honour was a personal quality essentially embedded in one's character that then extended itself to one's family and kinship group—and, in Elisha's case, to his company of prophets. The personal character of honour was nevertheless not limited to the elite. As we have observed, slaves, peasants, women, men, children and wandering healers, teachers, and prophets did manage to achieve honour in their respective courts of reputation. They would also have been characterized by esteem, and that esteem likewise clung to those attached to them. Needless to say, what constituted honour differed in the ancient world's respective social hierarchies. For instance, for peasants it might be liberation from debt and poverty—liberation, however, was converted into the common currency of honour.[24] For the demon-possessed, it was being released from the possessing agent and transitioning successfully back into the community, family and kinship group. They had managed to gain a new-found freedom worthy of respect. Elisha had honour granted to him when the company of prophets declared 'the spirit of Elijah rests on Elisha' (2 Kgs 2.17). They then proceeded dramatically to embody the declaration by walking over to meet him and bow to the ground before him (2 Kgs 2.17). The conferral of honour frequently exhibited itself in embodied form and was intentionally designed to confirm the recipient's honour standing. With Elisha's honour standing confirmed, the fifty-strong company of prophets immediately prevail upon Elisha that he grant them permission to seek his master—who in their estimation despite being caught up by the spirit of the Lord may have been hurled down on some mountain or into some valley (2 Kgs 2.16). Elisha resists at first but then acquiesces in shame to their persistent urging—their persistence put him to shame (ἠσχύνετο, LXX 2 Kgs 2.17). It would appear that even though Elisha's reputation in the company of prophets had been confirmed it was nevertheless still tenuous and had yet to be solidified in the crucible of testing.

The point is that possessors of honour were able to wield power because of the awareness that honour was a possession everyone desired, maintained and defended, and because of the enormous concerns that it not be lost. Honour had huge currency and was accepted as a medium of exchange. Little wonder, then, that the author of 2 Kings embedded his

23. Lendon, *Empire of Honour*, pp. 36-73.
24. Lendon, *Empire of Honour*, pp. 33-34.

stories of Elisha in the give-and-take exchange of honour challenges precipitated by competing notions of what constituted real honour between rival religious associations and prophets. Rival notions of true honour, doled out by the respective opinion communities, frequently became the locus of mocking commentary.

With the testing of Elisha complete the author quickly followed with a story designed to seal the honour of the prophet in the imaginations of his audiences—the cursing and mauling of those who dared to taint his reputation dramatically reinforced the power and standing of the prophet.

The Mockery of Hybris, Anger, and Honour/Shame: The Case of Elisha's Honour Defence

Everyone with a desire to excel strove passionately for honour and defended it when under attack. As we mentioned earlier, particularly offensive forms of shameful behaviours were those that precipitated anger, stimulated by the realization in action of the opinion of someone's worthlessness. In his excellent study of *hybris*, Fisher notes that slighting (derogatory, disparaging, belittling) commentary generates anger and also triggers three other distinct emotions—contempt (*kataphronesis*), spite (*epereasmos*) and *hybris*.[25] The *locus classicus* of *hybris* comes from Aristotle:

> The man committing *hybris* also slights: for *hybris* is doing and saying things at which the victim incurs shame, not in order that one may achieve anything other than what is done but simply from the pleasure of it. For those who act in return from something do not commit *hybris*, they avenge themselves. The cause of the pleasure for those committing *hybris* is that by harming people they think themselves to be superior (that is why the young and the rich are *hybristai*; they think that they are superior when committing *hybris*). Dishonour is characteristic of *hybris*, and he who dishonours someone slights him, since what has no worth has no honour, either for good or bad. That is why Achilles says when angry: 'He dishonoured me; for he has himself taken my prize, and keeps it' (*Iliad* 1.356) and 'he treated me as if I were a wanderer without honour' (*Iliad* 9.648=17.59), since he is angry for those reasons. (*Rhet.* 1378b23-25)[26]

Hybris was directly related to a whole subset of other mocking displays of speech and conduct, such as obscene language, quarrelling, outbursts of anger, derision hurled about shamelessly, and acts of injustice meant

---

25. N. R. E. Fisher, *HYBRIS: A Study in the Values of Honour and Shame in Ancient Greece* (Warminster: Aris & Phillips, 1992), pp. 7-8.

26. Translation from Fisher, *HYBRIS*, p. 8.

to harm another. Especially significant for this discussion is the relationship between *hybristic* conduct and dishonour. Fisher's study firmly placed the species of *hybris* into a collection of concepts having to do with the honour of individuals. He defines *hybris* as a 'form of slighting, of making clear that one does not value or honour someone else, which produces anger, involving a desire for revenge, the restoration of one's honour... [*H*]*ybris* is itself a behaviour designed to produce shame.'[27] A characteristic of conduct driven by *hybris* is the wish to dishonour someone intentionally. Clear from Fisher's assessment of Aristotle's discussions of *hybris* is that not all behaviours (e.g. adultery, theft, striking another) that ancients committed against others were perceived to be driven by the deliberate intention to dishonour the victims for pleasure. The actions were considered morally wrong, but if they were committed not with the express purpose of dishonouring someone and pleasing oneself, they did not amount to *hybris*. However, the intentional desire to dishonour someone by laughing or mocking so as to cause reputational damage amounted to *hybris*. While *hybris* manifested itself in calculated insulting behaviour, the agent also had to derive pleasure from its deployment, typically involving harmful or violent action against the victim. Fisher also notes that *hybris* is directly related to injustice (*adikia*) leading to dishonour (*atimia*) and shame (*aidos*), and the excessively strong emotions it stirs, such as anger (*orgē*) and rage (*thumos*). Mockery was a form of *hybris*, and the proclivity of the *hybristai* for offensive, honour-damaging abuse stimulated shame and anger in the abused. Desire for revenge was frequently the outcome.[28]

This brings us back to the issue of words, actions and the emotion of anger. There were moments for appropriate anger, especially expressions of anger perceived to be enacted in defence of the community—for example, the anger felt by kings, priests or assemblies protecting the standing of the community from harmful scandal. Harris argued that most Athenians equivocated between *orgilotēs* (irascibility), *aorgēsia* (routine absence of *orgē*) and *analgēsia* (indifference). For Aristotle, the point was not that one should avoid anger altogether, or that one's persona should be caught halfway between irritability and the routine absence of *orgē*; rather, 'one should be angry with the right people for the right reasons, in other words with people who have truly done one some injury, and also in the right manner and at the right moment and for

27. Fisher, *HYBRIS*, p. 10.
28. Fisher, *HYBRIS*, p. 1; Harris, *Restraining Rage*; Harris, 'The Rage of Women', pp. 212-43.

the right length of time'.[29] Achieving a healthy balance involved simply experiencing a moderate amount of anger—but if the circumstances were right and the provocation injurious enough, then vigorous and prolonged anger were justified.

Anger tended to be triggered when the immodest actualizations of opinions of a person's worthlessness took place, precipitating anger not only in the recipients but also in the observers. The emotional response was made all the more infuriating when derogating commentary displayed an irritating superiority in the perpetrators and indicated the pleasure they found in making insulting remarks. The victims were deeply shamed by the devaluations of their persons and associates, with the result that friends and family members of the victim bore the contagion of the victim's shame. Lydus, who was a tutor, complains bitterly about one of his students because he was 'making his father and me, his friends and relatives, into carriers of his disgrace' (Plautus, *Bacch.* 380-81).[30] Failure infected the entire kinship structure or the prophetic guild in the case of Elisha.

Full of rich social colouring, the author of 2 Kings illustrates the emotion of anger in Elisha's reaction to the boys' taunting him. With a sense of irritating superiority, the boys from Bethel observed Elisha,

---

29. Taken from Harris, 'The Rage of Women', p. 128. Aristotle, in his *Eth. Nic.* 4.5.1-3, wrote that 'Good temper is a mean with respect to anger; the middle state being unnamed, and the extremes almost without a name as well, we place good temper in the middle position, though it inclines towards the deficiency, which is without a name. The excess might be called a sort of 'irascibility'. For the passion is anger, while its causes are many and diverse. The man who is angry at the right things and with the right people, and, further, as he ought, when he ought, and as long as he ought, is praised. This will be the good-tempered man, then, since good temper is praised. For the good-tempered man tends to be unperturbed and not to be led by passion, but to be angry in the manner, at the things, and for the length of time, that the rule dictates; but he is thought to err rather in the direction of deficiency; for the good-tempered man is not revengeful, but rather tends to make allowances. The deficiency, whether it is a sort of "inirascibility" or whatever it is, is blamed. For those who are not angry at the things they should be angry at are thought to be fools, and so are those who are not angry in the right way, at the right time, or with the right persons; for such a man is thought not to feel things nor to be pained by them, and, since he does not get angry, he is thought unlikely to defend himself; and to endure being insulted and put up with insult to ones friends is slavish' (translated by W. D. Ross). [cited 6 August 2013]. Online: http://classics.mit .edu/Aristotle/nicomachaen. 4.iv.html.

30. Taken from C. Barton, 'Being in the Eyes: Shame and Sight in Ancient Rome', in D. Fredrick (ed.), *The Roman Gaze: Vision, Power, and the Body* (Baltimore: The Johns Hopkins University Press, 2002), pp. 216-35.

noted his baldness, and began to abuse him verbally. Filled with a sense of indomitable youthfulness and saucy insolence they made sport of Elisha just for the pleasure of it. Predictably it triggered a powerful anger in Elisha. We can also assume that because Elisha was in the eyes of the company of prophets still estimating his honour quotient, they were watching him carefully to assess his response to the boys.

The ancient Mediterranean world was a culture of spectacle—anything that was eye-catching, especially something remarkable in appearance or impressive in nature, became ocular feasts. Valuable recent studies have shown the significant role that the gaze or the penetrating look had in the self-definition or the annihilation/disregard of others.[31] Particularly significant is Carlin Barton's 'Being in the Eyes: Shame and Sight in Ancient Rome', which examines the social behaviour of the eye itself and helpfully explains what it meant for ancients to live visibly under the constant gaze of others.[32] Barton situates her discussion of being in the eyes of others in the context of honour and shame that in a culture of visibility took on special concern. The gaze of the other was ever present and inescapable—hiding from it ignited suspicions about one's character and raised the spectre of further, more intense, scrutiny. Ancient culture was one of visibility or public prominence, where everyone was easily noticed by and caught the attention of the public, groups of people and individuals. Being seen carried with it enormous risks, especially when one was seen unaware, unexpectedly, intentionally and calculatedly. Fully aware of the risk, however, those with a sense of honour and shame accepted the peril of visibility.[33] The thinking here was that one's nature required 'testing' and 'probing' to be real, actual and current.[34] Barton observes that the *spectator* was an inspector, judge and connoisseur, and in such roles he or she was meant to hear, behold, observe, see, think and judge.[35]

In an ocular culture constantly testing and weighing the character of ancient Israelites, Elisha could not have escaped scrutiny. And, avoiding it was not an option because of the suspicions it raised in the minds of the onlooker. Indeed, as noted, had Elisha tried to escape the public limelight the light would have been turned upon him with even greater

31. Barton, 'Being in the Eyes'.
32. Barton, 'Being in the Eyes', p. 221.
33. Barton, 'Being in the Eyes', p. 221.
34. Barton, 'Being in the Eyes', p. 221. Barton points out that terms such as these were used to describe the effect of visibility upon one's persona: *porbatus, spectatus, expertus, argutus*.
35. Barton, 'Being in the Eyes', p. 221.

intensity. Moreover, something as momentous as the mauling of forty-two boys by two she-bears surely was noticed and that it was the result of a curse called upon the boys for their rude disregard of Elisha's status also drew attention. Under such scrutiny Elisha could not afford to respond inappropriately without regard for aggressively maintaining his honour and standing in the community of prophets—derision was pragmatically linked to shamefulness of exposure. Indeed, the embarrassment of public exposure for failing vigorously to defend his standing in the company of prophets would have shamed him and by association those around him. A nonchalant attitude to being the target of scorn was recognized as an aberrancy—namely indifference was a symptom of having a deficient sense of honour. Victims of mockery were expected to seek occasions for revenge.[36] Under constant inspection and rooted in a social context where mockery at a moment's notice destroyed public reputations, he had no other recourse but to turn on the boys with a vengeance. Awe was instilled in the onlookers at the power of this prophet. Even his deity ceded to his request.

Conclusions

Mockery was a potent force that Elisha could not ignore. Because ridicule worked in tandem with honour and shame and the extraordinary sensitivity to the loss of respect, a strong response was required for Elisha to mitigate the damage to his status the boys caused him. Coupled with a culture of visibility in which conduct, character and standing were in constant evaluation, the desire to come back forcefully when status was under threat was heightened. The honour quotient of Elisha was being probed by the company of prophets to see whether he had the same mettle/spirit of his predecessor. Yes, the company of prophets had provisionally granted Elisha standing as a prophet in status equal to Elijah when they declared that 'the spirit of Elijah rests on Elisha' and then again when they came over to meet him and bow before him—a public display of embodied homage to the successor of Elijah (2 Kgs 2.15)—yet, questions must have remained in their minds about whether his status was equal in quality to that of Elijah. They insisted that a party should be sent out in search of Elijah. Elisha initially resisted, but under further pressure he eventually acquiesced. We are told that he relented because he had been shamed—before the company of fifty it appeared that he was still finding his honour footing. Not surprisingly, the author of 2 Kings followed up with the incident of the boys taunting Elisha and

36. Halliwell, *Greek Laughter*, p. 41.

his angry riposte to fortify the perception that Elisha was an equal to Elijah. The dramatic display of anger reinforced by a curse that invoked the name of his deity confirmed to the company that his deity was sanctioning Elisha's standing as a prophet equal to Elijah. They were therefore under obligation to validate Elisha's prestige in the company of prophets.

Elisha's honour defense was deadly but effective. It established his credentials as a powerful prophet to be given considerable respect. In Elisha's social context the violent outburst was understandable and even required, while to our modern sensibilities this is a story 'whose reason for existence is hard to fathom'.[37] Elisha's forceful defence of his honour, while disproportionate to the foolish taunting of the boys, was never intended as a moral lesson for the modern world. The story, moored in a particular social environment of mockery, honour and shame, and visibility, was intended dramatically to solidify the prestige of Elisha as the legitimate successor of Elijah.

37. Segal, *Sinning in the Hebrew Bible*, p. 2.

DEATH AND THE MAIDEN:
HUMAN SACRIFICE IN EURIPIDES' *ANDROMEDA**

C. W. Marshall

While the concept of human sacrifice did exist in ancient Greece (at *Iliad* 23.175-76 Achilles sacrifices twelve Trojans on the tomb of Patroclus, for example), it was not a part of the ritual life of Classical Athens.[1] In spite of this, the playwright Euripides made human sacrifice a central motif in a significant number of tragedies. The pattern established in these plays is regular enough that it is meaningful to generalize and speak of the 'plays of voluntary self-sacrifice' in Euripides:[2] *Children*

---

* This short chapter is happily presented to my colleague Paul Mosca on his retirement from the University of British Columbia.

1. A. Henrichs, 'Human Sacrifice in Greek Religion: Three Case Studies', in J. Rudhardt and O. Reverdin (eds.), *Le sacrifice dans l'antiquité* (Geneva: Fond. Hardt, 1981), pp. 195-235; D. D. Hughes, *Human Sacrifice in Ancient Greece* (London: Routledge, 1991); P. Bonnechere, *Le sacrifice humain en Grèce ancienne* (Kernos supp. 3; Liège: Centre International d'Étude de la Religion Grecque Antique, 1994), and see, for an overview, S. Scullion, 'Human Sacrifice', in H. M. Roisman (ed.), *The Encyclopedia of Greek Tragedy* (London: John Wiley & Sons, 2013). The pseudo-platonic *Minos* 315b apparently presents human sacrifice as still practiced in the fourth century (οὐ νόμος ἐστὶν ἀνθρώπους θύειν ἀλλ' ἀνόσιον, 'it is not legal to sacrifice people, but it is unholy'). Later accounts do provide some possible rare exceptions, but these are not normative: Themistocles before the battle of Salamis in 480 (Plut., *Them.* 13, which Henrichs takes to be fictional); contemplated by Pelopidas before Leuctra in 371 (Plutarch, *Pelop.* 20-22).

2. J. Wilkins, 'The State and the Individual: Plays of Voluntary Self-Sacrifice', in A. Powell (ed.), *Euripides, Women, and Sexuality* (London: Routledge, 1990), pp. 177-94, and see J. Schmitt, *Freiwilliger Opfertod bei Euripides* (Giessen: A. Töpelmann, 1921); P. Roussel, 'Le thème du sacrifice volontaire dans la tragédie d'Euripide', *Revue Belge de Philologie et d'Histoire* 1 (1922), pp. 225-40; H. Strohm, *Euripides. Interpretationen zur dramatischen Form* (Zetemata 15; Munich: Beck, 1957), pp. 50-63; P. Vellacott, *Ironic Drama: A Study of Euripides' Method and Meaning* (Cambridge: Cambridge University Press, 1975), pp. 178-204; E. A. M. E. O'Connor-Visser, *Aspects of Human Sacrifice in the Tragedies of Euripides* (Amsterdam: B. R. Grüner, 1987).

of Heracles (ca. 429 BCE), *Erechtheus* (fragmentary, dating to 422 or possibly a few years later),[3] *Hecuba* (ca. 421),[4] *Phoenician Women* (ca. 410), and *Iphigenia at Aulis* (posthumously produced in 405). In each of these plays, a young woman (or a young man in the case of Menoeceus in *Phoenician Women*) is killed as a sacrifice to a god or a deceased hero as part of the dramatic action. Sufficient variation exists that each death can be seen to be individual, even though the larger pattern stands apart from the presentation of human sacrifice elsewhere in tragedy.[5]

Other plays present human sacrifice as an action antecedent to the events of the play. Iphigenia's death precedes the events of Aeschylus' *Oresteia* (458; cf. *Ag.* 218-49), and the event is assumed in plays that engage directly with Aeschylus' narrative, including Euripides' *Electra*, *Orestes*, and Sophocles' *Electra*; *Iphigenia in Tauris* (ca. 417)[6] presents Iphigenia having been miraculously rescued from sacrifice but ironically about to sacrifice her own (unwilling) brother years later; Polyxena's sacrifice precedes Euripides' *Trojan Women* (415; cf. *Tro.* 622-23); etc. Euripides was not the only playwright to present plays in which young people were sacrificed (cf. the fragmentary *Iphigenia* of Aeschylus and the *Iphigenia* and *Polyxena* of Sophocles[7]), but there is not enough

3. See *TrGF* vol. 5.391-418 (and M. J. Cropp, '*Erechtheus*', in C. Collard, M. J. Cropp, and K. H. Lee [eds.], *Euripides: Selected Fragmentary Plays*, vol. 1 [Warminster: Aris & Phillips, 1995], pp. 121-47, and C. Collard and M. J. Cropp, *Euripides: Fragments. Aegeus–Meleager* [Cambridge, MA: Harvard University Press, 2008], pp. 362-401).

4. For this date (rather than the more usual ca. 424), see C. W. Marshall, 'The Consequences of Dating the *Cyclops*', in M. Joyal (ed.), *In Altum: Seventy Five Years of Classical Studies in Newfoundland* (St. John's: Memorial University of Newfoundland, 2001), pp. 225-41, at 228-29 n. 10.

5. Scullion, 'Human Sacrifice', suggests that 'it may be that Aeschylus himself invented the version ending in Iphigenia's actual sacrifice' (as in the *Oresteia*; such a conclusion requires Pindar, *Py.* 11 to be written in 454, following C. M. Bowra, *Pindar* [Oxford: Oxford University Press, 1964], pp. 402-405, and not in 474); T. Gantz, *Early Greek Myth: A Guide to Literary and Artistic Sources* (Baltimore: The Johns Hopkins University Press, 1993), pp. 582-88.

6. For this date (rather than the more usual ca. 413), see C. W. Marshall, 'Sophocles' *Chryses* and the Date of *Iphigenia in Tauris*', in J. R. C. Cousland and James Hume (eds.), *The Play of Texts and Fragments: Papers Presented to Martin Cropp on the Occasion of his Sixty-Fifth Birthday* (Leiden: Brill, 2009), pp. 141-56.

7. See *TrGF* vol. 3.213-4 (and A. H. Sommerstein, *Aeschylus: Fragments* [LCL; [Cambridge, MA: Harvard University Press, 2008], pp. 106-7]); vol. 4.270-74 (and H. Lloyd-Jones, *Sophocles: Fragments* [LCL; Cambridge, MA: Harvard University Press, 2003], pp. 138-41); 403-407 (and Lloyd-Jones, *Sophocles: Fragments*,

surviving to permit a measured understanding of how the sacrifice was handled dramatically in these cases. The uncertainty extends to Euripidean plays, too. Among several attested plays about Phrixus and Helle (children of Athamas and Nephale, and step-children to Ino), there are indications both of the unwilling and the voluntary sacrifice of Phrixus:[8] the source of Hyginus, *Fab.* 2.2-4 (= Eur. *Phrixus B*?) indicates that a voluntary self-sacrifice exists in the tradition somewhere, and Menoeceus is not unique as a male offering himself for sacrifice. There are, further, tragedies in which infants are threatened onstage with killing in a sacrificial context but survive, as with the young Orestes in Euripides' *Telephus.*[9]

Given what evidence survives, we may identify two narrative patterns within the plays of Euripides that involve human sacrifice of speaking characters during the dramatic action of a play. One of these is the noble self-sacrifice on the behalf of a community (an action that may have been presented with various shades of irony): this is seen in *Children of Heracles, Erechtheus, Hecuba, Phoenician Women,* and *Iphigenia in Aulis.* A second pattern has the sacrificial victim rescued by a god at the last moment with an animal being substituted as the creature sacrificed: this is seen in the antecedent action to *Iphigenia among the Taurians* (see lines 28-30), in the spurious (fourth-century) ending to *Iphigenia in Aulis* (lines 1578-1629) and possibly in *Phrixus B*; it also shares obvious features with the story of Abraham and Isaac, Gen 22.1-19. The only other Athenian play in which a young person is sacrificed and for which a conclusion may reasonably be drawn concerning its dramatic treatment is Sophocles' *Polyxena,* where there is reason to think that it was 'drastically different, with Polyxene begging for her life till the last

pp. 262-7; A. H. Sommerstein, '*Polyxena*', in A. H. Sommerstein et al., *Sophocles: Selected Fragmentary Plays,* vol. 1 [Oxford: Aris & Phillips, 2006], pp. 41-83).

8. Plays called *Athamas* are attested for Aeschylus (*TrGF* vol. 3.123-25; and Sommerstein, *Aeschylus: Fragments,* pp. 2-5), Sophocles (twice: *TrGF* vol. 4.99-102; and Lloyd-Jones, *Sophocles,* pp. 10-13), Xenocles (a satyr play, *TrGF* vol. 1.153), and Astydamas II (*TrGF* vol. 1.60 T 5); *Phrixus* for Sophocles (*TrGF* vol. 4.491-92; and Lloyd-Jones, *Sophocles,* pp. 338-39), Euripides (twice: *TrGF* vol. 5.856-76; and Collard and Cropp, *Euripides...Oedipus-Chrysippus,* pp. 423-27), and Achaeus I (*TrGF* vol. 1.125; and possibly Timocles or Philocles, *TrGF* vol. 1.252 T3); *Ino* for Euripides (*TrGF* vol. 5.442-55; and Collard and Cropp, *Euripides... Aegeus–Meleager,* pp. 438-59) and an unknown playwright (*TrGF* vol. 1.36 DID A 12a). For the dizzying mythography, see Gantz, *Early Greek Myth,* pp. 176-80.

9. See *TrGF* vol. 5.680-718 (and Cropp, '*Telephus*', in Collard *et al.* [eds.], *Selected Fragmentary Plays 1,* pp. 17-52, and Collard and Cropp, *Euripides... Oedipus-Chrysippus,* pp. 185-223).

moment and putting up physical resistance that had to be suppressed by force' as in a fifth-century painting of the scene by Polygnotus on display in the Athenian agora.[10]

My purpose here is to provide a modest addition to this framework, considering Euripides' presentation of the sacrifice of Andromeda. Produced in the same tetralogy as the extant *Helen* (412), *Andromeda* opens with the title character bound before a cave mouth, about to be devoured by a sea monster (*kêtos*).[11] Andromeda is not a willing victim, and her narrative offers a significant contrast to the patterns found elsewhere in Euripides.

Andromeda represents an unblemished offering: the noble daughter of the Ethiopian king Cepheus, she is a *parthenos* (fr. 125, 127, 129, 145; cf. *Hcld.* 408) who would otherwise offer a 'noble marriage' (fr. 137 γενναῖον λέχος).[12] Poseidon has demanded her specifically in recompense for a boast by her mother Cassiopia about her beauty.[13] Andromeda is therefore both the instrumental cause of Poseidon's wrath and the means by which it will be appeased.[14] By having the play begin with

10. Sommerstein, *'Polyxena'*, p. 63, and see pp. 43-44.

11. See *TrGF* vol. 5.233-60 (and F. Bubelm, *Euripides: Andromeda* [Palingenesia 34; Stuttgart: Steiner, 1991]; J. Gibert, 'Andromeda', in Collard *et al.* [eds.], *Euripides: Selected Fragmentary Plays*, vol. 2 [Warminster: Aris & Phillips, 2004], pp. 133-68, and Collard and Cropp, *Euripides...Aegeus–Meleager*, pp. 124-55. For discussion, see J. Gibert, 'Falling in Love with Euripides (*Andromeda*)', *ICS* 24-25 (1999–2000), pp. 75-91; M. Wright, *Euripides' Escape-Tragedies: A Study of* Helen, Andromeda, *and* Iphigenia Among the Taurians (Oxford: Oxford University Press, 2005); W. E. Major, 'Staging *Andromeda* in Aristophanes and Euripides', *CJ* 108 (2013), pp. 385-403; C. W. Marshall, *The Structure and Performance of Euripides'* Helen (Cambridge: Cambridge University Press, 2014), pp. 140-87. For other Andromeda plays, see R. Klimek-Winter, *Andromedatragödien* (Beiträge zur Alterumskunde 21; Stuttgart: Kohlhammer, 1993).

12. Wilkins, 'The State and the Individual', p. 182; J. Chadwick, *Lexicographica Graeca: Contributions to the Lexicography of Ancient Greek* (Oxford: Clarendon Press, 1996), pp. 226-29, identifies a *parthenos* as a post-pubescent (and so nubile) woman who is still part of her father's household.

13. Apollodorus, *Lib.* 2.43 places Cassiopia's beauty at issue, but Hyginus, *Fab.* 64 makes it about Andromeda. Marshall, *Structure,* pp. 167-69 argues that Apollodorus adheres more closely to the Euripidean version. For Poseidon's demand, cf. Hyginus, *Fab.* 64: *Neptunus expostulauit* (the same words used in *Fab.* 46 concerning Erechtheus).

14. There is no sense in any version that she is one of an ongoing series of offerings, as with the Athenian youths offered to the minotaur; cf. Hyg. *Fab.* 41, where Theseus does present himself as a willing offering, a detail shared with Eur. *Theseus* (*TrGF* 5.426-36; and Collard and Cropp, *Euripides...Aegeus–Meleager*, pp. 415-27).

Andromeda already exposed, Euripides establishes her as a victim, though it is possible that a lost portion of the play described details of Cassiopia's offense, the message from Poseidon, and other preliminary rites. Indeed, fr. 133 (ἀλλ' ἡδύ τοι σωθέντα μεμνῆσθαι πόνων, 'But it's sweet to remember sufferings [*ponôn*] after one has been saved') looks like a prompt from Perseus for just such a description (his own adventures are described with the same word in fr. 134). Though Andromeda will be rescued by Perseus, the offense of Cassiopia remains and Poseidon's demanded recompense is still unfulfilled. It is only with the destruction of the sea monster by Perseus (described by a messenger, whose speech included fr. 145) that the means by which Poseidon's wrath may be abated becomes deactivated. While his anger against the Ethiopians (and Cassiopia particularly) may persist, there is no indication of a lingering belief that Andromeda must be offered to him through some other means.

Perseus' actions mean that Poseidon will not be appeased, but this should not as a result lead to the conclusion that Andromeda is not an actual sacrifice, as some have claimed. Hughes excludes Andromeda and some other instances from his study, because 'the absence of sacrificial language in these stories is notable: the young victims are given either as nourishment or as sexual partners to the monsters, and they are exposed rather than killed in the act of sacrifice'; in a footnote, however, he admits that 'there is occasional sacrificial colouring'[15] and cites Sophocles, *Andromeda* fr. 126:

†ἡμιουτον† κούρειον ἡρέθη πόλει·
ἀρχῆθέν ἐστι τῷ Κρόνῳ θυηπολεῖν
γένος βρότειον τοῖσι βαρβάροις νόμος.

> ...was chosen as a...sacrifice for the city. For from ancient times the barbarians have had a custom of sacrificing human beings to Kronos.[16]

This fragment demonstrates there is nothing incidental about the association of Andromeda with sacrifice in Euripides' most immediate mythic precedent. Indeed, by tying the sacrifice of Andromeda to Cronus, Sophocles establishes a direct correlation between Andromeda and the Carthaginian practice of human sacrifice, as the Athenians understood it: the pseudo-platonic *Minos* 315c identifies the Carthaginian god to whom

15. Hughes, *Human Sacrifice*, p. 78 and pp. 227-28 n. 10
16. Text and translation by Lloyd-Jones, *Sophocles*. The text is corrupt and the word order uncertain, but the sacrificial context is evident in both κούρειον and θυηπολεῖν. It has been suggested that Sophocles' *Andromeda* was a satyr play, but the matter is uncertain.

child sacrifices are made as Cronus.[17] In Euripides, the god is instead Poseidon, but Andromeda nevertheless remains a sacrifice, even though the extant fragments phrase it in terms of a banquet: 'to set out food for the sea monster' (fr. 115a, ἐκθεῖναι κήτει φορβάν). The unusual ritual activity is appropriate for the exotic African context on the Atlantic coast (fr. 125 and 145).

Euripides' *Andromeda* therefore offers a different model for human sacrifice than is seen in his other plays. Though the offering of Androm-eda is part of the dramatic action, she is presented neither as a willing victim, nor is there any indication of an animal substitution as in *Phrixus B*. Instead, Andromeda conforms more closely to the pattern evident in Sophocles' *Andromeda* and *Polyxena*. That Euripides is capable of such variation, despite his clear interest in the ethics surrounding the voluntary self-sacrifice of youths, is not surprising, but it is salutary to have a clear example. It also authorizes some further conclusions about Euripides' play.

While much is made of the suddenness with which Perseus falls in love with Andromeda (fr. 125, 139),[18] there is some negotiation. Perseus asks, 'Maiden, if I should rescue you, will you show me gratitude?' (fr. 129, ὦ παρθέν', εἰ σώσαιμί σ', εἴσῃ μοι χάριν;), and a sexual dimen-sion to the use of χάρις here is often assumed (i.e. '…will I receive a favour?').[19] Andromeda's response is unequivocal: 'Rescue me, stranger, whether you wish a servant, or a wife, or a slave' (fr. 129a, ἄγου δέ μ', ὦ ξεῖν', εἴτε πρόσπολον θέλεις | εἴτ' ἄλοχον εἴτε δμωΐδ'…). Andromeda is a survivor, and any of these outcomes removes her from her present danger, even as it makes her sexually available to Perseus. Once she is no longer under her father's control, she is technically no longer a *parthenos* and consequently will no longer be an acceptable sacrifice.

In *Andromeda* a marriage rite becomes a means of circumventing a sacrificial ritual. As the play ends, Andromeda is taken from a land of death to Greece, where she becomes the mother of several children. This

---

17. The association of Baal with Cronus (and then Roman Saturn) is well estab-lished; cf. A. I. Wilson, 'Romanizing Baal: The Art of Saturn Worship in North Africa', in M. Sanader *et al.* (eds.), *Proceedings of the 8th International Colloquium on Problems of Roman Provincial Art, Zagreb 2003* (Zabreb: Opuscula Archae-ologica, 2005), pp. 403-408. *Minos* proceeds to tie human sacrifice to the mythical example of Athamas and Phrixus.

18. Gibert, 'Falling in Love'.

19. Cf. *Hec.* 830 concerning the relationship between Agamemnon and Cassandra. Even if the association is intended to be secondary, the power of erotic love on Perseus is established at fr. 136 and 138a.

pattern (which Guépin calls *anodos* drama[20]) is also shared with *Helen*, *Iphigenia among the Taurians*, and *Alcestis*.[21] *Andromeda* can therefore be seen as another dramatic example demonstrating how 'the sacrificial metaphor shapes and becomes an intrinsic part of Euripides' dramaturgy as a whole'.[22]

Within extant Euripidean drama, there is only one other play in which a speaking character is threatened with sacrifice, but the event is avoided completely: in *Iphigenia among the Taurians* the recognition between brother and sister, in an geographical area equally remote, means that bloodshed is averted and the title character may be restored to her home in Greece.[23] Through the narrative connection of a sacrifice averted, *Andromeda* and *Iphigenia* share an interest in ritual, rescue, and salvation. Significantly, these are themes that are under-represented in the companion play to *Andromeda*, *Helen*. Even though *Helen* and *Iphigenia* share a large number of narrative features,[24] it would appear that the focus on sacrifice and ritual present in *Iphigenia* is instead taken up in the companion play to *Helen*, *Andromeda*. This is an unexpected connection, and it helps to establish a third narrative pattern concerning sacrifice within the plays of Euripides: the idea of 'sacrifice averted', which may stand alongside 'sacrifice undertaken voluntarily' and 'sacrifice substituted'.

20. J.-P. Guépin, *The Tragic Paradox: Myth and Ritual in Greek Tragedy* (Amsterdam: A. M. Hakkert, 1968), p. 142, and see R. Rehm, *Marriage to Death: The Conflation of Wedding and Funeral Rituals in Greek Tragedy* (Princeton: Princeton University Press, 1994), and H. P. Foley, *Female Acts in Greek Tragedy* (Princeton: Princeton University Press, 2001), pp. 301-31.

21. In contrast, 'the structure of the *Iphigenia* [*in Aulis*] hangs on the performance of a sacrificial ritual that is disguised for a large part of the action as a fictitious marriage rite' (H. P. Foley, *Ritual Irony: Poetry and Sacrifice in Euripides* [Ithaca, NY: Cornell University Press, 1985], pp. 67-68). The association between marriage and death more generally in tragedy is discussed by Rehm, *Marriage to Death*.

22. Foley, *Ritual Irony*, p. 64.

23. *Telephus*, produced in 438 with *Alcestis*, also has a sacrifice averted, but the victim is an infant.

24. M. Platnaur, *Euripides: Iphigenia in Tauris* (Oxford: Clarendon, 1938), p. xv, identifies several structural parallels.

Part III

THEOLOGY AND RECEPTION

CHILD SACRIFICE:
A POLYVALENT STORY IN EARLY EUCHARISTIC PIETY

Paul C. Burns

Introduction

There is an assumption that the Jewish and Christian biblical traditions
have replaced human sacrifice of all kinds first with a substitution of an
animal and then with the replacement by the once-for-all character of
the sacrificial death of Jesus Christ. This abolition or the definitive act of
the sacrifice on the cross is certainly a distinctive aspect in the biblical
traditions and within the parameters of formal thought and teaching of
the Christian Church. However, there is a popular thread of late fourth-
century oral narrative which focuses on a Eucharistic apparition with the
graphic sacrifice of the child Jesus. This oral narrative gets written down
and also interacts with some liturgical symbols of human sacrifice. In the
present study I propose to examine this oral narrative from the fourth-
century ascetical movement in Egypt which, at some point, is written
down in Greek and then translated into Latin and several other languages. The early stage of the narrative is deeply informed by themes of
sacrifice inherent in the ascetical tradition which is reflected in sketches
or paintings near the altars of two monastic churches in the Sinai. To
explore the interpretations of this first stage of this narrative and subsequent adaptions in the Middle Ages I will appeal to several current
studies by art historians.

A Latin translation of this narrative is later employed by a ninth-
century Gallic monk within the first extended western treatment of the
presence of Christ in the Eucharist. In addition to the Egyptian story, the
author of that ninth-century treatise picks up a narrative about the
conversion of a Jewish boy who also sees the child Jesus in the Eucharist
and then gets seriously punished by his father. Within this conversion
story there is an interesting interaction between a painting and the
interpretation which the boy uses to account for his escape. Finally, in
thirteenth-century England, the original story from Egypt gets retold in a
handbook for the religious instruction of lay people. In one particular

manuscript of this handbook, there are two painted miniatures which retell two critical stages of the original tale. The point of the present study is to track the integration of narrative and art to reflect significant themes of Christian piety within three different cultural and religious contexts. The polyvalent applications of this tale might be linked to the perverse accusations against Jews for ritual child murder in the twelfth and thirteenth centuries. Therefore, this study focuses on the various narratives and artistic renderings of the Eucharistic apparition of the Christ child whose body and blood have been sacrificed.

A Written Text of the Original Oral Narrative

The first extant instance of the motif of an apparition of the sacrifice of the little boy Jesus occurs in the collections of *The Sayings of the Desert Fathers*.[1] A Greek version has survived in an alphabetical series which is attributed to Abba Daniel. There is also a version preserved in a thematic series which has not survived in the original Greek version but is extant in a Latin translation made in the sixth century. This is the version which Pascasius quotes within his somewhat different context in Carolingian Gaul in the ninth century and then becomes the basis for the version found in Anglo-Norman in the thirteenth century.[2] In the sixth-century Latin translation of the thematic collection, the narrative is listed under the theme, 'De Providentia sive contemplatione'. In their original setting in the early generations of the ascetical movement in Egypt, these 'sayings', in both the alphabetical and also in the thematic formats, demonstrate how basic teaching and moral guidance were provided to members of this ascetical movement. Some of the ascetics were educated and hence literate; others were uneducated and probably illiterate. These oral narratives, often cryptic and startling, were effective expressions for

1.   For the Greek text, consult J.-P. Migne, *Apophthegmata Patrum* in *Patrologia Graeca*, vol. 65, cols. 156-57. It is located under the name Daniel and is number seven in the list attributed to him. For an English translation, consult Benedicta Ward, *The Desert Fathers: Sayings of the Early Christian Monks* (London: Penguin, 2003), pp. 185-86, and her earlier *The Sayings of the Desert Fathers: The Alphabetical Collection* (Cistercian Studies 59; Kalamazoo, MI: Cistercian Publications, 1984), pp. 44-45. For an informative and, at times, critical assessment of Ward's text, consult Peter Jackson's review in *Cistercian Studies Quarterly* 40 (2005), pp. 328-31.

2.   This text is known as the *Systematic Collection* and was translated into Latin by the Roman Deacon Pelagius together with the Sub-deacon John. In his sixteenth-century edition, Heribert Rosweyde identifies this Pelagius with the person who became Pope from 555 to 560. For this Latin translation, see J. P. Migne, *Patrologia Latina*, vol. 73, 'De Vitis Patrum', liber V,18.3, cols. 978D to 980A.

the values and practices of the movement. The 'sayings' were normally ascribed to a specific elder, such as Antony, Arsenius or Daniel. Within the collections of 'sayings', two women, Sarah and Syncletica, are included among the authorities. In time, probably due to external pressures, these oral narratives were written down and preserved in both the alphabetical and the thematic series. They were originally written in Greek, or perhaps Coptic, but they were later translated into a range of languages, including Syriac, Georgian, Old Church Slavonic, Arabic and Latin.[3]

In both versions this particular 'saying', on the presence of Christ in the Eucharist provides more of a geographical and thematic context than is often the case in these collections. First, Daniel identifies his source of the story as Abbot Arsenius, who describes an unnamed elder living at Scetis. This person described the presence of Christ in the Eucharist as a 'symbol' (figura eius) and not the 'real body of Christ' (non esse naturaliter corpus Christi). The text which follows is from the thematic series in the Latin translation by Pelagius preserved under the title of 'De Vitis Patrum'. This Latin translation by Pelagius is the version quoted by the ninth-century treatise on the Eucharist. So we begin with the full account provided by Pelagius' Latin translation. He introduces the central character as an elder (senex) who has led an exemplary life but has a naïve (simplex) grasp of faith:

> Narravit iterum abbas Daniel, dicens: Dixit Pater noster abbas Arsenius de quodam sene, qui erat magnus in hac vita, simplex autem in fide, et errabat pro eo quod erat idiota, et dicebat, non esse naturaliter corpus Christi panem quem sumimus, sed figuram eius esse. (*De Vitis Patrum* V, 18.3)

Two elders intervene and repeat his erroneous claim and then point out that instead 'he should hold the view which the Church has passed down' (sicut Ecclesia catholica tradidit):

> Hoc autem audientes duo senes quod diceret hunc sermonem, et scientes quia magna esset, vita et conversatio eius, cognitavarunt quia innocenter et simpliciter diceret hoc, et venerunt ad eum, et dicunt ei: Abba, audivimus sermonem cuiusdam infidelis, qui dicit quia panis quem sumimus, non natura corpus Christi, sed figura est eius. Senex autem ait eius: Ego sum qui hoc dixi. Illi autem rogabant eum dicentes: Non sic teneas, abba, sed sicut Ecclesia catholica tradidit:... (*De Vitis Patrum* V, 18.3)

3. Consult Caroline T. Schroeder, 'Child Sacrifice in Christian Monastic Culture: From Familial Renunciation to Jephthah's Lost Daughter', *Journal of Early Christian Studies* 20 (2012), pp. 269-302. At 277 n. 15, she cites Kenneth Willis Clark, *Checklist of Manuscripts in St. Catherine's Monastery, Mount Sinai* (Washington, DC: Library of Congress, 1952), pp. 7, 15, 18, 36, and 129.

The two elders confront their colleague with the tradition handed down by the Church about the real presence of Christ in the Eucharist and repeat the false interpretation attributed to him.

Out of respect for their colleague's simplicity and ascetical labors, the two elders propose that they pray that God might reveal the truth to this misguided person. They propose a literal parallel with the Lord's words of institution at the Last Supper and the texts about the status of humans as 'the image of God' in two passages from Genesis. The naïve man, too, accepts this proposal and asks God to recognize that he has not spoken from malice but from ignorance and asks God to reveal to him the truth of the mystery. The two elders make the same prayer.

> ... nos autem credimus quia panis ipse corpus Christi est, et calix ipse est sanguis Christi secundum veritatem, et non secundum figuram: sed sicut in principio pulverem de terra accipiens plasmavit hominem ad imaginem suam, et nemo potest dicere quia non erat imago Dei (Genesis 2.7 and 1.26), quamvis incomprehensibilis; ita et panis, quem dixit: Quia corpus meum est, credimus quia secundum veritatem corpus Christi est.
>
> Senex autem ait eis: Nisi reipsa cognovero, non mihi satisfacit responsio vestra. Illi autem dixerunt ad eum: Deprecemur Deum hebdomada hac de mysterio hoc, et credimus quia Deus revelabit nobis. Senex vero cum gaudio suscepit sermonem istum, et deprecabatur Deum, dicens : Domine, si tu cognoscis quoniam non per malitiam incredulous sum rei huius, sed per ignorantiam errem, revela ergo mihi, Domine Jesu Christe, quod verum est. Sed et illi senes abeuntes in cella sua, rogabant et ipsi, dicentes: Domine Jesu Christe, revela seni mysterium hoc, ut credat et non perdat laborem suum. (*De Vitis Patrum* V, 18.3)

At the end of the week they went to church on the Lord's Day and all three sat on the same mat with the naïve old man in the middle. Then their eyes were opened and when the bread was placed on the holy table, a little boy (*puerulus*) became visible to these three alone. When the priest put out his hand to break the bread, behold an angel descended from heaven with a knife (*cultrum*) and poured the child's blood into a chalice. When the priest broke the bread into small pieces, the angel, also, cut the child (*puer*) into tiny pieces.

It is important to note two things about diction and about the repetitive quality throughout this narrative. The text does not employ the term, *infans*, but rather both the diminutive form, *puerulus*, and also the standard form, *puer*. The standard form applies to male children and even youths to age 17 and sometimes beyond. This will become significant when we identify some of the biblical passages through which this narrative was interpreted in the monastic liturgical tradition in Egypt. Moreover, the highly repetitive character of the narrative reflects the original oral form in which both the well-intentioned but simple character of the elder and also the real presence of Christ in the Eucharist is reinforced:

> Exaudivit autem Deus utrosque: et hebdomada completa venerunt Dominico die in ecclesia, et sederunt ipsi tres soli super sedile de scirpo, quod in modum fascis erat ligatum, medius autem sedebat senex ille. Aperti sunt autem oculi eorum intellectuales; et quando positi sunt panes in altari, videbatur illis tantummodo tribus tamquam puerulus iacens super altare. Et cum extendisset presbyter manus, ut frangeret panem, descendit angelus Domini de coelo habens cultrum in manu, et sicavit puerulum illum, sanguinem vero excipiebat in calice. Cum autem presbyter frangeret in partibus parvis panem, etiam et angelus incidebat pueri membra in modicis partibus. (*De Vitis Patrum* V, 18.3)

When they drew near to receive the sacred elements, the old man alone received 'a morsel of bloody flesh'. Seeing this he was afraid and cried out, 'I believe that this bread is your flesh and this chalice your blood'. Immediately the flesh which he held in his hand became bread according to the mystery and he took it giving thanks to God:

> Cum autem accessisset senex, ut acciperet sanctam communionem, data est ipsi soli caro sanguine cruentata. Quod cum vidisset, pertimuit, et clamavit, dicens: Credo, Domine, quia panis qui in altari ponitur, corpus tuum est, et calix tuus est sanguis. Et statim facta est pars illa in manu eius panis, secundum mysterium, et sumpsit illud in ore, gratias agens Deo. (*De Vitis Patrum* V, 18.3)

There follows a brief statement of explanation about God's use of bread and wine because he knows that humans cannot eat raw (presumably human) flesh:

> Dixerunt autem ei senes: Deus scit humanam naturam; quia non potest vesci carnibus crudis, et propterea transformat corpus suum in panem, et sanguinem suum in vinum, his qui illud cum fide suscipiunt. (*De Vitis Patrum* V, 18.3)

Then they gave thanks to God for the old man, because he had not allowed him to lose the reward of his labor. All three returned to their cells with joy.

> Et egerunt gratias Deo de sene illo; quia non permisit Deus perire labores eius, et reversi sunt cum gaudio ad cellas suas. (*De Vitis Patrum* V, 18.3)

There is no further comment. This story, with its repetitious reinforcement of the issue and graphic demonstration of the real presence, is allowed to stand on its own terms. In the collection the topic shifts to a different story also attributed to Daniel, but this time on the identity of Melchizedek.

Original Egyptian Ascetical Context

The repetition of the naïve person's issue and the graphic demonstration of the traditional teaching reflect the imaginative and oral character of teaching within the Egyptian ascetical tradition. However, other features in this narrative have attracted recent scholarly investigation. Two informative studies appeared in 2012. Dealing with this 'saying', both provide a survey of scholarly literature on Egyptian asceticism as well as an assessment of distinctive themes that are pertinent to our study. Nicholas Marinides explores the practice of tolerance within Egyptian asceticism.[4] He examines the constructive treatment of people within the movement who espouse unorthodox views as well as the similar approach to heretical visitors. He uses Daniel's story as an illustration of the first phenomenon. The naïve elder is not persecuted for his interpretation but rather is led to the traditional view of the Eucharist. Caroline T. Schroeder examines child sacrifice practices in narratives in the Egyptian ascetical tradition.[5] She makes the perceptive connection between narratives such as this one and later artistic representations of two biblical episodes which can be used to frame and to interpret the understanding of Eucharistic sacrifice in the ascetic tradition.

In its original context, this 'saying' is attributed to Daniel who identifies his source with his mentor, Abbot Arsenius. He joined the monks around Scetis in the desert south-west of the Nile valley in the 390s.[6] This centre experienced a number of challenges from Theophilus, the Patriarch of the Church of Alexandria, from 385 to 412.[7] He was a polarizing figure who promoted violent action against pagans and their sites in the city. He instigated the destruction of the temple of Serapis in 391. He also persecuted many of the Egyptian ascetics such as Arsenius and John Cassian because he claimed they were supporting a range of errors associated with interpretations of Origen's texts. He enlisted Epiphanius of Salamis and others to campaign against an alleged subordinationist Christology, the possible salvation of the devil, and

4. For the attitudes of the monks at Scetis, consult Nicholas Marinides, 'Religious Toleration in the Apophthegamata Patrum', *Studies in Early Christian Studies* 20 (2012), pp. 235-68, esp. 238-44.

5. Schroeder, 'Child Sacrifice in Egyptian Monastic Culture', pp. 269-302.

6. For the identity of Arsenius, see Ward, *The Sayings of the Desert Fathers: The Alphabetical Collection*, pp. 7-8.

7. For issues on the Eucharist among ascetics in the 390s, see Elizabeth A. Clark, *The Origenist Controversy: The Cultural Construction of an Early Christian Debate* (Princeton, NJ: Princeton University Press, 1992), pp. 64-66, 87, and 113.

non-physical interpretations of both the resurrection and also of the Eucharist. These monastic settlements at Scetis and elsewhere endured barbarian raids in 407 and in 434. These threats may well have motivated the monks to find some way to preserve their life and practices. These upheavals of the fifth century probably prompted them to gather the oral sayings into organized collections and to write them down.

Within Daniel's story there are two important hints about the original context. First, there is the identity of his source, Abba Arsenius. Arsenius had been born in Rome about 360. He was well-educated and, during the reign of Emperor Theodosius, he served as tutor to the future Emperors Arcadius and Honorius. In 394 Arsenius left for Alexandria and joined the ascetical movement around Scetis and remained there until his death in about 440. Although many of the sayings are brief and anecdotal, this one has a distinctive preamble and a reference to an argument about the physical reality of the Eucharist that also emerged in the disputes with Theophilus. In her masterful analysis of the Origenist controversies, Elizabeth Clark has pointed out that this issue about the physical presence of Christ flared up in the late 390s. She focuses on a dialogue between the monk Aphou and Patriarch Theophilus.[8] In that dialogue Aphou makes the claim that anyone who rejects the claim at Gen 1.26 that humans are the true images of God must also reject the reality of Christ's presence in the Eucharist.[9] She speculates that the monk Aphou and the author of the apparition story were defending the physicality of the image of God in all humans and the physicality of the presence of Christ in the Eucharist 'against visual evidence that might suggest otherwise'.[10] This same parallel between reality of the image and the reality of Christ in the Eucharist, as we have seen, also comes up in Daniel's story. So, this dispute may very well have provided the historical context for this particular 'saying' in its current extended form.

The Bible and Deaths of Young People

The intriguing question for each version of Daniel's story is why the apparition of Jesus is depicted as a little boy (*puerulus*). Why is it not a vision of the risen Christ, perhaps still bearing the wounds of the

8. For her evidence Clark uses the text of the exchange between Aphou and Theophilus provided in Étienne Drioton, 'La Discussion d'un moine anthropo-morphite Audien avec le patriarche Théophile d'Alexandrie en l'année 399', *Revue de l'Orient Chrétien*, 2d ser. 10 (=20) (1915–17), pp. 92-100, 113-28, esp. 98-99.

9. See Clark, *Origenist Controversy*, pp. 64-66.

10. See Clark, *Origenist Controversy*, p. 65.

crucifixion? There is no sign in this narrative of the experience of the Apostle Thomas in John 20.24-29. It is true that in both the Infancy Narratives of Matthew and Luke there are references to children and bloodshed. At Matt 2.16-18, there is the notice of Herod's slaughter of all male children two years and younger. In Luke at 2.33-34, there is Simeon's prophecy that this child is destined to be a sign that is rejected and that a sword will pierce Mary's soul. There are no hints either of the standard image of the innocent lamb of sacrifice which is central to the Jewish Passover and is employed at John 1.29 and Rev 5.12. But there are no indications that these scriptural texts were used by the Egyptian ascetics as the interpretive prism for Daniel's story, with its apparition of child sacrifice.

In her informative article on striking narratives on child sacrifice in this Christian tradition, Caroline Schroeder explores the ascetical objective for the repudiation of familial relationships. She goes on to integrate some of these narratives with some paintings which do provide two biblical episodes through which to interpret narratives such as Daniel's story about the apparition of the sacrifice of the Christ child.

After a brief comment on the numbers of children and their roles in the narratives of the Desert Fathers, she cites the telling injunction to an aspirant to sacrifice his son. In 'saying' 10 attributed to Sisoes a man expresses the wish to become an ascetic.[11] In response to an elder's question about any family relations, he admits he has a son. He is instructed to throw him into the river. Just as he was about to do so, another monk intervened to prevent this act. The candidate leaves his son and becomes a monk. Like its allusion to Abraham and Isaac at Genesis 22, the sacrifice is prevented at the last minute. So, in the ascetical tradition this narrative about child sacrifice prevented becomes a model for familial renunciation. Schroeder also notes two more examples of this theme which John Cassian took with him from Egypt to Gaul. He was roughly a contemporary of Arsenius and his teachings were probably a target for the attacks of Theophilus. In his *Collationes*, Cassian describes an imprudent monk who, under the influence of a demon, plans to kill his son in deliberate imitation of Abraham's willingness to sacrifice Isaac. The son notices, with alarm, that his father is sharpening a knife and so escapes.[12] Professor Schroeder argues that narratives of child killings

---

11. For 54 sayings attributed to Sisoes, see Migne, *Patrologia Graeca*, vol. 65, cols. 391-407.

12. At *Collationes* 2.7, John Cassian recounts a similar story of a father who is prompted by a demon to sacrifice his boy (puer). The son becomes alarmed when he sees his father sharpening a knife (cultrum) and escapes. See Cassianus, *Collationes*

became a striking narrative theme in Egyptian monastic literature to promote familial renunciation. I propose to use her evidence and her argument on the use of child sacrifice tales and images to dramatize familial renunciation in this ascetical tradition and to focus them on their understanding of the Eucharist.

Two important pieces of Schroeder's evidence are a pair of paintings found both in the Monastery of St. Catherine and also later in the Monastery of St. Antony in the Sinai.[13] The themes in both cases present a rendering of Abraham's sacrifice of Isaac, with its substitution of a ram, in Gen 22.1-19, and Jephthah's actual sacrifice of his daughter in Judg 11.29-40. In both cases the respective fathers are standing before altars, and both are nimbed. The son and daughter, in each painting, are kneeling.[14] In both cases the offspring could fit the age range reflected in the Latin word, *puer*. The paintings at St. Catherine's date from the seventh century; the ones at St. Antony are thirteenth century. At St. Catherine's, outline drawings are on pillars beside the altar. So, in a visual sense, they frame the altar for the worshipper in the nave and thus provide biblical themes by which to interpret the Eucharistic event. At St. Anthony's, the paintings are on the wall over the altar and visible from the vantage point of the celebrants behind the screen.[15] Professor

XXIIII (ed. M. Petschenig; CSEL 13; Vienna: Österrichischen Akademie de Wissenschaften, 2004), 2.7. In his *Institutes* 4.27 Cassian recounts the story of a person who wishes to become a monk and is instructed to throw his son into a river. See Cassianus, *De Institutis Coenobiorum* (ed. M. Petschenig; CSEL 17; Vienna: Österrichischen Akademie de Wissenschaften, 2004), 4.27. For English translations, see Boniface Ramsey, *The Institutes* (Ancient Christian Writers 58; Mahwah, NJ: Newman Press, 2000), pp. 92-93, and Ramsey, *The Conferences* (Ancient Christian Writers 57; Mahwah, NJ: Newman Press, 1997), p. 89.

13. For black and white prints of these four wall paintings, see Schroeder, 'Child Sacrifice in Egyptian Monastic Culture', pp. 273-75, 288.

14. For a helpful description of the examples at St. Catherine's and an informative survey of Early and Medieval Christian artistic treatments of Jephthah's vow and sacrifice, consult Lois Drewer, 'Jephthah and His Daughter in Medieval Art: Ambiguities of Heroism and Sacrifice', in Colum Hourihane (ed.), *Insight and Interpretation: Studies in the Celebration of the Eighty-Fifth Anniversary of the Index of Christian Art* (Princeton, NJ: Princeton University Press, 2002), pp. 35-59. For her treatment of the two paintings at St. Catherine's, see pp. 36-37.

15. For archaeological evidence for the use of screens and later textual evidence of them as applications of the biblical 'veils of the Temple', see Elizabeth S. Bolman, 'Visiting Sanctity in Christian Egypt: Visual and Spatial Solutions', in Sharon E. J. Gerstel (ed.), *Thresholds of the Sacred: Architectural, Art Histori-cal, Liturgical and Theological Perspectives, East and West* (Washington, DC: Dumbarton Oaks and Harvard University Press, 2006), pp. 73-104.

Schroeder points out that the paintings are at a sufficient height that they may have been at least partly visible to worshippers in the nave. She goes on to emphasize the application of the biblical sacrificial theme to the monastic life of sacrifice.[16]

The first episode from Genesis is a familiar scene which is normally understood in the Christian tradition as an anticipation of the Father's sacrifice of his only Son on the Cross. In the artistic examples in the two Egyptian monasteries, this scene is twinned with the more problematic sacrifice by Jephthah. He had made a vow that, if God granted a military victory to him, he would sacrifice the first living thing to greet him on his return home. His only child, a daughter, ran to meet him and he then killed her. Professor Schroeder cites several patristic treatments of Jephthah's sacrifice of his daughter. Many offer some criticism for Jephthah's judgment in making such a vow. Most highlight the willingness and the virgin status of the victim, which are both themes central to the ascetic ideal.[17] Schroeder links these two biblical passages and the sacrificial themes of the artwork to explain the choice of the ascetics who reproduce these perspectives in their own lives. This prominence of the sacrificial model within the ascetical tradition might account for the graphic use of sacrifice in the narrative about the child sacrifice in the Eucharist.

Carolingian Use of this Early Narrative

In the ninth-century monastery at Corbie, Pascasius Radbertus wrote his treatise *De Corpore et Sanguine Domini*, which is extant in 22 chapters, with four editions reflected in the format of the current critical edition.[18] He wrote his first version in 831, ostensibly for the use by Warin, one of his former students now charged with the instruction of novices at a daughter-house of Corbie in Saxony.[19] This is an area conquered by Charlemagne after tough military campaigns in the years 772–785.

---

16. See Schroeder, 'Child Sacrifice in Egyptian Monastic Culture', p. 276.

17. See Schroeder's citations from Philo, Ambrose, Jerome, Augustine, John Chrysostom and Ephraim in Schroeder, 'Child Sacrifice in Egyptian Monastic Culture', pp. 292-96. For the virgin's hymn at the end of Methodius' Symposium, which includes Jephthah's daughter, see Drewer's citation in her 'Jephthah and His Daughter', p. 48.

18. For the current critical edition, consult Bedae Paulus, *Pascasius Radbertus De Corpore et Sanguine Domini* (Corpus Christianorum Continuatio Mediaevalis XVI; Turnholt: Brepols, 1969).

19. This version is found in about 120 manuscripts.

Charlemagne enforced conversion to Christianity on his new Saxon subjects and used education in monastic schools as a deliberate policy to integrate his new subjects within his empire. Pascasius identifies the challenge to put the traditional teaching of the Fathers into terms understandable by these first-generation converts to Christianity. In his first *Prologue*, Pascasius says that he is appealing to the following Christian authorities to provide the appropriate material for the neophytes. He names Cyprian, Ambrose, Augustine, Hilary of Poitiers, Isidore of Seville, John Chrysostom, Gregory of Nyssa, Ysitius (Hesychius of Jerusalem) and Bede.[20] Pascasius endeavors to put his teaching on the Eucharist into terms that can be appreciated by the Saxon converts under instruction.[21] That audience accounts for his emphasis on the physical world and on the power of miracle stories. He revised his text for a presentation to Charles the Bald at either Christmas 843 or Easter 844.[22] The editor of the current critical edition has identified two more expansions of this text without assigning a date or context for either of them. For the fourth edition the editor identifies some additions to Chapters 6, 9, 14 and 21 and puts this material into a smaller font.[23]

The two stories that we will discuss appear in this fourth edition of the text. Daniel's story about the doubting ascetic is found in this additional material in Chapter 14. It has been inserted as the first among three other stories. They are all miracle stories to illustrate the real presence of Christ in the Eucharist. Then we will examine another Eucharistic apparition story back in Chapter 9 which is also identified by the editor as part of the fourth edition. This story also goes back to a Greek version. It involves a Eucharistic apparition to a Jewish boy with dramatic consequences.

20. See *Prologus Ad Warinum Abbatem*, lines 84-90: 'Haec autem ut securius tua perlegat infantia, placuit, karissime, catholicos ecclesiae doctores in principio adnotare, ex quibus pauca de pluribus quasi lac teneritudinis eliquaverim, Cyprianum scilicet, Ambrosium, Agustinum, Hilarium, Isidorum. Iohannem, Gregorium, Hieronimum, Ysitum et Bedam quorum doctrina ac fide imbutus melius possis ad altiora proficere'.

21. For adaptations of Christian thought for new Saxon converts, consult Rachel Fulton, *From Judgement to Passion: Devotion to Christ and the Virgin Mary 800–1200* (New York: Columbia University Press, 2002).

22. This version is found only in Paris Bibliothèque Nationale, lat. 2855 of the tenth century.

23. This version is found in three manuscripts: Paris, Bibliothèque Nationale, lat. 2854 of the ninth century; Paris Bibliothèque Nationale of the twelfth century; and Vatican City, Bibliotheca Apostolica Vat. Reg. lat. 73 of the twelfth century.

Pascasius begins his study on the Eucharist with the assertion that 'the communion of Christ is not to be doubted as his true body and blood'.[24] Like many of the headings to his chapters in this treatise, Pascasius may have been responding to specific questions posed to him by Warin.[25] Pascasius then proceeds to offer a traditional definition of 'sacrament' inherited from Isidore of Seville.[26] Pascasius says that 'a sacrament…is anything handed down to us in any divine celebration as a sort of pledge of salvation, with the thing done visibly simultaneously accomplishing something invisibly'.[27] To continue his discussion Pascasius employs the terms of 'figura' and 'veritas', which are very similar to the categories in the original 'saying' from the Egyptian ascetical tradition:

> Utrum sub figura an veritate hoc mysticum calicis fiat sacramentum.
> (IV.1-2)

Throughout the rest of the text Pascasius emphasizes both the presence of the physical and the historical Christ.[28] He states at the outset that the body is that of the body which was born of the virgin, suffered on the cross and was raised from the dead:

> Haec, inquid, 'caro mea est pro mundi vita (John 6.11)'. Et ut mirabilius loquar, non alia plane, quam quae nata est de Maria et passa in cruce et resurrexit de spulchro. (I.50-52)

At X.103-13 Pascasius uses a passage from Hilary of Poitiers' *De Trinitate* 8.13 to argue that the purpose of the Eucharist is to incorporate the believer into the body of Christ by consuming his body and blood. He concludes that by this we have a share in his relation with Father:

24.   See Pascasius Radbertus, *De Corpore et Sanguine* Domini I.1-2: 'Christi communionem verum corpus eius et sanguinem esse non dubitandum'.

25.   In her comprehensive survey of the language, the rituals, liturgical texts, the material elements and understanding of Eucharist in the Early Medieval period, consult Celia Chazelle, 'The Eucharist in Early Medieval Europe', in Ian Christopher Levy, Gary Macy and Kirsten Van Ausdall (eds.), *A Companion to the Eucharist in the Early Middle Ages* (Leiden: Brill, 2011), pp. 205-49. She makes the suggestion about the origin of Pascasius' headings on p. 236.

26.   See Isidore of Seville, *Etymologiarum sive Originum* 6, 19, 39-40.

27.   See Pascasius, III.2-4: 'Sacramentum igitur est quicquid in aliqua celebratione divina nobis quasi pignus salutis traditur, cum res gesta visibilis longe aliud invisibile intus operatur quod sancte accipiendum sit'. For a translation of this passage and a helpful discussion of themes and structure in Pascasius' treatise, see Patricia McCormick Zirkel, 'The Ninth-Century Eucharistic Controversy A Context for the Beginnings of Eucharistic Doctrine in the West', *Worship* 68 (1994), pp. 2-23.

28.   For an informative discussion of Pascasius' theme, consult Celia Chazelle, 'From Figure, Character and the Glorified Body in the Carolingian Eucharistic Controversy', *Traditio* 47 (1992), pp. 1-36.

... 'Et ideo' per hoc 'omnes' in Deo Patre et Filio ac Spiritu Sancto 'unum sumus quia Pater in Christo et Christus in nobis John 17.21)' esse probatur. Hinc igitur est, quod et nos in Christo naturaliter unum corpus efficiamur. (IX.111-13)

Moreover, unlike the earlier Egyptian weekly tradition, Pascasius repeatedly speaks of the daily offering of the Eucharist with the implication of the daily reception of communion by the monks.[29] By this period Carolingian monasteries had begun the practice of ordaining more members to offer votive masses at the request of benefactors.[30] When Charles received the second edition he apparently asked another monk at Corbie to address two questions provoked by the perspectives in Pascasius' treatise. So Ratramnus, troubled by the physical emphasis of Pascasius, provided a more figurative and spiritual interpretation of the Eucharist.[31] Historians often connect these two studies on the Eucharist by Pascasius and by Ratramnus within the broader Carolingian Eucharistic Controversy. This designation, however, may be a little anachronistic, by reading back into the 830s and early 840s the later issues between Gottschalk, Hincmar and John Scotus Erigena of the late 840s, the still later issues around 1050 between Lanfranc of Bec and Berengarius of Tours, then the issues in 1215 at the IV Lateran Council on transubstantiation and the canon on annual reception, and ultimately the Reformation debates. In a recent insightful paper Owen Phelan argues that there was no open debate between the two monks at Corbie. Rather, he argues that Pascasius was employing a 'horizontal' interpretation of the sacraments to incorporate people within the body of Christ while Ratramnus employed a more 'vertical' and spiritual approach of the

29. See Pascasius, III.80-82: 'Simili quoque modo et in baptismum per aquam ex illo omnes regeneramur, deinde virtute ipsius Christi corpore cotidie pascimur et potamur sanguine'. See also: VIII. 180: '...verissima caro Christi et sanguis cotidie ministratur'; and X.76-79: 'Unde idem panis Christus qui de caelo descendit, in hoc mysterio accipitur, sicut et caro quae in cruce pependit, cum integer deinceps Christus perseveret, licet ab omnibus cotidie edatur'. Also XI.58-59: '...rursus eum esuriendo et sitiendo cotidie potamus'. As well see XXI.83: '...dum cotidie Christi sanguinem de altare sumimus'. For the daily offering or immolation, see IV.41, V.37, IX.1-2, 4, 14-17, 60, 342, and 380, XIII.22, XIV.132, XXI.61-65. On the daily building up of the one body of Christ in all its fullness, see VII.5 and XII.64-66.

30. For her observation on this development, see Chazelle, 'The Eucharist in Medieval Europe', pp. 209, 221-22.

31. For the agenda of Ratramnus, see the effective summary in Zirkel, 'The Ninth-Century Eucharistic Controversy', p. 7. She points out that he seems to address two questions posed by Charles on distinctions between the 'real' vs. the 'symbolic' body and the 'historical' vs. the 'eucharistic' body.

believer to salvation and eternal life.[32] Although this disclaimer is
probably valid for the first edition of 831, some of the issues of the early
stages of the Controversy in the late 840s may have motivated the
additions for the as yet undated fourth edition, which alone is the source
for the two key stories in our discussion.

To strengthen his emphasis on the physicality and even historicity of
the body and blood of Christ, Pascasius collects a number of miracle
stories, particularly in his Chapter 14 but also in Chapter 9. The first
edition apparently had only one such story in Chapter 14. For the second
version for the presentation to Charles the Bald, Pascasius added two
more.

In the earliest version of Chapter 14 the only story is actually the
fourth one in the current expanded edition, at XIV.120-68.[33] In it the
English presbyter Plecgils, at a sanctuary dedicated to St. Ninian,[34] prays
for a vision of Christ in the Eucharist as a child (*puer*) held in his
mother's lap.

> *Te depraecor* inquid *omnipotens, pande* mihi exiguo in hoc mysterio
> *naturam corporis* Christi, *ut mihi lic*eat (sic) eum prospicere *praesentem*
> corporeo *visu* et formam pueri *quem* olim sinus *matris* tulit vagientem,
> nunc manibus contrectare. (XIV.139-43)

An angel says that he will see the infant Jesus, and Plecgils looks and
sees 'the infant child whom Simeon had held in the temple in Luke's
Gospel'. Plecgils then holds the boy and kisses him.

> Tum venerabilis *presbiter pavidus* ab uno vultum erigens vidit super aram
> *Patris* Fiium *puerum quem Simeon infantem portare* suis ulnibus
> *promerue*rat (Luke 2.28)… Deinde pro*fusus in amplexum dat oscula* Deo
> et suis *labiis* presssit pia *labia Christi*. (XIV.146-68)

---

32. For an excellent reappraisal of the actual issues under discussion by
Pascasius and Ratramnus, consult Owen M. Phelan, 'Horizontal and Vertical
Theologies: "Sacraments" in the Works of Paschasius Radbertus and Ratramnus of
Corbie', *Harvard Theological Review* 103 (2010), pp. 271-90.

33. The editor identifies textual parallels with an extant Life of St. Ninian by
using italics.

34. Ninian (ca. 360–412) was born in Cumbrian and visited Rome where he was
baptized. After consecration as a bishop in 394 he set out to convert Scotland. On the
way there he met Martin of Tours and, in fact, dedicated his church at Whithorn in
Wigtownshire in his honor. This became the centre for his missionary activity to the
Britons and the Picts. He was buried there and this became a pilgrimage site. For a
brief notice about Ninian and his sanctuary, see Bede, *Historia Ecclesiastica Gentis
Anglorum* 3.4.

Clearly this final episode in Luke's Infancy Narrative provides the biblical perspective through which to interpret this Eucharistic apparition. Although Pascasius' narrative does not explicitly quote Simeon (Luke 2.28), that Gospel passage did prophesy trouble ahead for the Christ child and his mother. Simeon predicts suffering, if not explicitly sacrifice. The story concludes with the specific observation that the Plecgils had been granted the vision of the Christ child, not in the form of the lamb as has been granted to others.[35] Thus the desire of Plecgils was fulfilled and our faith was confirmed in the telling of this story:

> Et mira Omnipotentis dispensatio qui ob unius desiderium ita se praebere dignatus est visibilem et non in figura agni, ut aliis quibusque sub hoc mysterio, sed in forma pueri, quatenus et veritas patesceret in ostenso et sacerdotis desiderium impleretur ex miraculo nostraque fides firmaretur ex relatu. (XIV.160-64)

The story expresses very distinctly that the figure in the apparition was not that of a lamb, as has been revealed to others, but rather in the form of a boy. This is an informative distinction between what Plecgils saw and the traditional biblical and Christian symbol of the Lamb. Christians had picked up the saving symbol of the blood of the Lamb from Exodus 11 and 12, the salutation of the John the Baptist to the Lamb of God at John 1.29 and the vision of the sacrificial Lamb between the throne with four animals and the circle of elders at Rev 5.6. The comment in Pascasius' report of Plecgil's vision is a pertinent observation since in the Carolingian art tradition there are several examples of the Lamb and the crucified Christ, but none, so far as I know of, which presents the victim as a child.

The sacrificial Lamb scene in the Revelation passage certainly informs the miniature in a manuscript of a Carolingian poem, *In Honorem Sancti Crucis*, contained in Vatican City, Biblioteca Apostolica Vaticana, Reg. lat. 124 folio 22 verso. It depicts the four animals in each quadrant of the folio with the Lamb in the middle. The Lamb also shows up in other Carolingian manuscripts such as the adoration of the Lamb in the *Codex Aureus of St. Emmeran*, Paris, Bibliopthèque Nationale, lat. 1141 folio 6 recto.

In the second edition prepared for Charles the Bald, Pascasius made a number of additions identified by the editor within square brackets. In Chapter 14 Pascasius added two more miracle stories both attributed to patristic sources. From Basil he tells the impact of the experience of

---

35. For an example of the Lamb motif, see the full page 'Adoration of the Lamb' in the Codex Aureus of St. Emmeran presented to Charles the Bald in 870.

mystery of the Eucharist on the conversion of a Jew at lines 30-43. From Gregory the Great he talks of a Eucharistic miracle to build up the faith of a Christian woman in lines 44-70.

In the story attributed to Basil,[36] a Jewish man enters a Church and 'joins in with the people as a Christian. He sees an infant (*infans*) in the hands of Basil. When he approaches communion he receives real flesh and real blood'.[37] He goes home and tells his wife and says he believes the Christian mystery. The next day he returns to Basil, who says the Eucharist is available to all who want salvation. So Basil baptizes him with his whole household.[38]

For this same second edition, Pascasius adds a second story, at Chapter 14 lines 44-70. He uses a miracle from Paul the Deacon's 'Life of Gregory the Great'.[39] The story deals with a lady who confuses the host offered in communion with bread she had brought as an offering. The celebrant asks the whole congregation to pray that she might see some visible appearance of Christ. She then finds a piece of the host covered in blood.[40] The celebrant now prays that this bloody host return to its prior form so that the lady might receive it in full faith.[41]

To identify the additions for the fourth edition of Pascasius' text, the editor employs a smaller font. In this format there appears the full version of the Egyptian ascetical narrative. Into Chapter 14, Pascasius

---

36. The editor identifies the quoted material by his use of italics. In this example he is referring to material assigned to Basil in *Patrologia Latina* 73 cols. 301D-302A.

37. See Pascasius, XIV.30-35: '...*Hebreus quidam se sicut Christianus populo commiscuit. Officii* ministerium et muneris *explorare volens vidit infantem* partiri *in manibus Basilii.* Et *communicantibus omnibus venit et ipse dataque est ei vere caro* facta. Inde accessit ad calicem *sanguine* repletum, ut vere est, et *ipsius* factus *est particeps.*'

38. See Pascasius, XIV.37-44: '*Atque de* utriusque servans *reliquias* abiensque *in domum suam ostendit uxori suae ad confirmationem* dictorum and narravit *quae propriis oculis viderat. Credens ergo* ait: vere quia horrible et ammirabile est *Christianorum misterium.* In crastino venit *ad Basilium* postulans se *sine dilatione accipere quod in Christo* est *signaculum.* Basilius autem santcus non differens, sed consuetam eucharistam volenti *omnes salvare* offerens *baptizavit eum cum omni domo sua credentem Domino.*'

39. See *Patrologia Latina* 75 cols. 52C-53B.

40. See Pascasius, XIV.60-65: '*Contuente* etaim illa *invenit partem* quam posuerat, in modum *digiti auricularis sanguine* superfusam'.

41. See Pascasius, XIV.66-70: 'Deinde sacerdos Christi continuo precibus egit, ut eadem caro et sanguis *pristinam* reciperet *formam.* Sicque *factum* est, ut omnes glorificarent Deum et infidelitas pelleretur feminae sacroque sancto communicata misterio sanaretur'.

adds the Egyptian tale from lines 71-119 ahead of the Plecgils tale. The story is a word-for-word quotation with a somewhat expanded introduction on the character of Arsenius. Pascasius then presents the full text with only a few minor alterations of diction. He introduces the doubtful ascetic who uses the term 'figure' or 'symbol' in distinction from the true nature of the body and blood of Christ. He is confronted by two elders who repeat his erroneous position. The doubtful ascetic agrees with their summary and then agrees with their proposal to pray for divine intervention. They go to Church the next Sunday. They see the child Jesus in the host and then an angel appears with a knife to sacrifice him. The blood is caught in a chalice and then when the priest fractures the host, the angel cuts the body into pieces. As they approach to receive communion, the sacrament reverts to its prior form of bread and wine. The doubting monk, however, receives a host with blood still on it. He then confesses his faith in the bodily presence of Christ. They go back to their cells giving thanks. This same story, as we shall see, reappears in thirteenth-century Anglo-Norman translation together with two colourful miniatures to illustrate specific stages of the striking story. But are there any representations of features of this story in Carolingian art?

Carolingian art normally presents Christ the victim as a figure on a cross looking straight out at the viewer.[42] Some of these examples show the crucified figure with blood flowing from his side. An early Carolingian example can be seen in the miniature for the 'Igitur' initial in the Gellone Sacramentary in Paris, Bibliothèque Nationale, lat. 12048 folio 143 verso. In two manuscripts from Tours in the 840s, the chalice is added to catch the flowing blood.[43] That is probably as close as the Carolingian art tradition gets to the specific details of Daniel's story as quoted at length in Pascasius fourth edition of his Chapter 14.

We need to complete our account Pascasius' Eucharistic apparition narratives with the ones added to Chapter 9. In the additions to Chapter 9, the stories are all attributed to Gregory the Great. To introduce him in lines 196-203, Pascasius describes him as 'the learned and blessed prelate of Rome'. From his learned writings, Pascasius inserts a series of

42. For a comprehensive study of the treatments of the sufferings of Christ in the Carolingian art tradition, consult Celia Chazelle, *The Crucified God in the Carolingian Era: The Theology and Art of Christ's Passion* (Cambridge: Cambridge University Press, 2001). See also her more recent comment on the Carolingian emphasis on Eucharist and sacrifice in her 'The Eucharist in Early Medieval Europe', pp. 227-28.

43. See the comments on the Arnaldus Gospels and the Bamberg Bible in Chazelle, *The Crucified God*, p. 248.

seven miracle stories. However, the first story is, in fact, from a different Gregory. It is an extended quotation from Gregory of Tours, *Liber Miraculorum* 1.9.[44] For the other additions to Chapter 9 Pascasius does use six stories associated with Gregory the Great with the first three drawn from his 'Homilies on the Gospels' and the final three from his 'Dialogues'.[45]

In the lengthy story from Gregory of Tours at IX.204-246, the Gallic author describes a Jewish boy (*infans/puer*) who entered the 'Basilica of Blessed Mary' with some of his friends. He received communion and 'went home rejoicing'. The father, who was a glass maker, angrily threw him into his furnace. Gregory alludes to the biblical narrative of three boys in the burning furnace at Dan 3.50. Then the mother searches for her missing son and wails when she finds what has happened. Christians come running. They see the child reclining among the flames as on the softest clouds (inveniunt puerum quasi super plumas mollissimas decumbentem). They rescue the boy and throw the father into the flames where he is totally consumed by the fire. They then question the boy about his protection and he supplies an interesting answer which connects a picture of a mother and child in the church where he received the Eucharist to the woman who protected him. Implicitly, the mother extends her care for her child in the picture to the young Jewish boy in danger. It is possible, with the introduction on Gregory the Great and the six other stories from his texts, that Pascasius may have assumed the church dedicated to Mary was the Roman Basilica of Mary Major with some painting or mosaic of Mother and Child. In his *Historia Francorum* at 10.1, Gregory of Tours had quoted the extensive sermon of Gregory the Great at his consecration in 390. At the end of that sermon Pope Gregory instructs different constituents within the community to gather at specific churches in Rome and then process to the Basilica of Mary Major. So, Gregory of Tours knew about the Marian Basilica in Rome, but whether he knew about any specific artwork in it of Mother and child is unknown. Perhaps the existence in the neighborhood of Tours of two churches dedicated to Mary reinforced the theme of Mother and Child

44. For a critical edition of the Latin text, consult Bruno Krusch, *Monumenta Germaniae Historica: Scriptores Rerum Merovingicarum*, Tomus I Pars II (Hanover: Impensis Bibliopolii Hahniani, 1885), p. 44

45. Pascasius adds the material from Gregory the Great in the following sequence. For IX.254-66 he borrows from *Ev.* 37, 8. For IX.272-346 he borrows from *Ev.* 9-10. For IX.346-51 he borrows from *Ev.* 7. For IX.358-83 he borrows from *Dial.* 4.42.57. For IX.393-96 he borrows from *Dial.* 4.61 and for IX.396-401 he borrows from *Dial.* 4.62

for Gregory in the selection of this story.[46] The narrator clearly connects the woman in the picture with the rescuer:

> Interrogantes autem infantulum Christiani, quale ei umbraculum fuisset, ait Mulier illa quae in baslicam ubi panem de mensa accepi, in cathedra sedebat parvumque infantem in sinu gestabat, haec ne pallio suo, me ignis voraret, operuit. Esca etiam illa quam de manu sacerdotis acceperam, in tantum me iuvit, ut ne spiraculum quidem ignis sentire me putarem. Unde indubitatum est beatam ei Mariam apparuisse. (IX.237-43)

Both the boy and his mother are then baptized.

> Agnita ergo infans fide catholica credidit in nomine Patris et Filii et Spiritus Sancti ac salutaribus aquis ablutus una cum genetrice sua denuo est renatus. (IX.243-45)

In conclusion, Gregory adds that many Jews in that city were baptized at a result of this episode.

Gregory, himself, seems to have borrowed this story from an earlier Greek source. In his *Ecclesiastical History* 4.36,[47] Evagrius Scholasticus recounted a miracle that had happened at Constantinople under Bishop Menas 536 to 552.[48] Here the Church is not named and the context is different. Apparently the custom, when there were hosts left over after a Eucharistic service, was to have 'uncorrupted boys' summoned to consume them. On one occasion a young Jewish boy joined them and then reported the experience to his father, who was a glass maker by profession. In anger the Jewish father threw the boy into the furnace. His mother spent three frantic days looking for him. On the third day the boy heard her and answered. She looked in and saw that he was unharmed. The boy explained that a woman in a purple robe visited him and provided water and food. When the Emperor Justinian learned of this he had the boy and his mother baptized and welcomed into the Church. Justinian also had the father impaled as the 'murderer of his child'.

46. For the church dedicated to Mary built by Omnatius and rebuilt by Eufranius after it had burned down, as well as the oratory at Marsat commissioned in her honor by Gregory of Tours, consult Martin Heinzlemann, *Gregory of Tours: History and Society in the Sixth Century* (Cambridge: Cambridge University Press, 2001), pp. 26, 65.

47. *Pace* Krusch, who identifies this passage as 4.26 in the apparatus in his critical edition of Gregory's *Liber Miraculorum*.

48. For the Greek text consult J.-P. Migne, *Patrologia Graeca*, vol. 86. For an English translation, see Michael Whitby, *The Ecclesiastical History of Evagrius Scholasticus* (Translated Texts for Historians 33; Liverpool: Liverpool University Press, 2000).

Gregory's version of this story about the conversion of the Jewish boy makes two contributions to our discussion. First, the interaction between narrative and art becomes a part of the narrative itself, not just a reflection of the larger cultural context to explain the reception of such a narrative. Then this appeal to Eucharistic apparitions reappears in some instances of hagiography and preaching in the next few centuries.[49]

In *Magna Vita Sanctis Hugonis*, for example, the monk, Adam, presents a lengthy biography of Hugh, the Carthusian monk who became Bishop of Lincoln 1186 to 1200. Adam recounts an episode in which an unnamed cleric has a Eucharistic apparition while Hugh is celebrating Mass. It resembles to some extent the narrative from the 'Vitae Patrum' and the treatise of Pascasius since the narrative does focus on the Christ child; it does not, however, have the explicit bleeding and wounding of the body:

> Cumque ceteris iam rite peractis, ad eum pervenisset locum ubi elevatam in altum hostiam benedicere moris est, mox in verum Christi corpus mistica sanctificatione convertendam, cuiusdam clerici oculos superna clementia dignata est apirire; eique sub specie infantis parvuli Christum suum demonstravit mudissimis digitis sacri presulis reverentissime contrectari. Erat vero idem puer forma quidem permodicus set divino quodam nitore atque candore super estimationem hominis nimium decorus. Clericus qui hec viderat mira devotione, nec mirum, succensus plurimumque compunctus, tempus omne continuabat in lacrimis quod intercessit ab illa elevatione usquequo interim eam levari cerneret, frangendam iam et sumendam sub trina sui partitione. In qua rursum elevatione sub eadem qua prius ymagine natum intuetur de virgine Filium Altissimi, seipsum offerentem pro humana salute. (*Vita Hugonis* 5.3)[50]

This episode clearly focuses on Christ as child and it also provides an explicit link to his virgin mother. Although this account does not address the graphic stabbing or shedding of blood, the observer is moved to compassion and copious tears over 'this offering for the salvation of humanity'. In view of the anti-Semitic use of this motif in the next generation in Lincoln and elsewhere, it is important to note, in the same biography at 5.20, the respect that the Jews of the city expressed for Hugh during his funeral in 1200.

In another adaptation of this theme there is a more sinister version in Thomas Eccleston's account of the Franciscans in England in a report on

49. For an overview of examples in preaching, hagiography, and popular culture, consult Leah Sinanoglou, 'The Christ Child as Sacrifice: A Medieval Tradition and the Corpus Christi Plays', *Speculum* 48 (1973), pp. 491-509.

50. See Decima L. Douie and Dom Hugh Farmer, *Magna Vita Sancti Hugonis* (London: Thomas Nelson & Sons, 1961), vol. 2, pp. 85-86.

Peter of Tewksbury.[51] After a Mass celebrated by Peter in the presence of a mother and her son, the boy took pains to avoid the priest. When questioned about this unusual behavior, the boy said that he had seen the priest consume a child at communion and did not want to be the next victim.

Across Europe there are many accounts of blood libel in which the Jewish community is accused of the ritual murder of Christian boys in order to use their blood in some of their own rituals around the time of their Passover. In some of these tales the Christian dates of Palm Sunday, Good Friday and Easter are featured. In 1150 Thomas of Monmouth, a Benedictine monk in Norwich, constructed an elaborate account of the life and death of a boy named William in order to promote his cause for canonization.[52] Rome never did approve this case but this text certainly supported a very popular local cult. Thomas claims to have been told by a convert from Judaism that European Jews had an annual meeting at Narbonne where they would decide from which country they would select a Christian to be killed in a ritual murder. In 1144 England was selected. Thomas proceeds to provide an extended and graphic account of the kidnapping of the twelve-year-old William. He describes gruesome torture and the crucifixion of William. This pattern was reflected in other accusations of ritual murder of children at Gloucester in 1168, at Bury St. Edmunds in 1181, at Bristol in 1183 and many places on the continent. In 1255 the body of a nine-year-old boy, named Hugh, was found in a well near Lincoln. It was assumed that he had been tortured and crucified by a local Jew. That person was identified, captured and executed. Then a local cult grew up in honor of Little Hugh of Lincoln. In the section of his *Chronica Majora* assigned to 1255, the Benedictine monk from St. Albans, Matthew Paris, certainly provided ample support for the popular cult of Little Hugh. He constructed an extended account of the torture and death of Hugh paralleled very closely with Christ's own beatings, the crowning of thorns, crucifixion, and stabbing with a spear. In this narrative Matthew added the gruesome detail of the disembowelling of the child's corpse. He further inflamed the population by stating that all the Jews of England were somehow implicated in the

---

51. See Thomas Eccleston: 'Cumque quaerit mater causa pro qua fugeret, dixit, quod viderat eum devorasse infantem in capella super altare et timuit ne faceret sibi similiter', in A. G. Little (ed.), *Fratris Thomas, vulgo dicti de Eccleston Tractatus de Adventu Fratrum Minorum in Angliam* (Manchester: Manchester University Press, 1951), p. 97.

52. See Thomas of Monmouth, *The Life and Miracles of St. William of Monmouth with Introduction, Text, Translation and Notes* (ed. Augustus Jessopp and Montague Rhodes; Cambridge: Cambridge University Press, 1896).

ritual killing of Little Hugh.[53] There are many such accusations against
the Jewish community, not only in England but throughout much of the
European continent. This demonstrates the potential for perverse distortions in the patterns of this polyvalent story from Egyptian asceticism.

Thirteenth-Century Version of the Story of the Doubting Ascetic

The original story reappears in an Anglo-Norman translation in a
miscellany prepared for the edification of a Noblewoman around 1260,
probably in the East Midlands or East Anglia in England.[54] In her
detailed study of this text, Professor Adelaide Bennett provides helpful
context. She points to the reforms of the IV Lateran Council of 1215 that
sought to improve the understanding and the practice of the Christian life
not only among clergy but among the laity. This handbook, which exists
in 27 manuscripts, reflects this basic educational renewal. This collection
consists of nine sections or chapters. The first deals with the 12 articles
of the Creed. Then there comes a treatment of the Ten Commandments
and then the Seven Deadly sins, followed by a treatment of the specific
sin of sacrilege. In the fifth section there is a treatment of the seven
sacraments. The sixth component provides a Sermon on love and fear.
The seventh provides guidance for making a good confession. The eighth
section is a treatise on prayer. The ninth and final section provides a
prayer to God and to the Virgin. A distinctive feature of the presentation
in sections two to five is the use of exempla, with a total of 60 in all. The
sources for this material follow a similar pattern to that in Pascasius,
three centuries earlier, with selections from the Bible, Gregory the Great,
the Vitae Patrum, and Bede.

Under the discussion of the Sacraments, there is a consideration of the
Eucharist and a prominent exemplum is the story from the Vitae Patrum
about the doubting ascetic. In the one manuscript with miniatures, this
story is found on folio 77 recto and proceeds through 77 verso and on to

53. See Henry Richards Luard (ed.), *Matthaei Parisiensis, Monachi Sanct
Albani, Chronica Majora, vol. 5 (AD 1248–AD 1259)* (London: Longmans & Co.,
1880), pp. 516-19.

54. This manual, entitled *Manuel des Péchés*, is found in Princeton University
Library, Taylor Medieval MS 1. I am very grateful to Professor Adelaide Bennett for
informing me about this manuscript and her informative article. See Adelaide
Bennet, 'A Book Designed for a Noblewoman: Illustrated "Manuel des Péchés" of
the Thirteenth Century', in Linda Brownrigg (ed.), *Medieval Book Production:
Assessing the Evidence: Proceedings of the Second Conference of the Seminar of the
Book to 1500; Oxford, July 1988* (Los Altos, CA: Anderson-Lovelace Red Gulf,
1990), pp. 163-81.

78 recto. At the bottom of the latter two folios there are two colorful miniatures which depict two specific stages of the story.[55] The first one has the celebrant elevating the host before three kneeling figures. Then with the host there appears the Christ child. From above comes an angel who stabs the child and collects the blood in a chalice. The second episode passes over the cutting of the child into pieces and depicts the stage at which the doubting ascetic receives a bloody host. So, unlike the paintings in the two Monasteries in the Sinai which provide two biblical scenes through which to interpret the Eucharist, these two paintings highlight and emphasize two critical stages in the narrative of the apparition of the child Jesus in the host.

During the thirteenth century there is considerable interest in the Eucharist at both the level of systematic theology but even more at the level of popular piety. In his treatment of the theology of the Eucharist written or collected together from 1271 onwards, Thomas Aquinas indicates that he is aware of apparitions that connect the Eucharist with the child Jesus. He poses the specific question about whether the body of Christ really remains in the Eucharist when there is an apparition of flesh or of the child.[56] In his 'Sed Contra' of this article, Thomas affirms that 'even when such an apparition appears, Christ still remains in the sacrament'. In his response Thomas makes two points. In a subjective appearance to a single beholder when everyone else still sees only the host, then there is no objective change or addition to the host. But then he adds that sometimes apparitions can also have an objective basis when everyone sees the same thing. Incidentally, this fits the case with the story of the doubting ascetic. He goes on to say that the glorified Christ can manifest himself to the un-glorified observer in its proper likeness, the fullness of the glorified manhood or in a borrowed version, ostensibly that of the child Jesus.

At the popular level, English plays associated with the thirteenth-century feast of the Corpus Christi cycle deal with a number of biblical episodes linked to our theme from the sacrifice of Isaac to variations of the presentation of the Child Jesus in the temple.[57] In the last instance the Child is placed not so much into the arms of Simeon but on the altar of sacrifice.

55. For the first miniature in colour, see http://ica.princeton.edu/images/princeton/t1.077va.jpg.

56. Consult Thomas Aquinas, *Summa Theologiae* Tertia Pars, Quaestio 76, Articulus 8.

57. For a detailed discussion of a range of evidence but particularly that of the Corpus Christi Cycle of plays, consult Sinanoglou, 'The Christ Child as Sacrifice', pp. 500-509.

Conclusion

This exploration demonstrates the enduring appeal of a striking oral narrative. In its first instance it is designed for the basic instruction of simple monks in the ascetical traditions of the Egyptian desert in the fourth and fifth centuries. The graphic connection between the apparition of the sacrifice of the child Jesus and the Eucharist dramatically replicates their understanding of the presence of Christ in this sacrament. Some of the art in two monastic churches demonstrate that the biblical passages of Abraham and Isaac and the tragic episode of Jephthah and his daughter reflect the emphasis on sacrifice in the ascetical tradition. That theme is applied to their Eucharistic sense of the sacrifice of Christ as a child. Later, in the Carolingian period, Pascasius employs the same story in a different context in order to provide instruction to relatively recent converts from early Germanic practices in Saxony to Christianity. He cites a range of patristic exempla to teach these relative neophytes about the presence of Christ in the Eucharist. His emphasis on physical presence and on miracle would resonate within the culture of the Saxon converts. His repetition of the Egyptian Eucharistic apparition explicitly highlights the distinctiveness of the Christ child image rather than the more familiar Lamb of God in the Carolingian period. Moreover, within Pascasius' selection of stories there are intriguing examples of the relationship between narrative and Church art. In one example in particular the image of Mother and child provides the model for the rescue of a child from a fiery furnace. Artistic representations linking the host and the child of sacrifice do not show up until the thirteenth century. There the exact episode in the original Egyptian tale reappears in a handbook designed for the edification of an educated Christian woman. At about the same time the depiction of the Christ child is certainly noted by Thomas in his major synthesis of Catholic thought in his *Summa Theologicae*. The same theme gets reflected in other forms of popular culture in the thirteenth century, such as the Mystery Plays of the Corpus Christi cycle and the sinister accusations of ritual child sacrifice against the Jews. Thus this story of the child of sacrifice is an effective way to present the belief in the real presence that can be accommodated to different audiences over time and space. At the same time, its very polyvalent power can also lead to very destructive applications.

DEUS NECANS:
JESUS IN THE INFANCY GOSPEL OF THOMAS

J. R. C. Cousland

'Who, then, is this infant child?'

—Clement of Alexandria[1]

Technically speaking, the *Infancy Gospel of Thomas* (*IGT*) does not contain an instance of child sacrifice.[2] Rather, it describes a young god killing human children, not humans offering young children to a deity. Nevertheless, the *Infancy Gospel* fits in a general way with the theme of this book—not sparing the children—and raises the question of why a compassionate deity, famed for his sacrificial love for humanity, should in his infancy 'sacrifice' those children who fall victim to his anger. As Paul Foster trenchantly asks, 'what motivated the creation of narratives that portray the young Jesus as insolent, uncontrolled and murderous?'[3] The present study is an attempt to explain this anomaly.[4]

1. Clement of Alexandria, *Paedagogus* 1.5 (ANF).
2. For recent editions of the *Infancy Gospel of Thomas* (*IGT*), see Ursula Ulrike Kaiser, 'Die Kindheitserzählung des Thomas', in Christoph Markschies and Jens Schröter (eds.), *Antike christliche Apokryphen in deutscher Übersetzung* (AcA I/1-2: Tübingen: Mohr Siebeck, 2012), pp. 930-59; Bart D. Ehrman and Zlatko Pleše, *The Apocryphal Gospels* (New York: Oxford University Press, 2011), pp. 3-29; Tony Burke, *Infancy Gospel of Thomas, De infantia Iesu Evangelium Thomae Graecae* (CCSA 17; Turnhout: Brepols, 2010); Ronald F. Hock, *The Infancy Gospels of James and Thomas* (The Scholars Bible 2; Santa Rosa: Polebridge, 1995); J. K. Elliott, *The Apocryphal New Testament* (Oxford: Clarendon Press, 1993); *idem, A Synopsis* of the *Apocryphal Nativity* and *Infancy Narratives* (NTTS 34; Leiden: Brill, 2006); O. Cullmann, 'The Infancy Story of Thomas', in E. Hennecke and W. Schneemelcher (eds.), *New Testament Apocrypha*. Vol. 1, *Gospels and Related Writings* (rev. ed.; Louisville: Westminster John Knox, 1991), pp. 439-53. The textual problems associated with the *IGT* are legion, and its transmission history extraordinarily complex. For a comprehensive overview of the issues and various recensions, see Burke, *De infantia Iesu*, pp. 127-222, 293-463.
3. Paul Foster, *The Apocryphal Gospels: A Very Short Introduction* (Oxford: Oxford University Press, 2009), p. 67.
4. The textual history of the *IGT* is notoriously complex. The discussion undertaken here will follow Tony Burke in assigning priority to the Greek manuscript S

The Problem of Jesus Necans

First-time readers of *IGT* are immediately confronted with the image of Jesus the killer.[5] In the space of four brief chapters (chs. 1–4), the five-year-old Jesus kills two other infants for trifling offences. At the beginning of the Gospel, when the son of Annas the High Priest disperses the pools of water Jesus had fashioned and dries them up, Jesus curses him, saying '"Your fruit be without root, and your shoot withered like a branch let off by a strong wind!" And immediately that child withered away' (*IGT* 3.2-3).[6] Shortly thereafter, another child (?) bumps into Jesus' shoulder. Jesus curses him, and he dies at once (*IGT* 4.1). When the child's parents go on to revile Jesus for this deed, he blinds them as well (*IGT* 4.2–5.1). And, later in the gospel, when Jesus is struck by his second teacher, he curses him and the teacher immediately falls down and dies (*IGT* 13.2). Jesus' parents confine him to the house thereafter so that he does not kill anyone else (*IGT* 14.3).

Several factors intensify the shocking effect of these incidents. One is that they occur at the beginning of the narrative so that that they help establish Jesus' character right from the outset. His curses immediately define Jesus and identify him through the course of the work. The second is that Jesus demonstrates absolutely no compunction for his killings. Even when he is recriminated for them by Joseph, he never acknowledges that he has done anything wrong. Although he twice decides to reverse his violent actions, this is viewed more as a concession on his part, not any sort of repentance. One gets the impression that he regards such actions as his prerogative. So, in marked contrast to the canonical gospels where Jesus suffers the little children to come to him, Jesus causes the little children to suffer—and die. This problem is certainly one of the most pressing questions that face scholars of the *IGT*, and for that reason, there have been numerous attempts at explanations.

and will follow (unless indicated otherwise) the translation that he provides in his Synopsis of the Greek versions (Burke, *De infantia Iesu*, pp. 465-539). For a brief account of Tony Chartrand-Burke's textual rationale and conclusions, see 'The Infancy Gospel of Thomas', in Paul Foster (ed.), *The Non-Canonical* Gospels (London: T&T Clark International, 2008), pp. 126-30.

5. François Bovon remarks that, 'the child Jesus acts ruthlessly and punishes with all his strength' ('Miracles, Magic and Healing in the Apocryphal Acts of the Apostles', in *idem*, *Studies in Early Christianity* [Grand Rapids: Baker, 2005], p. 254).

6. The English text of the *IGT* is that of Reidar Aasgaard, *The Childhood of Jesus: Decoding the Apocryphal Infancy Gospel of Thomas* (Eugene: Wipf & Stock, 2009), pp. 233-42.

Oscar Cullmann would attribute these episodes to the deficiencies of the author, who was wanting 'in good taste, restraint and discretion'.[7] He further observes that

> if the name of Jesus did not stand alongside *Infancy Gospel of Thomas* the description 'child' or 'boy', one could not possibly hit upon the idea that these stories of the capricious divine boy were intended to supplement the tradition about him… The cruder and more startling the miracle, the greater the pleasure the compiler finds in it, without the slightest scruple about the questionable nature of the material.[8]

Such an explanation seems to draw, however, on early twentieth-century assumptions about how the gospels were necessarily *Kleinliteratur*, and deficient in those cultured qualities that distinguished *Hochliteratur*.[9] And while Cullmann acknowledged that the author had 'a gift of vivid story-telling', more contemporary assessments of the *IGT* have tended to emphasize far more strongly the literary talent of the author.[10] Tony Chartrand-Burke, for instance, opines that, 'The *Infancy Gospel of Thomas* is a wonder of literature'.[11] These paired observations suggest, on the one hand, that the author possesses a considerable degree of literary sophistication, but that, on the other, like some literary Trimalchio, he is totally unaware of the crass impression he was creating. Can it really be that the author is oblivious or indifferent to the fact that his 'Jesus is an *enfant terrible* who seldom acts in a Christian way'?[12]

One explanation accounts for this difficulty by stressing that Jesus was indeed an *enfant*, and that it was his lack of maturity and self-control that caused him to act so inappropriately. Children in antiquity were thought

7. Cullmann, 'Infancy Story of Thomas', p. 442.

8. Cullmann, 'Infancy Story of Thomas', p. 442. Similar appeals to deficiencies in good taste can be found in Elliott (*Apocryphal New Testament*, p. 68), who speaks of crude sensationalism, and G. Schneider (*Evangelia Infantiae Apocrypha/ Apokryphe Kindheitsevangelien* [FC 18; Freiburg i.Br.: Herder, 1995], cited in Hans-Josef Klauck, *Apocryphal Gospels* [London: T&T Clark International, 2003], p. 77), who describes it as 'extraordinarily banal'.

9. Karl Ludwig Schmidt, *Der Rahmen der Geschichte Jesu: literarkritische Untersuchungen zur ältesten Jesusüberlieferung* (Berlin: Trowitzsch & Sohn, 1919), p. 17.

10. Cullmann, 'Infancy Story of Thomas', p. 442.

11. Tony Chartrand-Burke, 'Completing the Gospel: The Infancy Gospel of Thomas as a Supplement to the Gospel of Luke', in Charles Kannengieser, *The Reception and Interpretation of the Bible in Late Antiquity: Proceedings of the Montreal Colloquium in Honour of Charles Kannengiesser, 11-13 October, 2006* (Leiden: Brill, 2008), p. 116.

12. The phrase is from Elliott, *Apocryphal New Testament*, p. 68.

to be deficient in understanding and self-control until the onset of adulthood.[13] Ursula Ulrike Kaiser makes a strong case that the *IGT* deliberately portrays Jesus with the characteristics and immaturity of a five to twelve year-old.[14] She observes that Jesus is twice described as 'playing' (*IGT* 2.1; 9.1). Moreover, he is sent off to school to be educated, as would have happened with boys his age. These features suggest that Jesus was represented as a typical child. His intolerance, inability to control his emotions, and petulance are what would be expected of a young child.

This explanation accounts for some of the features of the *IGT*, but it is not free of difficulties. While it is true that Jesus is described as 'playing', on one of these occasions his playmate Zeno dies (*IGT* 9.1). Zeno's parents suspect that Jesus was to blame, so Jesus resurrects Zeno and asks him whether he was responsible. Zeno replies, 'No, *Lord*'.[15] The circumstance of having one little boy addressing his playmate as 'Lord' rather undermines the notion that Jesus is being portrayed as merely a little boy. Furthermore, as will be argued below, the second instance where Jesus is playing (*IGT* 2.1) likely has a strong theological subtext. And lastly, while Jesus is described as going to school, he is portrayed not only as vastly superior in understanding to his peers, but to his teachers as well. So, while Jesus does things that other children do, he is represented as being profoundly different from them.

By contrast, Tony [Chartrand-] Burke has sought to argue that Jesus resembles adults, and that his killings have affinities with the petulant and bad-tempered behavior typical of a Jewish Holy Man.[16] He argues that since the trope of the Jewish holy man was firmly established in the first century CE, it is likely Jesus was represented in a similar light. What makes this holy man figure so distinctive is that it was common for him

13. Ursula Ulrike Kaiser, 'Die sogenannte "Kindheitserzählung des Thomas": Überlegungen zur Darstellung Jesu als Kind, deren Intention und Rezeption', in Claire Clivaz, Andreas Dettwiler, Luc Devillers, and Enrico Norelli (eds.), *Infancy Gospels: Stories and Identities* (WUNT 281; Tübingen: Mohr Siebeck, 2011), pp. 474-79. Robert J. Miller (*Born Divine. The Births of Jesus and Other Sons of God* [Santa Rosa: Polebridge, 2003], p. 275) makes a similar observation: 'How would God act if he had the interests and emotions of a five-year-old?'

14. Kaiser, 'Die sogenannte "Kindheitserzählung"', pp. 474-75.

15. My italics.

16. Burke, *De infantia Iesu*, pp. 276-81; *idem*, 'Completing the Gospel', pp. 11-12. It is puzzling to me, therefore, that he is able to write elsewhere that the *IGT* 'seeks to portray Jesus as some kind of divine figure' ('Depictions of Children in the Apocryphal Infancy Gospels', *Studies in Religion/Sciences Religieuses* 41 [2012], p. 393).

to curse rather than bless; his 'power was believed to come from God, and God did not always act with mercy'.[17] Such traits can be discerned especially in the figures of Elijah and Elisha, who have notable affinities with Jesus—they curse those who are opposed to them and murder those who annoy them.[18] And, as he points out, Jesus himself shows anger in the canonical gospels by overturning the moneychangers' tables in the temple (Mark 11.12-22; Matt 21.18-19). He also curses the fig-tree (Mark 11.21) and disbelieving towns (Luke 10.13-15), and permits his disciples to curse individuals or cities (Matt 10.11-15; Luke 9.5; 10.10-12).[19] Burke concludes, therefore, that these features of Jesus' adult ministry readily mesh with the curses of Jesus found in the *IGT*.

Burke's observations are valuable, and bring up features that are often overlooked. Nevertheless, they do not entirely convince. First of all, on Burke's understanding of ancient biography, the picture of Jesus in the *IGT* is actually modeled on the behavior of the adult Jesus. Yet, the adult Jesus does not murder anyone, nor does he harm anyone, nor for that matter does he curse anyone. The only thing that Jesus actually curses in the canonical gospels is the fig tree (Mark 11.21; cf. Mark 11.12-14, 20-24; Matt 21.18-22). He certainly *condemns* the behavior of the Galilean towns, but this is categorically different from cursing them. Nor does Jesus sanction cursing on the part of his disciples (cf. Luke 9.51-56).

Second, Burke's category[20] of the cantankerous 'Jewish Holy Man' who is just as inclined to curse as to bless, is basically a construct consisting of only three people: Elijah, Elisha, and Artapanus' depiction of Moses (and given the relative obscurity of Artapanus' narrative, we are really looking at two individuals). This seems to be rather an insufficient basis on which to construct a paradigmatic group to which the *IGT*'s Jesus is supposed to belong.

Further, it is open to question how much the author would have been drawing extensively on *Jewish* exemplars. The *IGT* shows very limited reliance on the Old Testament.[21] Reidar Aasgaard's detailed chapter on biblical intertextuality in the *IGT* concludes that its 'ties with the OT are generally few and considerably weaker than with the NT. In itself, this is

17. Burke, *De infantia Iesu*, pp. 276-78.
18. Burke, *De infantia Iesu*, pp. 279-80.
19. Tony Burke, '"Social Viewing" of Children in the Childhood Stories of Jesus', in Cornelia B. Horn and Robert R. Phenix (eds.), *Children in Late Antique Christianity* (STAC 58; Tübingen: Mohr Siebeck, 2009), p. 41.
20. One of the topic headings in *De infantia Iesu* reads 'Jesus as a Young Jewish Holy Man' (p. 276).
21. Klauck (*Apocryphal Gospels*, p. 73) flatly states that, 'The Old Testament, which is so important for the Protevangelium, plays no role in the IGTh'.

a strong testimony for *IGT*'s distant relations to Judaism or Jewish influenced Christianity.'[22] He is, moreover, uncertain whether the author actually has any firsthand acquaintance with the Elijah, Elisha texts in 1 and 2 Kings or whether he is simply reliant on Luke.[23] Nor does the *IGT* display an obvious acquaintance with a Jewish milieu.[24] These tenuous connections with the Jewish world make it far more likely that the author has found his models elsewhere. So, intriguing as it is, Burke's theory does not account for Jesus' murderous behavior.

A third proposal has been advanced by Reidar Aasgaard. He suggests that the *IGT* should not be regarded as a production for adults, but one specifically designed for children. It is, in effect, Christianity's first children's story—'a story for children about Jesus, true God and true child. It is a story about a Jesus with whom they could identify, a story with both seriousness and humor, and a story well fit both to entertain and to edify.'[25] Yet, it also had a very serious dimension—it was designed as theology for children.[26] Aasgaard maintains that although its accounts of Jesus cursing might be problematic for our modern sensibilities, they need not have been problematic for early Christians.[27] Presumably, children would have found Jesus' vengeful deeds as somehow akin to the violence in fairy tales or modern-day cartoons.[28]

Aasgaard's proposal is refreshingly original. That being said, we know very little about the intended audience of the *IGT* (which, he acknowledges, would also have contained adults[29]) or, for that matter, about children's literature in antiquity. In addition, as Burke has forcefully argued, it 'strains credibility that a text in which the young protagonist

22. Reidar Aasgaard, *The Childhood of Jesus*, p. 134. Hock, *Infancy Gospels*, p. 98, observes that the Septuagint 'is not a source' for the *IGT*.

23. Aasgaard, *The Childhood of Jesus*, p. 129.

24. It is noteworthy, for instance, that even in his home village Jesus is taught *Greek* not Hebrew or Aramaic (cf. the version of the *IGT* at *Ga.* 14.1 where Jesus is to be taught 'First the Greek, then the Hebrew'). For a different view about the Jewish milieu, cf. A. G. van Aarde, 'The Infancy Gospel of Thomas: Allegory or Myth—Gnostic or Ebionite', *Verbum et Ecclesia* 26 (2005), pp. 826-50. He suggests that the context of *IGT* is that of Ebionite Christianity.

25. Aasgaard, *The Childhood of Jesus*, p. 216; *idem*, 'Uncovering Children's Culture in Late Antiquity: The Testimony of the *Infancy Gospel of Thomas*', in Horn and Phenix (eds.), *Children in Late Antique Christianity*, pp. 1-27.

26. Aasgaard, 'Uncovering Children's Culture', p. 23.

27. Aasgaard, *The Childhood of Jesus*, p. 213.

28. Aasgaard ('Uncovering Children's Culture', p. 22) observes that the children 'could identify with Jesus' anger, sympathize with his wish for revenge, and dream of having similar powers'.

29. Aasgaard, *The Childhood of Jesus*, p. 212.

maims or slays other children, disobeys his parents, and defies his teachers would be considered edifying subject matter for children by parents of that time'.[30] Would such an intrinsically subversive document mesh, for instance, with the proper 'management of children' advocated by 1 Timothy (1 Tim 3.4-5)?

A further objection that can be leveled against all the proposals mentioned above is their assumption that Jesus' anger would have been acceptable in certain contexts in antiquity.[31] This assumption, however, appears to be mistaken. In an excellent, carefully argued article Kristi Upson-Saia has sought to examine ancient constructions of anger and to assess how acceptable Jesus' anger in the *IGT* would have seemed to its audience.[32] She establishes that the repugnance that modern audiences feel for Jesus' anger and violence would have been just the same for early Christian audiences: 'Jesus' behavior would have been characterized as self indulgent, ignoble, unmanly and a threat to the community'.[33] Pagan discussions of anger that are roughly contemporaneous with the *IGT* indicate that anger was universally frowned upon; it was a passion characteristic of those of low social standing, the sick, and the young.[34] This aversion to anger was no less true for early Christians. Upson-Saia refers to a study by Michael McCarthy, which argues that 'patristic authors were deeply uneasy with references to divine wrath and used a range of strategies to minimize the potential harm, scandal, or misunderstanding that such biblical passages might engender'.[35] In light of these discussions Jesus, whether he was divine or human, would have been viewed as an ignoble figure who was a slave to his own anger.[36] Notwithstanding his great power, he would have been contemptible because he lacked the self-control to use it justly.

Given that this picture of Jesus is so unflattering, one wonders how it originated. Upson-Saia maintains that these stories were likely composed by opponents of Christianity, who wanted to malign Jesus, and used this

---

30. Tony Burke, 'Depictions of Children', p. 396.

31. Their view is also shared by Ursula Ulrike Kaiser, 'Die sogenannte "Kindheitserzählung des Thomas": Überlegungen zur Darstellung Jesu als Kind, deren Intention und Rezeption', in Clivaz, Dettwiler, Devillers, and Norelli (eds.), *Infancy Gospels*, pp. 462-63.

32. Kristi Upson-Saia, 'Holy Child or Holy Terror? Understanding Jesus' Anger in the Infancy Gospel of Thomas', *Church History* 82 (2013), pp. 1-39.

33. Upson-Saia, 'Holy Child or Holy Terror?', p. 3.

34. Upson-Saia, 'Holy Child or Holy Terror?', p. 14.

35. Michael McCarthy, 'Divine Wrath and Human Anger', *Theological Studies* 70 (2009), p. 846.

36. Upson-Saia, 'Holy Child or Holy Terror?', p. 16.

unflattering depiction of his youth to discredit him and his followers. She also argues at length that these stories were modified over the course of time as Christian tradents did their best to mitigate and smooth over the negative details of Jesus' actions and make them seem less offensive to believers.[37]

This is an ingenious theory but it raises a number of problems. She rightly points out that Celsus condemned Jesus for uttering threats and needlessly reviling men (Origen, *Contra Celsum* 2.76). But why would Christianity's detractors not do precisely what Celsus does and simply attack the adult Jesus directly? Why would they need to invent oblique and dubious stories about Jesus' infancy to condemn him? And, further, what are we to make of those aspects of the infancy stories where Jesus does act with rectitude and compassion? Were they also written by those wishing to subvert Christianity?

This brief overview indicates that while considerable progress has been made in assessing the infant Jesus' violent behavior, there is little in the way of unanimity. These very different outcomes stem in part from divergent assessments of the genre of the work, and so this problem will be addressed next.

Genre

The *IGT*'s genre continues to receive considerable attention.[38] Tony Burke, for instance, regards it as belonging to the biographical genre with further echoes from the canonical gospels. He points out that the figure of the infant Jesus is very similar to biographies of heroic and extraordinary children. Yet, a more considered examination of the gospel reveals that the *IGT* is not a biography of an exceptional human or a hero.[39] Jesus is not portrayed as a human or demigod, but as a god in human form.[40] Rather, it is the biography of a god. Over the course of the

37. Upson-Saia, 'Holy Child or Holy Terror?', pp. 21-37.

38. Burke, *De infantia Iesu*, pp. 281-84; Kaiser, 'Die Kindheitserzählung', pp. 937-38.

39. For a discussion of precocious heroes, see Charles H. Talbert, 'Prophecies of Future Greatness: The Contribution of Greco-Roman Biographies to an Understanding of Luke 1:5–4:15', in James L. Crenshaw and Samuel Sandmel (eds.), *The Divine Helmsman: Studies on God's Control of Human Events, Presented to Lou H. Silberman* (New York: Ktav, 1980), pp. 129-41.

40. Andries Van Aarde ('Ebionite Tendencies in the Jesus Tradition: The *Infancy Gospel of Thomas* Interpreted from the Perspective of Ethnic Identity', *Neotestamentica* 40 [2006], p. 358 n. 14) uses the term 'god-child', which is apt, except that he would also include exceptional humans within this category. Jesus' closest

Gospel, reference is frequently and repeatedly made to Jesus' divine traits.[41] The very fact that he is able to curse by divine fiat and on his own authority immediately sets him apart from any of the notable or heroic figures to whom he is compared.[42]

Moreover, the *IGT*'s first episode opens with an episode clearly designed to allude to Jesus' divinity.[43] Jesus' play with the earth and water recall God's actions at the beginning of Genesis when he separates the earth from the water.[44] Likewise, his fashioning of the sparrows from clay not only calls to mind God's creation of the birds and wild animals, but also the creation of Adam from the dust of the earth (Gen 2.7).[45] God gives life to all creatures, and Jesus is portrayed as doing the same things that his father had done. What is more, like his Father, he executes these deeds, too, by divine fiat.[46] When he cleanses the waters, 'he commanded it only by means of a word and without any deed' (*IGT* 2.1). Similarly, when he vivifies the sparrows, 'Jesus clapped his hands and commanded the birds with a cry in front of all. And he said: "Go, take flight like living beings". And the sparrows took off and flew away twittering'

classical analogues, however, would be Dionysus and Asclepius, who although they had mortal mothers, were still—unlike most Greek heroes—considered divine. Philipp Vielhauer, (*Geschichte der urchristlichen Literatur* [Berlin: de Gruyter, 1975], p. 676) rightly describes Jesus as a sort of 'heidnisches Götterkind'.

41. For a brief discussion of the *IGT*'s 'high christology', see Miller, *Born Divine*, pp. 274-75.

42. For instance, all the curses of the 'Jewish holy men' to whom Burke appeals as analogues to Jesus are enacted by God: they curse, but it is God who effectuates the curse. Burke acknowledges that, 'The power was believed to come from God, and God did not always act with mercy' (*De infantia Iesu*, p. 278). In Jesus' case, however, they are enacted on the basis of his own authority, and the immediacy with which his curses are enacted give expression to his own divine power.

43. Aasgaard, *The Childhood of Jesus*, p. 156: 'What we have in the Jesus of *IGT*, then, is a portrait of Jesus as a divine figure, but also as the all-too-human child described earlier'.

44. W. Baars and J. Helderman, 'Neue Materialien zum Text und zur Interpretation des Kindheitsevangeliums des Pseudo-Thomas', *Oriens christianus* 77 (1993), p. 205.

44. Richard Bauckham, 'Imaginative Literature', in Philip Esler (ed.), *The Early Christian World* (London: Routledge), p. 797. Cf. Stephen J. Davis, 'Bird Watching in the *Infancy Gospel of Thomas*: From Child's Play to Rituals of Divine Discernment', in Susan E. Myers (ed.), *Portraits of Jesus* (WUNT 2/321; Tübingen: Mohr Siebeck, 2012), pp. 130-31.

45. Aasgaard, *The Childhood of Jesus*, pp. 162-63, cites the *kosmopoiia* of 7.2 and 6.6, which would implicitly align Jesus' creative acts with those of God.

46. Other passages emphasize that Jesus' commands are fulfilled immediately: Cf. *IGT* 3.3; 4.1; 5.1; 8.2.

(*IGT* 2.4). That these events took place on the Sabbath illustrates that the infant Jesus was also Lord of the Sabbath. As Richard Bauckham notes, the infant Jesus 'claims his Father's prerogative to give life on the Sabbath, as the adult Jesus does in John 5'.[47]

Moreover, given that the author has certainly been influenced by the Gospel of John,[48] his decision to situate this 'creation' episode at the very outset of his narrative suggests that, in addition to Genesis, he may also have the prologue of John's Gospel in mind. Just as the latter hearkens back to the beginning of creation, the *IGT* also starts off with a creation narrative.

Consonant with this 'creation' imagery is a pronounced focus on Jesus' pre-existence and his heavenly origin. These examples also have a decidedly Johannine cast to them. For instance, Jesus addresses Joseph, saying, 'When you were born, I existed and came to you' (*IGT* 6.4). This statement has notable echoes with John 8.56-58, where Jesus famously asserts: 'before Abraham was, I am'. Both passages indicate not only that Jesus pre-existed Joseph or Abraham, but also that he was superordinate to merely human existence: he stands outside of the normal human continuum. This speculation about Jesus' pre-existence is furthered by Jesus' first teacher, who is brought to suggest that, 'Perhaps this child existed before the creation of the world?' (*IGT* 7.2). The question seems rather unaccountable unless the author expects us to come to precisely that conclusion. Jesus is distinct from creation. In short, Jesus is divine.

In addition to Jesus' pre-existence, his heavenly origin is repeatedly emphasized by the Gospel. In the same verse just cited, his teacher exclaims, 'The child is simply not of this earth (γηγενὴς)' (*IGT* 7.2), a fact that Jesus himself confirms when he asserts, 'For I have come from above (ἄνωθεν) in order to rescue those below from on high so that I may deliver those below and call them to what is above (τὰ ἄνω), just as the one who sent me to you ordered me' (*IGT* 8.1).[49] The parallels with

47. Bauckham, 'Imaginative Literature', p. 797.

48. See especially Table 1 in Geert van Oyen, 'Rereading the Rewriting of the Biblical Traditions in the Infancy Gospel of Thomas (Paidika)', in Clivaz, Dettwiler, Devillers, and Norelli (eds.), *Infancy Gospels*, pp. 499-503 (492-93), and Aasgaard, *The Childhood of Jesus*, pp. 121, 128. On Jesus' pre-existence in the *IGT*, see Burke, *De infantia Iesu*, p. 275; Klauck, *Apocryphal Gospels*, p. 77. Given the frequent echoes of the Gospel of John, Burke's reluctance to see any dependence of the *IGT* on it seems unduly skeptical.

49. Fred Lapham (*An Introduction to the New Testament Apocrypha* [London: T&T Clark International, 2003], p. 130) rightly remarks that, 'we are presented with a picture of one who is essentially not of this world'. He then adds without any warrant that this is a 'Docetic Christ'. But, as Klauck (*Apocryphal Gospels*, p. 77)

Johannine terminology are apparent, and speak vividly to his divine origin and divine calling. At John 3.31 Jesus says to Nicodemus, 'The one who comes from above (ἄνωθεν) is above all; the one who is of the earth belongs to the earth and speaks about earthly things', while at John 8.23 Jesus says to the Jews, 'You are from below, I am from above (ἐκ τῶν ἄνω εἰμὶ); you are of this world, I am not of this world'. Moreover, Jesus' emphasis on having been sent by the father, and his ability to deliver humankind, are stressed in both gospels.[50]

It is also striking that once Jesus has raised Zeno from the dead, Zeno's parents glorify (ἐδόξασαν) God and worship (προσεκύνησαν) the child Jesus. Given the context of the passage, their action is much more than obeisance. As with the disciple's reaction in Matt 14.33, they worship Jesus as divine after experiencing this epiphany.

Finally, the three teaching episodes in the *IGT* point to a strong Trinitarian focus within the Gospel. Jesus' discourses on the alpha have been analyzed in detail by Lucie Paulissen, who has convincingly demonstrated that there is a deliberate and sustained Trinitarian dimension to Jesus' exposition.[51] She concludes that,

> According to the theological plan, τάξις represents the rank in the hierarchy of each of the three persons within the Trinity, and Φύσις pertains to divinity. These persons form a whole (ξυνούς); they are separated (διαβαίνοντας), but reunited (συναγομένους). They are elevated in glory up to heaven, where they dance in a complex rhythm (ὑψου-μένους, χορεύοντας, τρισήμους); triple (τρισήμους), they are of the same family, in a perfect equilibrium, each with the same weight (ὁμογενεῖς, ζυγοστάτους, ἰσομέτρους).[52]

These assembled features strongly suggest that the infant Jesus is being portrayed not simply as a god, but as God with a capital G—a person of the Holy Trinity. It goes without saying that, if the infant Jesus is interpreted in this light, he is being portrayed in a manner entirely

germanely observes, Jesus' angry reaction when the second teacher strikes him on the head speaks against a docetic Jesus (*IGT* 14.2). Lapham seems to be subscribing to older presuppositions about the gnostic character of the *IGT*. Yet, as Tony Burke establishes in detail, 'There is no reason to associate *IGT* with Gnosticism at all' (Burke, *De infantia Iesu*, p. 280).

50. For deliverance and salvation in John, cf. C. K. Barrett, *The Gospel According to St. John* (2d ed.; Philadelphia: Westminster Press, 1978), pp. 78-81. On John's 'sending Christology', cf. Craig S. Keener, *The Gospel of John: A Commentary* (Grand Rapids: Baker, 2003), pp. 315-17.

51. Lucie Paulissen, Jésus à l'école. L'enseignement dans l'*Évangile de l'Enfance selon Thomas*', *Apocrypha* 14 (2003), pp. 153-75.

52. Paulissen, 'Jésus à l'école', pp. 162-63 (my translation).

distinct from gifted mortals, demigods, or even minor deities. The understanding of Jesus advanced in these passages of *IGT* is basically that of God himself. If such is the case, however, then it is misguided to compare him at the outset with human figures or heroes who are possessed of exceptional abilities. The ongoing refrain of the Infancy Gospel, especially in the first half, is that despite superficial similarities, the infant Jesus is fundamentally different from humans. While the *IGT*'s Jesus' narratives may owe something to the genre of *Wunderkinder* or preternaturally gifted youths, they focus more prominently on his distinctive divinity. In short, the attempts to confine the *IGT* to any genre that fails to take account of Jesus' divinity are inadequate and reductive.

Does this mean, therefore, that the *IGT* is somehow *sui generis* as far as its genre is concerned? Are there no comparable narratives about deities that would help cement this assumption? In fact, there are. Parallels to Krishna and other divine figures have sometimes been adduced as models,[53] but for a Graeco-Roman audience parallels lie far closer to hand. These are the popular stories told about the infancy of many of the male gods in the Graeco-Roman pantheon, Zeus included.[54]

The most celebrated instances of these stories occur in the so-called *Homeric Hymns*.[55] Although these works are not actually by Homer, they

53. Stephen Gero, 'The Infancy Gospel of Thomas. A Study of the Textual and Literary Problems', *NovT* 13 (1971), p. 47; Kaiser, 'Die Kindheitserzählung', p. 939; *idem*, 'Die sogennante "Kindheitserzählung"', pp. 469-70; Vielhauer, *Geschichte der Urchristlichen Literatur*, pp. 676-77.

54. Lesley Beaumont ('Born Old or Never Young? Femininity, Childhood and the Goddesses of Ancient Greece', in Sue Blundell and Margaret Williamson [eds.], *The Sacred and the Feminine in Ancient Greece* [London: Routledge, 1998], p. 80) makes the instructive distinction that while the male Greek gods are often represented as children, this is not usually the case with the goddesses. She accounts for this difference on the grounds of socially ascribed gender roles: female roles were delimited, but 'Contemporary religious sensibilities...seem to have required that the gods in their infancy demonstrate that their divinity was not limited by the dependency of the childhood state' (p. 93). They were able to use this childhood stage 'to display and explore aspects of the divine male' (p. 92). See further Lesley Beaumont, 'Mythological Childhood: A Male Preserve?', *Annual of the British School at Athens* 90 (1995), pp. 360-61.

55. Apostolos N. Athanassakis, *The Homeric Hymns* (Baltimore: The Johns Hopkins University Press, 1993); Jenny Strauss Clay, *The Politics of Olympus* (Princeton: Princeton University Press, 1989), pp. 95-151. On the *Homeric Hymn to Hermes*, see Nicholas Richardson, *Three Homeric Hymns: To Apollo, Hermes, and Aphrodite* (Cambridge: Cambridge University Press, 2010); Athanassios Vergados, 'The *Homeric Hymn to Hermes*: Humour and Epiphany', in Andrew Faulkner (ed.), *The Homeric Hymns: Interpretative Essays* (Oxford: Oxford University Press, 2011), pp. 82-104.

were regarded as having the stamp of Homeric authority, and their details came to be circulated throughout the Graeco-Roman world, forming a firm mythic foundation for an enduring reception history.[56] Given their continued popularity in the Graeco-Roman world, it is strange that they have been very largely overlooked by scholars of the *IGT*.[57] These episodes and related stories were very well known, and it is entirely plausible that they provided the author of the *IGT* with a model or template for constructing his own infancy narrative of Jesus.

While many of the *Hymns* are not concerned with the infancy of the gods, two of the longest—those to Hermes and Dionysus—narrate more fully the adventures of the gods in their youth.[58] These narratives are aretological and reflect on *divine* deeds. The *Hymn to Dionysus* recounts the kidnapping of the young Dionysus by pirates, who hope to hold him for ransom. Despite the repeated warnings of their helmsmen that they are angering a god, they ignore him until Dionysus fills their boat with wine and savage animals. The terrified pirates leap overboard and are transformed into dolphins for their slight against the god.

The narrative *Hymn to Hermes* is particularly famed for its lengthy description of the precocious Hermes, who immediately after his birth sets out to steal his brother Apollo's cattle.[59] The *Hymn* opens with a description of the nymph Maia giving birth to Zeus' son Hermes:

56. For overviews, see G. Siebert, 'Hermes', *LIMC* V (1990), pp. 285-387; Timothy Gantz, *Early Greek Myth* (Baltimore: The Johns Hopkins University Press, 1993); L. Preller, *Griechische Mythologie*. Vol. 1, *Theogonie und Götter* (5th ed.; Berlin: Weidmannsche Verlagsbuchhandlung, 1964), pp. 388-94.

57. Notable exceptions are Klauck, *Apocryphal Gospels*, p. 77, and David Litwa, *Iesus Deus: The Depiction of Jesus as Mediterranean God* (Minneapolis: Fortress Press, 2014). The *Hymn* is mentioned *en passant* in Burke, *De infantia Iesu*, p. 250, p. 252; *idem*, 'Social Viewing of Children', p. 38; Chartrand-Burke, 'The *Infancy Gospel of Thomas*', p. 134.

58. *Homeric Hymn* 4 ('To Hermes') and *Homeric Hymn* 7 ('To Dionysus'). In Hymn 7, Dionysus is a young teenager—'a stripling in the first flush of manhood' (7.3 LCL).

59. Apollodorus 3.10.2; Antoninus Liberalis 23; Ovid, *Met.* 2.679-707; Philostratus, *Imag.* 1.26; Schol., *Il.* 15.256; Alcaeus, Frag. 308 (retold by Horace in his Hymn to Mercury, *Carm.* 1.10.9-12). There are several vase-depictions of episodes from this hymn: T. H. Carpenter, *Art and Myth in Ancient Greece* (London: Thames & Hudson, 1991), p. 90, plates 105 and 106. Further examples are listed in Beaumont, 'Mythological Childhood', p. 342 n. 20.

> Then she bore a child who was a shrewd and coaxing schemer,
> a cattle-rustling robber, and a bringer of dreams,
> a watcher by night and a gate-keeper, soon destined
> to show forth glorious deeds among the immortal gods.
> Born at dawn, by midday he played his lyre,
> And at evening he stole the cattle of far-shooting Apollon.
>
> (*Homeric Hymn* 4.13-18 Athanassakis)

As these lines suggest, Hermes' precosity is remarkable. He leaves the cave in which he was born, invents the lyre, and then steals Apollo's cattle. He gets the cattle to walk backwards to avoid pursuit. He then invents firesticks, lights a fire and sacrifices two cows, dividing them into twelve pieces as portions for the gods. Though tempted to eat the meat, he does not, and he returns to his cave. Hermes' theft is revealed to Apollo by an old man, who in subsequent versions is named Battos and is punished by being turned into stone by Hermes.[60] Apollo accuses Hermes, who denies any involvement, and the matter is finally resolved by Zeus. Hermes gives his lyre to Apollo in exchange for his cattle. The work concludes by saying that Hermes endlessly beguiles 'the tribes of mortal men throughout the night' (4.577-78). Over the course of these narratives, therefore, readers are faced with the spectacle of youthful gods performing remarkable actions. The gods do things that human children do—Hermes sleeps in a crib, he passes gas—but they are nevertheless represented as being categorically different from humans.

Whether the author of the *IGT* had direct acquaintance with the *Hymn to Hermes* (or other *Hymns*) is difficult to establish. Nevertheless there are some interesting points of contact. Both Hermes and Jesus are remarkable for their divine knowledge and precocity. Each manifests divine wisdom and knowledge, as well as technical abilities and remarkable ingenuity. They also sometimes demonstrate an amoral disregard for others and, as a consequence, are both scolded by their parents for engaging in immoral behavior. Hermes and Jesus ignore these parental rebukes and continue to do whatever they wish. It is only near the end of these narratives that the problems raised by their immoral actions are resolved. At this point each enters into his divine father's house and acknowledges his authority. Both figures finish by achieving popular recognition for their exceptional abilities.

---

60. This episode has points of comparison with Jesus' withering of Annas' son. Richardson, *Three Homeric Hymns*, pp. 168-69, offers a helpful discussion of the antiquity of the Battos episode. The versions including Battos are found in Ovid's *Metamorphoses* 2.685-707 and Antoninus Liberalis 23.

It is noteworthy that each vacillates between human and divine behavior. Henk Versnel notes that, 'The Hymn constantly pictures Hermes as uniting two natures, that of the god and that of the mortal. Throughout the Hymn the author plays with this ambivalence, but his play is a precarious one. Blending a mortal and an immortal nature in one character *must* end up in inconsistencies.'[61] It is striking how germane his observations are to the picture of Jesus that emerges from the Infancy Gospel. Its depiction of Jesus as a pre-existent deity sits uneasily next to accounts of Jesus playing with the children of the village. These incongruities in identity are, in fact, defining features of the genre of the two works.[62]

Nevertheless, the developmental processes whereby the gods come to this point differ. Hermes' actions indicate that he is maturing, although he remains essentially unchanged so far as his *ethos* and character are concerned. He resists the temptations that humanity offers him—eating the meat he sacrifices—and his divine nature remains fundamentally unchanged until the end. The same cannot be said for the *IGT*, however. Jesus is faced throughout the work with a series of choices that arise from his being in human society. Unlike Hermes, his *ethos* does undergo a process of development, and is humanized in the process. The following section will deal with the nature of this development, and the section following that will address Jesus' humanization.

Development

Each poem emphasizes the protagonist's maturation and development. Sarah Iles Johnston and Adele Haft both argue that one of the key themes in the *Homeric Hymn to Hermes* is maturation.[63] Johnston maintains that

61. H. S. Versnel. *Coping with the Gods: Wayward Readings in Greek Theology* (Leiden: Brill, 2011), p. 324 (emphasis his).

62. These incongruities between child and god can also be exploited for humorous ends, and both the *Hymn to Hermes* and *IGT* have strong humorous undertones. On the humor in the *Hymn to Hermes*, see Richardson, *Three Homeric Hymns*, pp. 19-20, and Vergados, 'Homeric Hymn to Hermes', pp. 86-98. Lucian does the same things in his various dialogues of the gods, see R. Bracht Branham, *Unruly Eloquence: Lucian and the Comedy of Traditions* (Cambridge, Mass.: Harvard University Press, 1989). For Lucian's special attention to the comic possibilities associated with the figure of Hermes, see especially pp. 147-52.

63. Sarah Iles Johnston, 'Myth, Festival, and Poet: The *Homeric Hymn to Hermes* and its Performative Context', *Classical Philology* 97 (2002), pp. 109-32; Adele Haft, '"The Mercurial Significance of Raiding": Baby Hermes and Animal Theft in Contemporary Crete', *Arion* 4 (1996), pp. 27-48.

the reason that the poem focuses on Hermes' theft of Apollo's cattle is because cattle raids were commonly viewed as rites of passage: 'Hermes' myth, especially as it is narrated in the *Hymn*, can be grouped with other cattle-raid myths as a "coming of age" tale... [H]is precocious leap ahead to the activities of adolescents conforms to the way that Greek gods typically behave as infants.'[64] Hence, even though Hermes retains his infantile form in the *Hymn*, his actions reveal that he is fast leaving his childhood behind, and quickly maturing into an adult deity. And although the character of Hermes' actions remains the same—deceitful and deceptive—as a child and an adult, he is nevertheless portrayed as growing in stature, and as carving out his niche among the Olympian divinities.[65] Adele Haft points out that the two songs (ll. 57-61 and ll. 427-33) performed by Hermes in the *Hymn* confirm that there is a developmental process at work with respect to Hermes' status: 'In the first song, the baby god could identify himself only as the illegitimate offspring of Maia and Zeus. But by the second song, he has demonstrated his place among the gods.'[66]

In the *IGT*, we see the opposite process at work. Here Jesus elects to leave his place with god in order to become the offspring of two humans. And, as will become clear below, his task is carving out a niche among humans not among gods. This is the nature of his particular developmental process.

Some commentators, however, have taken it as axiomatic that the work shows no signs of development.[67] Various reasons are thought to justify this position. First, it is claimed that the *IGT* conforms to the dictates of ancient biography, which is thought by its very nature to be non-developmental. In ancient *Bioi*, the child was regarded as the father to the adult, and the infancy narratives of an individual were meant to show proleptically how their essential character remained unchanged

64. Johnston, 'Myth, Festival, and Poet', p. 114.

65. Clay (*Politics of Olympus*, p. 96) argues that part of the purpose of the Homeric *Hymns* is to show how deities acquired their particular honors. Since Hermes had not been included in this distribution, he was required to get his honors by theft or exchange. Cf. Haft, 'Mercurial Significance', pp. 31, 35.

66. Haft, 'Mercurial Significance', p. 43.

67. This point is repeatedly stressed, for instance, by Tony Burke, 'Depictions of Children', 393; *idem*, 'The *Infancy Gospel of Thomas*', p. 137; cf. Vielhauer, *Geschichte der Urchristlichen Literatur*, p. 674. For views to the contrary, cf. Aasgaard, *The Childhood of Jesus*, p. 46; Stevan Davies, *The Infancy Gospels of Jesus: Apocryphal Tales from the Childhoods of Mary and Jesus* (Woodstock: Skylight Paths, 2009), p. xxiii; Kaiser, 'Die Kindheitserzählung', p. 938; Miller, *Born Divine*, p. 275; Paulissen, 'Jésus à l'école', p. 170.

from youth.[68] The second is that structurally the *IGT* is not really a narrative whole, but a piecemeal composition that has been assembled on an ad hoc basis. As a result, it lacks any overall and fundamental narrative coherence, and cannot therefore be described as developmental.[69]

Yet, while it is true that a number of ancient biographies conform to a non-developmental pattern, it is by no means a hard and fast rule, and there are numerous examples of narratives that depart from this pattern.[70] Moreover, these 'departures' actually result from the narrative character of biography itself. As Thomas Hägg notes in his recent examination of ancient biography, movement was entirely characteristic of biography: 'development or (at least) change, a character confronted with a succession of events and influences'.[71]

As for the second objection, there is little doubt that the *IGT* is a loosely assembled compilation of narratives, but it is also the case that they have been fitted into a framework based on the age of the young Jesus.[72] The episodes begin when Jesus was five years of age (*IGT* 2.1, cf. 6.2), continue to when he is seven (10.1), then eight (12.1) and conclude when he is twelve (17.1). The last of these corresponds to Jesus' age at Luke 2.42, and it is probable that the *IGT*'s age-framework has been retrojected, based on Luke's indication of Jesus' age.[73] Richard Bauckham further makes the attractive suggestion that the *IGT*'s author is familiar with the *Protevangelium of James*, and that the chronology of the *IGT* is designed to fill the temporal gap between the close of the *Protevangelium* and Luke 2.41-51.[74] If his supposition holds, then the narrative and developmental tenor of the *IGT* is all the more firmly established, since it is designed to fill the major gaps in Jesus' biography from the annunciation up until his appearance in the temple.

68. Tomas Hägg, *The Art of Biography in Antiquity* (Cambridge: Cambridge University Press, 2012), pp. 6, 75, 330. On the *IGT*, see Raymond E. Brown, *The Birth of the Messiah: A Commentary on the Infancy Narratives in the Gospels of Matthew and Luke* (2d ed.; Garden City, NY: Doubleday, 1993), p. 481.

69. Hock, *Infancy Gospels*, p. 96; cf. Gero, 'Infancy Gospel', p. 58.

70. One need only consider the book of Acts (possibly known to the author), which in its three accounts of Paul's conversion imparts a developmental framework to Paul's life.

71. Hägg, *Biography in Antiquity*, pp. 4-5.

72. Frédéric Amsler, 'Les Paidika Iesou, un nouveau témoin de la rencontre entre judaïsme et christianisme à Antioch au IVe siècle?', in Clivaz, Dettwiler, Devillers, and Norelli (eds.), *Infancy Gospels*, pp. 433-58.

73. For age as a similar ordering principle in the *Alexander Romance*, see Hägg, *Biography in Antiquity*, pp. 122-27.

74. Bauckham, 'Imaginative Literature', p. 797.

Be this as it may, the author has certainly used Jesus' age as an ordering principle for his episodes, and while some of these individual episodes could feasibly be interchanged with no appreciable effect, there is a definite pattern at work and Jesus' character does develop. With the exception of the killing of his second teacher, all of Jesus' 'negative' deeds are concentrated in the first third of the work. Nor is it the case that these deeds simply taper off. Instead, he relents of his earlier actions twice, and undoes every instance of harm that he has previously committed, as the following list demonstrates:

1. Killing of Annas' child
2. Killing of the boy who ran into him
3. Threat to Joseph
4. Blinding of his accusers
5. **'And immediately all those who had fallen under his curse were saved' (*IGT* 8.2)**
6. Killing of second teacher (*IGT* 13.2)
7. **Saving of Second teacher (*IGT* 14.4)**[75]

In fact, whether intentional or not, Jesus' individual actions are almost systematically reversed. Although the first three actions are effectively countermanded by Jesus' words at 8.2, some of Jesus' other actions explicitly contrast with his initial misdeeds. The killing of Annas' child finds its counterpart in Jesus' raising of Zeno from the dead (*IGT* 9.1-3), and the killing of the boy who runs into him, in the raising of a young man from the dead (*IGT* 16.1-2). Joseph's recriminations of Jesus are transformed into thanksgiving that he possesses such a son (*IGT* 12.2). The result is, that by the time the work ends, Jesus has not only reversed all of his misdeeds, he has also embarked on a string of positive actions, which include:[76]

1. The raising of the dead child Zeno
2. Miraculous deeds on behalf of his parents
3. The donation of Jesus' miraculous harvest to the poor and orphans (*IGT* 11.2)
4. The saving of his brother James from a viper bite
5. The raising of a young man from the dead

---

75. The passages presented in bold type indicate the two points in the narrative where Jesus reverses his 'negative' actions.

76. Hägg, *Biography in Antiquity*, p. 178. This list does not include instances where Jesus' exceptional wisdom is demonstrated.

These episodes are typically accompanied by acclamation and thanks-giving on the part of the neighbors, and the crowds close with a pro-grammatic anticipation of Jesus' future ministry: "'He has indeed saved many souls from death. And he will go on saving all the days of his life'" (*IGT* 17.1).

The only anomalous incident in this developmental sequence is his killing of the second teacher.[77] This one incident apart, there is an obvious developmental tenor to the narrative. It needs to be added that this developmental arc is not to be seen as synonymous with the bio-logical arc of 'normal' childhood development. While there are certainly overlaps, the *IGT*'s Jesus is notably different from pictures of children in antiquity. O. M. Bakke in his study of children in the world of nascent Christianity notes that children in the Graeco-Roman world were widely regarded as lacking *logos* and power: they were perceived as 'weak and timorous'.[78]

In the *IGT*, however, *logos* and authority are constant features of Jesus' activity, especially in his teaching. As a consequence his teachers need to respond appropriately to his divine knowledge or they suffer. Thus, when the second teacher dismisses Jesus' authority and hits him, he dies. By contrast, when the third teacher responds appropriately to Jesus' divine wisdom, he is praised and the second teacher restored to life. Power and *logos*, therefore, are intimately associated in the child Jesus.

Nevertheless, some have sought to argue that Jesus is merely being portrayed as a child of precocious intellectual attainments, and exempli-fies the *puer senex* motif, where a child is described as being unaccoun-tably wise for their years.[79] Tony Burke, for instance, compares *IGT* 7.4—the onlookers' acclamation of Jesus as 'either a god or an angel'—with the epitaph of a little girl that states that she 'read much and played little'.[80] Both infants are mature for their years. Yet, surely the point being developed in the *IGT* is that Jesus' wisdom is not obtainable in this world however much one reads or is taught. As the *IGT* repeatedly

---

77. Why this episode occurs so late is unclear. It may that this is the only instance where Jesus is physically assaulted, provoking him to retaliate more harshly. Burke would understand this later curse by Jesus as an argument against there being any development in the *IGT*, but this one exception is not sufficient to call the overall findings into doubt.

78. O. M. Bakke, *When Children Became People* (Minneapolis: Fortress Press, 2005), p. 54.

79. Burke, *De infantia Iesu*, pp. 223, 266-68, 285-86; *idem*, 'Social Viewing', p. 37, cf. Kaiser, 'Die sogenannte 'Kindheitserzählung des Thomas', p. 472.

80. Burke, *De infantia Iesu*, p. 286.

emphasizes, Jesus needs no human teachers, but they emphatically need him. Throughout the work, Jesus is entirely in control: he acts, and everyone else reacts. This tenor extends from the very beginning of the work right through until his final acclamation in the temple.

Qui Deus Homo

This tenor also describes the process whereby Jesus the god becomes 'humanized'—that is, how god became human. Jesus tempers his temper. He learns how to redirect his power and to accommodate himself to human weakness. He moves from harming people to saving people. Finally, he becomes socialized and adjusts to the essential banality of human existence: fetching water, planting crops, working in crafts, all within a small village. He helps his parents with their day-to-day chores. He gives all of his miraculous harvest to the poor. Most importantly, he displays increasing reverence for human life. This also seems to be a process that he undergoes. He resurrects Zeno seemingly not so much because the child has died an untimely death, as because Zeno can vouch for Jesus being innocent of his death. Yet, by the time of his brother James' near-fatal snakebite, Jesus is evidently moved with deep concern for his wellbeing; he *runs* to James to blow on the snakebite (*IGT* 15.2). The same is true for the boy whom he raises from the dead. Jesus forces his way through the crowd so that he can immediately heal the wounded foot and raise the youth from the dead. His onetime divine indifference as a five-year old to the deaths of his peers has seemingly matured into a deep-seated compassion for stricken humans.

These observations suggest that the *IGT* is not concerned with Jesus 'growing up' so much as with Jesus 'growing down', that is to say, the process whereby Jesus *qua* god becomes Jesus *qua* human. Jesus' divine power is quelled and set aside in favor of a compassionate and controlled bearing towards humans, throughout this process Jesus still retains his divine wisdom and divine sense of identity.

This returns us the question of the *IGT*'s understanding of the divine and the problem raised at the beginning of the present study. If Jesus' developmental arc involves dispensing with 'divine' traits at the beginning of the *IGT* in favor of human ones, how is it that these 'divine' traits are so lacking in divinity? Is it appropriate to describe the killing and blinding of people as divine actions?

For a Graeco-Roman audience they could indeed be described as divine actions. In Graeco-Roman mythology such actions were typical of the gods. Images of violent, petulant, and self-absorbed deities were commonplace, so much so that the Greek philosopher Xenophanes was able to lament that Homer and Hesiod had attributed to the gods all that was shameful among humans (fragment 11). The gods were renowned for displaying prodigious power, but also for their blatant self-regard and profound indifference to the human condition.[81] As Hugh Lloyd-Jones succinctly puts it, in the Greek world Zeus was far from being mortals' benevolent father in heaven: 'The gods govern the universe not in men's interest but in their own, and have no primary concern for human welfare'.[82] In the realm of Greek mythology it is understood that if a human in any way obtrudes on the sphere of the gods or their prerogatives, the act is usually deemed *hubris*—'arrogance in word or deed or even thought'—and is followed almost invariably by *nemesis*—'punishment by a jealous deity'.[83] Divine power and wrath, of course, are hardly the exclusive preserve of the Greek gods—Yahweh's anger is well documented, and has definite affinities with the ire of the Graeco-Roman deities.[84] Nevertheless, in the Hebrew Bible this anger is usually furnished with a moral grounding of some description, whereas such

81.   The *Cypria*, a part of the Greek epic cycle, shows that Zeus' pity, such as it is, is rarely directed towards humans: 'There was a time when the countless races <of men> roaming <constantly> over the land were weighing down the <deep-> breasted earth's expanse. Zeus took pity when he saw it, and in his complex mind he resolved to relieve the all-nurturing earth of mankind's weight by fanning the great conflict of the Trojan War, to void the burden by death. So the warriors at Troy kept being killed, and Zeus' plan was being fulfilled' (*Cypria*, Fragment 1 in Martin L. West, *Greek Epic Fragments*, LCL).

On the nature and character of divinity in Graeco-Roman mythology, see J. R. C. Cousland, 'Gods and Goddesses (Greek and Roman)', in Graham Shipley, John Vanderspoel, David Mattingly, and Lin Foxhall (eds.), *The Cambridge Dictionary of Classical Civilization* (Cambridge: Cambridge University Press, 2006), pp. 395-99.

82.   Hugh Lloyd-Jones, *The Justice of Zeus* (Berkeley: University of California Press, 1971), p. 161. Cf. Aristotle, *Magna Moralia* 1208b: 'It would be strange for anyone to say that he loved Zeus'.

83.   E. R. Dodds, *The Greeks and the Irrational* (Berkeley: University of California Press, 1951), p. 31. This can even extend to a human being seen as too successful, happy, or fortunate: divine *phthonos* (jealousy) is immediately activated (pp. 30-31), hence the well-known Greek maxim—'call no man happy until he is dead'. See further, *OCD*, s.v. 'Nemesis'.

84.   It needs to be stressed that the Hebrew Bible also has a number of instances where the wrath and intolerance of Yahweh are much in evidence. For examples see Patrick Considine, 'The Theme of Divine Wrath in Ancient East Mediterranean Literature', *Studi Micinei ed Egeo-Anatolica* 8 (1969), pp. 85-159; M. L. West, *The East Face of Helicon* (Oxford: Clarendon Press, 1997), pp. 124-28, as well as the discussion in Gerd Lüdemann, *The Unholy in Holy Scripture: The Dark Side of the Bible* (Louisville: Westminster John Knox, 1997), pp. 33-75.

grounding is only intermittently the case in Greek myth. Occasionally these accounts are 'moralized', but this phenomenon is by no means consistent.[85]

It is highly likely, therefore, that these Graeco-Roman ideas of the divine inform and underlie the conception(s) of divinity at work in the *IGT*. When the son of Annas deliberately destroys Jesus' arrangement of the pools, he is understood to have committed an act of *hubris* (*insolent, godless behavior*). Jesus' responds immediately to this act of *hubris*: Annas' son has arrogantly challenged a god. In Greek myths such a challenge, almost without exception, is immediately followed by the destruction or punishment of the perpetrator, and so it is here: 'immediately (*eutheôs*) that child withered away' (*IGT* 3.3). The same holds true for the little boy who bumps into Jesus—he, too, has affronted a god. It matters little whether it was intentional or not; the Greek gods were not concerned with such niceties and nor is Jesus, who responds with immediate retribution. And when the boy's parents complain, they are rashly calling into question the decision and deeds of a god. Again, it does not matter if the parents' complaint is just—their recriminations also constitute *hubris*, and they are punished with blindness precisely because they fail to recognize Jesus' divinity. Accordingly, Jesus says that they 'shall receive their punishment' (*IGT* 5.1). It is the bystanders who signal the appropriate reaction to the boy's death. They ask, 'From where was this child born, since his word becomes deed?' (*IGT* 4.1). For them the point at issue is whether they had a divinity in their midst, and they are not slow to associate this violent act with a god.[86]

Finally, there is the instance of the teacher who strikes Jesus during his lessons, and whom Jesus kills in retaliation. As noted above, it is slightly anomalous because it occurs well along in Jesus' developmental arc. If Jesus was in the process of becoming human, why is this episode included so late in the process? There are likely two reasons. The first is the extreme nature of the act of *hubris*. This is the only episode in the *IGT* where Jesus is deliberately struck and *hurt*—a clear affront to his divine nature. It is also, of course, a clear affront to his divine knowledge. As was just mentioned, the *IGT*'s conception of Jesus' humanization does not involve a corresponding loss of his divine insight. The fact that the second teacher was ignorant of the meaning of the Alpha and was nevertheless punishing Jesus for his knowledge also precipitates Jesus' response. The third teacher demonstrates that the second teacher's

85. Dodds, *The Greeks and the Irrational*, pp. 31-32.
86. That this was thought to be a not uncommon occurrence can be inferred from Acts 14.8-18.

response should have been one of humble acclamation: namely, that Jesus was 'full of much grace and wisdom' (*IGT* 14.3).[87]

For the author of the *IGT*, therefore, Jesus' developmental arc involves him gradually moving from a Graeco-Roman 'divine' attitude to one that is increasingly human (and Christian). While Jesus' divine knowledge remains essentially unchanged, his divine power and arrogance come to be replaced with a compassionate and committed humanity. The author's understanding of the incarnation results in a Jesus with two natures, one divinely human and the other humanly divine. The years of Jesus' boyhood chronicle the process whereby this balance between the two natures is achieved. For the author the balance culminates with Jesus' visit to the temple where, in addition to his father Joseph's approbation, he also displays the approbation of his heavenly father.

The IGT as Preparation for the Gospel?

The chief problem that arises from this assessment of the development of Jesus' two natures, is why the *IGT*'s author should have initially relied upon a Graeco-Roman understanding of the divine. In many respects it does not seem to be a natural choice. One would have thought that the Hebrew Bible or Gospels would be far more apt. Even if the author was not especially familiar with either, he or she was evidently conversant with Luke and probably with John as well. So why did he not start off with a Christian understanding of god?

The simplest explanation is that the Graeco-Roman model of the divine was the one that had been most familiar to the author or at least the one most familiar to the *IGT*'s prospective audience. To show that Jesus' youth had parallels with the youths of the Greek gods makes him seem much more familiar. And for them to see that Jesus could actually act with the authority of the Greek gods makes him doubly so. In fact, one of Celsus' chief objections to Jesus being accounted a god is that Jesus does not act with the power and authority one should expect from a deity: 'And would it not seem reasonable that if you are, as you say, God's son, God would have helped you out of your calamity, or that you would have been able to help yourself?'[88] Since Jesus initially acts with the divine power and authority commensurate with the Graeco-Roman gods, potential converts would recognize that his developing of human

---

87. Paulissen ('Jésus à l'école', p. 169) remarks that he 'reconnaît l'enfant à sa juste valeur'.

88. Celsus, *On the True Doctrine: A Discourse Against the Christians* (trans. R. Joseph Hoffman; New York: Oxford University Press, 1987), p. 58.

compassion in no way implied that he was deficient in power. It would, therefore, be far easier for potential pagan converts to appreciate and appropriate the Christian proclamation, if they were to recognize familiar 'divine' attributes in the figure of Jesus. That the author has Jesus retain his divine knowledge and insight throughout the *IGT* means that Jesus continues to act as a god, despite his human traits.

The author's inclusion of the developmental motif is, therefore, meant to show his readers 'a better way'. This kenotic Christology whereby Jesus leaves off the divine arrogance and indifference of the pagan gods and replaces it with human virtues and compassion presents readers with an alternate understanding of the divine, one that is ultimately far more sympathetic and humane.[89] Nor is this sort of transformation unprecedented. In a recent discussion of the parallels between Christ and Dionysus in Nonnus' *Dionysiaca*, Hernández de la Fuente observes that, under Christian influence, Dionysus' savagery is transmuted into compassion: 'in clear archetypical correspondence with the Christian god, in Nonnus' version, Dionysus becomes once and for all the god who, furthermore, feels pity for the mortals and dedicates himself to heal or even revive them'.[90]

By the end of the *IGT*, the work has brought its readers to the point where they can take up the narrative in the canonical gospels and see Jesus' divine compassion and humanity reach their fullest expression in the words and deeds of the adult Jesus. The hostile Jesus of the *IGT*, therefore, is designed as a kind of *praeparatio evangelica*. It prepares potential Graeco-Roman converts for the Christian message by demonstrating that Jesus, despite his later crucifixion by the Romans, was just as powerful and deserving of respect and veneration as any of the pagan gods. But, unlike pagan gods such as Hermes, his purpose was not to achieve divine status on Olympus, it was ultimately to make divine salvation available to humans through Jesus' saving actions.

---

89. It needs to be called to mind that a great many Jews had expected (and continued to expect) a powerful, royal messiah who would 'smash the arrogance of sinners like a potter's jar' and 'destroy the unlawful nations with the word of his mouth' (*PsSol* 17.23-24 [*OTP*]).

90. David Hernández de la Fuente, 'Parallels between Dionysus and Christ in Late Antiquity: Miraculous Healings in Nonnus' *Dionysiaca*', in Alberto Bernabé et al. (eds.), *Redefining Dionysus* (MythosEikonPoiesis 5; Berlin: de Gruyter, 2013), p. 482.

Conclusion

This present study has sought to address the problem of Jesus as a *deus necans*. Why does the *IGT* portray him in such a violent and unsympathetic light? Even if the infants he kills are not human sacrifices per se, they nevertheless meet their demise as a result of Jesus' divine petulance and indifference to human life. The answer proposed above is that the Jesus who is initially portrayed in the Gospel embodies the popular pagan understanding of the divine, where gods are primarily acknowledged for their divine power and often their sublime indifference to human suffering.

By casting Jesus in this light, the *IGT* intends to show the superiority of the Christian conception of God, where God's—and Jesus'—power is second to his love and compassion for humans, in all their fallibility and ingenuousness. Readers will be brought to recognize the superiority of the Christian understanding of the divine, and readied for the divine character of the adult Jesus as it is expressed in the canonical gospels.

LIVING SACRIFICE:
RETHINKING ABRAHAMIC RELIGIOUS SACRIFICE USING FIELD NARRATIVES OF EID UL-ADHA

Michel Desjardins and Aldea Mulhern

1. *Introduction*

Sacrifice in common parlance means one of two things: subsuming a need, desire, or preference for the sake of something else; or ritualistic slaughter. The first meaning, which is far more discursively prevalent than the second, entails giving up something of value, either for what one imagines is a greater good, or with the hope of receiving something better in return. Thus, one might give up one's own life to save one's friend, child, or country; one might give up time with family on weekends to dedicate that time to paid work in the hope of a job promotion; or one might give up an umbrella to a stranger in the rain to model a selfless act. This notion of sacrifice is itself part of a socialization process in which one is taught from childhood to sublimate natural urges in order to reap greater rewards and avoid negative consequences, and to make oneself a good, or better, person.

The term's etymology, 'making sacred', points to its religious roots, which underscore the common use of this term. Most Christians, for example, believe that Jesus gave up his life in order to save humanity, and some Hindus will occasionally refrain from eating meat in order to show the kind of religious dedication needed to have the gods reward their acts, perhaps with the marriage of a daughter, or the health of a spouse. The model here, repeated in classical religious texts, is *do ut des*: I do something in order that You, the deity, may do something in return.

This social and psychological process takes on added force when a triangular relationship complicates the simple binary of religious adherent and deity—when we introduce another living being into the equation, whose life is taken to please the deity. That other being—it could be an animal or another person—becomes implicated in an individual's relationship with the spirit world. A chicken is killed in the hope that its death, and the spilling of its blood, will make the deity look favourably on the one offering that animal, the death of God ransoms all of humanity, or a son must be offered up in order to fulfill a divine command.

That story of the sacrifice of Abraham's son contains both the two-pronged and three-pronged relationship. The human life that is sought and offered is precious to Abraham. While it is another being who is about to be sacrificed, the filial relationship of that being to Abraham also makes it an extreme personal sacrifice for him. As the story presents it, Abraham is not (at least, not initially) offering an animal; he is offering his very best in service to his god. For those with historical sensitivity, a traditional worldview that considers a child—and a wife, who is written out of this story—the property of the patriarch[1] dampens the shock of that Abrahamic story, but the shock also gives the myth its enduring force.[2]

Substitution plays a key role in this particular triangular form of sacrifice. The foreskin replaces the firstborn Jewish male offering. Jesus stands in the place of humanity when he dies for 'us'—and bread and wine ritualistically come to replace his body and blood. And an animal, in the end, replaces Abraham's son, both for Abraham's sacrifice and later, during Muslim commemorations of it. We are not far here from the notion of the scapegoat, which includes not only replacement but a thorough cleansing: the sacrifice takes our place, and it also wipes clean the accumulated stains of our life.

Blood, too, is often also central to sacrifice. Beets and carrots might be offered but they are not sacrificed, except sometimes for those for whom the picking and eating of plants is also a form of violence. The gods—at least some of them—appreciate blood. And blood they get with the

---

1. Indeed, many would now identify this way of thinking as a form of patriarchy, and consider the story not only highly regrettable but also socially constructed. This move, notably, has been used by some scholars invested in these religious traditions as a way to push for change internally. The best-known such critique of the Abrahamic story is Carol Delaney's *Abraham on Trial: The Social Legacy of Biblical Myth* (Princeton: Princeton University Press, 1998). A variation of this approach can be found in Alice Miller, *The Untouched Key: Tracing Childhood Trauma in Creativity and Destructiveness* (New York: Anchor, 1990). Miller, a psychoanalyst whose career was dedicated to revealing the roots of child abuse, here considers the story of the Abrahamic sacrifice to have contributed to a worldview that justifies the abuse of children.

2. A further example is the Christian reframing of the story to represent Jesus' death as sacrifice.

slaughtering of animals, which can, by dint of the substitution at work in the above examples, carry overtones of human sacrifice. One need not go back to ancient Carthage; one need only take Christian communion seriously to appreciate this logic. Or one need understand the biblical message as Jean Soler does when he sees a significant alimentary separation between humans and God in the biblical evolution of eating practices: blood in his view remains set apart as God's food, so it is natural that one would seek it out to be close to God, and offer it to God.[3]

Outside of the Abrahamic traditions, animal sacrifice and the ensuing bloodletting in religious contexts is still pervasive. In many Indian-rooted and aboriginal religious traditions, for example, the spirit world is thought to be engaged through flesh and blood, as flesh and blood are engaged through food. We also see this in places where Christianity and Islam have fused with indigenous spiritual life—for example, in Cuban-based Santeria where Christian practitioners will kill an animal to entice the spirits or connect to the ancestors, or in parts of Indonesia where Muslims will offer the bloody head of an ox to the sea goddess before returning for noon prayers at the mosque.

The forms of sacrifice within the Abrahamic traditions are likewise varied. It is clear that the animal sacrifices that were so central to Jewish religious life were significantly curtailed with the destruction of the Temple in 70 CE, and the Christian appropriation of those rituals onto the body of Jesus has over time shrunk to a symbolic ingestion, not of a meal, but of a thin wafer, or a small piece of bread and a paper cup's worth of grape juice. Like the cellophane-wrapped meat that Canadian consumers buy in the supermarket, the link between that actual product and the original source is minimized or all but forgotten. The same can be said for the Baha'i tradition in which offerings to God are comprised of words, not flesh or food, offered in temples of prayer, not sacred sites with sacrificial altars.

---

3. Jean Soler argues that humans progress from eating a pure vegetarian diet (while God is offered meat and blood), to eating meat after the flood, but with the blood removed from it. See his 'Sémiotique de la nourriture dans la Bible', *Annales: économies, sociétés, civilisations* 28 (1973), 943-55; translated by Elborg Forster as 'The Dietary Prohibitions of the Hebrews', *The New York Review of Books* (14 June 1979), pp. 24-30; then reprinted as 'The Semiotics of Food in the Bible', in Robert Forster and Orest Ranum (eds), *Food and Drink in History*, vol. 5 (Baltimore: The Johns Hopkins University Press, 1979), pp. 126-38, and reprinted again in Carole Counihan and Penny Van Esterik (eds), *Food and Culture: A Reader* (New York/ London: Routledge, 1997), pp. 55-66.

But animal sacrifice lives on in Islam, particularly in Eid ul-Adha, the Festival of Sacrifice. This annual event, celebrated by Muslims around the world, provides valuable information to help scholars understand the nature and practice of religious sacrifice, particularly when combined with the work of scholars who theorize about sacrifice.

Our chapter is an exploration of sacrifice that is grounded in both sacrifice theory and fieldwork on the Festival of Sacrifice as witnessed in Egypt, China and Canada. We begin with an analysis of the academic discussion concerning religious sacrifice over the last century and a half. Then we turn to fieldwork on this festival to identify how sacrifice functions in the lived experiences of some Muslims. Our purpose is twofold: to create space for the social and personal complexities of religious sacrifice that are sometimes downplayed or ignored by theorists, and to identify the academic frameworks that have interpretive power for these examples.

We also have a third purpose. Religious sacrifices using humans and other animals have had deep cross-cultural and trans-historical resilience, and they continue to elicit passionate responses from both insiders and outsiders. It is certainly fitting for academics to use their resources to examine the particularities of this human practice, in the hope of increasing cross-cultural understanding. It is even more fitting to do so in a book that honours a consummate teacher who, throughout his long career, has insisted not only on developing critical thinking skills in his students, but also on nurturing the growth of the whole person.[4]

2. *Theories of Religious Sacrifice*

The academic study of sacrifice can be seen through approaches that classify or typologize sacrifice, theorize sacrifice in terms of something fundamental to human nature or society, and understand sacrifice in the context of discussions about power. Their three goals are mutually distinguishable, although analyses are often intertwined.

In the subsections that follow, we examine some significant ideas from theories of sacrifice that fall under each of these three major approaches. Broadly speaking, typologies of sacrifice seek to determine whether sacrifice is primarily about gift, homage, abnegation, magic, substitution, sacralization, or communication. The gift is arguably the most influential

---

4. The teaching lineage continues: Michel during his MA program was Paul's Teaching Assistant in the mid-1970s, and Aldea in her MA program was Michel's Teaching Assistant thirty-five years later.

of these categories, but these attempts at classification all share a general approach in which particular sacrificial acts (gleaned from sacred texts, myth, or anthropological reports) are juxtaposed and analyzed in order to attempt to show what the sacrifices do for the practitioners. Theories of sacrifice that hinge on a particular foundational view of human nature or society, for their part, tend to universalize in a different fashion, by explaining human life itself as fundamentally determined by a core impulse (usually violent) or mode of social organization. Finally, the more ideological analyses consider sacrifice primarily as an opportunity for intellectual explorations that address philosophical and political concerns.

2.1. *On Sacrificial Types*
A number of scholars have tried to make sense of sacrifice by gathering discrete examples of sacrifices and classifying them under a term or rubric that does justice to the characteristics they notice.[5] Iconic contributions in this vein begin with nineteenth-century scholars of religion such as Tylor, Spencer and Frazer.[6] These early works, as was typical of scholarship at the time, were largely based on examples drawn from other texts, including collections of myth and anthropological reports, and carried clear assumptions about primitivity and evolution. Contemporary awareness of these assumptions now troubles an easy deployment of certain conclusions they present—for example, about magic, survivals, the contagion of similarity—but their attention to elements of giving, giving up, and commensality still underpin much of contemporary scholarship on the topic.

Influential typologies of sacrifice represent sacrifice primarily as a commensal meal, a gift, or its own category altogether. The most important early reflection on sacrifice as meal occurs in William Robertson Smith's Burnett Lectures, which were given just before the turn of the twentieth century and later collected under the title *The Religion of the Semites*. Smith finds in sacrifice the essence of religion,

---

5. Mary Douglas has famously taken this approach. While she focuses on sacrifice in several places, including her work on Leviticus, she is not primarily interested in sacrifice as her object, but rather in the synecdochal modeling of larger worldviews onto particular systems of social regulation. See her *Leviticus as Literature* (Oxford: Oxford University Press, 1999).

6. Edward B. Tylor, *Primitive Culture* (New York: Brentano's Books, 1871); Herbert Spencer, *The Principles of Sociology*, vol. 1 (New York: D. Appleton & Co., 1882); and James G. Frazer, *The Golden Bough: A Study in Magic and Religion* (abridged ed.; New York: Collier Books, 1922 [1890]).

and argues that sacrifice in its original sense means a communal commensality, a religious feast where food is shared between a people and their god. He makes a distinction between private offerings and public rituals, and between non-meat oblations and animal sacrifices, distinguishing the latter as the kind 'which are essentially acts of communion between the god and his worshippers'.[7]

The commensality thread has been developed by other scholars of sacrifice in the contemporary period. For example, using Greek myths as their point of departure for an intracultural assessment of sacrifice, Marcel Detienne and Jean-Pierre Vernant argue, in *The Cuisine of Sacrifice among the Greeks*, that there is an 'absolute co-incidence of meat eating and sacrificial practice' in the ancient Greek polis.[8] In addition, they seek to show that hunting was conceived as a practice for destroying pests, and that domesticated animals were always sacrificially butchered and eaten as ritual food.

To commensality as a popular category for sacrifice scholars have added the notion of the gift. Tylor and Spencer are the iconic English-language theorists on this topic. Tylor posits three phases of sacrifice, evolving from ordinary gift-giving to homage to abnegation, which for him is the highest form.[9] Spencer uses the word 'offering' to describe food and non-food used to propitiate ghosts and deities.[10] Later, Marcel Mauss would characterize the gift largely independently from sacrifice, seeing sacrifice as a type of gift rather than the other way around.[11] Mauss's key point is that the gift always carries an attendant obligation: we are obliged to give, to receive, and to repay, often with interest, and possibly by destruction (e.g. the potlatch).

---

7. William Robertson Smith, *The Religion of the Semites: The Fundamental Institutions* (New York: Meridian Books, 1957 [1989]), p. 243.

8. Marcel Detienne and Jean-Pierre Vernant (eds), *The Cuisine of Sacrifice Among the Greeks* (trans. Paula Wissing; Chicago: University of Chicago Press, 1989 [1979]), p. 3.

9. Tylor, *Primitive Culture*.

10. Spencer, *The Principles of Sociology*.

11. Marcel Mauss, 'Essai sur le don: Forme et raison de l'échange dans les sociétés archaïques', *L'année sociologique* NS 1 (1923–24), pp. 30-186 (translated into English as *The Gift: The Form and Reason for Exchange in Archaic Societies* [New York: Routledge, 1990]). See also the earlier article that Mauss wrote with Henri Hubert, 'Essai sur la nature et la fonction du sacrifice', *L'Année sociologique* 1 (1898), pp. 29-138 (*Sacrifice: Its Nature and Functions* (Chicago: University of Chicago Press, 1981 [1964]).

Mauss develops a theory of sacrifice separately, with Henri Hubert, in which they argue that sacrifice is actually a *sui generis* type.[12] They consider sacrifice to be a ritual process by which the victim serves as mediator between the person on whose behalf the sacrifice is made (the sacrifier/*le sacrifiant*) and a god. They direct our attention to three sacrificial roles: the sacrificer, who carries out the sacrificial ritual; the victim, who is necessarily destroyed in the sacrifice; and most importantly the sacrifier (*le sacrifiant*), who is the person 'to whom the benefits of sacrifice accrue'.[13] Although destruction is a necessary component of their theory, they ultimately account for sacrifice as a mediation, negotiation, or exchange between the sacrifier (not the sacrificer) and the deity.

Kathryn McClymond shares Mauss and Hubert's attention to discrete moments in a ritual process, but takes issue with their argument about the necessity of destruction in sacrifice. She relegates violence to the background of sacrifice, and suggests a polythetic definition by which sacrificiality is determined by the presence and interdependence of seven major criteria: apportionment, association, heating, killing, identification, consumption, and transformation.[14]

For scholars who share this approach, then, the conversation is primarily about classification. Some intend their classificatory systems to be universalizable; others do not. What they share, though, is an intra-specific and typological focus. They are concerned with which things count as sacrifice, which parts of sacrifice count, and which parts can be subsumed to other parts.

2.2. *On sacrifice as Psycho-Social*

Other scholars explain sacrifice with recourse to what they perceive to be fundamental human needs or qualities. Many widely recognized studies in this vein have focused on violence as inherent to the human psyche or to human society—notably those of Walter Burkert and René Girard.[15]

---

12. Mauss and Hubert, like Smith whom they critique, claim an essence to sacrifice that can be generalized. Smith claims sacrifice as a type of meal before it is anything else (expiatory or propitiatory); Mauss and Hubert claim that sacrifice is its own type.

13. Mauss and Hubert, *Sacrifice*, p. 10.

14. Kathryn McClymond, *Beyond Sacred Violence: A Comparative Study of Sacrifice* (Baltimore: The Johns Hopkins University Press, 2008). The criteria are introduced on pp. 29-33.

15. See also Maurice Bloch, *Prey into Hunter: The Politics of Religious Experience* (New York: Cambridge University Press, 1991); Georges Bataille, *The*

These thinkers each in their own way consider violence to be not only central to the human psyche or sociability, but also the fundamental building block of religion.

Some of the best-known work on sacrifice in the latter half of the twentieth century was centered on the idea of a link between society and violence best expressed through sacrifice, and assumes an evolutionary model. Even in the 1980s Burkert and Girard were seeking explanatory models of religion by imagining a primitive social world where the origins of the modern, complex social structures might be found, in a manner that echoes the strategies of scholars like Emile Durkheim, William Robertson Smith (mentioned above), and particularly Sigmund Freud.[16]

Girard famously sees religion as controlling violence through the mechanism of the ritual substitution and the sacrifice of a surrogate victim, or scapegoat. Mimetic desire[17] in his view stimulates violent murder, which itself stimulates retribution or violent response, which invokes further retaliation from the social group. This cycle of violence would rapidly destroy any society were it not for what he terms the scapegoating mechanism, in which the society picks a surrogate victim to kill in a ritual ceremony, thereby breaking the cycle. A mob mentality

---

Accursed Share: An Essay on General Economy (New York: Zone Books, 1991 [1949]); and Sigmund Freud, *Totem and Taboo: Resemblances Between the Psychic Lives of Savages and Neurotics* (New York: Vintage, 1946 [1913]). Psychologizing and socially oriented studies that do not centre on violence include William Beers's study of women, sacrifice, and primary narcissism, *Women and Sacrifice: Male Narcissism and the Psychology of Religion* (Detroit: Wayne State University Press, 1992); and Nancy Jay's study of sacrifice and paternity, *Throughout Your Generations Forever: Sacrifice, Religion, and Paternity* (Chicago: University of Chicago Press, 1992). Jay's gender analysis recommends her especially to our third type below.

16. Both Durkheim and Smith argued that sacrifice contained the origin of religion. See Durkheim's *The Elementary Forms of the Religious Life: A Study in Religious Sociology* (London: Allen & Unwin, 1926 [1912]), and Smith's *The Religion of the Semites*. Freud, as is well known (e.g. *Totem and Taboo*), argued for violent origins of humankind that led to the construction of religious rituals to allay people's psychological trauma. Girard is a Freudian, with the added Christian bias that Jesus offers the way out of the endless repetition of violence.

17. To be precise, it is mimesis that is 'primordial' for Girard, and violence is simply the necessary and constant consequence of it. See especially René Girard, 'Generative Scapegoating', in R. G. Hamerton-Kelly (ed.), *Violent Origins: Walter Burkert, René Girard, and Jonathan Z. Smith on Ritual Killing and Cultural Formation* (Stanford: Stanford University Press, 1987) p. 123.

allows the scapegoating mechanism to operate, with people believing that the scapegoat is actually a malefactor whose execution will result in resolution. The scapegoat may thus paradoxically be a benefactor by becoming the victim of a collective act of violence that reunites the social group.[18]

Writing at the same time as Girard, Burkert finds ritual to be the mechanism of controlling aggression in order to construct and maintain society. He shares with Girard a sense of the problem of killing and the role of religious expiation, but theorizes it differently: he attempts to derive sacrificial ritual from Paleolithic hunting and Neolithic husbandry.[19] Ritual, for Burkert, is communicative, and is fundamentally about learning and transmission: it underpins religion, and allows it to self-perpetuate and refine. Ritual helps people overcome the guilt of the aggressive kill by allowing them to share the guilt, often by means of sharing the food, and thus ritually to overcome death in life: 'After all, ritual killing is real killing'.[20]

For both Girard and Burkert violence is imagined to be a function of human society, and sacrifice is a social valve to control the pressure of violence that threatens social organization. The thrust of their approach, like other social-psychological explanations of sacrifice, is that sacrifice is best understood as a practice arising not from symbol or story, nor from idiomatic situations, but from a fundamental human social nature. Here sacrifice is universalized, but not entirely abstracted: sacrifice itself is situated as an especially human phenomenon.[21]

2.3. *Theory of Sacrifice as a Point of Departure*
The theories discussed in this third subsection are united across their differences by using sacrifice as a point of departure to address ideas that merit deep reflection. Scholars such as Jacques Derrida, Bruce Lincoln, and Nancy Jay share an interest in deconstruction and critical theory, and focus on sacrifice as a cipher that underlines ideology.

18. René Girard, *Violence and the Sacred* (trans. Patrick Gregory; Baltimore: The Johns Hopkins University Press, 1977); see also his 'Generative Scapegoating'.

19. Walter Burkert, 'The Problem of Ritual Killing', in R. G. Hamerton-Kelly (eds), *Violent Origins*, pp. 164-70. On the issue of the hunt, see also Gary Lease, 'Hunting and the Origins of Religion', in Bron Taylor et al. (eds), *The Encyclopedia of Religion and Nature* (Bristol: Thoemmes Continuum, 2005), pp. 805-809.

20. Burkert, 'The Problem of Ritual Killing', p. 153. Cf. Bloch, *Prey into Hunter*, on this point.

21. McClymond, above, is responding especially to these theories when she argues for a more complex and nuanced understanding of sacrifice, and human nature.

Derrida engages religion and sacrifice in *The Gift of Death*.[22] Abraham's (secret, unbeknownst to the son or mother) sacrifice of Isaac fascinates him.[23] He finds a moral paradox in this story: responsibility to the wholly other (God) and to the others (family) are mutually exclusive, and this in his view is an ultimate failure of morality. 'Abraham is at the same time, the most moral and the most immoral, the most responsible and the most irresponsible.'[24] Derrida asks how the gift of death can ever be given in light of the fact that one cannot ever take on another's death. Ever kicking against the societal and academic goads of his day, he sees abstract and creative potential in the sacrificial economy, for individuals and for society. Sacrifice 'keeps what it gives up',[25] and because of this a sacrificial economy never exhausts itself.

Lincoln pursues a related question, but to a substantially lesser degree of abstraction. He argues that sacrifice is yet another systemic social legitimation of the domination of some by others, analyzing *who* is sacrificing *what* for the benefit of *whom*, leaving aside any glamorization of violent acts and instead pointing out the paths of power. Lincoln finds that sacrifice underscores an ideology that allows for structural modeling of ideas onto bodies and objects: 'sacrifice is most fundamentally a logic, language, and practice of transformative negation, in which one entity—a plant or an animal, a bodily part, some portion of a person's life, energy, property, or even the life itself—is given up for the benefit of some other species, group, god, or principle that is understood to be "higher" or more deserving in one fashion or another'.[26]

Jay traces another kind of power. She argues that sacrifice functions to join and separate.[27] Surveying a broad selection of sacrificial traditions, including Israelite, Christian, Ashanti, and Hawaiian, she finds that sacrifice inscribes social distinctions, chief among them the turning of natural birth through the mother into socially constructed descent

22. Jacques Derrida, *The Gift of Death* (Chicago: University of Chicago Press, 1995 [1991]).

23. As it is told in the *akedah* and testamental traditions; the qur'anic version, for example, does not feature the element of secrecy on which Derrida places so much emphasis.

24. Derrida, *The Gift of Death*, p. 72. There is some affinity with Mauss on the point of relationship between the gift and responsibility/duty/obligation.

25. Derrida, *The Gift of Death*, p. 8.

26. Derrida, *The Gift of Death*, p. 204.

27. Nancy Jay, *Throughout Your Generations Forever: Sacrifice, Religion, and Paternity* (Chicago: University of Chicago Press, 1992), p. 17. Her work in this respect has affinity with that of Mary Douglas on purity and pollution.

through the father.[28] Jay argues that motherhood is easy to establish[29] and fatherhood, conversely, is among the social distinctions that must be inscribed ritually.[30] She perceives patriarchal underpinnings in sacrifice, underpinnings that are exported in universalizing theories. Sacrifice joins and separates: one eats commensal sacrifices because they join the eaters; one never eats expiatory sacrifice because one is trying to separate from that which is polluting or threatening. Sacrifice and its attendant social organization in Jay's view functions to naturalize and universalize a contingent historical order in which men dominate women.

2.4. *Summary*
The typological, psychological and ideological approaches to understanding sacrifice reviewed in this section are grounded to varying degrees on data gathered from contemporary lived religion. To help move the discussion forward, we now turn to an exploration of ritual practices that are commonly observed by hundreds of millions of Muslims every year.

3. *The Festival of Sacrifice*

Like every major religious festival, the Muslim Festival of Sacrifice, or Eid ul-Adha,[31] is agglutinous. Whatever its origins may be its current practice has several distinct components, which differ regionally. This section outlines these key components, paying special attention to the sacrifice proper, and concludes by situating this sacrifice within the

---

28.   Jay finds this true even among the matrilineal Ashanti. See Jay, *Throughout Your Generations Forever*, Chapter 5.

29.   Stanley Stowers has critiqued Jay on this point: 'Greeks Who Sacrifice and Those Who Do Not: Toward an Anthropology of Greek Religion', in L. Michael White and O. Larry Yarborough (eds), *The Social World of the First Christians: Essays in Honor of Wayne A. Meeks* (Minneapolis: Augsburg Fortress, 1995), pp. 293-333.

30.   'Sacrifice cannot be infallible evidence of begetting and therefore obviously cannot constitute biological paternity. It is the social relations of reproduction, not biological reproduction, that sacrificial ritual can create and maintain'; 'Sacrificially constituted descent, incorporating women's mortal children into an "eternal" (enduring through generations) kin group...enables a patrilineal group to transcend mortality in the same process in which it transcends birth' (pp. 37, 40).

31.   This festival has different names across the world—for example, Eid ul-Adha (Feast of Sacrifice), Kurban (Sacrifice), Bakrid (Cow), and Hari Raya Hajji (Pilgrimage Celebration Day).

complex set of lived experiences of those who celebrate the festival.[32] The key point we want to make is that 'sacrifice' should not be treated independently of the broader ritual context to which it belongs.

3.1. *Remembering Abraham and his Son*

The ideological core of Eid ul-Adha is the qur'anic rendering of the biblical *akedah* ('binding', Gen 22), in which Abraham is called by God to sacrifice his son. The qur'anic version of this story (Q 37.100-110) is short and summative, and engages the son, who is not named in the text, and is later understood by most Muslims to be Ishmael rather than Isaac. Abraham dreams that he will sacrifice his son, and asks his son what he thinks of this. The son gives his assent, encouraging his father to sacrifice him as God has requested. Both father and son are depicted as fully submissive to the divine request; if anything, it is the son's plea ('my father, do as you are commanded'; 102) that is most poignant. The sacrifice is undertaken mutually and without secret, and the compliant son requires no binding. God intervenes and prevents the filicide, praises Abraham's obedience, indicates that he has passed the test, and substitutes a sacrificial animal in the son's place ('we ransomed him with a mighty sacrifice'; 107).[33]

What is remembered and celebrated by the community are Abraham and his son's extraordinary acts of obedience. The central commemoratory ritual is the sacrifice, or slaughter, of a large animal. The degree of submission shown by these two men in this enduring story becomes the quintessential model for a Muslim, or 'one who submits' to God.[34]

---

32. Data for this section comes from interviews conducted by the authors with former and upcoming pilgrims in India, Egypt, China and Canada from 2006 through 2013, and through participant observation of this festival in Cairo (2007) and Lijiang (2012).

33. The meaning is clearer in Gen 22; the qur'anic version assumes that the reader or hearer knows the more extensive (re)telling of the story that includes, *inter alia*, the substitution of a ram for the son.

34. The Christian appropriation of the Genesis story goes down a similar path. In this case, the willing son dies, in full submission to God, and the celebratory feast, Easter, honours Jesus' overcoming of death. In commemorating this founding story the early Christian anti-sacrificial rhetoric (e.g., Matt 9:11, 'I desire mercy not sacrifice') certainly accords better with the Eucharist than with an actual animal sacrifice. Given Muhammad's knowledge of Christians and Jews it is tempting to imagine the qur'anic story as a reworking of the Christianized version of the *akedah*, but the many Jewish re-interpretations of Gen 22 over time also support an independent Muslim adaptation of that primal story—or Muslim borrowing from a variant Jewish version of that story.

The commemorative sacrifice is later embedded in the Meccan pilgrimage, or *hajj*, where it becomes the penultimate ritual, capped by the
circumambulation of the Kaaba. Each pilgrim is expected to slaughter an
animal, or have one slaughtered for them. These days, relatively few
people slaughter their own animal, or even see the animal slaughtered.[35]
Almost all now simply buy a voucher when they arrive in Mecca; they
will give that voucher to someone later to have an animal killed for them.
The meat from that animal is quickly frozen and distributed to the poor
across the world. When the middleman returns and announces the names
of the people who have had their animals slaughtered, the sacrificial
ritual is over. Although the pilgrimage is not quite over when their
animal is slaughtered, it is at this point in the multi-day ritual when
pilgrims begin to use the honorific, *hajji*, for themselves.

The use of '*hajji*' underlines the significance of what has happened.
When a person's animal is killed, with their name uttered over it, that
person's current life also dies, along with their sins. They experience
themselves reborn, sinless. This ritual is an extension of the stoning of
Satan that takes place before the sacrifice; here the pilgrims cast out their
sins with the stones they throw onto the pillars. The animal sacrifice
takes away the rest of the sins.[36] Within religious traditions that emphasize sin and eternal punishment, rituals that in effect can set the clock
back to zero are vital to adherents.[37]

The fresh start brought about by this sacrifice puts moral pressure on
those considering the *hajj*: lapses committed after the *hajj* seem, in the
eyes of many, particularly disrespectful to the individuals themselves and

35. Before the mid-1980s pilgrims typically slaughtered their own animals.
Muslims who participated in the *hajj* in those years depict scenes of animal slaughter
in the desert that are quite unlike what the vast majority of pilgrims now experience.
For those who now do slaughter their own animal, the meat simply gets burned,
since inspection laws now prevent individually slaughtered meat from being added
to meat that gets given to the poor.

36. This removal of sins is only accomplished when Muslims do the *hajj* in
Saudi Arabia. Muslims who celebrate this festival elsewhere do not consider their
animal a sin offering.

37. The Jewish Day of Atonement traditionally served this function with the
killing of a scapegoat who bore the community's sins; currently Orthodox Jews
swing chickens (or other items) over their heads to transfer sins to the chickens, and
then slaughter them on the eve of the Jewish Day of Atonement. Christians went one
step further by arguing for a one-time, all-inclusive removal of sins through Jesus'
sacrifice. Muslims are given access to this thorough cleansing as part of the *hajj*
sacrifice. Note the logic in all three: animal or human blood and death, in the proper
context, removes a person's failings, and the deity accepts that replacement.

to God. Not surprisingly, people more often participate in this ritual when they are elderly, and are less apt to act and think improperly when they return home.[38] The animal sacrifices in particular bear considerable psychological weight.

The *hajj* sacrificial ritual is collective but for many pilgrims it is primarily an individual experience. Because of the presence of pilgrims speaking many different languages there are no collective sermons pronounced. The experience can thus be intensely personal, consisting in doing something among, rather than with, people, and doing it for personal and salvific reasons.[39]

A remarkable feature of this ritual is that it has a complementary existence outside Saudi Arabia in the form of a major religious festival. At the same time as Muslims are having animals sacrificed as part of the culmination of their pilgrimage, other Muslims around the world are also celebrating the Festival of Sacrifice. The core to those celebrations is still an animal sacrifice, as a remembrance of that qur'anic story of submission, and the festival is also accompanied by the charitable distribution of meat. Gone, as indicated above, is the remission of sins. Moreover, the festival celebrated outside Saudi Arabia is a far more family- and community-based event. Prayers at a local mosque start the process, children receive new clothes and other presents, women typically prepare delicious meat-based meals, and people gather to enjoy one another's company. Charity is often also far more visible, with the slaughter of animals leading directly to distribution of meat to the extended family and the poor, locally and globally.

In Muslim-dominant countries and areas the presence of an unusual number of animals tethered in the streets and alongside homes characteristically marks the imminent arrival of the celebration, and on the morning of Eid ul-Adha animals are slaughtered in a variety of public and private spaces, including the courtyards of mosques, people's backyards, underground parking lots, and farms. The carcasses are butchered, and the meat is divided and distributed. Animals, blood, and meat fill the public spaces, while meat, cooking, laughter and hospitality fill the private spaces.

38. Cf. some early Christians who, based in part on a literal meaning of Heb 10.26 ('For if we choose to go on sinning after we have learned the full truth, there no longer remains a sacrifice for sins'), delayed their baptism into the faith until their deathbed.

39. An Iranian Canadian informant, who had done the *hajj* four times, explained that he experienced his *hajj* in important ways as a solitary journey, 'just as all people will face judgment individually'.

It is common practice for those who are able to purchase an animal to give away two thirds of the meat: half to close friends and extended family, and half to strangers. Moreover it is becoming increasingly common, in both Muslim-dominant and Muslim-minority countries, to take the money that it would cost to buy an animal and donate it to a food bank or an organization that will ensure that the poor are fed. From the perspective of the poor themselves (a perspective severely under-represented), this is one of the few times in the year that is about being fed. Here, the Festival of Sacrifice becomes a Festival of Feasting.

Religious festivals, in general, are primarily about the cooking, laughter and hospitality that so deeply shape the Festival of Sacrifice. The sacrificial element in Eid ul-Adha, however, combines the actual death of an animal with the religious experience. That said, sacrifice does not stand alone, and the point we would like to make in closing this section is how a sacrifice-based festival like this one is as complex and rich as the people who participate in it, and how sacrifice needs to be understood within a much broader celebratory context. Societies con-struct feasts, as they do religion, in order to address multiple needs, and those special religious occasions that have survived over the centuries are particularly effective at representing those needs.

Animal sacrifice, we argue below, shapes a religious event in particu-lar ways. It strengthens communities; facilitates quality family time, charity, and innovation; and creates a particular set of challenges. We untangle a few of these by providing fieldwork examples (in first-person narrative) that bring them to life.

3.2. Narratives of Eid ul-Adha Outside the Hajj

Kunming, Yunnan Province, China, 2012. A sunny courtyard in a down-town mosque fills up with middle-aged and older people carrying and rolling large, heavily taped, old suitcases. They're preparing to leave for Mecca to do the *hajj*, and the whole community has come out to wish them well, and give them presents. These people are not the jet-setting community that arrives in Saudi Arabia in comfort, or the well-off from Canada who will be staying in good hotels during their time in Saudi Arabia. These are the poor who have saved their entire lifetime to take this trip. Their community has helped by raising money for them. Those who have gone before are held in high esteem, as these pilgrims will be when they return. There are tears, and hugs, and nervousness in the eyes of the elderly. 'Would you like to go too?' I ask a young woman photographer who I hope speaks English. 'Oh, I'm not ready yet', she responds, examining me closely. 'I'm too young to make that lifetime commitment to purity [smile], but I've worked hard the last few years to support my grandmother, the one over there, who has been waiting her whole life to make the pilgrimage.'

Lijiang, Yunnan Province, China. 2012. 'Will you be celebrating Kurban [Eid ul-Adha] this year?', I ask a middle-aged university English teacher. 'Not me personally, but my brother. He'll provide a feast for Muslims here, as he usually does. He runs a restaurant in town. It brings us all together once a year.' 'How about your family—are your parents still alive?', I ask. 'My mother will stay in her town. She wouldn't consider coming here. As the eldest member of her community who is known to be a really devout Muslim, she will be honoured by other women with the choice portions of the slaughtered animals.'

Cairo, Egypt, 2007. The morning mosque service has just concluded, and families are lingering in the courtyard before heading home—the young girls in their pretty new clothes which they wear self-consciously, adults distributing treats to all the children as they emerge from prayer, people chatting in the cool December morning sun. Goats, sheep and bulls are tied to trucks in the distance, and some are pacing in holding pens beside the mosque. You can identify the butchers by their rubber boots and the knives sticking out of the leather sheathes that cover their calves. They too are pacing in the background, smoking, caught up in a personal world that seems distant from the crowd that has emerged from the mosque, who in turn seem oblivious to the animals and the butchers.

When the last family is about half a block away, the children walking arm in arm with their backs to the mosque, attention turns to the animals. The first, the largest bull, unexpectedly escapes as he is being brought from the holding area in the back of the mosque. We all scatter. He is eventually corralled and killed. It is not as things should go, but there's always danger and the unexpected in these encounters. Then the small group of butchers starts the process of killing the rest of the animals, one by one, and preparing the meat. I have seen animals killed before but it still surprises me how much blood can come out of a cow.

Beside me is a recent convert to Islam, a young Black American, who is capturing the images on his iPhone and transmitting them to family in Chicago. His excitement is palpable. 'What are you thinking about now?' I ask as we both stand beside the next cow that's being prepared for slaughter. 'Becoming part of the *ummah*', he responds. 'I am now part of all this! And I know that Muslims around the world are sharing in this event as I am.'

I lift my eyes and see several young boys who had climbed the fence and were watching. I thought of a previous conversation I'd had with a Somali Canadian family who had noted the significance of the rite of passage for a young male when he kills his first animal for Eid ul-Adha. I wonder whether these boys are thinking of the time when they would be personally involved in the slaughter.

Five hours later, after seven animals had been slaughtered, the court-yard is almost as it had been when the families emerged from their morning prayers. Skin and bones and entrails are gone, and the stones have been hosed clean. What remains are the last of what had been several tables of cut-up meat, ready to be distributed. The faces of the poor looking through the courtyard fence make it clear that the meat is welcomed.

Cairo, Egypt. 2007. A small backyard of a suburban home not far from the mosque. An elderly couple has hired someone to kill their sheep, which they bought two days before, and which is tethered to the fence. The animal cost half of what it would if bought in Saudi Arabia for the *hajj*, but that $200 is still more than a month's income for them ('an imported sheep would have cost us less but who can trust the sellers?'). So there they are, in their pyjamas, both of them wearing pink slippers with pompoms, the woman with her arm around the husband's waist, and the husband with his left hand on the shoulder of the man who is about to slit the animal's throat.[40] 'Why is the sheep not resisting?', I think to myself. 'Will the blood get on the pompoms?' The cut is quick, there is remarkably little blood, and as the butcher begins to skin the animal the couple make their way back to their kitchen, where two pots are ready for the meat. The kitchen shows signs of considerable preparation, and the woman and her three daughters launch into a cooking frenzy.

Lijiang, China. 2012. Young people are tumbling out of the mosque following their morning prayers. Many, it turns out, are university students who have moved here to study in this ancient town. Somebody notices my wife and me standing at the base of the stairs, and two bus rides later we find ourselves on the outskirts of town in a restaurant with about seventy people enjoying an Eid meal. The food, which keeps coming, course after course, is provided gratis by the owner who is delighted to have foreigners share the experience. Without the help of

40.   Traditionally the one sacrificing the animal also slaughters it. The next best thing, for some at least, is to touch the person who is killing the animal. That practice likely explains the Egyptian man putting his hand on the butcher's shoulder, and the woman touching her husband.

alcohol, the conversations get louder, people's faces get happier, two professors, being true to their profession, make speeches (to the importance of learning, and the need to care for one another wherever we may be), and the owner beams.

Waterloo, Canada, 2010. Two university colleagues are in conversation over lunch, in earshot. 'I've become increasingly concerned about the maltreatment of animals in factory farms, and in slaughterhouses. Even those run by Muslims.' 'So what do you do for Eid?', asks his colleague (great question, I think). 'I used to drive to a farm an hour away to have a goat slaughtered for us, but this past year I bought a locally raised, hormone-free, organically fed goat. Don't laugh. It wasn't fair trade and grown in the shade! I had it butchered at a local abattoir by the owner I got to know. The meat was not halal. But I felt more Muslim doing this. For the first time in her life my wife prepared this non-halal meat for our meal. When we gave some to the food bank we told them that it wasn't halal.'

3.3. *Closing Reflections*
The tie that binds this section is the recognition that a sacrifice-based gathering can be both ordinary and exceptional. Eid ul-Adha, on the one hand, is like every major religious festival. It addresses multiple personal and collective needs, and if one could observe all its global expressions one would notice both striking commonalities and remarkable variations. On the other hand, the presence of so much meat during this festival helps to accentuate the sorts of activities we have exemplified through some fieldwork stories. Food in general brings people together, it solidifies the importance of women's work, and it heightens concern for those who are not as fortunate.

4. *Conclusion*

The picture that emerges of Eid ul-Adha re-orients our understanding of the sacrifice at the centre of this festival, and sacrifice itself as it is usually depicted by scholars. Had we introduced case studies of animal sacrifice by practitioners of other religious traditions—e.g. at the Dakshinkali Temple outside Kathmandu, among santeros and santeras in Miami, in rural Chinese villages—there might have been more blood and more frequent animal offerings. But our overall point would not have changed: animal sacrifice, far from being exotic, is best understood as part of broader, quite normal—though no less remarkable—set of social and cultural practices. In this closing section we offer a few thoughts about the applicability of current scholarship on sacrifice.

4.1. *Typology*

We have approached the Festival of Sacrifice much like scholars who have been drawn to identify the core characteristics of sacrifice, but rather than pulling our data from different traditions, as many of them did, we have taken data for sacrifice from different expressions within the same tradition. Comparison inevitably reveals commonalities and points of departure and difference. Scholars make much of the links between sacrifice and commensality, as they do between sacrifice and giving. Both of these characteristics also occur in our fieldwork examples and descriptions of Eid ul-Adha celebrations, though 'giving' in these cases turns out to be far less about 'giving to God' than 'giving to the poor'.

If we were to apply a typological framework to this festival we would lean towards a polythetic model, acknowledging fluidity and complexity, as well as multiple defining characteristics that need not all be present at any one time. Such a model would need to accommodate the presence of two types of Eid: an intra-*hajj* Eid that is private and expiatory, and an extra-*hajj* Eid that is more communal and consumption-oriented. We would also turn our attention to the differences that emerge between individuals, and with the same individual across time. One person's awe at the slaughter of an animal is another person's horror; one person's response at age 14 might be quite different from their response at 44 or 84.

4.2. *On Violence*

Our journey through different expressions of Eid ul-Adha has also made us appreciate the value of scholarship that uses sacrifice as a way of thinking about more fundamental human traits. Meditation on violence is both a frequent and understandable response to the confrontation of animal slaughter in connection with a deity. Indeed, as the present authors both continue to conduct fieldwork cross-culturally on this topic, an obvious question is whether the thousands of animals across the planet that are killed on a daily basis as a way to reach out to the spirit world indeed underscore a troubling human trait. The same could be said about animal slaughter in general.

Yet perhaps because of our own worldviews and interests in sitting with our data on recent Eid ul-Adhas, violence did not emerge as a fundamental feature across the diversity of Eid experiences. Yes, animals are killed, but for the most part the meat is prepared and shared, people enjoy one another's company, and the broader context binds people to a community that is diachronic and translocal, extending into the spiritual imaginary. These characteristics, if we were to extrapolate, might point to the value for some humans in feeling connected to something larger, and in coming together to rejoice and reflect, and eat. Sacrifice as experienced by Muslims during the *hajj* adds to this base a desire to be forgiven and radically transformed, or at least to fulfill a duty. In sum, if one were to take a set of sacrificial examples and deduce a human essence from them, the humans that emerge at their core might just as easily be vulnerable, socially engaged, and morally sensitive as they might be fundamentally dangerous, discrete, and violent. There is animal killing, and danger, and personal solitude in these stories, but we quite easily also found and focused on age, community support, gift-giving, food charity, and communal feasting that deeply connects one's own hunger with the hunger of others.

4.3. *On Power*

Scholars who approach sacrifice—and religion—as a window that allows them to see fundamental social and political issues also shed light on this festival. It is instructive to reflect on issues of power and gender in the context of religious myth and ritual in general, and the broadly based Eid ul-Adha in particular. In a festival like this it matters if one is rich or poor, male or female, child or adult, Saudi or non-Saudi, Canadian or Indonesian, human or animal. Moreover, the ways in which individuals participate in this festival, and the degree to which they accept its mythical substructure, offer heuristic sites for reflecting on how we structure our communities at large—including how we think about non-human animals.

We would add to this type of reflection two other categories, which extend out of concerns about power: the charity model, and the shaping of a global Muslim identity. Eid ul-Adha reflects a model of addressing poverty that runs counter both to the emerging model of social entrepreneurship and to the current critique of the charity model, which mutually insist that fundamental change to power imbalances comes, not by giving food and other forms of aid to the poor, but through making significant changes to social structures. In addition, Muslims are now interconnected to a degree never before imagined—via the internet, and through faster and less expensive modes of physical travel—and the economic disparities among them remain staggering. Eid ul-Adha is already being reshaped as a result of these factors, as it is by the increasing growth of the American empire. A global festival like this, viewed in its complexity and with this sort of lens, is a prime site on which to reflect on these issues of poverty and privilege.

4.4. *Closing Thoughts*

In reflecting on the journey taken in this chapter, we close by noting that religious rituals are successful to the extent that they engage the whole person in all its complexities, and offer different entry points for a wide range of individuals. Eid ul-Adha, not surprisingly given its long history and global spread, is thick with possibilities. It can be a platform for compassion, community and personal development, and deep reflection on moral responsibility; it can just as easily exist without connecting to any of those things. The opportunities that Eid ul-Adha offers for bodily knowing reminds us as scholars that religious festivals—all the more so those with animal sacrifice—need to be approached with a researcher's toolkit at least as deep as are the examples themselves.

JOHN MILTON'S POETICS FOR CHRIST VERSUS MOLOCH

Lee Johnson

In the modern, civilized world it can be unsettling to think about human sacrifice, especially the sacrifice of children, despite the historic prevalence of these seemingly barbaric rituals. They have often been well-intentioned, of course, as ways of trying to placate implacable forces and deities—usually in response to inexorable feelings of guilt and mortality. Indeed, some scholars have classified up to nine different purposes for human sacrifice: to release souls into the service of dead ancestors, to bind deities to human beings through propitiation, as a communion meal for the assimilation of life, as a redemptive process for past transgressions, for atonement, earthly fertility, immortality, to transform human conditions, and, perhaps most significantly in general, to unify divine and mortal realms.[1] To make these sacrifices doubly sure, the young, the innocent, and the virginal represent the greatest investments in the shedding of blood to obtain favours and protection.

Our concern here is to examine the ways in which seventeenth-century English epic poet John Milton focused on Moloch-worship and the child-sacrifice associated with that worship as the epitome of everything that was wrong with religion. Our main theme thus concerns Milton's championing of the Christ-child as a source of life, of spiritual life in particular, against the sacrifice of children to a violent pagan deity. We shall also be concerned with Milton's poetic art in his presentations of Moloch and the Son of God, who takes on the role of the historical Christ. We shall examine the artistic contrast Milton devises between the empirical or sense-perceptible structures associated with the depiction of Moloch and the conceptual forms additionally associated with the symbolism attending the Son of God. Along the way, we shall reflect on a spectrum of interpretations that have been brought to bear upon Moloch as they range from the 'literal' to the 'figurative', although our

---

1. Kay A. Read, 'Human Sacrifice: An Overview', in Lindsay Jones (ed.), *Encyclopedia of Religion* (2d ed.; Detroit: Macmillan Reference USA, 2005), vol. 6, pp. 4182-85.

main interest will be in perspectives that prevailed in the seventeenth century, which tended to integrate literal and figurative aspects of Moloch-worship into an admonitory indictment of paganism. By the conclusion of our exploration of Milton's attitudes towards the Christ-child in relation to child-sacrifice in Moloch-worship, we should appreciate anew the distinctions he makes between sacrifices performed out of love versus those done out of fear.

Were Milton living at this hour, he would undoubtedly be keen to inquire into the latest scholarship on ancient religions and on Moloch-worship in particular. His own knowledge of these matters was highly advanced in his own time, given his study of biblical and classical languages and of the Bible itself, along with relevant commentaries. Probably what would now engage his curiosity most fully are the competing insights, since the seventeenth century, as to what the word or words associated with Moloch mean: whether there even was such a deity, whether it was a word simply meaning 'king' or ruler, or whether it referred not to a god but to a sacrificial ritual only, a ritual that may have literally involved children or, more symbolically, surrogates from the animal kingdom. In earlier centuries, the status of Moloch, Molek, Molech (or other variation) as a Canaanite or Ammonite deity was disputed but assumed to be a 'literal' historical fact, although when dealing with the nebulous nature of historical facts, we must always be careful to understand that the word 'literal' is a fiction. The disputes were over details of that fiction, not the main point, which assumed the deity's historical existence, as based on biblical and other ancient texts.

In the mid-1930s, however, Otto Eissfeldt changed the direction of scholarship on Moloch with his *Molk als Opferbegriff in Punischen und Hebräischen und das Ende Gottes Moloch*.[2] In this work, Eissfeldt argued that there was no such deity—note the dramatic ending of his book's title *das Ende Gottes Moloch*—but that a *molk* was a sacrificial offering. Subsequent scholarship has basically refined, qualified, or disputed Eissfeldt's argument or has even emphasized other more 'figurative' possibilities, such as Moloch-worship as a form of idolatry by marrying pagan women and having children outside one's faith, which metaphorically reinterprets the literal pain of 'passing through the fires of Moloch' in favour of the more symbolic critical aspirations of the rabbinical tradition. Thus, 'the common denominator of all these traditions is the understanding of Moloch-worship as the transfer of Jewish

---

2.   Otto Eissfeldt, *Molk als Opferbegriff in Punischen und Hebräischen und das Ende Gottes Moloch* (Beiträge zur Religionsgeschichte des Altertums 3; Halle: Max Niemeyer, 1935).

children to paganism either by delivering them directly to pagan priests or by procreation through intercourse with a pagan woman'.[3]

All these matters are impressively reviewed in the detailed, annotated bibliographies and commentaries of George C. Heider's *The Cult of Molek: A Reassessment*,[4] in which Heider surveys contributions on Moloch from the seventeenth century onwards and pays particular attention to the problems Eissfeldt presents, along with a considerable engagement with Paul G. Mosca's 'Child Sacrifice in Canaanite and Israelite Religion: A Study in *Mulk* and מלך'.[5] Rarely has an unpublished dissertation received such extensive published attention and commentary. That dissertation is also footnoted in John Day's *Molech: A God of Human Sacrifice in the Old Testament*,[6] as Day rejects Mosca's suggestion that *mlk* could mean 'an offering of an infant citizen' because, without additional words, *mlk* does not seem to entail a human sacrifice but an unspecified offering.[7] Day's work is a qualitative refinement of recent views, as he disassociates Moloch from other deities (Baal, Kronos [Saturn], the Ammonite deity Milcom) but associates Moloch with underworld deities of Sheol, as Day relies deeply and repeatedly on Isa 57.9: 'You journeyed to Molech with oil and multiplied your perfumes; you sent your envoys far off, and sent down even to Sheol'.[8] As Day says, 'We have seen above that there was a god Malik who was equated with Nergal and who therefore is the same as the Old Testament Molech and that there is not simply a coincidence of names, is indicated by the fact that there is evidence that Molech was likewise an underworld god'.[9] These writers, then, suggest the range of contemporary interest in the subject, an interest that corrects some of the assumptions of Milton's age about Moloch as a sun-god or as an Ammonite deity but also, on balance, reestablishes Moloch as a deity associated with human sacrifice, especially that of children.

---

3. Moshe Weinfeld and S. David Sperling, 'The Cult of Moloch', in Michael Berenbaum and Fred Skolnick (eds.), *Encyclopaedia Judaica* (2d ed.; Detroit: Macmillan Reference, 2007), vol. 14, pp. 427-29.

4. George C. Heider, *The Cult of Molek: A Reassessment* (JSOTSup 43; Sheffield: JSOT, 1985).

5. Paul G. Mosca, 'Child Sacrifice in Canaanite and Israelite Religion: A Study in *Mulk* and מלך' (Ph.D. diss., Harvard University, 1975).

6. John Day, *Molech: A God of Human Sacrifice in the Old Testament* (Cambridge: Cambridge University Press, 1989).

7. Day, *Molech*, p. 8

8. Day, *Molech*, p. 84.

9. Day, *Molech*, p. 50.

Milton would also be interested in the more exclusively 'figurative' or metaphorical references to Moloch in our own era. An example of this figurative application is found in Martin S. Bergmann's *In the Shadow of Moloch: The Sacrifice of Children and Its Impact on Western Religion.*[10] This book is not about any 'literal' Moloch at all and contributes nothing to serious historical, linguistic, and biblical scholarship on the subject. Instead, it uses Moloch as a metaphor to discuss human sacrifice throughout the world's religions, political holocausts, Freud and the Oedipal complex, classical tragedies that entail sacrifices, and so on. What is of interest, for our purposes, is Bergmann's choice of Moloch as the attention-grabbing word in his book's title, as if this word has such disturbing denotations and connotations that it symbolizes, better than any other word, the fascination that this abomination represents. It is as if we would have to invent such a compellingly negative word, if the word 'Moloch' did not come to hand so readily. It seems made to serve its ultimate purpose as the worst word one can find.

Perhaps the very sound of 'Moloch' to a poet's ear may help to explain not only Milton's fascination with this deity but also Allen Ginsberg's, even though it would be hard to adduce two more contrastable sensibilities whose poetic arts are far apart on the spectrum of expression. In *Howl*, Part II, Ginsberg begins by asking: 'What sphinx of cement and aluminum bashed open their skulls and ate up their brains and imagination?' The answer, repeated thirty-nine times in this relatively short section of the poem, is 'Moloch', as in: 'Moloch! Moloch! Nightmare of Moloch! Moloch the loveless! Mental Moloch! Moloch the heavy judger of men!'; or as in: 'Moloch whose mind is pure machinery! Moloch whose blood is running money! Moloch whose fingers are ten armies! Moloch whose breast is a cannibal dynamo! Moloch whose ear is a smoking tomb!'[11] What this has to do with a biblical and historical Moloch is unclear; there is no specific reference to child-sacrifice—just a general sacrifice of one's humanity to modern corporate greed and the military-industrial complex. In fact, the issue of money seems to be of principal importance and interest; perhaps 'Mammon' would have been a more accurate deity to invoke. Mammon, however, does not have the verbal punch of Moloch. Mammon is too much like manna, mamma, mama, and other 'soft' words; by comparison, Moloch has a lock on malice. Ginsberg was also a great admirer of the poetry of William

10. Martin S. Bergmann, *In the Shadow of Moloch: The Sacrifice of Children and Its Impact on Western Religion* (New York: Columbia University Press, 1992).

11. Allen Ginsberg, *Howl and Other Poems* (San Francisco: City Lights Books, 1996).

Blake, whose 'Urizen', as a symbol of the paralyzing reason's war against 'Los', the imagination, is evidently part of Ginsberg's conception of Moloch as an imprisoning tyrant. Overall, Ginsberg's Moloch is essentially a Blakean figure, having very little to do with the historical Moloch but everything to do with a prophetical denunciation of modern capitalism and its dehumanizing impact on creativity, freedom, and the imagination. How much more powerful as a rhetorical device and as a sound is an incantation on 'Moloch' rather than on 'Mammon' or 'Urizen'!

Milton's Moloch, by contrast, is decidedly a figure of death, violence, and the sacrifice of children, which is the sacrifice of one's future. He referred to Moloch throughout his career and featured this deity's particularly destructive nature among all the pagan deities he described, who once were angels in Heaven but who, after the War in Heaven, fled through Chaos to Hell and thereafter took up residence on Earth as various gods and goddesses: 'And Devils to adore for Deities' (*Paradise Lost* [hereafter *PL*], I, l. 373). These deities flourished throughout the ancient Mediterranean world and ranged across male and female examples: 'For Spirits when they please / Can either Sex assume, or both…' (*PL*, I, ll. 423-24). They disappeared as active objects of worship about the time Christ was born, and hence, to Milton as to many others, 'the silencing of the oracles' was of supreme significance. That significance forms a large part of 'The Hymn' from Milton's early and first major lyric *On the Morning of Christ's Nativity* (1629, as the poet approached his 21st birthday). Stanza XXIII is relevant here:

> And sullen *Moloch*, fled,
> Hath left in shadows dread
> His burning Idol all of blackest hue;
> In vain with Cymbals' ring
> They call the grisly king,
> In dismal dance about the furnace blue;
> The brutish gods of *Nile* as fast,
> *Isis* and *Orus*, and the Dog *Anubis* haste. (*Nat.* ll. 205-12)

As William B. Hunter points out, in considering William Blake's illustration *The Flight of Moloch* for the stanza just quoted, 'The god who exacted from parents the sacrifice of children is shown fleeing as the Christ-child stands miraculously, triumphantly, before the idol'.[12] In other words, Blake captures perfectly and exactly the opposition of the

---

12. William B. Hunter, 'Moloch', in William B. Hunter (ed.), *A Milton Encyclopedia* (8 vols.; Bucknell, Pa.: Bucknell University Press, 1979), vol. 5, p. 151.

Christ-child to the children who had been sacrificed and also accurately notes Moloch's departure in the presence of the Christ-child.[13]

Even at this early stage of Milton's poetical career, Moloch stands out as the antithesis of the themes and imagery associated with divine solicitude and the life of Christ. The stanza just quoted is full of dissonance and darkness, unlike the central stanzas of 'The Hymn', which mark the centre of a great circle that encloses the rude and regal manger scenes, respectively, of the opening and closing stanzas of this sacred ode. To the shepherds, the angels appear as 'A Globe of circular light' (*Nat.* l. 110) and sing the 'unexpressive' or inexpressible music of the Gloria in full cosmic harmony (l. 116):

> Ring out ye Crystal spheres,
> Once bless our human ears,
> (If ye have power to touch our senses so)
> And let your silver chime
> Move in melodious time;
> And let the Bass of Heav'n's deep Organ blow,
> And with your ninefold harmony
> Make up full consort to th'Angelic symphony. (*Nat.* ll. 125-32)

Of compelling interest is Milton's distinction between harmonies that only the mind can appreciate versus those that strike the physical ear. The spheres of light and the metaphysical music associated with 'Heav'n's new-born Heir' (l. 116) could not contrast more starkly with the 'blackest hue' and the clashing 'Cymbals' and physical noise of Moloch-worship.

Miltonists have provided many speculations on the sources of the poet's views of Moloch-worship, but a succinct summary—and one that, for ever-thoroughgoing Miltonists, does not include an excess of questionable information—appears in *A Variorum Commentary on the Poems of John Milton*:

> *Moloch* or Molech (meaning 'King') was a god of the Ammonites (1 Kings 11.7) whose cruel rites of child sacrifice are much condemned in the O.T. (Lev. 18.21; Ps. 106.37-8; 2 Kings 23.10). [Thomas] Warton noticed what Milton might have learned from George Sandys' *Relation of a Journey* (London, 1615, 186): wherein [i.e., in the valley of 'Gehinnon'] the Hebrews sacrificed their children to Molech, an Idoll of brasse, having the head of a calfe, the rest of a kingly figure, with armes extended to receive the miserable sacrifice, seared to death with his burning embracements. For the Idoll was hollow within, and filled with fire. And

13.   See http://artbuttz.tumblr.com/post/38290876125/william-blake-the-flight-of-moloch-illustration, accessed 20 March 2014.

lest their lamentable shreeks should sad the hearts of their parents, the Priests of Molech did deafe their ears with the continuall clangs of trumpets and timbrels... Warton remarked on the vividness of Milton's scene, which, avoiding the actual rites, presents the god as fled and the priests striving to recall him by the sounds with which they drowned the cries of his victims.[14]

We may entertain Sandys's account of Moloch-worship as a seventeenth-century starting-point for John Milton's elaboration of what this deity meant in his poetry. Sandy's observations seem at least consistent with the stanzas quoted above from 'The Hymn' to *On the Morning of Christ's Nativity*. What Milton adds to any sources is his sense of archetypal relationships of various religious and mythological figures to one another. Thus, he relates Moloch to Chemos, and both of these figures to Greek gods, as he adapts the epic roll call of heroes in Bk. I of *Paradise Lost* to his presentation of the devils in Hell:

> First *Moloch*, horrid King besmear'd with blood
> Of human sacrifice, and parents' tears,
> Though for the noise of Drums and Timbrels loud
> Thir children's cries unheard, that pass'd through fire
> To his grim Idol. Him the *Ammonite*
> Worshipt in *Rabba* and her wat'ry Plain,
> In *Argob* and in *Basan*, to the stream
> Of utmost *Arnon*. Nor content with such
> Audacious neighborhood, the wisest heart
> Of *Solomon* he led by fraud to build
> His Temple right against the Temple of God
> On that opprobrious Hill, and made his Grove
> The pleasant Valley of *Hinnom*, *Tophet* thence
> And black *Gehenna* call'd, the Type of Hell. (*PL*, I, ll. 392-405)

Milton writes a bloc of fourteen lines, divided roughly in half (ll. 392-99; ll. 399-405); and he follows this simple two-part structure with thirteen lines immediately thereafter: 'Next *Chemos*, th' obscene dread of *Moab's* Sons' (ll. 406-18), which arithmetically sets up another two-part structure, an equivalence between these two deities, infamous for their violence to children and to women. This kind of empirical structure is typical of Milton's methods in his blank verse, and it directs the attentive reader to parallels and correspondences in his material. Thus, when we finally come to the Greek gods, the parallels continue, as David Quint has pointed out, in relating Moloch to Saturn and Chemos to Comus:

14. Douglas Bush and A. S. P. Woodhouse (eds.), *A Variorum Commentary on the Poems of John Milton*. Vol. 2, Part 1, *The Minor English Poems* (New York: Columbia University Press, 1972).

'Moloch and Saturn are thus one and the same horrifying deity/devil'.[15] What needs to be added is that these parallels are inspired by Milton himself and by the equivalences set up in the design of his verse paragraphs.

Why Moloch is 'first' is of particular interest. The entry on 'Moloch' in *A Milton Encyclopedia* suggests Milton placed Moloch at the head of the devils because this deity was the 'first idol invented by superstition and thus the source of all idolatry'.[16] In this reading, Milton alters the usual infernal hierarchy by displacing Beelzebub with Moloch as a dramatic way of putting idolatry in the forefront of religious worship, 'the chief representative of 'false gods…adored as idols'.[17] However compelling this may be to explain Moloch's preeminence in Milton's poetry, I think the most compelling reason is, again, the antithesis Moloch represents, through child-sacrifice, to the Christ-child who brings peace and love instead of death and violence. In both *On the Morning of Christ's Nativity* and in *Paradise Lost*, Milton tells us that the two great events in the history of things are the creation of the universe and the birth of Christ. Thus, the Gloria sung by angels at the birth of the infant god repeats their angelic joy at the creation of the World: 'Such Music (as 'tis said) / Before was never made, / But when of old the sons of morning sung, / While the Creator Great / His constellations set, / And the well-balanc't world on hinges hung' (*Nat.* stanza XII). The same equation between the Creation and the birth of Christ reappears in Bk. VII of *Paradise Lost* as the angelic host celebrates the new universe by singing: 'Glory they sung to the most High, good will / To future men, and in thir dwellings peace' (ll. 182-83). With this parallel of having the angels sing the Gloria at both the Creation and the birth of Christ—a parallel distinctly Milton's, given his emphasis on it—we are at the very core of this poet's deepest beliefs. In relation to these existential principles, what could be more of a contrast than the anti-creative violence of child-sacrifice to Moloch?

Moloch even attempts to dominate the Council in Hell from Bk. II of *Paradise Lost*. Satan convenes the council and asks for tactical advice after the disastrous results of their War in Heaven. Moloch, Belial, and Mammon respectively offer their views, but hot-headed Moloch, as militarist in extremis, is first, again: 'My sentence is for open War…'

15.   David Quint, 'Milton's Book of Numbers: Book 1 of "Paradise Lost" and Its Catalogue', *International Journal of the Classical Tradition* 13, no. 4 (Spring, 2007), pp. 531-33.

16.   Hunter, 'Moloch', p. 150.

17.   Hunter, 'Moloch', p. 150.

(*PL*. II, l. 51). Basing his appeal on the repeated words 'ascend' and 'ascent', Moloch urges his associates to rise from Hell and retake Heaven, even if they lose their very beings in the attempt. The rhetoric of his appeal consists of three roughly ten-line passages (ll. 51-60, 60-70, 70-81), concluding with two roughly twelve-line sections (ll. 81-93, 94-105), as each part of his speech is in parallel with other parts in order to amplify the rhythm and weight of his language. As such, the structure of his speech maximizes its simple, sense-perceptible, auditory impact, requiring no great intellection to appreciate its implications. Of course, the desperate rhetoric of his speech immediately leads to Belial's cowardly call to inaction and then to Mammon's much more praise-worthy call to the action of building a counter-Heaven in Hell, a popular idea that threatens Satan's command over his followers. What is true of the structure of Moloch's speech, however, is also true of Belial's and Mammon's: the simple stacking of parallel sections of verse to clarify rhetorical relationships and associations, while augmenting, through simple symmetry, the emotive dignity or gravitas of its impact.

Milton's use of parallel structures and simple symmetries certainly gives the devils' speeches their due. A strategic challenge for the poet, therefore, is how to distinguish, beyond obvious differences in content, the rhetorically powerful speeches accorded to Satan and his minions from speeches by the Father, Son, good angels, Adam, and Eve. What follows is a discussion of the poet's remarkable solutions to this problem by means of a sustained and representative example: his presentation of what we may call 'Three Acts of Love' involving Satan, the Son, and Eve. Moloch, as we have seen, is 'first' in the epic roll call of Bk. I and first among the speakers in the Council in Hell; but he is representative of the values of his leader Satan, who sums up his followers in their entirety. The dilemma Satan faces in the Council in Hell is that he is essentially confronting a leadership review convention, thanks to his having led his followers down to an ignominious defeat. Common opinion in Hell, after the first three major speeches, is tilting in favour of Mammon as the new leader; and this must be stopped, at all costs. To that end, Satan's right hand, Beelzebub, suggests guerrilla warfare against God by locating the newly created Earth and then subverting its human inhabitants. But who will be brave enough to scout out this new creation and find ways to undo its 'puny habitants'? (*PL*, II, l. 367). After no one volunteers to undertake this mission, Satan breaks the silence by magnanimously proposing to 'seek / Deliverance for us all' in an apparent 'act of love' that is the political epitome of self-love, of self-aggrandizement.

In the first fifteen lines of his speech (ll. 430-44), which divide sym-
metrically into eight followed by seven, Satan emphasizes and inflates
the perils of making the journey to Earth: 'These past, if any pass, the
void profound / Of unessential Night receives him next / Wide gaping,
and with utter loss of being / Threatens him...' and so forth. After
frightening his auditors, he then in two roughly eleven-line passages (ll.
445-56, 456-65) generously offers to do precisely what he claims cannot
be done, in no small part because of his sense of civic duty: '...if aught
propos'd / And judg'd of public moment, in the shape / Of difficulty or
danger could deter / Mee from attempting'. He shrewdly concludes:
'...while I abroad / Through all the Coasts of dark destruction seek /
Deliverance for us all: this enterprise / None shall partake with me'. By
excluding his associates, he reconsolidates his sway over them and in
every sense gets the hell out of Hell where his leadership cannot easily
be challenged in his absence but only be admired for its apparent courage
and audacity.

The Council in Hell in Bk. II is essentially a parody of the Council in
Heaven, which occurs immediately thereafter in Bk. III. The heavenly
council is an extraordinary dialogue in the mind of Milton's Supreme
Being, whose voices divide into two parts: a Father insisting on justice
for those who try to undo the original perfection and harmony of the
Creation, and a Son responding with the greater vision of grace, of divine
love, as the means by which creatures may freely choose to reestablish
their harmony with one another and with their Creator. The Father's call
for justice includes a literal and physical death for the breaking of a
figurative and spiritual bond of trust: 'He with his whole posterity must
die, / Die hee or Justice must; unless for him / Some other able, and as
willing, pay / The rigid satisfaction, death for death' (*PL*, III, ll. 209-12).
One of the contentions here is that Moloch-worship, in its sacrifice of
children, is an example of literalism applied to an act of propitiation. By
comparison, the self-sacrifice of the Christ-child as an adult is to die a
physical death out of love for others in order to encourage a return to
spiritual life. In his *Christian Doctrine*, Bk. I, Chapters XII and XIII,
Milton joins those theologians who discuss Four Degrees of Death: the
Original Sin of the Fall, which brings about a symbolic death between
the creatures with one another and with their Creator; the repeated
propensity to sin, which is Spiritual Death and ever-greater alienation
from others with ever-greater devotion to oneself; the third form of
death, Physical Death, which puts a stop to unending and increasing
Spiritual Death; and finally, Eternal Death, which is appropriate to the
state of those who, like the fallen angels and the damned, are forever lost

in their own sin.[18] Another way of putting all this is in terms of selfless love versus self-love. Self-love, or pride, leads to death in literal and symbolic terms, a 'Hell within', as the epic narrator says of Satan's soul in Bk. IV (l. 20). Selfless love, which is the basis of Milton's redefinition of epic heroic ideals, leads to 'a paradise within', as Michael indicates in Bk. XII (l. 587), and a restoration of spiritual life. That restoration is so important that it becomes 'the act whereby man, being delivered from sin and death by God the Father through Jesus Christ, is raised to a far more excellent state of grace than that from which he had fallen'.[19] In other words, a Fortunate Fall is attainable for those who freely choose it.

Silence greets the Father's request for any of the angels to undertake the role of dying for the sake of humanity—a parallel to the silence in Hell when a similar request was made for a deliverer, of sorts—until the Son expounds the nature of grace. It is one of the most important passages in the whole of Milton's works; in a sense, it is the passage to which his entire life as a poet and thinker has been leading. Its thirty-nine lines are the antithesis of Moloch-worship, of Satanic self-regard, and move from Heaven to Earth and the birth and life of Christ, and then from Hell and Earth back up to Heaven in their completion of a great circle from life to death and a return to eternal life:

> Father, thy word is past, man shall find grace;
> And shall grace not find means, that finds her way,
> The speediest of thy winged messengers,
> To visit all thy creatures, and to all
> Comes unprevented, unimplored, unsought?
> Happy for man, so coming; he her aid
> Can never seek, once dead in sins and lost;
> Atonement for himself or offering meet,
> Indebted and undone, hath none to bring:
> Behold mee then, mee for him, life for life
> I offer, on mee let thine anger fall;
> Account mee man; I for his sake will leave
> Thy bosom, and this glory next to thee
> Freely put off, and for him lastly die
> Well pleas'd, on me let Death wreck all his rage;
> Under his gloomy power I shall not long
> Lie vanquisht; thou hast giv'n me to possess
> Life in myself for ever, by thee I live,
> Though now to Death I yield, and am his due

18. John Milton, 'The Christian Doctrine', in Frank Allen (ed.), *The Student's Milton* (New York: F.S. Crofts & Co., 1930).

19. John Milton, *Christian Doctrine*, Bk. I, Chapter XIV.

All that of me can die, yet that debt paid,
Thou wilt not leave me in the loathsome grave
His prey, nor suffer my unspotted Soul
For ever with corruption there to dwell;
But I shall rise Victorious, and subdue
My vanquisher, spoil'd of his vaunted spoil;
Death his death's wound shall then receive, and stoop
Inglorious, of his mortal sting disarm'd.
I through the ample Air in Triumph high
Shall lead Hell Captive maugre Hell, and show
The powers of darkness bound. Thou at the sight
Pleas'd, out of Heaven shalt look down and smile,
While by thee rais'd I ruin all my Foes,
Death last, and with his Carcass glut the Grave;
Then with the multitude of my redeem'd
Shall enter Heav'n long absent, and return,
Father, to see thy face, wherein no cloud
Of anger shall remain, but peace assur'd,
And reconcilement; wrath shall be no more
Thenceforth, but in thy presence Joy entire. (III, ll. 227-65)

The speech opens with a rhetorical question (ll. 225-31) that emphasizes the key repeated word 'grace'; its five lines then lead to ten lines (ll. 232-41) in which the Son freely chooses to take on the life of the historical Christ, from birth to Crucifixion, as this section of the speech concludes with the apparent triumph of 'Death'. These fifteen lines then modulate into twenty-four lines (ll. 242-65) that divide into a simple binary structure of twelve + twelve and are semantically unified by four main clauses ringing changes on 'I shall' with two of these clauses in each half or twelve-line section. These concluding twenty-four lines return almost immediately to the word 'Death' and foretell Christ's Resurrection in the first of its two twelve-line sections (ll. 242-53), after which the remaining twelve lines (ll. 254-65) depict the general resurrection of the dead and the final and eternal attainment of heavenly 'Joy'. The Son of God's descent from Heaven to Earth, to the life and death of Christ, and the ascent back to Heaven, even to the end of historical time on Earth, is celebrated with the repetition of the key word 'Heaven' in the final lines. As we may infer, Milton characteristically builds up his verse paragraphs on the repetition of key words; here they are 'grace', 'Death', and 'Heaven', with grace and heaven encircling death in accordance with the overall theme and structure, the essential idea, of the speech.

Although the content of the Son's speech, with its theme of selfless love, could not be more antithetical to the themes of speeches by characters such as Moloch and Satan, its structure appears to be rather similar: the use of key, repeated words to build up a paragraph in conjunction with simple symmetrical subsections of verse. At least, this is how the issue of variety among Miltonic speeches appears at first glance. A closer look at the Son's speech, however, reveals another level of unity between theme and form that distinguishes it from anything accorded to the rebel angels. Although this key speech is a two-part structure, it does not, overall, divide into a simple binary or ternary structure, easily perceived by the senses. Instead, its main division into two parts is between the first fifteen lines, depicting the descent of the Son and the Incarnation represented by the life of Christ, and the remaining twenty-four lines, chronicling the ascent of the resurrected Christ back to Heaven as the Son of God. The asymmetry of this division appears only five other times in Milton's works, and all six examples symbolize the ratio of Heaven to Earth in the Incarnation, the figure of Christ. It is the ratio of the Divine Proportion, which in this historical epoch is described by Luca Pacioli in his book *De divina proportione* 1509), to which we will turn shortly in considering why this conceptual geometrical form was thought of as such as an appropriate way of describing the nature of God.

Here, the ratio of fifteen to twenty-four is, in lowest terms, five to eight. Continuing the ratio, one sees that 5:8::8:13. Thus are the transitions from Heaven to Earth and Earth to Heaven exemplified in geometrical symbolism. In the opening paragraph of *Paradise Lost*, the twenty-six lines present two sentences: one sixteen lines long followed by ten lines, with the 'greater Man'—the second Adam—(l. 4) being proclaimed as its main theme, as the key words 'Man' and 'men' build up the verse paragraph and dominate its vocabulary in the ascent from earthly things to heavenly inspiration. In lowest terms, the final ten lines are to the first sixteen as 5:8::8:13. At the other end of *Paradise Lost*, Michael describes the life of Christ to Adam in a grand, summarizing verse paragraph of eighty lines (Bk. XII, ll. 386-465), whose opening fifty (ll. 386-435) divide exactly into a simple binary of twenty-five + twenty five and whose concluding thirty lines (ll. 436-65) divide exactly into another simple binary of fifteen + fifteen: in lowest terms, the final thirty are to the opening fifty as 3:5::5:8. In the contest between 'death' and 'life' in its first fifty lines, the Resurrection prevails over the Crucifixion at the place of divine proportion: 'A gentle wafting to immortal Life' (l. 435). The return to Heaven and the establishment of a new Paradise round out the final thirty lines. After hearing this account of the second Adam who will redeem him, Adam bursts into a version of *O Felix Culpa* (Bk. XII, ll. 469-84) which exactly replicates the ratio of Michael's much larger speech by showing ten lines followed by six: 3:5::5:8. This harmony between Adam and his mentor is thus geometrically secured, along with Adam's accurate understanding of the theme

Michael has brought to his attention. In fact, in his final speech in the epic (Bk. XII, ll. 553-73), Adam acknowledges his 'Redeemer ever blest' in an utterance of twenty-one lines that are encircled by the word 'blest' and unfold as eight + thirteen: 8:13::13:21. Adam moves from 'this transient World, the Race of time' (l. 554) and eternity, reaches the divine proportion of the verse paragraph, and proceeds to the internal spiritual insights that the example of Christ provides 'to the faithful' who will also find 'Death' to be 'the Gate of Life' (l. 571).

These five examples from *Paradise Lost*—one from Bk. 1, one from Bk. III, and three from Bk. XII—are anticipated much earlier in Milton's career, 'Through the dear might of him who walk'd the waves' in stanza ten of *Lycidas* (ll. 165-85), in which the rhymed stanza of a *canzone* presents its *fronte* and *sirima*—its two main parts—in geometrical terms, with the entire stanza ascending from Earth's ocean to Heaven and back down to the ocean as the opening thirteen lines shift to the final eight in another completion of a great Miltonic circle of theme and form: 8:13::13:21. It is a grand vision that again unites the concerns of both Earth and Heaven through the agency of Christ. As such, *Lycidas* may be deemed the early key to the passages of greatest thematic significance in Milton's epic, passages which reveal *Paradise Lost* to be a work whose main theme is love, a concept of love that goes back to the archetype of divine love of things eternal to things temporal in the Incarnation, the life of Christ. In Milton's poetics, this conceptual, symbolic form occurs nowhere else: it appears only in conjunction with reflections on the birth and life of Christ.

The distinction between a structure, such as the simple symmetries in speeches given to Moloch and the rebel angels, and the conceptual form that serves as the basis of the speeches in the epic and of the stanza from *Lycidas* just noted is, in ontological terms, a difference between things which are easily perceptible to the senses and things which are purely conceptual in nature: hence, the distinction between an empirical structure and a conceptual form. The conceptual nature of the geometrical form we have just been considering was, during the Renaissance, the inspiration for Luca Pacioli's treatise *De divina proportione* (1509)[20] and its juxtaposition of this mathematical ratio with traditional descriptions of God, as Pacioli indicated by pointing to five key similarities:

---

20. Luca Pacioli, *De divina proportione* (ed. and trans. into German by Constantin Winterberg from Venetian edition of 1509, printed by Antonio Capella (Vienna: Carl Graeser, 1889). Reprinted in *Quellenschriften für Kunstgeschichte und Kunsttechnik*, N.F. II (Hildesheim: Georg Olms, 1974).

1. the divine proportion is a unique form of unity, which unity is the supreme epithet of God;

2. just as one and the same substance is found in the three persons of the Holy Trinity, so one and the same proportion is always appropriately found in the three terms of the ratio;

3. just as God cannot be properly defined and made comprehensible to us through words, so the proportion cannot be expressed through rational numbers;

4. just as God is always unchanging in every part, so the proportion is always continuous in all its parts;

5. just as God's quintessence is conferred on the four elements of earth, water, air, and fire and through these on all other things in nature, so the proportion is inherent in the pentagonal dodecahedron and thereby accounts for the other regular solids and their four elements which cannot be made proportional to one another without the ratio.

As I noted in an earlier article, 'Pacioli's third and fifth properties, which concern the ratio's status as a concept and its application to the natural world, represent principles that are central to modern discussions of the golden section', which, along with the phrase 'golden ratio', is typically used as a current name for this concept.[21] In algebraic terms, the ratio is like *pi* in that it is an infinitely non-repeating decimal fraction, as the square root of five, minus one, divided by two, indicates. In other words, numbers cannot express the ratio exactly, which exists only as a geometrical equation: $a:b::b:a+b$. Numbers, like sequences in time, can only variously approximate the geometrical limit that exists solely as an unchanging concept like eternity. Thus, Pacioli makes a parallel between verbal language and rational numbers, both of which fail to express something inexpressible in their symbols. In relation to the natural world, the ratio is often cited for its exemplification in the equiangular spiral, found in seashells, pinecones, the sequence of branches on various plants...all the way to spiral galaxies. Again, however, these natural structures do not exactly express the ratio but only approximate its ideal form. What is evident in Milton's use of the ratio is his reliance on the most basic of Fibonacci Series to approximate it: 1, 1, 2, 3, 5, 8, 13, 21... as each successive term is the sum of the two that precede it. Obviously,

---

21. Lee Johnson, 'Milton's Mathematical Symbol of Theodicy', in Istavan Hargittai (ed.), *Symmetry: Unifying Human Understanding* (New York: Pergamon Press, 1986), pp. 617-28.

3/5 is not the same as 5/8, and so on, but, as the numbers grow larger, the more closely they approach the limit that governs their successions.

It is instructive that Milton uses the first and easiest of the Fibonacci series as the most basic, and, really, the simplest set of approximations to the divine proportion for showing, geometrically, his idea of the relationship of divine to human realities. In some cases, the asymmetrical division is in the first three-eighths of a paragraph or stanza, as in the Son's speech in Bk. III; and in some cases the division is five-eighths through the set of lines, as in the opening verse paragraph of *Paradise Lost*. What is of primary importance is that this conceptual form expresses the ratio of the heavenly Son to the earthly Christ as a continuous geometrical proportion that encompasses both realms. The conceptual form of the divine proportion is the idea surrounding the empirical structure and specific verbal experience of words and their sounds and their rhythms that move in accordance with that idea in a way that does not exist in the verse paragraphs assigned to the rebel angels. In all this planning of his verse paragraphs, Milton relies, as we have noted, on a simple Fibonacci sequence rather than on more complicated ways of calculating approximations to the divine proportion. The advantage of this approach is that he is able to make a dramatic distinction between simple symmetrical forms that divide perceptibly into two or three parts and the clearest expression of the asymmetrical form of the divine proportion, which is known only to the mind's conceptual insights, even though it governs and gives significance to the space accorded to actual phrases and verbal structures.

Milton's use of poetic forms also reveals fundamental attitudes towards moral values. A form, by definition, is something positive, something constructive. In his era, a negative form would have been, on its own terms, a self-contradiction. One would not expect Moloch, Satan, or the rebel angels to employ a divine proportion in their utterances; for it would thereby support the imperatives of the divine realm. What evil characters can do, however, is to take a different and suitable pre-existing form and pervert it to their own purposes. Here is an instance in which a conceptual form can be turned on itself. Although the divine proportion is excluded from this kind of poetic inversion, Milton's brilliant use of the unrhymed or blank verse sonnet can be so used. Our third 'Act of Love' is from Eve, and her evidently unconscious use of sonnet-form becomes an extraordinary echo of language from the Son's self-sacrifice in Bk. III and leads to dramatic examples of sonnet-form elsewhere in the epic. In Bk. X, Eve approaches Adam and is denounced and utterly rejected: 'Out of my sight, thou Serpent...' (l. 867), as he blames her for all their woe. Rather than retaliate in kind, Eve completely stuns Adam by offering to go to the place of judgment where she will give her life in place of his so that he may live:

> While yet we live, scarce one short hour perhaps,
> Between us two let there be peace, both joining,
> As join'd in injuries, one enmity
> Against a Foe by doom express assign'd us,
> That cruel Serpent: On me exercise not
> Thy hatred for this misery befall'n,
> On me already lost, mee than thyself
> More miserable; both have sinn'd, but thou
> Against God only, I against God and thee,
> And to the place of judgment will return,
> There with my cries importune Heaven, that all
> The sentence from thy head remov'd may light
> On me, sole cause to thee of all this woe,
> Mee mee only just object of his ire. (ll.923-36)

This fourteen-line passage divides into an octave, on Eve's relationship to Adam, and a sestet, on her further relationship to God. In its repeated use of emphatic personal pronouns, it recalls the Son's 'Behold mee then, mee for him, life for life / I offer, on mee let thine anger fall' (Bk. III, ll. 236-37); but Eve cannot be aware of this parallel, given her state of 'vehement despair' (Bk. X, l. 1007). In the poem's textual intentions, however, Milton has put her impassioned speech into an unrhymed sonnet that appropriately expresses her love for Adam in accordance with the traditions associated with the form.[22]

This is, for the human pair, the most important moment in the poem; for this love-lyric breaks down Adam's hatred, reminds him of his love for Eve, and together they go to the place of judgment. Adam's immediate response is a subtle conception on Milton's part: at first, Adam uses pronouns of 'I' versus 'thou' (ll. 947-57) but modulates into 'let us' and 'we' as his speech unfolds (ll. 958-65). Thanks to Eve's offer of her life for Adam's, she has unwittingly enacted the pattern of divine love expressed by the Son in Bk. III. She has thus prepared herself and Adam to receive further 'Prevenient Grace' leading to the idea of a 'paradise within' (Bk. XI, l. 3; Bk. XII, l. 587).

We have already seen how Adam, in his final speech near the end of Bk. XII, has come to 'Acknowledge my Redeemer ever blest' (l. 573) in a verse paragraph governed by the divine proportion. The angel

---

22. Lee Johnson, 'Milton's Blank Verse Sonnets', *Milton Studies* 5 (1973), pp. 129-53 (142).

Michael's immediate reply to Adam is an unrhymed sonnet that emphasizes its theme of divine love:

> To whom thus also th' Angel last repli'd:
> This having learnt, thou hast attain'd the sum
> Of wisdom; hope no higher, though all the Stars
> Thou knew'st by name, and all th' ethereal Powers,
> All secrets of the deep, all Nature's works,
> Or works of God in Heav'n, Air, Earth, or Sea,
> And all the rule, one Empire; only add
> Deeds to thy knowledge answerable, add Faith,
> Add Virtue, Patience, Temperance, add Love,
> By name to come call'd Charity, the soul
> Of all the rest: then wilt thou not be loath
> To leave this paradise, but shalt possess
> A paradise within thee, happier far. (ll. 574-87)

The octave, with its repetition of the word 'all', is devoted to the pleasures and limits of *scientia*. The sestet repeats the word 'add' as it gathers together the greater attainments and imperatives of *sapientia*. The tradition of the Italian sonnet suggests earthly contexts in the fourness of the octave which here highlights the four physical elements of classical science, just as it could highlight the four points of a square or the four directions of a compass. A more spiritual context usually prevails in the threeness of the sestet—the three points around which a circle, an unending line, may be drawn, or the threeness of the Trinity— which here highlights the nature of love and the paradise it creates. Paradise is a state of the soul, not so much a geographical location, which, when Adam and Eve leave the Garden of Eden, will be removed. Paradise is a state of the soul that depends on selfless love, however, and inheres in the consequent interdependence of Adam and Eve with one another and with their Creator—which is why our final glimpse of the human pair shows them 'hand in hand' (l. 648).

At the other end of the poem, Satan provides a parody of the very form and idea of Michael's valedictory love-sonnet by uttering what we may term a 'hate-sonnet' in one of his most memorable and classically heroic speeches:

> Is this the Region, this the Soil, the Clime,
> Said then the lost Arch-Angel, this the seat
> That we must change for Heav'n, this mournful gloom
> For that celestial light? Be it so, since he
> Who now is Sovran, can dispose and bid
> What shall be right: fardest from him is best
> Whom reason hath equall'd, force hath made supreme

Above his equals. Farewell happy Fields
Where Joy for ever dwells: Hail horrors, hail
Infernal world, and thou profoundest Hell
Receive thy new Possessor: One who brings
A mind not to be chang'd by Place or Time.
The mind is its own place, and in itself
Can make a Heav'n of Hell, a Hell of Heav'n. (Bk. I, ll. 242-55)

Here Heaven occupies Satan's thoughts in the octave, and Hell in the sestet; it is the inversion of what one would expect of traditional sonnet-form. Satan treats love as possession and power over a place: it is a state of the soul that consumes its surroundings. The final two lines are a rhetorically grand but thematically impoverished version of Michael's 'paradise within thee, happier far'. A mind that can turn heaven into hell or hell into heaven because the mind is its own place is a mind that has detached itself from the ontological reality of the scale of creation. Such a mind, through its self-absorption, sinks into itself, creating the inexorable 'Hell within' which the epic narrator assigns to the state of Satan's soul (Bk. IV, l. 20); for it is a Hell within that is ontology's exaction of judgment on solipsistic self-love, turning Satan's emptiness into a parody of itself.

Here, as elsewhere in the epic, Satan, Moloch, Mammon, and the rest of the rebel angels exist only in relation to, and as a parody of, the Son, Michael, Raphael, and the rest of the faithful angels. In Milton's universe, evil has no authentic existence of its own. It has no authentic 'form' by which it can define itself. It can realize its modes only by taking the forms of the good and inverting them, turning them inside out, or otherwise deconstructing what, by its nature, was constructive. Milton's view of evil as a privation of good—a rather traditional concept in Christian history—is predicated on the idea that one could have a universe that is entirely good, with no evil in it. The idea that one could have an evil universe with no good in it is not rational, in this way of looking at the problem, because such an evil universe, being unable to show sustainable interrelationships among its elements, would self-destruct. Ontologically, then, good is prior to evil; and, for its part, evil defines itself only in relation to the pre-existing good because it never had an original existence of its own. In poetics, this dependence of evil upon good is perfectly illustrated by the two blank verse sonnets we have just examined. Michael's celebration of 'Love, / By name to come call'd Charity, the soul / Of all the rest', fulfills the nature of sonnet-form in a sweet union of verbal and non-verbal and conceptual components. Satan's hate-sonnet, by contrast, is virtually devoid of meaning without its relationship to pre-existing sonnet-form and to Michael's articulation of the relationship of a 'paradise within' to the further forms and harmonies of the Creation itself. Satan drains the conceptual purpose of octave/sestet relationships until only the literal and rhetorical power of verbal language alone is left. His anti-sonnet can create heavens and hells at will, for they are empty of any reality external to his own mind.

In Milton's universe, the rebel angels are empty of everything except parodies of the good that descend into literal-mindedness. Moloch-worship, so far as Milton was concerned, required literal rather than figurative sacrifices. Satan's seduction of Eve ends up being literal, too, as he says in his victory speech in Hell in Bk. X: 'Him by fraud I have seduc'd / From his Creator, and the more to increase / Your wonder, with an Apple' (ll. 485-87). Satan makes a literal interpretation of the prophecies that talk about his punishment: 'True is, mee also he hath judg'd, or rather / Mee not, but the brute Serpent in whose shape / Man I deceiv'd' (Bk. X, ll. 494-96). He winds up his victory speech by dismissing his fate: 'I am to bruise his heel; / His Seed, when is not set, shall bruise my head: / A World who would not purchase with a bruise...?' (ll. 498-500). Feeling secure in his literal hermeneutics, Satan concludes his final appearance in the epic by being transformed into a serpent, as he and his followers begin hissing like snakes in the greatest sustained passage of sibilance in the history of poetry. They hungrily eat fake fruit that turns to ashes, and the devils end up as literal objects of satire and allegorical derision. Allegory and satire are also reserved, in *Paradise Lost*, for Satan, Sin, and Death in Bk. II and for the Limbo of Vanity and its Paradise of Fools towards the end of Bk. III (ll. 430-97) as Satan wings his way through Chaos to the World and its little world of Earth. The flattening effect of allegory and satire is well suited to the literalness and simplicity of motive and action of characters who seem incapable of conceptual complexity. Moloch was always a flat character, and, even if Satan seemed to be a round or complex character at the beginning of the epic, his final appearance is utterly flat, like a pathetic stage villain in an inferior theatrical event. His final appearance in *Paradise Lost* helps to explain the continuation of this kind of character in *Paradise Regained*.

A very different conclusion attends heavenly and earthly characters in Bk. XII of the epic, as the conceptual forms of the divine proportion and the blank verse sonnet come to dominate the poem. We have already examined speeches designed in divine proportion: Michael's account of the life of Christ, Adam's joyful responses to that account, and Adam's final speech in the epic. In addition, there is Michael's unrhymed sonnet on physical knowledge, metaphysical wisdom, and the 'paradise within'. Finally, Eve is given the last speech by any character in the poem (other than the epic narrator); and her speech is a love-poem, appropriately another blank verse sonnet. In its sestet, Eve rings changes on the word 'all', as she understands the literal and figurative role she will play in human history:

> ...thou to mee
> Art all things under Heav'n, all places thou,
> Who for my willful crime art banisht hence.
> This further consolation yet secure
> I carry hence; thou all by mee is lost,
> Such favor I unworthy am voutsaf't,
> By mee the Promis'd Seed shall all restore. (Bk. XII, ll. 617-23)

The 'Promis'd Seed' is the Christ-child, the 'paradise within' 'our Mother *Eve*' (l. 624). As such, Eve is the living refutation of Moloch, who, in stark contrast, carries children to their deaths within the fires of his belly. Also notable is Eve's understanding of language, compared to Satan's: the Monarch of Hell dismisses being bruised by mankind's 'Seed' as an empty threat (Bk. X, l. 499), in no small part because he is not thinking figuratively and symbolically. His vision is circumscribed by the immediacy of his political ambitions. The larger and longer vision of a conceptual design does not seem to engage or worry him.

The conclusion of *Paradise Lost* is remarkable for the predominance of its conceptual forms, far beyond the capacities of a Satan or a Moloch to appreciate. Three examples of the divine proportion—one from Michael and two from Adam—and two examples of the blank verse sonnet—one from Michael and one from Eve—pervade the epic's final pages. The entire poem is 10,565 lines long; it was fifteen lines shorter in its ten-book form of 1667, in which its concluding Bk. X, with nearly 1,550 lines, was the longest. In 1674, that original Bk. X was split into the new books, Bks. XI and XII. In that final arrangement, Bk. XII has 649 lines, of which the concluding 264 are dominated by the three divine proportions and the two blank verse sonnets. Together, these symbolic forms occupy 145 of those final 264 lines. In other words, conceptual forms dominate and elevate the entirety of the epic's final pages; and in the twelve-book form that conceptual domination is much more apparent than in the ten-book version. Nowhere else in Milton's poetry is there such a frequency of his ultimate symbolic poetical forms. The epic ends in a conceptual blaze of metaphysical designs, giving Bk. XII pride of place in the exemplification of Milton's poetics. That outburst of conceptual power augments the 1674 edition's emphasis on the Fortunate Fall and tempers humanity's loss of a literal, geographical Paradise by the greater insight and gain of a 'paradise within'.

The role of Moloch in Milton's thinking now seems clear: the worship of this deity represents the triumph of ignorance, literal-mindedness, and fear. The belly of Moloch is the sum of horrors in its destruction of new life. It is the direct opposite of the celebration of the Christ-child in a mother's womb; and Eve in *Paradise Lost* and Mary in *Paradise Regained* are the characters who, in this context, most vividly embody Milton's critique and rejection of Moloch-worship. The poet's celebration of the Christ-child is at the heart of his deepest values, from the early *On the Morning of Christ's Nativity* to *Lycidas* and eventually to the final summations of *Paradise Lost* and *Paradise Regained*; and Eve and her daughter Mary are the vessels who make possible that celebration. Reading this essay, Moloch would be perplexed by its examination of conceptual form, by its emphasis on divine inspiration from the Christ-child, and by its celebration of the supreme importance of women in human history; but it is no matter: his fires have gone out.

INDEXES

INDEX OF REFERENCES

INDEX OF AUTHORS